Language Planning and Education in Australasia and the South Pacific

Multilingual Matters

Please contact us for the latest book information:
Multilingual Matters, Bank House, 8a Hill Rd,
Clevedon, Avon BS21 7HH, England

MULTILINGUAL MATTERS 55
Series Editor: Derrick Sharp

Language Planning and Education in Australasia and the South Pacific

Edited by

Richard B. Baldauf, Jr and Allan Luke

MULTILINGUAL MATTERS LTD
Clevedon · Philadelphia

Library of Congress Cataloging-in-Publication Data

Language planning and education in Australasia and
the South Pacific.
(Multilingual matters; 55)
Bibliography: p.
Includes index
1. Language planning—Australasia. 2. Language
and education—Australasia. I. Baldauf, Richard B.,
1943– . II. Luke, Allan. III. Series: Multilingual
matters (Series); 55.
P40.5.L352A78884   1989   409'.9   88-34561

British Library Cataloguing in Publication Data

Language planning and education in Australasia and
the South Pacific (Multilingual matters: 55)
1. Minority languages
I. Baldauf, Richard B (Richard Birge), *1943–*
II. Luke, Allan
400

ISBN 1-85359-048-7
ISBN 1-85359-047-9 pbk

Multilingual Matters Ltd
Bank House, 8a Hill Road   &   1900 Frost Road, Suite 101
Clevedon, Avon BS21 7HH   Bristol, PA 19007
England   U.S.A.

Index compiled by Meg Davies (Society of Indexers)
Typeset by Editorial Enterprises, Torquay
Printed and bound in Great Britain by WBC Print, Bristol

Contents

PART IV: LANGUAGE PLANNING AND USE IN SOUTHEAST
ASIA

Foreword

Over the last decade, a substantial interest in language planning and language education in multicultural nations has developed. Yet much of the research and theorizing has concentrated on North American, European and African contexts. The purpose of this volume of original papers is to introduce and survey the language planning and language education issues which have arisen in Australia, the South Pacific and Southeast Asia. A selected annotated bibliography at the end of each of the three major sections of the volume is provided to give readers an indication of the readily available literature related to the situations and issues characteristic of each region.

With the colonization of the South Pacific rim by European and Asiatic powers came not only economic, political and military imperialism, but processes of language change were set in train by the confrontation of exogenous and indigenous languages and cultures. In some areas, indigenous languages were eradicated or rendered marginal; in others, pidgins and then creoles emerged. Often language became a key terrain for both colonial imposition and nationalist dissent and, in some sites, matters of language became embedded within larger questions of political and cultural autonomy. With the intrusion of imperial powers into the South Pacific and Southeast Asia came new languages of power: in various colonies and spheres of influence, Portuguese, English, French, German, Chinese and Japanese supplanted indigenous Australian, South Pacific and Southeast Asian languages, many of which had long standing historical traditions in the conduct of government, trade and cultural exchange.

Throughout the region, colonial education systems were imported and developed to facilitate training in both colonial ideology and exogenous languages. Often these had the hegemonic intent of training indigenous peoples to support and co-operate with, or at the least to accept, colonial economies and social organization. In other cases, these systems yielded an élite within indigenous populations; differential levels of oracy and literacy in the new colonial languages became markers of class and economic status.

Following the Second World War, most nations throughout the region began to move towards self government. However, in areas such as New Caledonia and French Polynesia, conflict over colonial status continues to this day. Other nations have become involved in the complex web of international political relations and multinational economics as North American, European and Asian nations again have begun to recognize the strategic and economic importance of the South Pacific. Of course, language issues have become focal points of dispute within the larger questions of national, ethnic and regional identity, neo- and post-colonial economic development, and sociopolitical organization. New élites have emerged, and within many nations, multinational economic relations have generated a further set of perceived imperatives in language planning and education: tourism, trade relations and the need for access to scientific knowledge and expertise have become the catalysts for language policy. In more recent years, at the behest of governments, formal language planning procedures have been used to introduce deliberate language change in the region. In such a complex situation, the 'technical' aspects of language planning inevitably have become entangled with political and social issues.

In Australia and many South Pacific countries, then, imperialism from within and from without has threatened indigenous languages and cultures. In some respects, the widespread proliferation of Western educational systems and practices is at the forefront of this process. Nevertheless, there is an increasing body of research into Australian and other indigenous languages in the Pacific region with an eye not only to their preservation, but to their active use and further development.

This volume looks at an array of language problems and issues in the South Pacific and Southeast Asian region, and it introduces issues related to the structure and status of Australian languages. Throughout the following papers, a range of shared problems facing governmental officials, language planners and consultants, and educators is identified: What languages should be taught and used? How should language be used and to what ends? Who should be involved in decision making processes relating to language and education? And, how can educational policies and practices at once enhance economic development, while maintaining cultural and linguistic diversity?

This anthology features papers from the Australian and New Zealand Association for the Advancement of Science (ANZAAS) Conference, subsection on 'Language and Identity', which was convened in Townsville, Queensland from 23–28 August 1987. Several augmenting papers were solicited expressly for this anthology. In this way contributions by Kaplan, Lo Bianco, Thomas and Gonzales were added. All articles are previously unpublished.

We have endeavoured to provide a balance between issues related to language planning theory and practice. Both general discussions of issues and problems, and more detailed case studies are provided. This is, of course, not an exhaustive sample of the range of national and regional issues. However these articles should be of value to researchers, language planners and educational administrators, post-graduate students and advanced undergraduates studying educational policy and sociolinguistics. They will also be of interest for those interested in the politics, language and culture of Australia, the South Pacific and Southeast Asia.

Finally, we wish to acknowledge the help and support we have had from a number of sources: the Applied Linguistics Association of Australia for their co-sponsorship of our ANZAAS sub-section, Björn Jernudd and Roger Keesing for their input at critical junctures, Diana Rayward for her technical assistance in the preparation of the manuscript and the Cartographic Centre, James Cook University and Reg Chapple for their work on the maps and cartoons in this volume.

Richard B. Baldauf, Jr & Allan Luke
James Cook University, Australia
4 July 1988

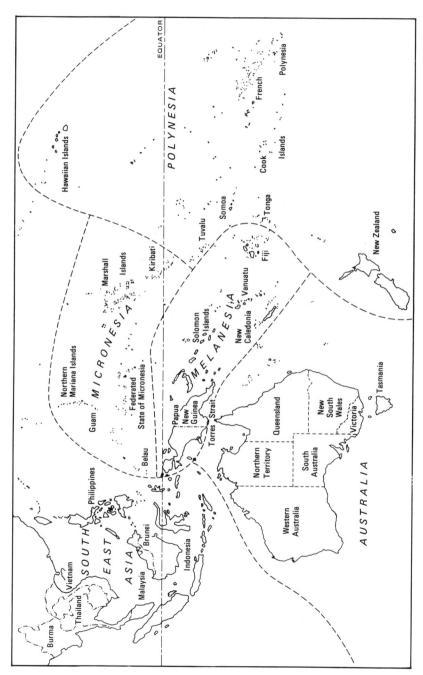

Map of Australasia and the South Pacific

Part I:
An Overview on Language Planning Issues and Change

Introduction: Language planning in theory and practice

ROBERT B. KAPLAN

In the past two or three years, the question of 'cultural literacy' has resurfaced in academic and popular discussions in the United States (e.g. Bloom, 1987). This discussion has given rise to a curious phenomenon. Arising from a concern that youngsters do not have broad knowledge of the cultural artifacts of their society, the discussion has tended to reduce culture to a static commodity which can literally be passed from those who own it to those who want it (or, by the same token, withheld); the possession of the commodity makes possible equality between those who have recently acquired it and those who have always had it. This is an unfortunate view of culture. The educational establishment is, typically, the culture carrier. Such a view of culture places the educational establishment in the position of being the vendor of this commodity. It is probably true that university education, when it was made available to the economic élite, had precisely this function; it was intended to provide the ruling class with a commonality of world knowledge that would enable the members of that group to rule amicably without great friction among themselves and with a sense that they were 'doing the right thing' for those who were being ruled. Language is, of course, the essential tool for the transmission of culture. Such a view of culture forces an interpretation of language as a natural resource which can be managed in the same manner that any other natural resource (oil, coal, water, etc.) can be managed for the general good of the commonwealth.

Language planning, which came into existence after the Second World War, at a time when resources were being managed and when the desire was to create a more efficient, more scientific, more objective mechanism for resource management, was first perceived as 'language engineering' —

as a potentially efficient, neutral, scientific mechanism for the determination of answers to questions related to the uses of language(s) in various societies. This conceptualization of language planning was seized upon by nations emerging *de novo* out of the demise of 19th century colonial empires to make such decisions as those involved in choosing a national language. This notion of language-planning was, indeed, closely tied to the concept of nationhood, and permitted a reduction of the underlying activities, in part at least, to the discovery or invention of an 'authentic' tradition for the chosen language through which the values of the common culture might be said to be shared among all the speakers of that language. It mandated the notion of a group of persons who could be described as 'mother tongue' speakers of that language, and it was entirely compatible with a structuralist view of language which perceived of language as a separate structure composed of phonemes, morphemes, and sentences which, like any other set of tokens, might be manipulated in isolation. It lent itself to a conceptualization of *nation* as a monolingual entity (Bartsch, 1987; Scaglione, 1984; Wardhaugh, 1987).

A quarter century of experience has shown that language is not an isolate and that language planning is a somewhat more complex activity. As early as 1971, Alisjahbana pointed out that 'language deals with all activities of man', and Fishman (1972) cautioned that those who dealt with language in a planning environment had to be aware of 'the presence of so many ambivalent factors.' The history of language change shows that the process is as old as human history. The fact is, however, that in the period before the rapid emergence of nations, language change moved at a stately pace. The emergence of large numbers of new nations, the explosive growth in communication media, and the evolution of a high technology directly tied to economic growth all combined to increase the pace of language change. Further, the rapid development of technology and its application to the military has created an environment in which vast numbers of persons have been displaced from their traditional habitats and forced to seek refuge in new locales which have been linguistically different. Rapid urbanization has also contributed to that movement. Linguistic diversity is now a widespread phenomenon, and that diversity has created 'language problems' requiring systematic solutions.

Language planning remains an attempt by some organized body (most commonly, some level of government) to introduce systematic language change for some more or less clearly articulated purpose (commonly stated in altruistic terms but often not based on altruistic intents). But new questions have been introduced into the process; now, it becomes important to understand *whose* language is being modified to what end by what means (LaPonce, 1987). In the very recent past, there has been a dawning recognition of the notion of language rights and of the fact that the manipulation of language invariably occurs in a political environment in which the authority of some group is at issue.

Because language is so central to the functioning of entire nations (which are themselves not isolates but exist in geographic, political, economic, and cultural relationship with other nations), language planning ought to be a function of the highest levels of government; unfortunately, the centrality of language in the operations of government is not widely perceived, and language planning activities have tended to be relegated to the educational structures of government. Educational structures have engaged in language planning largely in a negative sense; that is, they have tended to exclude some languages from consideration, to minimize the effectiveness of language dissemination by underfunding language teaching operations, and to support the notion of the identity between the nation and some single language. These practices have served to disenfranchise some segments of the population and to disadvantage the entire population by diminishing the cultural value of multilingualism even in polities which were already multilingual.

This behavior of educational structures has tended to create a category of experts wielding tremendous power. As Trueba notes:

> ... issues regarding 'language handicaps' and 'academic underachievement,' are social phenomena that surface in the form of linguistic deviance and are then 'interpreted by the experts.' The traditional assessment of concept formation is based on the assumption that, if the child does not demonstrate in an appropriate linguistic form that he/she recognizes a concept (or concepts) and its (their) interrelationships in those domains 'all normal children' know, the child is handicapped. A perfectly normal child who has just arrived from a linguistically, socially, or culturally different country, by not being able to produce in oral or written text the expected linguistic forms, becomes *ipso facto* 'abnormal' in the eyes of the educator.
>
> (1986: 48)

In sum, language planning has been invested in structures in which specialists who understand language or its social interactions are not likely to make decisions but in which decisions are almost certain to be made on political or economic grounds by individuals having a vested interest in the structure but not in the language process.

In a paper delivered at the sixth InterAmerican Symposium on Linguistics of the InterAmerican Program for Linguistics and Language Teaching, held in San Juan, Puerto Rico, in June 1971, Lichtveld (not a linguist but a diplomat) said:

> With all our respect for pure science we cannot lose sight of the basic fact that no science is only an isolated, unrelated discipline. Even the most absolute science has to serve the fundamental goals of life: our togetherness and happiness, our development and our self-fulfilment, our realization of a better world.

> As everyone will know by now, the whole Caribbean area is in a state of turmoil, of deep trouble. This is not a mere political matter, not a matter of parties or social controversies and allegiances, not even a matter of economic arrangements. In all these scattered islands and continental enclaves where in the course of a few centuries people from all parts of the world have been thrown together under very diverse circumstances for each group, there is now a frantic search and an outcry for an identity, an identity of their own. They want to be themselves. . . They all want an identity of their own, as a prerequisite for their human dignity, for their micro- and macro-togetherness, for their nationhood. They are (but not yet feel) obliged to amalgamate, compromise, and above all: communicate. They are compelled to devise common means of understanding, to go outwards from their old groups to others, without completely losing themselves. Therefore, they are bound to create something new: a culture of their own, a communication system which may serve as many of them as are confined within their natural or inherited national boundaries, and make them respectable and understood, not only there but also in the world beyond.

> Here we have linguistic problem number one, the most urgent, the most paramount one . . . . Something new, something creative is needed; something that appeals to the hidden foundations of all linguistic science.

I apologise for quoting at such length, but it seems to me that this statement goes a very long way toward defining a program for language planning in terms quite different from those that gave rise to the birth of language planning as a scholarly activity. It seems, further, that the problem defined by Lichtveld, though he defined it in terms of the Caribbean area, is precisely the problem that this volume attempts to deal with. One of my purposes in quoting at such length is to show that the problems of the Southwest Pacific Basin are not absolutely unique to this segment of the world but that they exist elsewhere, have existed elsewhere for some time, and have been given at least some attention.

Lichtveld points to two conflicting issues — the need for local identity through local language, *versus* the need for access to the wider world through the use of languages of wider communication. Elsewhere (Grabe & Kaplan, 1986; Kaplan, 1983; 1987), I have argued for the importance of English as a language of wider communication. Not to repeat those arguments, but to summarize them, for reasons which are essentially accidental, English *is* the world language of science and technology (and a number of other functions), and polities aspiring to access to science and technology to serve the function of improving local standards of living simply must have high-level access to English. It is not economical in terms of time or the expenditure of scarce resources to re-invent science in some other language or to re-create the information networks that serve to disseminate science.

At the same time, one simply cannot ignore the local needs for identity and for participation in government. It is equally inefficient to re-invent culture in a language of wider communication or to re-create governance structures that permit local participation. Elsewhere (Kaplan, 1987), I have tried to show the relatively parallel spread of English and Chinese through the Pacific Basin but to claim that the spread has, in each case, served entirely different purposes. While the spread of English has been related to the spread of colonial structures and, more recently, to the hegemony of English in science and technology, the spread of Chinese has simply accompanied immigration. While English serves the needs of modernization, Chinese serves the need of identity with a 5,000 year old culture, connectivity with a tradition, and unification in diversity (in the sense that standard Mandarin has become the unifying variety for speakers of a diversity of other Chinese varieties in the relatively recent past (cf. Tay, 1985; 1986)). Chinese and English are, of course, not the only languages spreading through the Southwest Pacific Basin; as the various papers in this volume suggest, a creole variously named in various sectors of the area, is also spreading and may yet come to have an intermediate regional function — neither a language of wider communication for purposes of modernization nor a language of the heart/hearth (if such an absurd metaphor may be applied in the South Pacific), but a language of local regional participation, of political empowerment.

It is a function of language planning not to reduce all linguistic functions in a polity to one language but to recognize and support the diversity necessary to both local need and global need within the scarce resources available to devote to these activities (Jernudd, 1986). That is not to say that the resources are absolutely constrained; rather, the problem is that governments (which control the allocation of whatever resources exist) see the language issue as far less important than the management of natural resources, the protection of the identity of the polity, and the construction of the educational system to provide mathematical literacy, cultural literacy and, in some more advanced cases, scientific literacy and even computer literacy, but not necessarily linguistic literacy; thus, even in industrialized states, the rate of functional illiteracy is increasing.

Language planning, as an activity undertaken by scholars in the employ of polities, is impelled to recognize the dichotomy Lichtveld identified — the need within any given polity for a language which permits all the citizens of that polity to have the absolute right to aspire to socioeconomic mobility and political power *and* the need for a language which permits some of the citizens of that polity to have access to the scientific and technological information available elsewhere in the world in rich profusion. The first need may well be served by a language variety previously stigmatized (e.g. Part III of this volume). If such is the case, language policy — the inevitable outcome of language planning, whether formally stated or merely implicit in the actions of agencies of government — must include broad-scale activities to overcome the stigmatization (i.e. advertising campaigns to 'sell' the validity of that particular variety). In order to determine whether such is in fact the case, language planning depends upon a multiplicity of survey activities, the function of which is to describe as accurately as possible the language situation which may be subject to change.

Language policy, then, requires an attempt to predict what will occur if certain aspects of the language situation are modified in certain directions. It has been more or less traditional to think of language planning as an activity undertaken by professional linguists. Professional linguists have an important role to play, particularly in corpus modification, but a variety of other academic disciplines are equally involved in language planning — anthropologists, economists, historians, industrial engineers, international relations specialists, learning psychologists, management specialists, political scientists, public administrators, to give only an emblematic list. Language planning is an activity of a well-coordinated team, not an activity of a single scholar of whatever discipline. If some minority within a polity is disproportionately represented in the expenditures of the judicial and penal systems, the causes of that disproportionate representation must be investigated to determine the effects of language, and such an investigation simply cannot be managed solely by a linguist. Status planning is, by definition, so sensitive that it may not be entrusted solely to the linguistic community, but by the same token it may not be entrusted solely to the government education structure either. The two views of how language planning may be accomplished are well represented in this volume, in the papers by Lo Bianco (showing how the activity may be structured by and through government) and by Luke, McHoul, and Mey (exemplifying a neo-Marxist approach).

It has been suggested that language planning should be a function of government at the highest level but that, in fact, it is most commonly the function of the education sector. This is not to suggest that the education sector does not have an appropriate role to play; to discuss the role of the education sector, it is important to differentiate between language planning and language-in-education planning. In an ideal environment, a government authorizes the development of a language plan, leading to a language policy; within that language policy, it is assumed that certain languages will be used for certain purposes (e.g. the plan calls for an increase in economic exchanges with neighboring polities whose languages are significantly different); language-in-education planning would then undertake to establish curricula to inculcate those languages in some segment of the population. It is not the function of the education sector to decide *de jure* what languages will be taught in such a context; rather, it is the function of the education sector to decide who will teach those languages at what point in the educational system, to what segment of the population, through what methodologies, with what materials, at what cost. It is then the function of the education sector to turn to central government for the resources to accomplish the job, and it is the function of central government either to allocate the resources or to modify the plan, extending the time for achievement of the objective, changing the objective, etc. A serious problem in the history of language planning has been the confusion of these two functions. Indeed, in contemporary New Zealand (a participant in the region though not in this volume) precisely what has been here described as undesirable confusion of functions is happening. A broad national review of curriculum has surfaced a language problem, and central government is about to relegate the solution of the language problem to the education sector. In an environment in which central government has not recognized the causes of the language problem, the likely effects of various solutions, and so on, it is predictable that any solution proposed by the education sector is likely to be too narrow and is further likely to be unimplementable except in the most rudimentary sense because the resources necessary to resolution are not available to central government, not having been planned for at that level.

The critic George Jean Nathan has suggested that the theater is the point at which all the arts come together and are actualized; it has been suggested that, by analogy, applied linguistics is the point at which all the social sciences come together and are actualized. Language planning is the activity in which applied linguistics is most fully realized. The case studies in this volume serve as exemplification of the validity of this claim. They demonstrate the inseparability of corpus and status planning, the inter-relatedness of language with all the functions of a populace, and the importance of planning which involves all segments of a society rather than only the education sector.

In the long history of language change, the roles of other sectors have frequently been overlooked. The fact is that, over the last several hundred years, as European (and other) imperialistic expansion occurred, it was not government which played the most critical role in language policy development. Masagara (in preparation) demonstrates the vital role played in language policy in East Africa by institutionalized religion. The success of language activity in this sector has depended significantly on three stages of development: first missionaries *interacted* with the population to understand the needs and behaviors of that population in order to deliver a new message; second they *de-constructed* the existing environment by providing attractive alternatives to existing practices and beliefs, thereby creating new structures and new needs; third they set in motion a *dialectic* process designed to adjust the new model to the evolving situation. These stages are rarely found in more formal language planning activities under the auspices of government. It may be that the needs of government are such that the requisite flexibility is simply not possible, yet the success of the missionary model must not be overlooked. It is possible that government can learn from this example. There is no question that, in the Southwest Pacific Basin, religion has played a role in language change, but so too have economic activities, political activities, and demographic realities. The varieties of language which have evolved are functions of these variables rather than of systematic planning. The functions of these variables are not well understood and require serious analysis. Crucially, the function of language planning involves under-standing the forces that are already in motion and learning to take advantage of existing forces to achieve its planned objectives. An obvious problem lies in the fact that the moving forces may be working against the objectives of government, and here lies the moral dilemma of the language planner, since a language plan may be used to disenfranchise some segment of the population as well as to create a condition in which communication functions to the benefit of a whole population rather than as a territorial defense. The case studies in this volume illustrate both conditions — those in which communication works for the common good, and those in which communication is a function of the territorial imperative, guarding the good of some at the cost of excluding others.

This volume constitutes the first analysis, in my experience, of the complex language problems of the polities of the Southwest Pacific Basin; and this volume, through the diversity of its analyses and discussions, illustrates the applicability of Lichtveld's passionate cry to the Southwest Pacific Basin as well as to the Caribbean. The region is composed of polities of two different sorts — those which have a long political tradition of monolingualism, and those which are by definition polyglot. Even those which have a history of political monolingualism are not in reality monolingual; rather, they have promulgated the myth of monolingualism to preserve the political advantage of some through the relegation to oblivion (by the simple act of failing to recognize their existence) of others. It is a sign of the greatest hopefulness that a volume like this one has come into print. The existence of this volume is a recognition, by scholars if not by governments, that vast linguistic diversity characterizes the region and that it is in the best interests of all to deal somehow with that diversity. The problem of how to deal with this great linguistic diversity is a 'language problem'. That problem may be left to resolve itself (as it eventually will simply because the problem involves flexible human beings), or it may be approached through systematic planning, not only by individual governments but even on a regional basis. Systematic planning may serve to solve the problem either by reducing diversity or by preserving diversity and at the same time allowing essential central activities to occur efficiently. One of the polities (Australia) has recently put in place a 'National Language Policy'; it will be of the greatest interest to watch the workings of that policy unfold. But Australia's policy is inward-looking; the existence of this volume makes possible the articulation of a policy for the region. In truth, such a policy has always been possible. This volume raises the issue to visibility and thereby in some small way increases the probability. This volume announces to the governments of the region that the experts exist, that the problem has been studied to some extent, and that more effective solutions can be achieved given the creation of opportunities for these experts and others to engage in purposeful dialogue. It is unlikely that those whose names are inscribed in this volume will live to see the resolution. We will have to be content with having brought the problem into consciousness, and we will have to hope that, if and when some resolution is in its turn printed, the names inscribed will be more representative of the populations affected.

References

ALISJAHBANA, T. (1971), New national languages: Problems modern linguistics has failed to solve. *Lingua* 15, 515–530.

BARTSCH, R. (1987), *Norms of Language*. New York: Longman.

BLOOM, A. (1987), *The Closing of the American Mind: How Higher Education has Failed Democracy and Impoverished the Souls of Today's Students*. New York: Simon and Schuster.

FISHMAN, J. A. (1972), The relationship between micro- and macro-sociolinguistics in the study of who speaks what language to whom and when. In J. B. PRIDE & J. HOLMES (eds.), *Sociolinguistics*. Harmondsworth: Penguin.

GRABE, W. & KAPLAN, R. B. (1986), Science, technology, language, and information: implications for language and language-in-education planning. *International Journal of the Sociology of Language* 59, 47–71.

JERNUDD, B. H. (1986), Introduction. In E. ANNAMALAI, B. H. JERNUDD & J. RUBIN (eds.), *Language Planning: Proceedings of an Institute*. Mysore: Central Institute of Indian Languages. (Co-sponsored by the Institute of Culture and Communication, East-West Center.)

KAPLAN, R. B. (1983), Language and science policies of new nations (Editorial). *Science* 221, 4614. (September).

— (1987), English in the language policy of the Pacific rim. *World Englishes* 2 (6), 137–148.

LAPONCE, J. A. (1987), *Languages and Their Territories*. Toronto: University of Toronto Press.

LICHTVELD, L. (1971), Linguistic problems in the Caribbean area. Unpublished talk delivered at the VIth InterAmerican Symposium on Linguistics of the InterAmerican Program for Linguistics and Language Teaching (PILEI). San Juan, Puerto Rico (June 15).

MASAGARA, N. (In preparation), Religion as a dynamic resource base for language change in East Africa: The case of Christianity and Islam. Ph.D., Los Angeles, CA: University of Southern California.

SCAGLIONE, A. (ed.) (1984), *The Emergence of National Languages*. Ravena: Longo Editore.

TAY, M. W. J. (1985), *Trends in Language, Literacy, and Education in Singapore*. Singapore: Department of Statistics (Census Monograph No. 2).

— (1986), Bilingual communities: National/regional profiles and verbal repertoires of Southeast Asia/SEAMEO. In R. B. KAPLAN, A. d'ANGLEJAN, J. R. COWAN, B. B. KACHRU, G. R. TUCKER & H. G. WIDDOWSON (eds.), *Annual Review of Applied Linguistics*. VI.

New York: Cambridge University Press.

TRUEBA, H. T. (1986), Bilingualism and bilingual education (1984–1985). In R. B. KAPLAN, A. d'ANGLEJAN, J. R. COWAN, B. B. KACHRU, G. R. TUCKER & H. G. WIDDOWSON (eds.), *Annual Review of Applied Linguistics*. VI. New York: Cambridge University Press.

WARDHAUGH, R. (1987), *Languages in Competition*. New York: Basil Blackwell.

1 Language planning and education[1]

RICHARD B. BALDAUF, JR

Defining Language Planning

Language planning is a complex process which has been defined as
involving *deliberate* language change in the systems of language code
and/or speaking by organizations that are established for these purposes.
In theory at least, language planning develops language problem-solving
strategies that are future oriented. Language planning does not take place
in vacuo, but considers language facts in their social, political, economic,
psychological and demographic contexts (Rubin & Jernudd, 1971). An
analysis of this definition of language planning suggests that it consists of
three underlying entities: plans, planners and planning (cf. Baldauf, 1982).
In what follows I want to consider each of these entities briefly and then
to see how language planning is often 'realized' through language-in-
education policy.

A 'plan' in Rubin and Jernudd's terms is a future oriented, problem-
solving language change strategy which has been developed to meet
particular language needs. The basis on which plans are developed and
how needs are determined — through cost-benefit analysis, needs analysis,
sociolinguistic surveys, political decision making, and so forth — is an
ongoing theme in this volume of papers. Haugen's (1983: 275; see also
Table 1) revised model for language planning can be seen as an example
of a generalized plan or strategy which sets out the major elements
common to language planning, some or all of which may be used to
develop a particular language policy.

The well developed language plan, as the definition implies, 'requires
the mobilization of a great variety of disciplines because it implies the

channeling of problems and values to and through some administrative structure' (Rubin & Jernudd, 1971: xvi).[2] That is, ideally at least, those charged with developing a language plan, the individuals or agencies, must consult widely and consider all aspects of the language situation before a plan is developed. The reality, of course, is that planners come from particular backgrounds and operate under social, cultural, economic and political constraints. They also must operate within the bureaucratic structures and resources available to them. Cobarrubias (1983: 58ff) reviews some of these issues and cites historical examples of the sometimes conflicting forces with which language planners have to contend.

TABLE 1 *Haugen's (1983: 275) revised language planning model*

	Form *(policy planning)*	*Function* *(language cultivation)*
Society (status planning)	1. Selection (decision procedures) (a) problem identification (b) allocation of norms	3. Implementation (educational spread) (a) correction procedures (b) evaluation
Language (corpus planning)	2. Codification (standardization procedures) (a) graphization (b) gramatication (c) lexication	4. Elaboration (functional development) (a) terminological modernization (b) stylistic development

Finally, there is the dimension of 'planning' or the implementation of the plan designed by the planners. The planning process itself is a complex one located as it is in a society which is growing and changing based on a particular set of historical, economic, cultural and social circumstances. As planning occurs over time, it is subject to a variety of bureaucratic pressures and to changes in personnel (Baldauf, Chapter 14, this volume) which can mediate and alter significantly the nature and direction of the planned language change. Furthermore, effective planning implies the continued evaluation and revision of a plan during the implementation of language planning process, although Rubin (1983: 338) indicates that in practice 'this is only rarely done'.

Intervening Variables

While language planning can broadly be seen as planners working on future oriented language plans and on the implementation of those plans to create language change, the real world seldom works in such predictable ways. Language planning, as Kaplan points out in the Introduction to this volume, is a process always *in situ*, and therefore open to the influence of key individuals, bureaucratic structures and institutions. These subjects, groups and institutions act as intervening variables in the language planning process. It may then be appropriate to ask: What are the key intervening variables? What influence do those variables have on the development and implementation of a particular language plan? What influence do they have on those responsible for plans and planning implementation?

Some of the intervening variables which have been suggested as influential in planned language change or language maintenance as they relate to language planning are: perceived economic demand (e.g. trade, tourism), the need for information and scientific exchange (cf. Grabe & Kaplan, 1986; Jernudd & Baldauf, 1987), nationalism (cf. Fishman, 1971), ethnic identity (cf. Edwards, 1985), religion (cf. Das Gupta, 1971), historical circumstances, the growth of urbanization (Jourdan, Chapter 9, this volume), bureaucracies and education. In differing situations, these variables may influence to varying degrees the character and development of language planning policy.

Given the potential impact of such intervening variables on the language planning process, it is perhaps surprising that the language planning literature related to them is very limited. In Haugen's model (Table 1), we can see that these intervening variables relate most closely to 'status planning' issues. Indeed, the papers selected for this monograph have as their primary concern status planning issues related to problems of 'selection' (i.e. historical, political and social variables) or 'implementation' (i.e. education). In Chapter 2, Luke, McHoul and Mey look at some problematic issues related to 'selection' variables although they might be reluctant to put it in these terms. While their position is that language planning as it stands is a contradictory and in some senses, futile activity, I would argue that it occurs, either on a *de facto* or *de jure* basis, the former often under the auspices of language-in-education programs. Hence, my focus here is to raise issues related to implementation and education.

Education as a variable in language planning is of particular importance in Australasia and the Pacific rim since it is often implicated in all four of Haugen's stages and not just restricted to the implementation phase. For example, most language planning agencies in Southeast Asia are attached to Ministries of Education and/or Culture; their principal duties involve corpus planning (Noss, 1985). This creates the curious situation where:

> the formation of language corpus policy, which is relatively unimportant to education as such, is the province of language planners closely associated with schools, universities, and Ministries of Education, while the formulation of language status policy, which is of vital importance to curriculum development, teacher training, instructional methods and approaches, and examination policy, is often left at the mercy of all sorts of uninformed political pressures.
>
> (Noss, 1985: 84)

In Australia, Melanesia and Polynesia language planning agencies have not been established (Australia is only a recent exception to this, see Lo Bianco, Chapter 3, this volume) and departments of Education, individuals from universities, missionary and other pressure groups interested in language issues have taken on many of the corpus and status planning roles.

These situations, which I have previously referred to as 'language without planning' events because of the absence of a formal language planning body and the often idiosyncratic nature of planning decisions (cf. Baldauf, 1982; Russo & Baldauf, 1986), have often been a major driving force behind language change and language shift in modernizing countries in this region. Typically in these situations, very little in the way of formal language planning is done. Instead, the educated élites, whether they be of the exogenous or indigenous variety, opt for a modern Western educational system, like the one in which they were educated. Within a bare bones framework, typified by conflicting language development requirements, the educational system is left to plan for much of the language development that is meant to occur in that country. This scenario creates a language-without-planning situation at the political level in which the educational system has the role of language planner thrust upon it. The resultant developments are very often manifest in 'language-in-education programs' (cf. Eggington & Baldauf, Chapter 5, this volume) rather than in the implementation of a more general language policy.

Education as an Intervening Variable

But what evidence exists for the hypothesis that education is an intervening variable? The discussion of this proposition is also a major theme in a number of chapters in this book. Stated in simple terms the question is whether education often acts as a *de facto* language planner (i.e. language-in-education policy development) or whether education is simply one of many tools available for implementing language planning (i.e. that education plays mainly a reactive role in the planning process).

In a number of papers that relate language planning and education, the underlying assumption seems to favour the weak form of the hypothesis, that education is a tool, part of the process of language development, rather than a major force in 'directing' language change. For example, Kennedy (1983) argues that language planning is important for educators because:

> the close relationship between the use of a language and political power, socioeconomic development, national and local identity and cultural values has led to the increasing realisation of the importance of language policies and planning in the life of a nation. Nowhere is this planning more critical than in education, universally recognised as a powerful instrument of change. At the focal point of educational language planning is the teacher, since it is the successful application of curriculum and syllabus plans in the classroom, themselves the instruments of higher levels of language planning, that will affect the realisation of national level planning. . . . Because of this link between national language planning and classroom practice (see Lewis & Massad, 1975), an understanding of language planning can provide explanations to the teacher . . . (introduction: ix)

One significant implication here is that teachers and perhaps educators in general are, in a comprehensive analysis, just 'the instruments of higher levels of language planning'.

Edwards (1985: 138) can find little to support education as a key variable in the retention of ethnic identity and he indicates that:

> There is no evidence to suggest that any meaningful aspects of ethnicity can be held in place by outside intervention, much less ones which are visible markers (like language).

These citations suggest that language-in-education programs are not major instigators of language change, but rather support other more potent variables in the language change process.

There is, however, another way to view the role education may play in language change. In the English-speaking world there has been relatively little in the way of formal language planning or language planning bodies. Instead English has been left to evolve (cf. Heath & Mandabach, 1983). One might argue that this attitude towards language change and development has carried over into many of the English influenced colonial and post-colonial situations in the Pacific. Language planning decisions are not made in detail, but left implicitly for the education system to develop and implement. As we will see in the chapters in this book, the degree to which such a generalization is valid varies with the situation. In the Solomon Islands and Papua New Guinea, for instance, it would appear the generalized hypothesis is more accurate than in Malaysia and Brunei. Now let us briefly review some of the specific evidence available which suggests that education functions as an intervening variable.

Studies of Education and Language Planning

A review of the literature on education and language planning located a number of studies in which both topics were a major focus of concern.[3] Twelve of these studies are briefly summarized in Table 2. The studies look at colonial, post-colonial and national political situations in many parts of the world for a variety of language concerns. Many of them are taken from the two issues that were published of the *International Education Journal* which had as its primary focus education and language issues.

The studies seem to provide evidence for the existence of both language planning and language-in-education policy development. Four of the studies discuss education as a contributing variable in developing a language plan or policy. Abu-Absi (1984), for example, looks at the two main issues of language policy common to all Arabic speaking countries: Arabization and modernization. Given the changes which have occurred in both these areas in recent years, language instruction in both Arabic and foreign languages is then discussed and the implications for bilingualism and minority languages examined. In these post-colonial situations, education is described as a medium of implementation for broader language policy, although the specific sources of that policy are not made clear.

The development and implementation of educational language policy is also the focus of Ekka's (1984) paper which describes the language scene in India and the constitutional safeguards for minority

TABLE 2 *Studies on education and language planning*

Author (Date)	Country/ Area	Language Concerns	Situation	LP Type
Abu-Absi (1984)	Arab World	Arabic	Post-colonial	Lang plan
Baldauf (1984)	Amer. Samoa	English	Colonial	Lang-in-edn
Burns (1984)	Bolivia	Quechua/ Spanish	National	Lang-in-edn
Chrishimba (1984)	Zambia	English	Post-colonial	Lang-in-edn
Ekka (1984)	India	Minority Languages	National	Lang plan
Fuller (1984)	Navajo	Navajo/ English	National/ Colonial	Lang-in-edn
Ikwue (1984)	Nigeria	Local/ English	Post-colonial	Lang-in-edn
Noss (1985)	S.E. Asia	5 studies	Post-colonial	Lang-in-edn
Russo & Baldauf (1986)	Australia	Australian	National/ Colonial	Lang-in-edn
Santiago (1984)	Puerto Rico	Spanish/ English	Colonial	Lang-in-edn
Stewart (1984)	Guatemala	Indian	National/ Colonial	Lang plan
Zimmerman (1984)	Namibia	Multilingual	Colonial	Lang plan

languages. The states, which are responsible for education and the provision of minority languages in schools, seem to prefer to develop the dominant literary languages rather than mother-tongue education, potentially creating a conflict between constitutional rights and policy implementation.

In Guatemala the political situation is seen as the major influence on the development of bilingual programs for Indian children (Stewart, 1984). The government, which does not seem to be overly concerned with the education of its Indian minority, is determined to produce a Spanish-speaking population, while the Protestant missionaries champion literacy development in the Mayan languages. In this national intra-colonial situation education serves mainly as the tool for political and economic domination on the one hand and on the other, for religious conversion of the minority Mayan Indian population.

Finally, Zimmerman (1984) describes the linguistic situation in Namibia and its implications for education. Recent attempts to develop a language policy for education are described. Although vernacular education was being used as the *de facto* medium of instruction throughout primary education, official policy is that a switch to a European language should occur in standard second. Here again there seems to be an attempt at a language planning for education solution in this multilingual colonial situation.

There are, however, a number of studies which describe how a language-in-education policy develops. Baldauf (1984; see also Chapter 14, this volume) argues that once the broad political decision was made to modernize colonial American Samoa, how that was done was left primarily to educators to implement and to Directors of Education to make changes in direction. In the Northern Territory, Australia, a similar process occurred (see Russo & Baldauf, 1986; Eggington & Baldauf, Chapter 5, this volume) where after an initial decision by the federal government to implement bilingual education, language development has been left primarily to the educational authorities and has been assessed primarily on educational criteria. In both these cases general language development and change for whole communities has been driven by the needs of the educational system and has been evaluated from an educational perspective, with little consideration for the more general language planning implications of these educational policies.

The literature provides a number of other examples of language-in-education policy development. In Bolivia the split between the urban Spanish-speaking literates and the rural Queshua-speaking campesino, who see no need for literacy, is deep. The basic philosophy of educational administrators in Bolivia was for 'an unbending preference for the direct method of imposing Spanish as the language of education at all levels' (Burns, 1984: 211). The development of a bilingual program, with USAID funding for a demonstration project, sought to break this cycle and to create a greater sense of national pride in Queshua language and culture. Burns argues that this three year project, which was continued by the Bolivian government when funding lapsed, did create some 'appreciation for the vernacular language as a legitimate tool for education' (1984: 213). It can be argued that this externally funded language-in-education program may provide the beginnings for a more broadly based language policy.

In Zambia a language-in-education policy, in which English is adopted as the *lingua franca* and medium of instruction, has been justified on the basis that to select a Zambian language(s) would be an invitation to tribalism. However, Chrishimba (1984) argues that in southern Africa factors such as urbanization, labour oriented economies, white racism, urban–rural migration and language contact have created detribalization, and that non-linguistic arguments are being used selectively to solve linguistic problems to the detriment of Zambian children. A more broadly based language plan might result from the National Language Committee which was being set up to advise the government on language policy, but this body was still to be answerable to the Ministry of Education and Culture.

For the Navajo, 'schools are instrumental in contributing to the complete shift of a vernacular language, i.e. to the extinction of language' (Fuller, 1984: 93). However, schools can contribute to the development and revival of vernacular languages if they give them meaningful roles to play in school. If one accepts Fuller's view, bilingual Navajo–English language-in-education programs could lead not only to a better education for Navajo children but to the promotion of 'the dignity and solidarity of an ethnically unique people' (1984: 98).

Other studies by Ikwue (1984), Noss (1985) and Santiago (1984) highlight further ways in which language-in-education policies can lead to language development. As a group, these eight studies suggest that language-in-education can be a powerful force for language change. It is difficult, however, to categorize neatly the situations, represented by the studies listed in Table 2, into either language planning or language-in-education policy situations. Most contain some elements of both approaches and indicate that impact of education as an intervening variable is itself strongly influenced by other situational factors.

Conclusions

I have tried here to demonstrate that in both theory and practice education is an important variable in most language planning situations. Studies of language planning and education, however, show that the role education takes in language development situations varies across linguistic, political and cultural situations. Thus, it is important not to isolate education from other contextual variables when looking at language issues.

The distinction also needs to be made between the legitimate role that education has to play in language planning situations and the consequences of letting educational considerations dominate programs for language development. Language selection is in Haugen's terms a matter of form and a matter for political decision making. Language implementation is a matter of function and a matter for educational spread using the best educational methods available. These two roles should not be confused if language planning is to be sensitive to the needs of the communities it is meant to serve.

Notes

1. This chapter had its beginnings in discussions with Björn Jernudd at the Culture Learning Institute, East West Center, and has benefited greatly from comments from Allan Luke.
2. Jernudd & Baldauf (1987) describe the multiple components needed to plan a science communication network.
3. Chapters 7 (Luke and Kale), 15 (Teleni) and 19 (Bo) of this volume provide a further annotated list of studies related to language planning and, to varying extents, education. I have not listed most of those studies here.

References

ABU-ABSI, S. (1984), Language planning and education in the Arab world. *International Education Journal* 1 (2), 113–132.

BALDAUF, R. B., Jr (1982), The language situation in American Samoa: Planners, plans and planning. *Language Planning Newsletter* 8 (1), 1–6.

— (1984), Language policy and education in American Samoa. *International Education Journal* 1 (2), 133–150.

BURNS, D. H. (1984), Quechua/Spanish bilingual education and language policy in Bolivia. *International Education Journal* 1 (2), 197–220.

CHRISHIMBA, M. M. (1984), Language policy and education in Zambia. *International Education Journal* 1 (2), 151–180.

COBARRUBIAS, J. (1983), Ethical issues in status planning. In J. COBARRUBIAS & J. A. FISHMAN (eds.), *Progress in Language Planning: International Perspectives.* Berlin: Mouton.

DAS GUPTA, J. (1971), Religion, language and political mobilization. In J. RUBIN & B. H. JERNUDD (eds.), *Can Language Be Planned?* Honolulu: East-West Center.

EDWARDS, J. (1985), *Language, Society and Identity.* Oxford: Basil Blackwell.

EKKA, F. (1984), Status of minority languages in schools in India. *International Education Journal* 1 (1), 1–19.

FISHMAN, J. (1971), The impact of nationalism on language planning: Some comparisons between early twentieth-century Europe and more recent years in South and Southeast Asia. In J. RUBIN & B. H. JERNUDD (eds.), *Can Language Be Planned?* Honolulu: East-West Center.

FULLER, E. (1984), Educational language planning in a Navajo community. *International Education Journal* 1 (1), 91–102.

GRABE, W. & KAPLAN, R. B. (1986), Science, technology, language, and information: Implications for language and language-in-education planning. *International Journal of the Sociology of Language* 59, 47–71.

HAUGEN, E. (1983), The implementation of corpus planning: Theory and practice. In J. COBARRUBIAS & J. A. FISHMAN (eds.), *Progress in Language Planning: International Perspectives*. Berlin: Mouton.

HEATH, S.B. & MANDABACH, F. (1983), Legal status decisions and the law in the United States. In J. COBARRUBIAS & J. A. FISHMAN (eds.), *Progress in Language Planning: International Perspectives*. Berlin: Mouton.

IKWUE, I. O. (1984), Effective educational language planning in Nigeria. *International Education Journal* 1 (1), 39–60.

JERNUDD, B. H. & BALDAUF, R. B., Jr (1987), Planning science communication for human resource development. In B. DAS (ed.), *Language Education in Human Resource Development*. Singapore: RELC [Anthology Series 20].

KENNEDY, C. (ed.) (1983), *Language Planning and Language Education*. London: George Allen & Unwin.

NOSS, R. B. (1985), The evaluation of language planning in education. *Southeast Asian Journal of Social Science* 13 (1), 82–105.

RUBIN, J. (1983), Evaluating status planning: What has the past decade accomplished? In J. COBARRUBIAS & J. A. FISHMAN (eds.), *Progress in Language Planning: International Perspectives*. Berlin: Mouton.

RUBIN, J. & JERNUDD, B. H. (1971), Introduction: Language planning as an element in modernization. In *Can Language Be Planned*? Honolulu: East-West Center.

RUSSO, C. & BALDAUF, R. B., Jr (1986), Language development without planning: A case study of tribal Aborigines in the Northern Territory, Australia. *Journal of Multilingual and Multicultural Development* 7 (4), 301–317.

SANTIAGO, I. S. (1984), Language policy and education in Puerto Rico and the continent. *International Education Journal* 1 (1), 61–90.

STEWART, S. O. (1984), Language planning and education in Guatemala. *International Education Journal* 1 (1), 21–37.

ZIMMERMAN, W. (1984), Language planning, language policy and education in Namibia. *International Education Journal* 1 (2), 181–196.

2 On the limits of language planning: Class, state and power[1]

ALLAN LUKE, ALEC W. McHOUL and JACOB L. MEY

The Politics of Language Planning

Language planning as a social scientific enterprise is roughly three decades old. It arose as an extension of sociolinguistics into the domain of social planning, and the job of describing and tracing patterns of language change thereby was tied to the normative task of prescribing such change. The enabling historical conditions which led to the formalization of language planning had their bases in postwar concerns with the systematic 'scientific' engineering of social and educational policy. As a result, many language planners embrace the discursive strategies of what Habermas (1972) has called 'technicist rationality': the presupposition that the linear application of positivist social science could transform problematic, value-laden cultural questions into simple matters of technical efficiency.

Our purpose here is to critique in broad terms some of the practical and theoretical assumptions of language planning. We should note at the onset that our backgrounds are not in language planning: working in language education, ethnomethodology, discourse analysis and pragmatics, we have found that these fields have been informed increasingly by developments in contemporary social theory. We intend here not to provide a new or revised model for language planning. Instead, we want to raise a range of contentious and polemical issues which might be further explored as part of research, theorizing and critique by sociolinguists and language educators.

Language planning and education in the developing nation states of Southeast Asia and the South Pacific — focal areas of interest in this volume — pivot around the historical problematic of decolonization. In the aftermath of postwar decolonization by European and Asian powers, various political systems have arisen in countries of the South Pacific rim. Governmental intervention in cultural and linguistic practices by minority and majority groups — perhaps exemplified most clearly by the Malaysian language policy — has become the focus of regional and national debate. The continuing role of colonial culture and language is thus a crucial matter, for, on the one hand, governments are eager to establish national and regional identities and economic autonomy and, on the other, many strive for the preservation and further development of economic, scientific and cultural ties with both former colonial powers and multinational trading partners (Carnoy, 1974). At the same time, political and geographic expediency has led to the invention of nation states (e.g. Papua New Guinea, Indonesia) which have attempted to incorporate, at times coercively, a diversity of indigenous and migrant cultures and languages. As in industrial and post-industrial nations, the establishment of educational and language policies which reflect *a* national identity in the midst of cultural and linguistic diversity has posed myriad political and social problems.

Is what has come to count as 'language planning' adequate to the task of unknotting these matters? Language planning, as an academic and policy exercise, has set out to render explicit and to influence directly the interlocking sociological and cultural factors which effect linguistic change. Indeed, prior to such programs of linguistic research and development, a range of social influences acted as *de facto* forces for the deployment, development, registration, formalization and use of language, often unintentionally establishing a seemingly natural path of institutional and bureaucratic intervention and non-intervention in language development, change and death. Larger agendas of educational, social and economic policy tended to circumscribe *a priori* any deliberate language planning.

Yet it would appear that much of the subsequent literature on language planning has slipped into the very mystification which it once sought to avoid. Many linguists and educational planners saw their task as an ideologically neutral one, entailing the description and formalization of language(s) (corpus planning) and the analysis and prescription of the sociocultural statuses and uses of language(s) (status planning). Those involved in status planning have worked under a range of stated and unstated constraints which reflect political interests of those who have commissioned language plans — whether these be regional educational authorities, national governments or international development agencies — and have not had purely linguistic or (social) 'scientific' interests. This aspect of the endeavour has been largely ignored:

> It is high time that we recognize that language planning is undertaken by those who are in a position of power to undertake such policies and is therefore designed to serve and protect their interests.
> (Williams, 1981: 221)

It is somewhat ironic, then, that while language planning set out to study and control various sociological factors which influence language change, its very character as a form of 'interest-bound' modern social planning has led, in many cases, to a failure to tackle explicitly the hidden agendas — political, social, educational and otherwise — of particular forms of government, economic relations, politics and social organization. Instead, a technical discourse of 'norms' and 'treatment' has been imported from structural–functionalist sociology (e.g. Neustupný, 1974). Social organization has been *treated* as if it were an organism. Partly as a result of this orientation, a curious phenomenon has emerged: those social and economic forces, institutions and structures have come to be viewed in what pass for 'neutral' terms (Edwards, 1985: 88–96). That is, as a discourse of governmental policy, language planning has tended to avoid directly addressing larger social and political matters within which language change, use and development, and indeed language planning itself, are embedded.

Despite the veneer of scientific objectivity gained by the continuing development and fine tuning of theoretical matrices to guide planning, language plans have always arisen from socially and politically defined 'language problems' (Neustupný, 1974), and language planning implementation, Haugen (1983: 286) candidly states, is subject to 'political constellations'. Crucial to our present purposes, Haugen observes that for those involved in language planning 'an attempt to dislodge a well-established élite may result in backlashes and tactical retreat'. In a recent revision of his prototype for language planning, he concludes with a call for

> further research ... [on] how much influence can be consciously exerted by the manipulation of sources of power and how much linguistic change is due to underlying and uncontrollable social forces
> (Haugen, 286–7).

The need now is for a broader theoretical understanding of specific aspects of social organization which mediate the planning of language, and for that matter, influence the contractual briefs laid out by governments for linguists undertaking corpus and status planning activities (Kennedy, 1984; Edwards, 1985; Jernudd, 1989).

Still, only a few of the commentators indicate what kind of political analysis might be appropriate. Jernudd and Neustupný (1987), for example, end their call for due consideration of sociopolitical context with an invocation of the need for further 'scholarly reflection'. What is omitted is an exploration of the complex theoretical relationship between language, discourse, ideology and social organization. These are precisely the central concerns of neo-Marxist social theorizing, post-structuralist discourse analysis and critical theory. In what follows, we want to draw from these three fields which are, we duly acknowledge, disparate and, in their current states, occasionally incommensurate — for all their shared concern with political understanding and critique of concrete social practices on the terrains of class, state and power. First, we examine the question of the relationship of language selection and class within societies. Second, we move on to draw upon the work of Habermas (1976) to identify how different and competing systems within society generate and sustain contending forms and methods for the legitimation of language and discourse. Third, we turn to post-structuralist theory to clarify how the Foucauldian reconceptualization of discourse and power sets an agenda for a complete rethinking of language planning.

Class

In a superficial sense, the relationship between language planning and social control seems to fall within a common-sense version of social power: those who are able to decide what language use(s) can be deemed acceptable, which should be encouraged and furthered, respectively demoted and discouraged, are in positions of political power and hence can control the development of language (*planning*), in addition to controlling to some extent actual discursive practices. The classical case of 'linguistic oppression' (Mey, 1985: 26f) is that of 'high' and 'low' prestige dialects, or that of pidgin versus 'standard' languages, where pidgins are considered to be merely degraded variants of 'the' language (see Keesing, Jourdan, Smith, Kale, Chapters 8–11, this volume). Gross cases of linguistic oppression include the total or partial criminalization of the use of local or vernacular idioms, as in the case of the 'Basque stick', a punitive device used in Basque area schools, to be carried by pupils on outstretched arms as punishment for using a Basque word or expression (Mey, 1985: 27). In many Australian mission schools in the early and mid-twentieth century, Aboriginal children were punished for reversions into 'language' (Glen, 1989); parallel cases have been documented in Canadian government and mission schools developed in the early twentieth century for Indian children (Ashworth, 1977).

As a prelude to the analysis of such cases, we can ask the rudimentary question of 'whose language' is being planned, and correlatively, 'whose language' is the controlling norm or guideline for such planning. This question boils down to asking *who* is planning *for whom*, and *what* (overt and covert) *aims* planning pursues; similarly, *whose behaviour* is to be the standard of language use, and *what aims* such a use should set for itself.

We can begin to address such questions by quoting Brecht's dictum that 'morals are for the rich'. That is, moral behaviour is something you should be able to afford (but as a rule, cannot); however, by appealing to some universally valid laws of justice and equity (which are strictly valid only under idealized circumstances, *viz.* in perfect societies), governments allow the rich man to get away while they string up the sheep thief and the poacher. In the case of language, the term 'linguistic repression' has been used to characterize this subtle, but pernicious form of planning and control (Mey, 1985: 26; cf. Pateman, 1975). This latter concept of repression is particularly important in defining and describing the paradoxes that arise in contemporary pedagogical thinking, whereby the student (*qua* 'client') is considered a passive receptacle for the ideas and knowledge to be imparted by the teacher (see Freire & Macedo, 1987: xvi), or by which, alternatively, students are supposed to be in the possession of exactly those qualifications, as a prerequisite to learning, with which the teaching is supposed to imbue them.

These various contradictions arise from the asymmetrical relationships of power still implicit both at the everyday level of conventional pedagogical settings and at the structural level of 'the plan'. The general problem becomes even more remarkable in specific cases where planners work on behalf of what Haugen called 'élite' interests: language rulers contract plans for language users; linguists, bureaucrats and politicians determine what language is fit for the rest of the people to use. It is this reality of language planning that is most obvious in the case of such South East Asian states as Malaysia, Singapore and Brunei where, to use the current euphemism, the 'clients' of a language plan have limited, if any, effective electoral franchise, and insofar as the illusion of franchise exists, legislators' options are delimited by the authoritarian mandates of a ruling class, party or élite. Further, what Freire (1972) calls the 'banking ideology' has ramifications within language planning. In the following, we will examine how a particular brand of this ideology, which we shall call 'supply side' thinking, has had widespread and damaging effects in the language planning industry.

In general, supply side planning considers the people it plans for as manipulable objects of economic, political and educational engineering. In order to plan ahead, an ideal picture of the 'client' is constructed. Further, planners need to determine what kinds of values customers can be expected to react positively to, so that they will be able to promote business and 'make the economy flow smoothly'. In economics, this translates into marketing analyses, the establishment of 'customer profiles' and the production of a commercial discourse for 'selling' the plan to both clients and fellow planners (Haug, 1986). The result of this is a process of production exclusively geared to the selling, or 'supply', side of the economy, which has little or no concern for its other aspects, such as global production patterns, the consumers' situation, ecological requirements and so forth (cf. Habermas, 1976: 42–44; Wilden, 1986).

What are the effects of this supply side ideology on language education and planning? First, it should come as no surprise that this kind of ideology operates as a kind of 'selective tradition' (Williams, 1977); it has as its preferred customers those who are willing and able to purchase the product. The anomaly of modern education, whether in post-industrial or developing countries, has been the conflict between its stated aim of generating 'equality' and 'mobility' and its historical mission which actually reproduces inequality:

> Education may well be, as of right, an instrument whereby every individual ... can gain access to any kind of discourse. But we well know that in its distribution, in what it permits and what it prevents, it follows the well-trodden battle-lines of social conflict. Every educational system is a political means of maintaining or of modifying the appropriation of discourse with the knowledge and the powers it carries with it.
>
> (Foucault, 1972: 227).

Nowhere has the role of formal education in the social, economic and cultural reproduction of inequality been more obvious than in colonial and neo-colonial settings (Carnoy, 1974). Similarly, language education involves a paradox, that of 'exclusive club' membership: to become a member, one has to qualify, but the only way to obtain the necessary qualifications is through membership of the club. Bourdieu (1970: 2) puts this more directly in terms of the prerequisites for obtaining cultural and linguistic capital:

> . . . by doing away with giving explicitly to everyone what it implicitly demands of everyone, the education system expects of everyone alike that they have what it does not give, which consists mainly of linguistic and cultural competence.

Historically, in order to ensure their survival, élite groups have used the educational provision of linguistic competence and literacy for purposes of self-reproduction (cf. Graff, 1987). Hereditary political bodies, such as the upper chambers of parliamentary democracies, are a classic example, and post-colonial élites, generally educated in colonial institutions and language, constitute a parallel group in Southeast Asia and the South Pacific.

To learn a language effectively, those who already have some knowledge of it, and of the sites and rituals, speech and literacy events within which it is used, are at an advantage. Hence, in those cases where — in the name of 'development', 'national unity' or 'identity', or 'scientific' advance — a language which is *other* to specific groups within the populace is selected as the medium for discourses of power (e.g. mass media, legal systems, commerce and trade, schooling, governmental policy, research), these groups in turn will suffer cyclic disadvantage. The continued use of English as the language of instruction in Papua New Guinean schools is a case in point and, throughout Melanesia, the push towards *de jure* or *de facto* state monolingualism is in direct contrast to most peoples' multilingual heritages. Any plan for the future of *a* language, moreover, implicitly expresses a projection of the future of the polity, insofar as it expresses the *means* of representation and reproduction. Both matters return us to the kernel issue: 'Whose language' is it that the language planner takes as a norm for teaching and use, and to what end?

Yet the problem of supply side ideology extends beyond the authority or class devising the 'language plan' to implicate the social scientists contracted; indeed the scientist frequently is a member of that class. For the language planner is not only the employee of such groups, but is more than likely to possess facility with the language and educational competence deemed 'desirable'. Hence, supply side planning by definition is a task undertaken by those with access to the cultural and linguistic capital which is to be valued. It thereby all too readily excludes the interests of the powerless 'plannees', framing these in a series of abstractions (e.g. 'equality', 'economic growth', or for that matter, the 'right' to cultural/linguistic preservation) rather than offering a concrete analysis of their relationship to structures of power and labour.

How, then, are we to get beyond either empirical, acritical or abstract, rhetorical descriptions of the social and linguistic problems of those for whom language is allegedly being planned? Simply consulting and surveying groups, ascertaining actual functions and uses of language and attitudes towards language shared in a speech community — the staple approach offered in many planning models (Fasold, 1984) — is indeed an obvious recourse. But such straightforwardly positivist procedures in and of themselves beg key questions. Again, we can turn to Freire's (1972) argument, that those without access to (analytic) language and literacy may be precluded from a concrete analysis of their own (economic, political *and* linguistic) oppression. Nowhere is this matter more problematic than in the case of Aboriginal peoples, where the positions voiced by or on behalf of the 'client' group in question may reflect a post-contact, hegemonized understanding of their own position, rather than unsullied 'native' wishes. We find a contrasting situation in the case of those ethnic groups whose stated self-interests may reflect privileged class-position or status on the part of an élite *within* the community, internal power struggles within the group, and so forth. For example, as Keesing (Chapter 8, this volume) has indicated, the views of tribal authorities in the Solomons *vis-à-vis* the appropriate domains of use of vernacular languages are a reflection of their own vested interests in retaining power locally and cross-generationally. So to accept at face value statements by 'plannees' themselves, especially when mediated by empiricist social science research methods, can be as misleading as to ignore them altogether.

An analysis of the question of 'Whose language?', then, requires an understanding of how languages gain legitimacy, and how, in differing forms of social organization, particular economic, cultural and political contingencies serve as the basis for establishing mass loyalty towards and use of *a* language, and discourses of power. Overall class relations and interests, as we have seen, are crucial, but this 'top-level' realization needs supplementation by those more specific questions of language and discourse at definite sites of power. It is to this that we now turn.

State

Rationales for language selection are framed in rhetoric designed to generate consensus among the populace in question. Hence, throughout

Southeast Asia and the South Pacific, we encounter language plans justified on the basis of 'cultural preservation', 'scientific development', 'international trading links' or 'national unity'. These arguments often are adopted without critical analysis by those involved in language planning and the analysis of language planning: in policies developed in Singapore, Indonesia, Brunei and Malaysia, for instance, such goals are given in the planning process, mandated by the government/contractor and ostensibly facilitated by the language plan. All such rationales address the question of 'Whose language?' by reference to the (generic) populace and to the ostensibly non-problematic goals of the state; in some cases the argument has been made that nation building requires compromises and sacrifices on the part of ethnic and minority language speakers. Such stated aims, and the hidden political agendas which lie therein, stem from the perceived imperatives of differing systems within the state.

Habermas (1976), in his analysis of patterns of 'legitimation crises' in industrial and post-industrial societies, argues that capitalist states, both 'liberal democratic' and 'advanced', have developed an increasingly differentiated structure, and that to generalise the needs and imperatives of the state (as is often done in 'dominant ideology' critiques) may be to misrepresent the complexity of modern capitalism. He analytically differentiates three systems operating within modern nation states: the economic (both private and public), the political/bureaucratic, and the sociocultural. The three stand in complex, interlocking relationships, so that problems and crises which arise because of the tendency of capitalism to traverse a 'crisis ridden' path of development are transferred, mediated and relocated from one system to another. Complex modern states, then, are able to deflect possible crises perhaps without coercive police state tactics, overt class antagonism or economic collapse by engaging in a continual balancing act whereby the imperatives of one system are played off against another. Mass loyalty, for instance, can be maintained by deploying or perpetuating cultural traditions, myths and symbols which rationalize economic problems or political oppression (Barthes, 1973). Alternatively, they may develop public economic institutions (e.g. welfare) which modulate problems generated by the private economy.

A full exposition of Habermas's model is beyond the scope of this paper (cf. Luke, 1988), and it should be noted that in more recent work Habermas reconceptualizes the workings of state systems as well as their manifold institutional constraints on communicative competence. However, several examples from the South Pacific rim exemplify how state systems can balance and counterpose the imperatives of one system against another. Consider, for example, the situation in Malaysia. There the language issue, historically a focus of contending sociocultural systems of particular ethnic groups and classes, is intricately tied to the political and economic situation (see Ożóg, Chapter 17, this volume). Government and the Chinese minority groups battled in 1987 over the possible replacement of Mandarin-speaking administrators in Chinese schools by Malay-speaking teachers and administrators. Minority language rights, and the crucial issue of whose language and culture should dominate which sociocultural domains, became a flash point for historically deep-seated political questions. The outcome was that opposition party leaders and members of the Chinese community were jailed for illegal dissent over the national language and education policies. These policies, supposedly designed to generate national identity and solidarity, thus led to overt political conflict between ethnic minorities holding specific class positions within the economy. The conflict in turn was used by the government as a means not only to quash opposition to changes in the educational system but moreover to silence the political opposition representative of a particular socioeconomic/ethnic group.

By contrast, the state can effectively employ cultural allegiances and institutions to generate mass political loyalty and thereby deflect attention from economic problems. For an example of this, we can turn to the Fijian situation where in 1987 the Rabuka military government repeatedly attempted to mask the political situation, and questions of class and economic stability, by justifying itself as the only protector of indigenous culture, customs and language.

What we are arguing here is that whether and how a language gains legitimacy, and how a language plan or policy may serve other political ends, can only be understood in terms of the interlocking imperatives of the economic, political and sociocultural systems (see Jourdon, Chapter 8, this volume). In order to gain legitimacy, or mass loyalty, acceptance and actual use, a language must indeed have apparent value and use within the cultural traditions and social practices of the latter sphere; it must serve a political structure; and it must be congruent with the demands of the economic system or subsection in question. Regardless of how language is planned, authorized and 'implemented' by language planners on behalf of governments, without these complementarities what we might term a language-related 'crisis' can arise, for language is never .hermetically sealed off from the broader political domains which surround it. It is always already political.

The Habermasian framework, then, allows us to analyze contending claims made on behalf of a language plan or policy in terms of its possible concomitants and consequences in each of the three systems. Most often, a language plan purports to serve economic purposes (e.g. 'national development and trade'), and the development of sociocultural solidarity (e.g. post-colonial 'national identity'). Too often hidden, though, is how that plan may facilitate political ends (e.g. the linguistic repression of particular groups or classes, the perpetuation or transformation of class stratification, the perpetuation or transformation of aspects of residual cultural tradition which serve to uphold or undermine a political system). In similar fashion, the call for language standardization and change under the auspices of 'technological development' may serve an economic and ultimately political agenda (e.g. the development of multinational resource or tourist industries, the selling of resources to offshore interests and the further accumulation of wealth by a domestic, colonially educated élite).

Of course, the priorities, differentiation and complexity of each of these societal sub-systems will vary depending upon the kind of social system. Habermas (1976: 24) argues that in tribal societies, where kinship relations and primary roles demarcated by gender and age form the basis of social organization, there is little 'differentiation between social and system integration'. Hence, in the case of indigenous groups in the New Guinea Highlands, for example, economic imperatives remain intimately interwoven with cultural and administrative imperatives; the matter of 'whose language?', *within* the tribal system, is non-problematic *until* the tribal culture's homeostatic character is threatened by 'externally induced identity crises', e.g. unequal contact with economies and social forces extrinsic to the tribe itself. In Melanesia and Australia, languages thrived in many precolonial historical situations characterized by interethnic and intertribal coexistence. There languages served as important sociocultural boundary markers. However, once contact with a colonial or post-colonial economy occurred — based on asymmetries of power and exchange — the generation of differentiated (and hegemonic) interests began. This again calls into question naive readings of 'cultural preservation'.

In what Habermas (1976: 20) calls 'traditional social formations' — non-secular aristocracies — the principles of social organization are based on class domination in a political form. Aristocratic kinship remains the principle of social organization, but a concomitant bureaucratic machinery (the State/Crown) has developed to organize administratively the transmission and reproduction of wealth and labour. From this, we might generalize that the role that language plays in the maintenance of social solidarity, and its potential use in the economic and political systems as both a tool and issue, largely will depend on the kind of social organization of the state in question. To analyze the language and education situation in present day Brunei, for instance, we would have to consider how the blending of 'traditional' and 'advanced capitalist' systems has generated differing imperatives in the economic, political/bureaucratic and sociocultural systems. At this stage, the Sultanate views the maintenance of colonial language and educational systems, alongside of traditional Muslim cultural practices, as necessary for the perpetuation of economic and political privilege.

We have argued here that language planners need to consider not only the question of 'whose language?', but also how this question in turn can lead to a more critical, systemic analysis of the imperatives and interests operative within the specific sites of state, region or jurisdiction, for example. But, given this reconsideration of language planning in light of critical theory, the related question must be whether any sociolinguistic analysis as such is capable of theorizing language in non-neutral terms, for the very question of 'analysis' may be fraught with political considerations. We have looked at the politics of *sites* of planning, but now we must turn to the politics of the planning discipline itself: linguistics.

Power

Any history of linguistics in the twentieth century would surely have to record that it saw the birth of structuralism (Saussure), its scientistic fruition (Chomsky) and also, perhaps, its death. With respect to the latter, we refrain from appending a name, even tentatively. The first major stab wound, however, came from within, from Hymes (1972), who simply reminded linguists that their 'positive science' was also a social science; that language has a context as well as a calculus. This was the moment in which linguistics, by the mid-1960s the most rigorous of the human sciences (and so much so that even biology was borrowing its metaphors), took a social and political turn. But the turn was only through some 90º. Linguistics, in order to remain linguistics, had to take 'society' as a topic of analysis just as before it had considered grammar (phonology, syntax, semantics) its proper object (Fowler et al., 1979). This first social and partly political turn most clearly is associated with the sub-discipline of sociolinguistics, but would also include ethnomethodology, conversation analysis, the ethnography of communication and pragmatics.

To a certain degree, then, concepts of society have been amply inscribed within linguistics and its related fields. However, the relation between linguistics and society is still, to invoke a further metaphor, a colonizing one. That is why we want to mark what we consider a further development in the demise of a structuralist, authoritative and positivist linguistics: namely the advent of discourse.

If traditional linguistics construed language in terms of the triple division of phonology/syntax/semantics and has now added 'social' topics to these, it has *necessarily* ignored discourse, in the sense that we use it here. For discourse, in the seminal work of Foucault (1972) and also of such theorists as Bakhtin (1986) and Bourdieu (1984), is not identical with 'talk' or 'conversation' or even 'text'. It is not the utilitarian end of language (with language construed linguistically). Rather discourse is that central, yet also diverse, analytic field in which language, power and discipline(s) come together.

Foucault inaugurates a moment in the critique of the social and human sciences at which they become highly self-conscious of themselves as parts of the very social terrains that, previously, they would merely have turned into scientific topics on a par with the atom, the dendrite, the axon: thus to control the same. If linguistics' social turn was away from positivism and towards humanism, Foucault's has been away from both of these and towards a dissolution of the traditional distinctions between social science and society, linguistics and language, corpus and status, theory and practice and the other dualisms that we have relied upon for so long. The result was that while the pragmatists amongst us were pleading for linguistics to become 'socially relevant', we were all fairly blind to the disciplinary 'effectivity' of linguistic knowledge. Moreover, it was particularly the applied aspects of linguistics that, in quite local, yet widespread locales, were having their effects as parts of the armatures of *power*. Pedagogic linguistics was, all along, providing a theoretical base and legitimation for strategies of power in the classroom (cf. Lemke, 1984). Linguistic stylistics encoded, recoded, decoded and digitalized the space of literary production (e.g. Freeman, 1970). The 'demystifications' of the language of advertising were nowhere more readily received and used than in the copywriter's office, the latter relying particularly on the psycholinguistics of reading, with peculiar results. But on a much more global scale, and following the fault-lines of traditional divisions closely, was another and much more central discourse of applied linguistics, central at least as far as the repetition and enforcement of power-relations was concerned: language planning. And this is not to mention its associates: the spread of pan-anglicism (TEFL), the normalization of 'special' (i.e. handicapped) populations (ESP), the isolation (with an eye to destruction) of putative 'class codes' within natural languages, and some others.

What then, in the theoretical space which follows the transformation of linguistics from positivism to humanism, is power?

> ... power must be understood in the first instance as the multiplicity of *force relations* immanent in the sphere in which they operate and which constitute their own organization; as the process which, through ceaseless struggles and confrontations, transforms, strengthens, or reverses them; as the *support* which these force relations find in one another, thus forming a chain or system, or on the contrary, the disjunctions and contradictions which isolate them from one another; and lastly, as the strategies in which they take effect, whose general design or institutional crystallization is embodied in the state apparatus, in the formulation of the law, in the various social hegemonies (emphases added; Foucault, 1979: 92–3; cf. Eco, 1987: 239–55).

On this score, language planning is the classic incarnation of a linguistics which is blind to the very networks of power through which it operates. One need not dwell too long on the simple demographic matters:

— that 'language', in language planning, always means 'natural' or 'national' language, relying as it does on those twin scientistic fictions of objective natures and nationhoods;
— that, relatedly, language planning texts have been written *in* English, American English, French, Dutch, German ... *about* the languages of the developing world, Southeast Asia, the South Pacific, about regional and minority languages home and abroad, about the languages of indigenous peoples colonized (or 'imported') in preceding centuries by the English, the Americans, the French, the Dutch, the Germans ..., in short *about* all those languages whose very national status is 'officially' dubious;
— that the first *de facto* language planners (doing some of the first linguistics) were colonial administrations, churches and missionary bodies;
— that many of today's language planning organizations are organs of, or at least funded and sponsored by, the descendants of those bodies;
— that, historically speaking, nothing has constituted a better precondition for social and cultural independence than the existence of forms of communication outside the 'natural' language of the administration;
— that well-meaning attempts to understand those indigenous forms are, in terms of power, structurally identical with attempts to control

and eliminate them, thereby equating humanistic with more overtly colonialistic endeavours within language planning (cf. Bates, 1966);
— that, finally, language planning is knowledge: knowledge which is frequently statistico-demographic in character and therefore politically strategic knowledge (cf. Hacking, 1981), whatever the intentions of its 'producers' towards 'understanding', 'preservation' and 'scientific endeavour' (cf. King & McHoul, 1986; Muecke, 1982).

While language, in the sterile sense linguistics has attached to it, can be 'planned', discourse cannot. In planning 'language', discourse continues as before: it continues as discipline. For example, the national language plan for Ireland, constructed in the 'best' humanist terms by English speakers and writers, fails or refuses to acknowledge that the dominant medium of transmission in modern Ireland is no longer the pub conversation or even the pedagogic dialogue, but television and, though only marginally, radio and print. The only possible means for the survival of the Gaeltacht, in this situation, is the establishment of pirate television stations. This is an incredibly risky business, a business in which language planners can have less say than speakers of Irish and in which the Irish can only have a say by virtue of continued illegal activity. Irish is surviving, if at all, not because of any language planning but, on the contrary, by virtue of *discursive strategy*. And discursive strategy is clearly not something that language planning can take on board as part and parcel of its procedure. For one procedure of discursive strategy, resistance, works in the face of official planning.

The discourse of language planning, then, is opposite to that of strategy in the way that the discourse of criminology opposes the discourse of the prisoner. The former are scientific, official, dominant. The latter are marginal, quotidian, dominated. But this separation is part of a political facticity which language planning can neither analyze nor change — for it depends for its very existence on that political facticity being in place, as firmly as possible. To give a blunt example: Turkish 'guest workers' in Germany are not taught their 'host's' language for the sake of intellectual advancement (Mey, 1985). The networks of power include employers, German and multinational, yet it would be difficult to argue that employers *control* those networks. Rather they are consistent with largely public, tax-funded agencies teaching German-for-workers on just such an intellectualistic or humanistic pretext. (It should be added that this is with the usual proviso that local managers, for example, get a say in the curriculum.) The existence of a perfectly good rationale (e.g. intellectual advancement) neither cancels nor undermines the general, impersonal, constraining *and* enabling relations of language and power here. It is simply an accompaniment: a humanistic irrelevance. If one insists, for all this, upon a more traditional class analysis, it has to be said that any humanist language planning rationale would be nothing more than a useful fallback legitimation for (German) capitalism and/or the multinationals. There is, then, no political or economic conspiracy involved in this. It is the result, to abbreviate Foucault's comments, of a complex, localized, historical conjunction of force relations and their associated processes, forms of support and strategies.

The advent of discourse, in the face of linguistic construals of 'language', is the advent of a realization which can be called neither analytic, methodological or theoretical. It is something which language planning can neither allow for (especially not statistically) nor challenge. It is a realization which construes language as a political condition in a sense crucially outside the parameters of language planning. That realization is aptly expressed by Deleuze and Foucault:

> *Deleuze*: In my opinion, you were the first . . . to teach us something absolutely fundamental: the indignity of speaking for others . . . . [O]nly those directly concerned can speak in a practical way on their own behalf.
> *Foucault*: And when the prisoners began to speak, they possessed an individual theory of prisons, the penal system, and justice. It is this form of discourse which ultimately matters, a discourse against power, the counter-discourse of prisoners and those we call delinquents — and not a theory *about* delinquency.
>
> (Foucault, 1977: 209)

If discourse is political, in the same sense language planning itself can only be construed, in Barthes' (1973) terms, as 'depoliticised speech'. The other term Barthes uses for this is 'myth'. Paradoxical as it may appear to the structural linguist, we can now show that discourse is not something that language *does*. Discourse is not a mere function of language. Rather discourse is, to put it crudely, the condition by which language as a structure or a system exists:

> . . . discursive processes being at the source of the production of meaning effects, language constitutes the *material space* where these meaning effects are realized. This specific materiality of language relates to the idea of 'functioning' (in the Saussurean sense), as opposed to 'function'. The characterization of this materiality constitutes the whole problem for linguistics.
>
> (Pêcheux cited in Muecke, 1982: 99)

If discourse is the condition of language, then language planning must strictly be said to remove language from that condition, or at least to try. Like a fish out of water, language becomes, more or less instantly, dead. Language planning, then, can only 'plan' the language(s) which it constrains, delimits, controls and, metaphorically, kills. By contrast, living language remains immersed in its discursive conditions. It has to be construed as both repressed and repressing, as both constraining and enabling. Like the alphabet which both limits available phonetic possibilities and at the same time enables expression, linguistic conditions of possibility are both determining, and capable of, change through intervention (cf. Eco, 1987: 239–55). But it is equally clear that language planning is incapable, at present, of either theorizing the determination or organizing the intervention. This incapacity has to do with the absence of a power/political concept of discourse in the field of language planning. On the positive side, however, this absence provides an irresolvable blockage and contradiction for any imperialist tendencies of those who would commission or generate plans and policies. Further, were language planning to begin theoretical moves in the direction of the discursive — at least as it is construed in these remarks — it would no longer *be* language planning. It would, simply, have defected. That language planning requires such a radical move in order to become political shows, finally, just which side it is on at present.

What Is To Be Done?

As noted in articles in this volume and elsewhere (Mey, 1985; Jernudd, 1989; Jernudd & Neustupný, 1987), the development of language plans has tended to reflect the political and economic imperatives of particular social groups, rather than what could be construed as linguistic or cultural concerns *per se*. The interrelationship between political economy and language is particularly apparent in Southeast Asia and the South Pacific, where questions of 'whose language' and 'for whom', 'by whom' and 'by what', lead us to larger issues of self-determination, regional identity, class structure, and post-colonial politics. But in the absence of a critical analysis of the complex dynamics of economics, politics and culture, language planning has aspired to a technicist value-free neutrality, only to be viewed by many of its practitioners and sceptics alike as a formalization and legitimation of politically preordained developments, policies which with uncanny consistency concur with or reinforce extant relations of power and authority.

What is to be done? We have tried to show here that it may not be a simple matter of language planners evolving more sophisticated theoretical grids and demographic methods which incorporate and thereby negate, the insights of critical social theory. Attempting to graft critical categories onto the 'grids of specification' which characterize positivist social science (cf. Foucault, 1981; Hacking, 1981) would be not only bizarre theoretically, but would seriously threaten the continuing existence of 'planning' as an apparently unified practice. What we have argued here is that without an understanding of its own status as discursive (and political) practice, language planning will remain the ready tool of language rulers. For it not to be so may mean for it not to be at all.

Notes

1. The authors thank Richard Baldauf for critical comments, informed scepticism and suggestions, and Björn Jernudd for providing access to materials in press.

References

ASHWORTH, M. (1977), *The Forces Which Shaped Them*. Vancouver: New Star.

BAKHTIN, M. (or VOLOSHINOV, V. N.) (1986), *Marxism and the Philosophy of Language*. Cambridge, MA: Harvard University Press.

BARTHES, R. (1973), Myth Today. In *Mythologies*. London: Paladin.

BATES, D. (1966), *The Passing of the Aborigines*. Melbourne: Heinemann.

BOURDIEU, P. (1970), Cultural Reproduction and Social Reproduction. Paper presented at the British Sociology Conference, London.

— (1984), *Distinction: A Social Critique of the Judgement of Taste*. Cambridge, MA: Harvard University Press.

CARNOY, M. (1974), *Education as Cultural Imperialism*. New York: Donald McKay.

ECO, U. (1987), *Travels in Hyper-reality*. London: Picador.

EDWARDS, J. (1985), *Language, Society and Identity*. Oxford: Blackwell.

FASOLD, R. (1984), *The Sociolinguistics of Society*. Oxford: Blackwell.

FOUCAULT, M. (1972), The Discourse on Language (L'ordre du discours). In *The Archaeology of Knowledge*. New York: Harper and Row.

— (1977), *Language, Counter-memory, Practice: Selected Essays and Interviews*. Oxford: Blackwell.

— (1979), *The History of Sexuality, Vol. 1: An Introduction*. London: Allen Lane.

— (1981), Questions of method. *Ideology and Consciousness* 8, 4–8.

FOWLER, R., HODGE, R., KRESS, G. & TREW, T. (1979), *Language and Control*. London: Routledge and Kegan Paul.

FREEMAN, D. (ed.) (1970), *Linguistics and Literary Style*. New York: Holt, Rinehart and Winston.

FREIRE, P. (1972), *Pedagogy of the Oppressed*. New York: Herder and Herder.

FREIRE, P. & MACEDO, D. (1987), *Literacy: Reading the Word and the World*. South Hadley, MA: Bergin and Garvey.

GLEN, S. (1989), *Missionary Education, Yarrabah and the Royal Readers III: An Essay on the Dynamics of Imperialism*. Unpublished MEd (Hons) thesis, James Cook University.

GRAFF, H. J. (1987), *The Legacies of Literacy*. Bloomington: Indiana University Press.

HABERMAS, J. (1972), *Knowledge and Human Interests*. London: Heinemann.

— (1976), *Legitimation Crisis*. London: Heinemann.

HACKING, I. (1981), How should we do the history of statistics. *Ideology and Consciousness* 8, 15–26.

HAUG, W. F. (1986), *Critique of Commodity Aesthetics*. Cambridge: Polity.

HAUGEN, E. (1983), The implementation of corpus planning: Theory and practice. In J. COBARRUBIAS & J. FISHMAN (eds.), *Progress in Language Planning*. The Hague: Mouton.

HYMES, D. (1972), Models of interaction of language and social life. In J. GUMPERZ & D. HYMES (eds.), *Directions in Sociolinguistics*. New York: Holt.

JERNUDD, B. H. (1989), The texture of language purism: An introduction. In B. H. JERNUDD & M. SHAPIRO (eds.), *The Politics of Language Purism*. Berlin: Mouton-De Gruyter.

JERNUDD, B. H. & NEUSTUPNÝ, J. V. (1987), Language planning: For whom? *Proceedings of the ICRB*. Québec: Université du Laval.

KENNEDY, C. (ed.) (1984), *Language Planning and Language Education*. London: Allen and Unwin.

KING, D. & McHOUL, A. W. (1986), The discursive production of the Queensland Aborigine as subject: Meston's proposal, 1895. *Social Analysis* 19, 22–39.

LEMKE, J. (1984), *Semiotics and Education*. Toronto: Toronto Semiotic Circle Monographs.

LUKE, A. (1988), Building mass loyalty through education: Rereading

Habermas's 'Legitimation Crisis'. Unpublished manuscript, James Cook University.

MEY, J. L. (1985), *Whose Language? A Study in Linguistic Pragmatics.* Amsterdam: John Benjamins.

MUECKE, S. (1982), Available discourses on Aborigines. In P. BOTSMAN (ed.), *Theoretical Strategies.* Sydney: Local Consumption Publications.

NEUSTUPNÝ, J. V. (1974), Basic types of treatment in language planning. In J. FISHMAN (ed.), *Advances in Language Planning.* The Hague: Mouton.

PATEMAN, T. (1975), *Language, Truth and Politics.* Lewes: Stroud.

WILDEN, A. (1986), *The Rules are No Game.* London: Routledge and Kegan Paul.

WILLIAMS, G. (1981), Review of 'Variance and Invariance in Language Form and Context'. *Journal of Multilingual and Multicultural Development* 1, 363–370.

WILLIAMS, R. (1977), *Marxism and Literature.* London: Oxford University Press.

Part II:
Language Planning and Use in Australia

3 Making language policy: Australia's experience

JOSEPH LO BIANCO

Introduction

This paper describes the Australian experience in formulating a national language policy and analyses some of the more important features of the policy and of the process which led to its adoption. The description of the process, and any generalisable validity it may contain, may be a valuable contribution which the Australian experience can offer to language policy (theory and practice) in the world. The development and acceptance of the national policy on languages has been essentially a process of status attribution. It was the evolution of a language constituency which was sufficiently coherent and strong to find unifying common ground among widely disparate groups which, ultimately, was the determining factor in bringing about the acceptance of the policy by government.

Fishman, Das Gupta, Jernudd & Rubin (1971: 293–302) and Fishman (personal communication, 1987) have called for the documentation of language policy processes focusing, among other aspects, on the interest basis which underlies them and on how this is manifested in particular situations. This paper addresses the development of the policy as a social process — a social process viewed from the perspectives of politics, social psychology and sociolinguistics.

The Status of the Policy

Language issues have attained a prominence in Australian public life which is unprecedented. At the highest levels of government there are frequent declarations about language questions and their intersection with important economic, nation-building and equity goals.

On the 26th April 1987 the Prime Minister, the Hon R. J. Hawke, announced the Commonwealth (Federal) government's endorsement of the National Policy on Languages. He stated:

> let me turn to another initiative of my government . . . the implementation of a national policy on languages . . . . The Government commissioned [the preparation] of a report on a national policy on languages . . . the Government endorses that report. . . . Let me take this opportunity to announce that we are committed to fund an integrated package in the August budget to implement the national policy on languages.

> (Hawke, 1987a)

The policy was released in the Senate on the 4th May 1987 (Hansard, May 1987: 2240) with Senator Susan Ryan, then Minister for Education, repeating the government's endorsement. On the 5th June the Federal Cabinet voted a budget towards the initial phases of implementation of the policy. On the 18th June 1987, launching the Immigration and Ethnic Affairs platform of the Australian Labor Party, the Prime Minister announced a 'package of measures' which were to be regarded as the concrete, implementing programs of the language policy. A press release jointly issued by the Prime Minister and Minister for Education accompanied the platform statement. Both stressed such aspects of the policy as the support for the maintenance of ethnic community languages, Aboriginal languages and the extensions to programs for teaching English as a second language. Mention was also made of some economic aspects of the policy. At the opening of the new Parliament following the July 1987 election, on the 14th September, the Governor-General, Sir Ninian Stephen, repeated the government's commitment as part of its program for the present term of office. The commitment was officially confirmed by the Treasurer in his 1987–88 budget and in the accompanying papers.

On the 15th December 1987 the government reconfirmed its funding of the Policy and its endorsement of it, as well as announcing the composition of the Australian Advisory Council on Languages and Multicultural Education (AACLAME) which will oversee its implementation and further development.

This statement stressed the economic aspects of the policy. It focused on the labour market and the ways in which tackling adult illiteracy levels, extending English proficiency and teaching 'trade languages' would benefit

Australia's economic performance. Already some ambiguity about goals and some tension about priorities is evident in the different emphases revealed in the various statements.

On the 9th and 10th March 1988 AACLAME held its inaugural meeting, the first occasion in which a constituted representative body has attended to broad issues of language policy and the implementation of explicit Commonwealth policy on language in Australia.

The content of the policy will be described after an account is given of the history of language planning in Australia. The recent history of the process which led to the adoption of the National Policy on Languages will also be discussed.

Seeing Language and Acting on it

To the dominant sections of society language is virtually invisible. 'Language' is their medium for exercising their influence over affairs but since *'their'* language — their particular dialect and the registers they command within their linguistic repertoire — is neither in a state of attrition, nor stigmatised, deficient or aberrant in any important way, it is rarely an issue. The society reinforces and reflects their language. There is no contrast, no problem which is encountered frequently and which is predictable which can, in the common-sense judgments of ordinary people on language issues, lead them to regard language as a social question requiring explicit 'treatment' or attention.

For linguists, and others who care about language (whether for aesthetic, cultural, social justice or other reasons), it seems natural to advocate deliberate planning of language development in society and in its institutions. For such people language has a natural salience. They are used to detaching language from its 'embeddedness' in social relations between groups, in ideology, text, schooling, culture and so on and making it visible.

Language professionals investigate language in systematic ways. Language artists use it to create. They are conscious of the social correlates of language such as the present and predicted sociolinguistic patterns of language in society; the trends towards attrition or the evolution of stable inter-generational maintenance of more than one language in a given speech community. They attend to issues such as the cultural impact of the loss of a minority group's language; the intellectual benefits of bilingualism; the location of language in the brain and the strategies learners employ to make meaning in a language over which they have only partial control. This constant attending to language and its correlates makes it highly visible.

For groups whose language is not society's dominant language — whether they are an immigrant minority, an indigenous minority or a group with a communication disability — the same is true. For these groups the contrast between their language and the society's dominant instrument for conferring power, access to information and knowledge is encountered daily. Language becomes a problem in the ways it restricts access and social participation and in the ways it makes these possible. Language is seen and felt to be important.

For some whole societies language is a salient question. Its correlation with issues of politics, with the institutionalisation of conflict and compromise is a constant reminder of language questions. For many countries, recently independent, which are trying to reconcile public administration and education in an inherited colonial language with the revival of an indigenous language, or the selection and elaboration of one among competing varieties, language is a social problem of great magnitude. The felt need for nationalism impels them towards the propagation of indigenous norms; the felt need for access to advanced technical skills and the literature of powerful knowledge especially in new technologies impels them towards preserving the 'foreign' language. The inherited colonial language is often the means for communicating with a wider world.

Other countries become conscious of language when institutionalised arrangements for containing linguistic conflict change or break down or cannot be set in place. Among such countries are many developed nations. Others have expressly externally-oriented economic needs which dictate the ways in which language comes to be seen, resulting in language planning which is centred around economic goals.

It seems inevitable, then, that in the absence of a dominant group whose language interests correlate with a practical pressing problem societies will not regard language as an issue requiring the attention of policy makers. Language policy — and indeed the sort of explicit, deliberate, conscious attention to language which can be considered language planning — will not occur. Power-holders in developed countries invariably seem to regard language policy and planning as either a phenomenon of Third World countries or as a peripheral concern of major interest only to domestic minorities in developed countries. It is interesting to note in this regard that one of the first and still a seminal text on language planning is subtitled Sociolinguistic Theory and Practice for *Developing Nations* (Rubin & Jernudd, 1971).

In developed countries like Australia conscious and deliberate language planning seems only to occur in response to social or economic problems which derive from language questions, or which have a strong language dimension. In addition to such 'problem-solving' language planning, there is the explicit attention to language planning and language policy development which is undertaken to facilitate the achievement of established or emerging social, political or economic objectives of given societies.

The absence of explicit policy on language issues does not mean that policies on language do not exist. Rather, such policies are implied in related actions which the society takes. Explicit treatment of language issues in policy is usually a consequence of a highly salient set of language derived problems which the society must confront. The conceptual basis of the Australian National Policy on Languages is socio-political language planning. It is largely concerned with status planning for languages in Australia, especially for language education. The more technical linguistic dimension of language planning (corpus planning) is concerned with the issues of the codification of languages (dealing usually with orthographies) and the elaboration of languages through various means. Much technical linguistic work has been undertaken on Aboriginal languages in Australia, some on Australian English and some on Australian Sign Language and some on Australian non-English community languages. Although this is technical work undertaken by linguists, it invariably also will involve some attention to status questions since the norms which are developed by linguists, no matter how rational they may be, will require propagation to ensure their acceptance both by the ordinary users of the language and, importantly, by the power holders in the language community concerned.

At the societal level, however, the absence of any explicit, overall, guiding set of principles until recently requires that previous policy be induced from practice. Organisational theory tends to view policy as the elaboration of explicit principles to guide action. A more useful definition might be action directed by an intention to achieve a predetermined result, regardless of how unconscious this may be. Whatever problems or deficiencies the National Policy on Languages may have, at least the principles underlying the policy have been enunciated clearly and the choices which flow from these have been asserted. These can be modified and improved if and when review and evaluation of the policy find this necessary.

At some points in Australian history direct, forceful and unambiguous decisions were made about language questions. The amendments brought into the education acts of several states to repress bilingual education in the second decade of federation are the clearest examples. Despite this, and the only recently repealed regulations restricting electronic media use of languages other than English, English has had no officially sanctioned status in Australia.

Historically, then, Australia has 'planned' for English monolingualism modelled on southern British norms. This has rarely been explicitly aimed for — usually it has been implied in other actions and can only be discerned by analysing these actions. What are the main ways this has been done? First, there has been a pervasive stigmatisation of Australian English. English as it is used in Australia has often been compared negatively with southern British norms of English, characterising the Australian variety as uneducated, rough, unsophisticated and so on. These associations usually are transferred to the speakers of the language varieties with the clear message that more desirable and prestigious qualities are attainable through modifying Australian speech habits. Recent years have witnessed a major breaking down of this sort of stereotyping.

Second, there has been the active, deliberate denigration and repression of Aboriginal languages. This resulted in the extinction of most of the languages of the southeastern part of the continent by the time the colonies federated to become a nation in 1901. Of the approximately 260 Australian languages assumed to have been spoken at the time of Captain Cook's arrival in Australia only a handful may still be spoken by children in the year 2000. (See entries in Kale and Luke, Chapter 7, this volume.)

Third, a wide range of forms of opposition has been directed at non-Aboriginal ethnic minority languages. Although the last decade and a half has seen a dramatic turn around in the appraisals of and intentions towards these languages, the rate of language shift away from their use and the degree of failure to acquire proficiency in their use among youth is high.

Fourth, in addition to this there has been a major neglect of second language education in schools. This has permitted a situation of serious crisis to emerge in which the numbers of students taking languages has declined dramatically at all but the primary levels, where, due to the community languages movement of the 1970s and 1980s there has been a substantial growth in language offerings, course and program types.

A fifth historical problem area has been the treatment of the language and communicative needs of the deaf. Although this factor could not obviously lead to English monolingualism, in some cases as recently as ten years ago attempts were made to stamp out the use of sign language among the deaf.

Australian language planning has been, insofar as broad generalisations are possible, firmly within the implicit and often unconscious categories of the continuum of socially directed actions on language. This has been punctuated by occasional deliberate intervention, usually for negative purposes representative of particular political positions and cultural values.

The Interest Bases of Advocacy on Language Policy

By origin the Australian population comprises the following elements:

(1) Aborigines and Torres Strait Islanders; comprising approximately 1% of the total population;
(2) Australians from the United Kingdom and Ireland of three or more generations and comprising approximately 60% of the total population;
(3) Australians from non-English speaking backgrounds of three or more generations ago comprising approximately 5% of the total population;
(4) Australians of first and second generation English speaking background comprising approximately 14% of the total population;
(5) Second generation Australians of non-English speaking background comprising approximately 8% of the total population; and
(6) First generation Australians of non-English speaking background comprising approximately 12% of the total population (CAAIP, 1987:11).

These groups approximate the broad divisions of the constituency for language issues in Australia. What are the interests which these groups perceive as their own and how do they advocate them?

In linguistic terms all these groups are varied though none so much as the first. Despite being the smallest group, Aborigines and Torres Strait Islanders are by far the most heterogeneous linguistically. Indigenous Australians include speakers of over 150 Australian languages, several Papuan languages, at least two stable creoles and some distinct varieties of English. The state of these languages can vary enormously, as do the sociocultural contexts in which the speakers reside. The attachment to the language spoken varies greatly too, influenced by both communicative and symbolic factors. A heightened attachment to the language spoken cannot always be predicted from the state of health of the language, although it seems generally to follow that the serious attrition of a language tends to produce heightened attachment to it as emblematic of the group's identity and, consequently, tends to lead to agitation for action on behalf of the language. Perception of the strength of a language sometimes leads to concerted advocacy for continued support — non-speakers of the particular language who may have lost their own ancestral language sometimes will, for symbolic reasons, advocate support for the strong languages. In all, the relationship of a group of speakers to its language(s) is highly complex and that complexity is well represented among Aborigines and Torres Strait Islanders.

English speaking Australians are, of course, a linguistically more homogeneous group. The positions which they take on language issues are varied. The history of deprecation of Australian English has produced a continuum of opinions about it from 'whether it exists', to 'is it not ugly or intellectually impoverished', all the way to sophisticated advocacy for it in terms of the 'national character', of 'our language', to the relativist acceptance of linguistic divergence and variation. To this day it embarrasses some Australians that Australian English is used overseas. The language issues which most agitate this group, however, are not about English but about the choices made for second language teaching in schools and the policies regarding the teaching of minority languages — whether immigrant or indigenous.

Australians of non-English speaking background, particularly the more articulate English-speaking younger generation are at the forefront of advocacy for the maintenance of minority languages — immigrant and Aboriginal — in addition to English. There are major differences between different ethnolinguistic groups. As with the Aboriginal communities it follows that the perceived state of health of the groups' language often indicates the predicted position, for example, a perceived shift away from its use by children and young adults often leads to supportive action for the language. This is not always the case since the perceived strength of the language within some groups can impel them to supportive action and among other groups the perceived weakness by the group of the language can lead them to utilitarian judgments that transference to English is desirable as well as inevitable. The next two sections deal briefly with past policies towards ethnic minority languages and Australia's indigenous languages.

Language Policy and Community Languages

English monolingualism seems to be an accurate brief description of Australian educational practices in relation to immigrant and Aboriginal students until relatively recently. If these practices have changed it is only slightly. The prevailing slogan could still now be said to be English proficiency with residual family or immediate community directed skills in the mother tongue. It was as though policy makers had intuitively understood the language ecology trends revealed by sociolinguistic research in North America, that shift to English by non-English speakers, whether immigrant or Aboriginal, would occur primarily as a result of the greater prestige of English, that is, its exclusive association with social and economic mobility. In both financial terms and in terms of clear policy, the efforts made either to teach English as a second language (for many Aborigines English as a foreign language) and to support non-English languages either in education or more generally have been less than would be required if the true policy had been aiming at bilingualism.

Since the post-World War II migration program, four distinct phases have characterised language policy approaches to ethnic minority languages. First, there was the period until 1969. This could be called the *laissez-faire* phase since there was no intervention by the Commonwealth or State/Territory authorities as far as either mother tongue development for non-English speaking children is concerned, nor was there even any systematic attempt to teach English as a second language. It was simply assumed that English would be 'picked up'. In the late 1960s and early 1970s the Commonwealth set up the Child Migrant Education Program whose purpose was (and still is) to teach ESL. This became law with the Immigration (Education) Act of 1971 in which the Commonwealth assumed the responsibility for English instruction as a consequence of its constitutional responsibility for recruiting immigrants.

From the early to mid-1970s there was the phase that can be called the 'rights-equality' phase. There was much agitation during these years. This was a part of a broader social activism which characterised urban Australia at the time and reflected somewhat the so-called 'ethnic revival' in the U.S.A. Articulate and active ethnic community groups began to agitate for public intervention on behalf of a wide range of claims including language issues: primarily interpreting/translating services and English teaching. This advocacy was fuelled by much government sponsored research which seemed to be showing that, contrary to the expectations and beliefs of the previous phase, there were persistent and predictable social inequalities correlated with non-English language ethnicity, especially in terms of occupational and educational prospects.

The third phase began towards the middle of the 1970s. It could be called the 'culturalist' or 'multicultural' phase. In part, it took off from an aspect of the previous phase involving advocacy of mother tongue teaching of ethnic minority languages, largely because it was believed this would enhance the acquisition of English. The emergent discourse renamed these languages 'community languages' largely to connote their greater immediacy in Australian schools. The main feature of this phase, which was partially engineered by governments as an ideological corrective to the overtly political character of the rights-equality phase, was that it replaced equality as the focus of debates with culturalist explanations of the positions of migrants in Australian society. Accordingly, the purposes of the multicultural programs which were initiated by the key text of this time — the Galbally report — were to encourage social harmony, social enrichment, diversity within an adherence to certain core values in the society. The target was the whole society (Galbally, 1978).

Hence, by the early 1980s the debate on programs and policies for ethnic minorities had evolved to the present one in which there is a pattern of gravitating to one or other pole of the 'rights-equality' and 'culturalist' phases — pursuing the goals of overcoming disadvantages and therefore targetting programs at minorities on the one hand and, on the other hand, pursuing socially enriching and harmonious relations by targetting the whole community. Two other key factors had also emerged, holdovers from the mid-1970s. The first was the very pronounced economic and, in particular, trading relationship the nation now increasingly conducted with Asian non-English speaking countries. The second was the serious decline of school second language education. Both are too complex to deal with in detail here but both came to have a significant impact on the present state of conceptualising language issues in Australia.

The decline in school second language education impelled professional language people — linguists, applied linguists and language teachers — to call for national action to correct the situation. In so doing they came to examine the situation in terms of the language ecology trends of minority languages. At the same time, the economic directions brought about a coincidence of national economic goals with language goals converting some of the lobbying into a more 'hard-nosed' advocacy which was more acceptable to government.

In two states in particular — Victoria and South Australia, and to a lesser extent in New South Wales as well — the state governments had set up community language and bilingual programs. In most primary schools this innovation was the first bilingual education since the forced closure of the Lutheran German language bilingual schools during 1916–1918. In addition Commonwealth *per capita* funding support for ethnic community schools had stimulated a growth in the language maintenance efforts of communities themselves. A decisive change occurred in 1982 when the Federation of Ethnic Communities Councils of Australia convened conferences around the country on the theme of calling for a national approach to language issues. In organising these conferences, the Federation assured the participation of other groups with an interest in language questions: the deaf, language professionals of various kinds and, of course, Aboriginal groups (FECCA, 1987). It was out of this agitation and advocacy that the Senate investigations commenced.

Language Policy and Australian Languages

The history of the treatment of Aboriginal languages in Australia is more longstanding and more extreme than that of the ethnic community languages. Furthermore, given that language shift away from an Australian language results in the death of the language itself the urgency of responding positively to the demands of the Aboriginal community is greater.

When the British first arrived in Australia it is calculated that there were approximately 260 languages being spoken. Estimates put dialectal variation at between 500 and 600. The results of a survey by Black in 1979 found that only 115 of these languages then remained. The majority had less than 500 speakers, and many languages stood on the verge of extinction. The rapidity and finality of the deaths of 145 languages in 186 years will be hard to match elsewhere in the world.

(Fesl, 1987: 13)

Fesl identifies the Early Period during which 'land grabs' and the introduction of diseases to which the indigenous population did not have immunity resulted in the deaths of many people — especially children who would have been the transmitters of their languages to successive generations. The setting up of reserves for the 'protection' of Aborigines followed and many people were removed to these reserves forcibly. This continued with the forced separation of families and the distribution of children and adults to work as free menial domestics and as labourers for white families. A wide range of measures including a prohibition on the use of Aboriginal languages, the forcing together of groups which did not share a common language, the denigration and stigmatisation of Aboriginal languages contributed to the extensive death of Australian languages. By the time the colonies had federated into the Commonwealth of Australia, most of the languages of the southeastern corner of the continent were no longer used. Due both to the remoteness and sparseness of the population, and to the discouragement of the learning of English by Aboriginal people to ensure their dependence in some areas in northern Australia on the dominant English speaking white society, Australian languages survived. Fesl then describes the assimilation periods during which concerted attempts to bring Aboriginal people together in centralised reserves was extended to the northern parts of the continent. This aggregation of people was accompanied by education programs which stressed English alone. The reaction to these attempts was the outstation movement whereby Aboriginal groups moved away from reserves to attempt to re-establish traditional life. In the early 1970s the Commonwealth government set up the first bilingual schools in areas of Commonwealth jurisdiction in education. (See also Russo & Baldauf, 1986: 303–310.)

Some bilingual education had existed prior to these programs being set up but these were isolated, private initiatives. By the late 1970s a few programs, especially those controlled by Aboriginal communities themselves had evolved into maintenance programs which attempted to secure and extend the proficiency of children in their non-English mother tongue as well as to impart skills in English. These are the exception since the majority of the existing programs, although many seek to impart literacy in the Aboriginal language, are very much transitional programs reflecting a belief that this is more efficient insofar as the acquisition of English language skills are concerned.

Despite the progress which has been made many linguists and Aboriginal people can still ask rhetorically: How many Australian languages will be spoken by children at the turn of the century? If the present rate of attrition continues unabated and the new threat of satellite television, broadcast to the remotest parts of the continent, is unable to be converted to the task of using local languages, the answer may be very few indeed.

By the early 1980s Aboriginal language activists, linguists and community representatives had evolved an alliance of interests with ethnic communities in lobbying for a national approach to language policy which supported the maintenance and development of Australia's non-English languages. The social process whereby this, and other alliances, produced a constituency for language issues in Australia is described in the next section.

The Principles and Programs of the National Policy on Languages

Following the very strong advocacy by professional groups and ethnic and Aboriginal groups, the Senate decided in May 1982 to refer the question of language policy to its Standing Committee on Education and the Arts. Their investigation produced the report entitled 'A National Language Policy' in October 1984. The first recommendation of the Senate's report was that:

language policies should be developed and coordinated at the national level on the basis of four guiding principles, namely:

(1) competence in English
(2) maintenance and development of languages other than English
(3) provision of services in languages other than English
(4) opportunities for learning second languages.
(Senate Standing Committee on Education and the Arts, 1984)

Almost two years after the Senate's report was published, no decisions had been taken on it. The 114 recommendations made — including the first, that there be nationally developed policies on language — had represented major problems for government. Internal attempts within the Commonwealth Education Department and cross-departmental committees had been unable to draw from the Senate's report a policy and a coherent set of programs acceptable to government.

I was engaged as a consultant from July 1986 to draft a policy for the government in response to the Senate's investigations. At its simplest, this whole process consisted of converting the best principles which have underpinned language planning in the past into explicit statements of desired objectives and into the establishment of programs to take these towards realisation. To do this involved describing the context for language policy at the national level and the factors which shape it. Four which were important in developing the policy are dealt with briefly here.

The first crucial factor which constrains national policy development on language is the Federal nature of Australia. Schooling, for example, remains primarily the responsibility of the states and territories. The Commonwealth is responsible for setting broad policies which act as the parameters for education as well as for resourcing schools and higher education. The policy on languages had to take this into account and it had to attempt to establish a consensus on the principles underlying the policy, and on the jurisdiction and roles of the different bodies. This consensus seeks to evolve a partnership between a wide range of virtually autonomous bodies on issues of language. The task is especially complex in cases involving English as a second language programs and in Aboriginal education. In such instances there is an explicit constitutional responsibility of the Commonwealth or a responsibility conferred on it by virtue of referendum. The neglect of such shared responsibilities — shared because both educational domains are also state and territory responsibilities — and the inadequate appreciation of the importance of evolving a partnership of shared goals have resulted in past language policy failures.

A second crucial factor is Australia's geographical proximity to a large number of culturally very different non-English speaking countries. Whatever other justifications exist for language teaching and learning in Australia, the proximity of large and small non-English speaking neighbours is significant. Australia's role as an English language centre for the purposes of providing aid and for economic purposes, as well as the widespread teaching and promotion of Asian and Pacific languages, are among the implications which flow from this consideration. The motivations thus tend to be instrumental and utilitarian. It should be noted that community based advocacy of language policy in the past has neglected, naively, to acknowledge the pragmatic (economically and politically derived) perspective which in Australia has proved to be a critical factor in attaining government support for a national policy on language.

A third crucial factor is the great diversity of Australia's linguistic demography. Given the dominance of English in Australian society and the presence of a significant number of non-English speaking groups including speakers of various Aboriginal languages, the questions of bilingualism, bilingual education, language ecology, interpretation/-translation, and the media are central considerations. The political strength of a broadly based constituency of groups interested in language issues was the single biggest factor in the successful campaign for language policies to be acknowledged as a legitimate function of the Commonwealth government.

Less obvious than the previous three, the fourth factor concerns the impact of modern technologies. Technological innovations will have a dramatic impact on the prospects for the survival of Aboriginal languages, on the prospects for the maintenance of other community languages, and on recreational and employment opportunities in language related areas. The displacement of workers from the jobs traditionally held by non-English speakers by the application of advanced technologies to manufacturing creates increased demand for English courses specifically designed for industrial retraining. Further to this, the growth of information and communications technologies will have major ramifications for the place and development of literacy and oracy in schooling, especially with such developments as voice instruction modes on computers. Yet, the learning of second languages can be diversified and enriched by the application of advanced technologies and the maintenance of community languages can be enhanced by increased access to the language variety and vocabulary of their native-speaking peers. Children prefer to model their language on their peers and contact with such varieties can be highly motivating. The imminent expansion of satellite based transmission of television to remote areas of Australia carries with it both potentially positive and potentially destructive prospects for the survival of Aboriginal languages. All these factors were able to sustain a rhetoric associated with the advocacy of the language policy which assisted in its being perceived as 'modern' and 'contemporary' and not 'backward-looking' or 'nostalgic'. This perception, furthermore, positively assisted the claims made before political bodies.

The policy is related to broad social goals summarised under the headings of *Equality*, *Economics*, *Enrichment* and *External*. These capture four key themes and were crucial in the development of a set of arguments to justify Commonwealth government involvement in language policy making, for each of these themes intersects with areas of distinctive Commonwealth responsibilities.

Equality refers to the correlations between social and economic inequalities and language. The obvious issues are communication disabilities such as deafness, lack of proficiency with standard Australian English because the speakers use either a dialectal form of English or another language and, also, negative attitudes to varieties of language which are different from the socially prestigious ones. Since clear patterns and relationships between such language issues and social or economic inequalities are manifest in indicators like unemployment rates and inadequate standards of English, poor success in schooling, and Aboriginality the involvement of the Commonwealth is justified in language policy making. For some individual members of Parliament, for some Ministers in Cabinet and for some factional groupings in the political parties it was this broader social goal, this dimension of the policy, which formed the basis for discussions and which engaged their interest and support.

Economics refers to the promotion of bilingualism for economic purposes, to the promotion of the vocational implications of second language learning, and to the economic value of Australia's expertise in teaching English to speakers of other languages. It has become widely accepted that it is in the national interest to address language questions seriously because of the relationship between the broad economic, specifically trading, directions of Australia and the nation's available language resources. At a critical time in the debate on language policies in Australia, this pragmatic, nationally self-interested dimension came to be shared by many powerful political and economic figures, and hence, the prospects of successful advocacy improved greatly.

Enrichment consists of the advocacy of second language learning for all on the basis of the traditional arguments for second language teaching: the cultural and intellectual benefits of such learning, and the maintenance of languages other than English in Australia.

External concerns Australia's role in its region and in the world. This deals with foreign aid and technology transfer and the facilitation of bilateral and multilateral relationships between Australia and other countries.

The principles on which the policy and related programs of action are based are as follows. The first section of the policy (Lo Bianco, 1987) consists of a series of normative statements about the status of language in Australia. These begin with a recognition of Australian English as the national, convenient and shared language of Australia and its major official institutions. This is followed by a recognition of the rights to use community languages other than English; including the languages and language systems of the deaf and a recognition of the indigenous and unique status of Aboriginal languages, Torres Strait

Islander languages and Australian creoles. Nonetheless, these statements do not carry the force of law, nor could they. In the Australian legal system, class action is either completely absent or exists in only a restricted way in some states. This, combined with the absence of any legal position for English and the absence of a Bill of Rights, greatly minimises the prospects that language questions could be taken into the legal arena as in the U.S.A.

The main section of the policy deals with education. Three principles underlie this: 'English for All', 'Support for Aboriginal and Torres Strait Islander Languages' and 'A Language Other than English for All'. 'English for All' contains specifications for English mother tongue education for English-speaking Australians, English as a Second Language teaching and English as a Second Dialect education where this is required, and internal and external provisions of English as a Foreign Language teaching where this is required.

'Support for Aboriginal and Torres Strait Islander Languages'[1] entails elements of bilingual and bicultural education for native speakers in all cases where this is possible. It further involves language awareness programs and language learning programs for non-speakers of Aboriginal languages and the expansion of descriptive linguistic work (e.g. recording and restoring).

'A Language Other than English for All' entails the teaching of community languages as part of a larger aim of mother tongue maintenance for children of non-English speaking background, the teaching of community languages as second languages to others for intercultural reasons and academic development, the teaching of languages of geo-political and economic importance to the nation, and the continued teaching of 'enrichment' second languages for general cultural and intellectual enrichment purposes.

In addition to language education policy the national policy on languages deals with non-educational language issues such as the provision of language services on an equitable and widespread basis. Specifically, these services include library provisions for ESL/ESD; LOTE teaching for recreation/information and services for the communication disabled. Interpreting/translating services (e.g. domestic provisions for the deaf, for immigrants and Aborigines) and external provisions for interpreting and translating in trade and diplomacy. A further language service is the use of the media to support the maintenance, learning and diffusion of languages. Of particular importance are the needs of the communication disabled, and speakers of small or widely dispersed community languages. A final language service is that of language testing. This calls for the establishment of a service for providing adequate, appropriate, fair and simple testing of languages for educational, vocational and other purposes.

The policy, completed at the end of November 1986, was distributed by the Commonwealth Minister responsible for co-ordinating the government response to the Senate's enquiry. Since the Australian states and territories have jurisdiction over education, their co-operation is crucial for a truly national approach to language planning. Most welcomed the policy and stated that they would co-operate in its implementation. This could be said to represent a national consensus on languages issues. Nonetheless, opposition to some of its goals, especially the support for ethnic minority languages and Aboriginal languages, from some sections of the broader community should not be under-estimated.

The Commonwealth government has made financial allocations of $15.1m in 1987–88; $28m in 1988–89; $27.3m in 1989–90 and $23m in 1990–91 towards the implementation of the policy. In addition, an advisory council charged with a monitoring and evaluating role has now been set up to provide for the further development and modification of the policy. Generally speaking, federal financing is intended to supplement existing state effort in the languages area or existing Commonwealth allocations to language programs. The next section describes the programs which have been funded by the Commonwealth.

Some programs are ongoing programs; others are to be reviewed prior to decisions about their life expectancy being made. All programs are meant to operate on the basis of co-operation between state, territory and non-government systems with the Commonwealth. The Commonwealth funds are intended to be matched, though not dollar for dollar, by the implementing authority. The matching can be of 'effort', and not necessarily a financial contribution. Given the severe financial stringency which has been in place at the Commonwealth level, the allocated amounts represent significant breakthroughs in many language policy areas — particularly at a time when the financial stringency coincides with a devolution of responsibilities away from the Commonwealth in many areas of activity, particularly in education.

Expansion of the new arrivals component of the English as a second language program

The English as a second language program has been expanded so that eligible students are able to participate for up to twelve months in intensive English courses both in language centres prior to schooling, and in schools. The largest component, the 'general support' element of the ESL program which provides ongoing support for students in schools, has not been expanded. The net additional cost is $13.2m in 1988.

Australian second language learning program

This new program provides funding to State, Territory and non-government school authorities for innovative and high quality projects of national relevance in languages other than English, reflecting a balance between all languages. These include community languages (e.g. Greek, Turkish or Vietnamese), languages of economic and geo-political importance (e.g. Arabic, Mandarin or Japanese), languages taught as part of mother tongue maintenance programs for non-English speaking background children, and those taught as second languages. The net additional cost is $7.44m for each of three years, as both a supplement for existing programs and for new programs. A national component for this program has also been funded.

The adult literacy action campaign

This consists of the implementation through the Commonwealth authorities of a two-year campaign to improve levels of adult literacy. This will include publicity on the need for literacy and existing tutoring and courses, curriculum and materials development, research and, of course, program provision and teaching. The total program cost is $3.93m but other funds of approximately $2m may be diverted to this activity.

Initiatives in Asian studies

This is the first Commonwealth program of this type. Its aim is to boost Asian studies in Australia, including, for example, initiatives to develop curriculum materials for school teaching and establish centres in tertiary institutions for research and teaching. The program will make available funding to promote the learning of Asian languages of economic and geo-political importance to Australia such as Indonesian, Japanese and Korean. The net additional cost will be $1.95m *per annum*.

Cross-cultural training programs

This program is intended to boost multicultural and intercultural studies in tertiary education institutions and post-school accredited educational authorities. Funds will be offered to intitiate or extend existing courses in cross-cultural attitudinal training and community languages, to develop curriculum materials for teaching such courses, and to include cross-cultural awareness content in a wide range of professional and para-professional courses. The program will target professional and para-professional training to enhance the quality of service delivery to Aboriginal and ethnic community populations. The net additional cost will be $1.5m.

The National Aboriginal Languages Program

This is the first Commonwealth program whose express goal is to assist in the maintenance of Aboriginal languages since the Commonwealth ceded jurisdiction on education to the Northern Territory government. It will provide supplementary funding to State, Territory and non-government authorities for initiatives in Aboriginal languages, including bilingual education programs, literature production, language maintenance and language awareness programs. The net additional full-year program cost is $0.5m in the first year and $1.0m in the following years.

Language testing unit

Although it had been decided to set up such a unit, this is now to be reviewed. The unit was to attend to the co-ordination and development of Australian tests of English for academic, occupational and other purposes and to review the language testing done by a wide range of official bodies in both English and languages other than English. It was intended to rationalise the existing language testing functions of various departments, including the Council on Overseas Professional Qualifications. Funding beyond 1988–89 was to be conditional on the Unit's full or partial recovery of its operating costs. The net additional full-year program cost which was allocated was $0.25m *per annum*. The current review of this item will delay any implementation for the time being.

Australian Advisory Council on Languages and Multicultural Education

The purpose of AACLAME is to monitor the development and implementation of the National Policy on Languages, to develop it further, and to address language and multicultural education issues generally.

The Process and Stages

Australia seems to have arrived at a delicate truce — a consensual stage — in resolving the interest-laden bases of language advocacy. The process of arriving at this position was complex and intriguing. It appears to have taken only about a decade and a half. Within the present consensus, however, is at least one issue which threatens to render it asunder. Prior to describing this situation I will describe the process of evolution and behaviour of the language constituency in social psychological and socio-political terms. This is an attempt to abstract from the practice of contested language policy making in Australia during the late 1970s and early to mid-1980s. What follows derives from my participation in and observation of the process. My position is influenced by the theories on intergroup relations (Tajfel, 1982; Taylor & Moghaddam, 1987). It is expressed in general theoretical terms in an attempt to find some generalisable validity in Australia's experience during this time. The following four stages were traversed.

(1) *Consciousness of group identity as language-determined or language-specific deriving from felt language 'problems'*. This process involved the gradual internal definition by ethnic, Aboriginal and other groups (e.g. the deaf) of language as a salient, if not the exclusive, defining characteristic of the group. This, like most group identity formation, emerges from a process of examination by the group of its boundaries with 'outgroups', particularly with those which are relevant and dominant. The contrast which emerged from this comparison was one which gave prominence to linguistic characteristics as the 'content' of the ingroup; different languages were seen as representative of the boundaries between different groups. This self-understanding emerged in many groups, especially ethnic and Aboriginal ones, at approximately the same time. Individually it impelled each to identify

self-interested advocacy of redress through various activities. This in turn involved the transfer of private language based problems to public issues which were claimed to require servicing.

This transference is never fully resolved within the group, because advocacy of an internal issue for public responsibility usually generates an opposite reaction from within the group for 'authenticity', for the group to retain 'ownership' of the language issue. The critical factors which move most groups to agitation for public intervention are:

(a) the perception of the attrition of the language, and/or
(b) the correlation between group membership status and socio-economic disadvantage which derives from a linguistic mismatch between the group and its language, on the one hand, and the dominant language code of the larger society on the other.

This must initially be accompanied by at least partial exclusion by the powerful outgroup which makes wholesale assimilation undesirable or, at least, temporarily difficult.

Initially, the group targets itself. For instance, teachers advocate that the members need to be more vigilant in preserving the language or enhancing its status; newspapers carry letters from vigilant members of the community that the children are abandoning the language; parents admonish the children for replying to them only in English. Ultimately this leads to external advocacy, for example, the demand for interpreting/translating services, governmental and public recognition and legitimacy, and forms of bilingual education or other teaching of the language.

There are usually two dimensions involved in describing the way groups advocate their claims — those of power and morality — though these are never far apart. The first involves generating a sufficiently strong internal group coherence with strongly marked boundaries between the group and outgroups recognised as such by the power-holding group. The group's perceived strength derives either from its size, or the positions and resources it holds and can mobilise from its strategic locations. Having established power, it is in a position to bargain. The second involves appealing to the moral sympathy of members of the dominant group. This requires a perception from the ingroup that the outgroup is predisposed to responding to such appeals; hence, evidence is presented to evoke sympathy (e.g. problems, family breakdown, disadvantage, irreparable cultural damage). Both strategies require recognition by the dominant outgroup, but often internally as well. To achieve this the group usually evolves a rhetoric of 'rights' based either on inherent rights which transcend considerations of polity (i.e. human rights) or 'earned' rights, those which derive from the contribution the group's members have made to the well-being of the society.

Both strategies tend to be determined by leaders from the ingroup; those who mediate between their own group and the powerholding group and tend to define the relationships between them. In both cases a range of possible responses exist by the powerholders, from 'pork barrelling', co-option of leaders, rejection and polarization, to the creation of 'alliances' based on 'clientelism' and mutual dependence. More positive responses are possible but these seem to require a judgement from the powerholding outgroup of the validity of the claims, and the perception that it can benefit by conceding, at least partially, to the claims.

(2) *These processes and behaviours require the identification and demonstrable existence of language 'problems'.* The second phase in the Australian experience emerged from the generalisation of these problems beyond single self-interested groups to 'issues' sufficiently well focused to allow the specific groups to perceive individual benefit in adhering to a broader constituency — but sufficiently broad issues to constitute a claim that could be put to the powerholding authorities uniting otherwise disparate separatist claims. This process was complex and difficult. It required the abandonment of many of the separatist claims in exchange for the achievement of a broader alliance built on the issues which all groups could deduce as flowing logically from their private claims. The prerequisites involved at least a perception of the commonness of the claims; a small or negligible degree of success as individual groups acting on their own: the perception of themselves as unlikely on their own to modify their relatively powerless position or to extract sufficient sympathy from powerholders; a minimisation of the compradour tendencies of any or each group or at least the key ones (i.e. 'holding the ranks').

Invariably the evolution of a broader constituency requires the creation of a new public, political discourse to describe the new, larger, united ingroup. First, it directs this new self-description to itself to enable a new self-description to be accepted by all the members and second, this new self-description is presented to the outgroup. This discourse seemed to require a rhetoric of 'national interest' and good citizenship. This seeks to reassure the powerful outgroup that the lobby is 'responsible', that it is concerned for the well-being and cohesion of the polity and that its advocacy and claims are consistent with the well-being of the polity. At the same time, the expanded ingroup will, very clearly, demonstrate its size, power and cohesion as an indicator both to itself and the powerholders of the relative strengths involved and to calculate the relative power distribution in the relationship.

In addition to its power it will publicly and obviously 'carry' the least powerful groups. The purpose of this appears to be to demonstrate the moral basis of the claims it is making. This involves carrying whole groups while protesting not to speak 'for' any single group (avoiding paternalism) but, to some extent, doing so nevertheless (claiming moral virtue). Sometimes this means 'presenting' evidence of disadvantage (family distress, discrimination, suffering). The other crucial feature is the early evolution of a composite log of claims. This is a vital process for bolstering internal cohesion and reinforcing to each constituent group the value of belonging (democratic decision making, 'getting somewhere'). It is also very important externally in that it unites the many problems into 'a case' which authorities/bureaucracies can deal with efficiently. This log usually is both specific and general. It will contain the discourse of the 'overall good', the 'national interest', and it will minimise the appearance of 'self-seekingness'. In addition the log will probably include the principles which underlie the separatist claims, extracting these from their specific manifestation as claims on the public purse and seeking that these be adopted as a guiding set of principles by the authorities.

(3) *Contact between representatives of both groups.* A third phase involves contact between the leaders or representatives of the lobby and the powerholding outgroup. This is a crucial stage since the lobby must delegate authority, always previously affirmed to rest indissolubly in the ordinary, 'voiceless' members. It is likely that attempts at co-option, defusing the growth of the movement, will occur at this time. Further, the system may wish to establish a compradour class among the lobbyists. Matters become more public — the authorities are asked by the media to 'respond', to 'react'. At this stage, the initiative is held by the constituency, which now strives to perfect a series of key words or themes in the evolving political discourse. These will stress language issues, not individual *languages*; the group will parade 'cases' of individual absurdity: of trade deals lost due to poor linguistic preparation by the nation, of intellectual and cultural benefits forgone. This will all be specific, of course, to the nation's self-perception. If it perceives itself as successful and modern, then the discourse will argue that language policy change is a correlate of this. If its great traditions are salient in the national self-consciousness, then

heritage and connection with the great ideas of the past will be stressed. If it is seeking to develop, to become a successful modern society then language issues pertinent to this will be the flag bearers of the language constituencies' public case.

The critical issue for the constituency is its cohesion. Its breadth needs to be sufficiently wide to enable individual groups to continue to attach specific problem-related aspirations to their membership of the lobby and to have their ordinary members perceive this. It also needs to encompass breadth enough to make 'pork barrelling' difficult. The discourse, then, involves a tension between localised interests and the broader case. Reconciling these is more difficult when entering open-ended dialogue with a powerful resource holding outgroup, than when engaging in a relatively closed internal monologue. The former tends towards practicalities, compromises, deals and bargaining, conceding and gaining. The latter tends towards purist positions. The constituency starts to introduce caveats and escape clauses in its log. It will tell the outgroup that although it is united there are different 'perspectives', 'affinity groups', 'streams', 'schools of thought' — all euphemisms for factions. It may be offered places on working parties, steering groups, committees, consultancy selection groups. The selection of these representatives is invariably difficult. A tension between the technical expertise which the bureaucracy will demand and the 'authenticity' and 'representativeness' demanded by the groups may be acute. Constant gravitating between these two is likely but, with good leadership, progress can be made.

(4) *Characterising the outcome.* When a policy is agreed — a compromise reached, a result obtained — all groups seek to own it. It may be characterised by the same group in different ways depending on the audience it is addressing. The lobbies will claim a victory for their power, a concession to their moral rightness. The authorities will claim to have made a responsible deal with the lobbies and to have responded to their claims by 'ensuring' that national interests were kept paramount.

The adoption of the National Policy on Languages in Australia has evolved through processes similar to those described above. The groups involved in achieving this result have maintained internal cohesion. In the last year language issues have been prominent in the media, particularly focusing on economic (trade and tourism) needs which Australia has in key Asian languages: Chinese, Japanese, and to a lesser extent, Indonesian. Recent political changes have made the media attention a source of great tension as far as the language constituency is concerned. The present tension, which may well worsen, is between two key groups. The following characterisation contains both the self-definition of the group's core adherents and the attributed definition by its opposing group. For the sake of making the points both simple and clear, the following is a slight oversimplification of the reality. For purposes of argument, I will label the first group the 'Anglo-Asianists' and the second group the 'Community Language – Multiculturalism Advocates'.

The former group caricatures the latter as being overly concerned with, 'obsessed by', 'useless' languages, atavism and naive rationales. They accuse them, at their most extreme, of ignoring Australia's 'real' language needs, of subordinating national interests to sectarian ones. At the same time, the latter group caricatures the former as being ignorant of what will motivate students to become bilingual, of being ignorant of schools and their communities, of exaggerating the relationship between economics and languages, of underestimating the usefulness of English and its position of strength as a *lingua franca*, in Asia in particular. At their worst they accuse them of not 'trusting' Asian–Australians who, by the community language thrust, would 'inevitably' be more proficient speakers of the so-called key languages than would Anglo-Australians.

The Asianists have the dominant position at present. A reflection of their position is the extent to which they control the language of the debate. The term 'community languages', which in the early 1970s was used in contradistinction to modern and foreign languages to connote greater immediacy and relevance, is now characterised as parochial, limited and domestic. Asian languages (really only Chinese and Japanese with Indonesian a long way behind) were labelled originally by their supporters 'key' languages, and then relabelled 'national interest' languages. As the debates became more contested more belligerent labels were employed: 'strategic' languages was popular for a time. The belligerence has given way to an uneasy truce, but preparations for battle continue, manifest in an increasing militarisation of the language for arguing about language. The Anglo-Asianists now speak of 'front-line' languages — the community languages advocates talk of 'holding the line' with the major community languages ('rearguard languages'). The stakes are the distribution of the existing allocations of resources and the deployment of any new or marginal resources.

The Community Languages – Multiculturalism group, although its largest components would be southern Europeans, is led by north and east Europeans. The group contains, of course, many Asian communities.

They are not usually the same as those considered most economically important; they would include Vietnamese, Cantonese, Hokkien and Hakka Chinese, Laotian and Kampuchean speakers. This places these groups in a somewhat ambiguous relationship overall, but usually they have adhered to community language justifications and rationales.

ESL is the central issue which has generated consensus among community languages groups. This is despite the fact that for the largest groups, the southern and northern Europeans, this is scarcely a relevant consideration since they are now enrolling their third generation, which is largely English-speaking, in schools. This group seems to have more supporters among the language professionals: linguists, applied linguists and language teachers, although many of these are associated with the 'traditional' languages of the curriculum, especially French, which in the past has been repudiated by both of the key groups mentioned above. The first group is supported by business and government. The second group is perceived by government to be a strong electoral constituency.

We must surmise that unless significant concessions can be made by both groups to the interests and needs of the other, the successful language constituency may evaporate. Unlike the U.S.A., where the status of English has emerged as the major issue in debates about bilingual education (Marshall, 1986), the only conflict which seems likely to emerge in Australia in English language education (apart from hardy perennials like the 'standards' debate) is the question of the relative priority to be accorded to English as a second language teaching as against the new economically more attractive English as a foreign language teaching. The latter is now regarded as a major potential export income earner for Australia.

Many of the elements of the tension described above are present in this emerging issue also.

Problems and Prospects

The Senate concluded its enquiry by declaring that a national — as distinct from a Commonwealth — approach to planning action on language matters was not only justified but necessary. Language policy making which deals with status attribution is not usually undertaken by or entrusted to linguists. This is a reflection of a political perception that language has powerful symbolic importance and group identity functions beyond its more obvious communicative functions and that, as a consequence the contested, disputed interests of different social groups are inextricably bound up with language issues. Policy making is not, therefore, a technical application of formulae, but rather one of negotiating consensus, of haggling out workable agreements about desired outcomes on language questions. Australia's languages policy has come about this way. A quick consideration of the following list of what may be called 'language problems' in Australia should be ample demonstration that policy is political and that, therefore, policy involves making choices. These choices are often between equally morally defensible claims and needs, balanced against economically imposed stringencies.

Some of these language problems are:

(a) Almost half of Australian students of migrant background who need extra help and instruction in English at school do not receive any such instruction. There are serious gaps in both the adequacy and appropriateness of much of the ESL provision for non-English speaking background Australian students. The most comprehensive studies undertaken of ESL provision in schools, the Campbell reports, attest to a serious inadequacy in the level of provision. They estimate that an increase of up to 30% of resources is justified and that there exist serious deficiencies in the ESL effort. Since the Campbell calculations the ESL program was cut sharply in the 1986 budget, thus further damaging the level of provision (Campbell et al.,. 1984, 1985a, b).

(b) Although in the U.S.A. deaf people can study to Ph.D. level in American Sign Language, it is extremely difficult for deaf Australians to study and attain qualifications in Australian higher education institutions.

(c) The rate of extinction of Aboriginal languages is over one per year and only a handful of the over 50 still spoken may be spoken by children in the year 2000.

(d) There is a consistent pattern of language shift among immigrant background Australians who learn a non-English language at home away from their mother tongue to using English all the time. This is despite the not insignificant successes in having community language bilingual and immersion second language programs introduced in primary schools.

(e) Australia's interpreting and translating provisions are inadequate and stretched. Although in recent years community interpreting has been the main planning emphasis, the provisions of interpreters and translators are inadequately and poorly used. There is virtually no high level accreditation provision (levels four and five of the National

Accreditation Authority for Translators and Interpreters) in languages of key economic significance and poor provisions for Aborigines and the deaf.

(f) Well over 300,000 Australians of immigrant non-English speaking background speak English poorly to very poorly. The majority of those of workforce age occupy jobs in industries undergoing the greatest degree of employment dislocation and attrition due to economic restructuring. The retraining of these workers, not to mention their economic and social prospects generally, is severely constrained by their inadequate proficiency in standard English.

(g) Over 3.7% of Australians, i.e. English-speaking background Australians, are functionally illiterate in English; a much higher percentage has only rudimentary reading skills and, when written skills are included, the proportion increases dramatically. Social class correlations are strong. This means that almost one million Australian adults have problems with English literacy. In its recent study in Victoria, the Victorian Adult Literacy and Basic Education Council (VALBEC, 1987) calculated that about 430,000 adults — migrants *and* others — require literacy help but only 4,000 receive tuition. Clearly, in addition to being an issue of individual social justice, adult illiteracy also carries significant economic and social costs to the country. In Victoria well over 80% of adult literacy students who work are employed in unskilled and semi-skilled jobs. Such jobs account for only 33% of all jobs — a proportion which is declining (VALBEC, 1987).

(h) Although only 7% of Australian undergraduate students were enrolled in language courses in 1982, and overall some 30 languages are taught, three languages attract 60% of students.

(i) Whereas over 44% of Australian students completed the Higher School Certificate — the pre-tertiary school year — with a second language in 1967, that figure had dropped to a national average of about 10% by 1986. This is particularly acute when the recommendations of the Economic Planning Advisory Committee (1986) are considered. EPAC argued that Australia must move away from dependence on extractable goods and agriculture products in its exports, and greatly improve its export of manufactured goods. It argued that Australia as an exporting nation must select and create niches in the economies of its trading partners and target goods at these. Inevitably this would require a much more sophisticated knowledge of these societies, and linguistic and cultural competence beyond present levels. Such instrumental reasons strengthen traditional 'cultural enrichment' arguments for lamenting such a serious decline in second language learning.

(j) Despite the potentially enormous impact which communications and information technology will have on literacy genres and skills, practically no serious attention has been paid to examining the implications of these changes for education and particularly for teaching.

It is around such issues, perceived and felt by the particular communities concerned in each case as 'problems', that the advocacy for language policy commenced and the processes described above took place. Despite the adoption of a National Policy on Languages, severe deficiencies remain in Australia's response to the pressing issues of language. It is important that permanent structures for overseeing language planning be set up.

A body entrusted by legislation with the authority to examine linguistic/technical aspects of language planning, especially in the case of Aboriginal languages, is an important goal. Although such a body — perhaps a National Institute of Languages — would be regarded by many as 'institutionalising' the issues, it could be constructed in such a way as to be representative of different interests. One of the urgent tasks of such a body would be to tackle the standardisation of existing orthographies, teacher training for Aboriginal bilinguals and literature production. These are essential if there is to be any prospect of producing significant long term curriculum improvements in the teaching of Aboriginal languages. Much of this must be done locally with Aboriginal management of the decision making, but some tasks can and ought to be done nationally.

Furthermore, for the languages policy overall it is also essential that an ongoing evaluation mechanism be set in place. The purpose would be to monitor, review and improve practice and to refine the work in this area continuously. Investigating ways of exploiting modern technologies for distance teaching and organisational variety to provide language maintenance in community languages is also a great need. Many schools in Melbourne and Sydney enrol speakers of over 30 languages and the total number of ethnic community languages is over 100. Inevitably such numbers of languages present practical, organisational and resource problems to planning mother tongue teaching provisions.

Conclusion

This paper has attempted to provide a description not merely of Australia's policy on languages but also of some of the more important social processes involved in producing it. It has also attempted to consider distinctive Australian language needs and some of the deficiencies of the present policy framework. This concluding section addresses the role of policy makers in developing language policy in complex multilingual societies like Australia.

It is the responsibility of policy makers to extricate themselves from the interest-based lobbies, generalising from specific instances, principles which meet four key criteria:

(1) Those which can be defended and sustained intellectually (e.g. by taking account of sociolinguistic evidence about the role of schooling in language maintenance or revival efforts, by gathering evidence about how proficiency in second languages is gained, by examining resource configurations which are reasonable to the goals of programs).

(2) Those which are feasible in terms of a fair measure of realistic or probable allocations of resources (e.g. setting realistic, attainable goals; acknowledging the jurisdictional roles of different bodies; explicitly stating the basis for the selection of options for the choices made; matching reasonable resource configurations to the meeting of goals of particular programs).

(3) Those which are both humanitarian and just in the context of democratic societies promoting equity in the broader society for minorities (e.g. ensuring that due consultative processes are engaged in; being as comprehensive as possible about the needs, rights and demands of disadvantaged groups).

(4) Those which are efficient and achievable in consideration of the national interest, which address the linguistic needs and opportunities of the mainstream sections of the society.

These principles involve the reconciliation of needs, demands and interests which are perceived to be national and those which are perceived to be important by the community. It is extremely important that an explicitly principled way of doing this is constructed so that through later refinement, changes can be made. It is also important that the value positions of the policy makers be stated. Policies need also to be practical and politically wise; attainable goals should be set; evaluation mechanisms and processes set in train. Actions should be embedded in existing structures where this is possible and proper account needs to be taken of minority/majority power positions, symbolic acts and practical tasks.

Some of these have occurred in the Australian experience — others have not. The setting up of a representative Advisory Council may ensure that the strengths of the present policy positions are reinforced, that the gaps and deficiencies are corrected, and that further refinements and developments take place regularly.

Note

1. Aboriginal and Torres Strait Islander languages will, for sake of brevity, be
   referred to as Aboriginal languages.

References

CAMPBELL, W. J., BARNETT, J., JOY, B. & MCMENIMAN, M. (1984), *A Review of the Commonwealth ESL Program*. Canberra: Commonwealth Schools Commission.

CAMPBELL, W. J. & MCMENIMAN, M. (1985a), *Bridging the Language Gap: Ideals and Realities Pertaining to Learning ESL*. Canberra: Australian Government Publishing Service.

— (1985b), *The English as a Second Language: Factors and Index Study, Commonwealth Schools Commission*. Canberra: Australian Government Publishing Service.

CAAIP, Committee to Advise on Australia's Immigration Policies (1987), *Understanding Immigration*. Canberra: Australian Government Publishing Service.

EPAC, Economic Planning Advisory Council (1986), *International Trade Policy*. Council Paper No. 18. Canberra: EPAC.

FECCA, Federation of Ethnic Communities Council of Australia (1987), *National Language Policy Conference Report (1982)*. Sydney: Federation of Ethnic Communities Council of Australia.

FESL, E. (1987), Language death among Australian languages. *Australian Review of Applied Linguistics* 10 (2), 12–23.

FISHMAN, J. A., DAS GUPTA, J. D., JERNUDD, B. H. & RUBIN, J. (1971), Research outline for comparative studies of language planning. In J. RUBIN & B. H. JERNUDD (eds.), *Can Language be Planned — Sociolinguistic Theory for Developing Nations*. Honolulu: University of Hawaii Press.

GALBALLY, F. J. (1978), *Review of Post-Arrival Programs and Services for Migrants: Migrant Services and Programs*. Canberra: Australian Government Publishing Service.

HANSARD SENATE, 4 May 1987, *Commonwealth of Australia Parliamentary Records*. Canberra: Australian Government Publishing Service.

HAWKE, R. J. (1987a), *Speech to the Ethnic Communities Meeting, Melbourne*. Canberra: Office of the Prime Minister and Cabinet.

— (1987b), *Statement by the Prime Minister, Australian Labor Party. Immigration and Ethnic Affairs Policy Launch, Melbourne*. Canberra: Office of the Prime Minister and Cabinet.

Lo Bianco, J. (1987), *National Policy on Languages*. Canberra: Australian Government Publishing Service.

Marshall, D. F. (1986), The question of an official language: Language rights and the English language amendment. *International Journal of the Sociology of Language* 60, 7–76.

Rubin, J. & Jernudd, B. H. (eds) (1971), *Can Language Be Planned? Sociolinguistic Theory and Practice for Developing Nations*. Honolulu: University of Hawaii Press.

Russo, C. & Baldauf, R. B., Jr (1986), Language development without planning: A case study of tribal Aborigines in the Northern Territory, Australia. *Journal of Multilingual and Multicultural Development* 7 (4) 301–17.

Senate Standing Committee on Education and the Arts (1984), *A National Language Policy*. Canberra: Australian Government Publishing Service.

Tajfel, H. (1982), Social psychology of intergroup relations. *Annual Review of Psychology* 33, 1–39.

Taylor, D. M. & Moghaddam, F. M. (1987), *Theories of Intergroup Relations. International Social Psychological Perspectives*. New York: Praeger.

Valbec, Victorian Adult Literacy and Basic Education Council (1987), *Literacy Matters*. Melbourne: Council of Adult Education.

4 Some competing goals in Aboriginal language planning[1]

PAUL BLACK

Once upon a time a young man sat for an examination, and he had a question something like this: 'Discuss the North Atlantic fishing treaty from either the point of view of the British or the point of view of the Americans.'

He wrote: 'I know nothing about the point of view of the British, or of the Americans, so I will write from the point of view of the fish.' (Sharpe, 1982: 36)

Much of literature on language planning leaves the impression that goals can somehow be set objectively by the language planner, perhaps 'mediating between the individual's good and the society's good' (Rubin, 1971: 479–84). Thus planning has typically been seen as a function of high level — often national — institutions (e.g. Karam, 1974: 104–5), with policy for minority groups being set by policy-makers who are not members of these groups (e.g. Paulston, 1985: 2, 35–6). Along similar lines, Russo & Baldauf (1986: 314–15) have described the need for more highly organised language planning for Aboriginal Australians, which they see as involving an overall co-ordinating and policy making body.

As Nahir (1984: 298) notes, however, even the language planning goals of a single organisation can be contradictory; his example involves a conflict between the Hebrew Language Academy's goals of lexical modernisation and external purification. There should be considerably more room for minority groups to have goals that conflict with mainstream opinion; in this regard consider Paulston's (1980: 39–75) discussion of the 'conflict paradigm' as applied to bilingual education and Apter's (1982) examination of conflict over national language policy. This suggests that there is no objective (value free) basis for selecting goals. If not, how are such conflicts to be resolved?

There are, in fact, several areas of real or potential goal conflict in language planning for Aboriginal Australians. What I want to argue here is that language planners and educators should not be deciding between competing views, but rather should be helping the groups involved come to better understandings of their own and each other's views in the hope of being able to reach consensus.

Bilingual Education and Language Maintenance

Bilingual education can promote either of two main types of goals. One is to improve the overall educational achievement of the children involved, not only by introducing them to content and such skills as reading through the medium of their own language, but also through increasing their self-esteem and by promoting better attendance. This is essentially the goal of the Northern Territory Department of Education (1986: 7–9) in its support of bilingual education for Northern Territory Aborigines.

A second goal of bilingual education can be to promote language maintenance. Bilingual programs in most Northern Territory communities may well be doing a good job of doing this even while they provide improved education, but the two goals are nonetheless distinct. This is made especially clear when the success of bilingual programs are evaluated in terms of the extent to which they have led to an improvement in English alone. (See Eggington and Baldauf, this volume, Chapter 5.)

There are certain situations in which the goals of improved education and language maintenance can come into competition. In the Fitzroy Crossing area of Western Australia, for example, many adults still speak such traditional languages as Walmajarri, but most school children are fluent speakers only of Kriol, often with some passive knowledge of a traditional language. To reach the children educationally one might want to have a bilingual program involving Kriol. Adults would find this unacceptable, however. Although they recognise that the children speak Kriol, they believe that the use of Kriol in a bilingual education would consume resources they would rather see devoted to teaching their traditional languages to the children. Their goal would thus be to have the children master a traditional language and English.[2]

This particular conflict has been dealt with by ignoring Kriol in the school and by having (at times) a Walmajarri program that is not a fully-fledged bilingual program — a solution that in practice probably does not promote either goal well. In contrast, Barunga (formerly Bamyili, in the Northern Territory) has dealt with a similar situation by developing a bilingual program for Kriol and largely ignoring the traditional languages of the community. For several years Ngukurr (formerly Roper River) has been on the brink of adopting a similar solution, but at the same time interest in reviving the local traditional languages has also been growing — as it may also be in Barunga.

One could, of course, try to combine language maintenance with other educational goals in such a situation by having bilingual programs involving Kriol and other 'languages other than English' (LOTE) programs for traditional local languages. The goals nonetheless remain in conflict to the extent that the use of Kriol for educational purposes makes the continued use of the traditional languages by the children less likely than it might otherwise be. The language planner could suggest that language maintenance was relatively unimportant because it rarely succeeds in the long run, but the concerned group may not share this evaluation — as in the Fitzroy Crossing situation.

Language maintenance can conflict with other educational goals even within a bilingual education program. This seems to be the case with the Tiwi bilingual program at St. Therese's School in Nguiu, on Bathurst Island. Here children and young adults speak a form of the traditional Tiwi language that has been simplified phonologically and heavily influenced by English. For example, they might say *yiya wantim yinkiti* for 'I want food', with *yiya* (or *ya*) as a pronunciation of the more traditional *ngiya* 'I', *wantim* for 'want' from English, and *yinkiti* 'food' from Tiwi. The more traditional Tiwi expression would be *Ngiya nguwurtimarti yinkiti*. (Kuipers, 1987; cf. Lee, 1983.)

The Tiwi of Bathurst Island are very concerned about maintaining their traditional language as much as possible, and they use their bilingual program to do this. Since the traditional Tiwi of the oldest speakers would be too difficult for the children, the school tends to use 'Modern Tiwi': essentially the more careful speech forms of middle aged adults. The considerably more simplified and contaminated 'New Tiwi', spoken by children and some young adults, is not written in the school, which has firmly rejected efforts by an SIL (Summer Institute of Linguists) linguist to produce literature in this variety.

Perhaps the goal of Tiwi language maintenance can be combined successfully with the general educational goal of bilingual education, but conflicts between the two goals are nonetheless apparent. The solution has been to compromise in favour of one goal or the other at various points. For example, to introduce literacy in the language as actually spoken by the children, with many words from English, would require different orthographic conventions from those used for more traditional forms of the language. In practice most of the words from English are avoided in writing, although strict adherence to more traditional grammar is not required from younger children: Tiwi teachers scribe such sentences as *Mutika kapi makatinga*, literally 'car to river', for example, even though Modern Tiwi would require a verb. Where language maintenance would require increasing use of more traditional language orally as well as in writing, some Tiwi teachers seem to be concerned that this is not actually happening in the classroom. To some extent this may be because younger Tiwi teachers find it difficult to speak Tiwi in the way it is supposed to be written. In any case chances seem good that relatively traditional varieties of the language will be maintained only as a written language, which at the moment has few functions in the general community.

The Roles of English

A second potential source of conflict is related to the possible roles of English as a second language for Aboriginal people. Many Aboriginal people consider it important to learn English, as well as such other skills as mathematics, especially so that they are better prepared for employment and other practical concerns within their own communities.

Harris *et al.* (1985: 26) have suggested somewhat more ambitious goals with regard to English:

> Social acceptance of Aborigines in the wider Australian society is probably assisted by the fluency with which they can (when they need to) use a variety of English which is fairly close to that spoken by native speakers of Western-world English.

They accordingly emphasise the importance of having 'standard' Australian-English models as teachers in Aboriginal schools.

There may seem to be no conflict between having enough English to get along in one's own community and having enough for wider Australian society: one can imagine just learning as much English as one can, the more the better. However, the two can come into conflict because of what seems to be required for the two learning situations. Whereas Aboriginal second language speakers of English should be able to teach functional English, it may be vital to have first language speakers of English if people want to end up sounding like first language speakers. To the extent that the available first language speakers are non-Aboriginal, this means having non-Aboriginal teachers in the community. But one reason why some Aborigines want to learn English is to reduce their dependence on non-Aborigines and the need to have non-Aborigines in their communities. Thus Penny (1975: 16–17) reports the following from Pitjantjatjara people in South Australia:

> I want school for children. Too many white fellers come little bit, don't stay. Too many white fellers here. When our children learn more, white people go.

> My people want our boys and girls learn teaching ... We don't like interfering whites. Some of the whites we do like don't stay. Better our own people learn teaching.

The goal of 'standard' English acquisition can thus be in conflict with Aboriginal aspirations for self-determination in some communities.

Standardisation

Another potential source of conflict arises from the tendency for many linguists and educators, both non-Aboriginal and Aboriginal, to seek standardisation of languages, especially those used in bilingual education. Perhaps they are simply assuming that Aboriginal languages should be like English in having standard spellings, or perhaps they find standardisation helpful for linguistic description and dictionary making, or perhaps they believe that it makes it easier for beginners to learn how to read.

Such points are debatable. In order to cope with dialect differences and variation within dialects it was decided that Kriol speakers should simply spell words as they pronounce them (Meehan, 1981: 16); the word for 'snake' might thus be spelled as *sneik*, *sineik*, or *jineik*. There is no requirement for consistency even within a single piece of writing. Spelling is thus less of a burden, and there is no evidence of which I am aware that the variability in spelling makes reading more difficult. With regard to dictionary making, ignoring variants in favour of a single 'standard' spelling is certainly convenient for the lexicographer, but it certainly does not contribute to the completeness of the description.

An actual situation in which lack of standardisation could seem to have caused problems involved two Groote Eylandt communities that came to have different orthographic conventions for Anindilyakwa, for which bilingual education programs were started but later discontinued. This led Russo and Baldauf (1986: 310, 314) to propose the establishment of a committee to develop standards for orthographies. The Groote Eylandt situation was complicated by linguistic debate on the relative merits of the two orthographies, but to the extent that each community was happy with their orthography (as they seem to be today) the alternative solution would be simply to allow them to maintain their distinct orthographies. That is, the problem was not inherent in the lack of standardisation, whether or not it was perceived to be.

Whether or not standardisation has real merits it is also potentially detrimental. It implies having authorities who determine and maintain the standards. Shirley Brice Heath (in a lecture to a class in 1985) has suggested that the introduction of literacy to a society leads to the introduction of a hierarchical structure of authority: certainly this tends to happen to the extent that standards are enforced. Standardisation can also promote the stigmatisation of non-standard varieties as inferior. This can involve entire communities, and when it does it can also conflict with the aspirations of people to keep their communities distinct.

I have observed a number of situations in which standardisation has led to major or minor problems. Tiwi bilingual education was discussed earlier; the fact that people are supposed to write a variety of Tiwi in which few speakers are fully competent can be very inhibiting — adult writers often have to consult a Tiwi dictionary or any elders in the vicinity. At an early stage in their bilingual program, Lajamanu people were learning to write Warlpiri not as they spoke it, but rather as it was spoken and written in Yuendumu, which had had bilingual education for a number of years. Now that bilingual education is well established in Lajamanu people seem happy to write Warlpiri as they speak it locally, and apparently no one finds it difficult to read material produced in the other community. In Arnhem Land, even though such pairs of varieties as Gupapuyngu and Djambarrpuyngu were traditionally spoken by different moieties, so that a wife might speak one and the husband the other, the perceived need for a single standard led one variety to be specified for the bilingual education of children from both moieties in any one community, thus Gupapuyngu in Milingimbi and Djambarrpuyngu in Galiwinv́ku (Elcho Island). Fortunately local staff increasingly recognise that it is unnecessary to favour one subvariety over another, and more sophisticated narrative writers feel free to have different characters use whichever subvariety is appropriate to their moiety — even though children in some communities have largely lost the distinction.

Conclusion

In each of the above cases one could debate the merits of either position in any particular situation. However, the present paper is not concerned with how defensible the positions are — for example, whether or not standardisation is appropriate in any particular case — but rather with the fact that different individuals or groups can have conflicting goals, such as the goal of standardisation as against goals of local or individual control.

Perhaps language planners tend to resolve such conflicts in ways that suit their particular clients. Especially when potential conflicts are more subtle, however, language planners may well think that their training gives them an objective basis for choosing the 'best' solution. For example, they may assume that standardisation is always a desirable goal. They may even feel constrained to make such choices: an educator once wrote in a letter to me that, since he was employed as an adviser, he felt obliged to advise. In the context this sounded as if he had to advise, whether he knew anything about the matter or not. In such cases it is entirely possible for language planners to resolve (or ignore) conflicts in ways that are even detrimental to their clients.

My position is that it should not be the business of the language planner, as a language professional, to decide between such conflicting goals. Perhaps 'language planner' is simply an ill-chosen term. What is needed in the Aboriginal context are language educators who can work closely with particular Aboriginal groups to gain a clear idea of their situation and to help them become better able to assess possible goals and consequences for themselves. This is in fact an increasingly common mode of working with Aboriginal groups. Indeed, in 1981 there was even a Workshop to Develop Aboriginal Leadership in Language Planning (see Bell, 1982).

Although consideration for client education in language planning is not new in the Aboriginal context, thus far it seems to have few parallels in the more general language planning literature. Perhaps this is why this literature, with its emphasis on centralised decision making, has tended to make language planning seem irrelevant and even antagonistic to Aboriginal concerns over language.

Notes

1. I am grateful to Richard Baldauf and Allan Luke for their continued encouragement and for their comments on an earlier draft of this paper, and to Mari Marett for her stimulating observations on some of the points raised.
2. This discussion is based on Aboriginal opinion expressed at the Aboriginal Languages Association meeting held in Batchelor, Northern Territory, 4–7 April 1982.

References

APTER, A. H. (1982), National language planning in plural societies: The search for a framework. *Language Problems and Language Planning* 6:3, 219–40.

BELL, J. (ed.) (1982), *Language Planning for Australian Aboriginal Languages: Papers Presented at the Workshop to Develop Aboriginal Leadership in Language Planning, Alice Springs, February 16–20, 1981*. Alice Springs: Institute for Aboriginal Development.

HARRIS, S., GRAHAM, B. & ODLING-SMEE, D. (1985), Aboriginal teachers and bicultural schooling. *Aboriginal Child at School* 13:3, 24–33.

KARAM, F. X. (1974), Toward a definition of language planning. In J. A. FISHMAN (ed.), *Advances in Language Planning*. The Hague: Mouton.

KUIPERS, L. (1987), Language shift and maintenance in Tiwi. Paper delivered at the Conference on Cross-Cultural Issues in Educational Linguistics held in Batchelor, Northern Territory, 9–11 August.

LEE, J. R. (1983), *Tiwi Today: A Study of Language Change in a Contact Situation*. Canberra: ANU, PhD Thesis.

MEEHAN, D. (1981), *Kriol Literacy: Why and How . . .: Notes on Kriol and the Bamyili Bilingual Education Program*. Katherine: Bamyili Press.

NAHIR, M. (1984), Language planning goals: A classification. *Language Problems and Language Planning* 8:3, 294–327.

NTDE (Northern Territory Department of Education) (1986), *Handbook for Aboriginal Bilingual Education in the Northern Territory*. Darwin: Northern Territory Department of Education.

PAULSTON, C. B. (1980), *Bilingual Education: Theories and Issues*. Rowley, Mass.: Newbury House.

— (1985), Linguistic consequences of ethnicity and nationalism in multilingual settings. Paper presented to the Conference on the Educational Policies and the Minority Social Groups Expert's Meeting, Organisation for Economic Co-operation and Development, Paris, 16–18 January.

PENNY, H. H. (1975), *The Training of Pitjantjatjara Aborigines for Greater*

Responsibilities in South Australian Tribal Aboriginal Schools. (Report and recommendations to the) Education Department of South Australia.

RUBIN, J. (1971), Evaluation and language planning. In J. RUBIN & B. H. JERNUDD (eds.), *Can Language Be Planned?* Honolulu: University of Hawaii Press.

RUSSO, C. & BALDAUF, R. B., Jr (1986), Language development without planning: A case study of tribal Aborigines in the Northern Territory, Australia. *Journal of Multilingual and Multicultural Development* 7:4, 301–17.

SHARPE, M. (1982), Aboriginal Education Policies Prior to 1973, with Special Reference to Language. In J. BELL (ed.), *Language Planning for Australian Aboriginal Languages: Papers Presented at the Workshop to Develop Aboriginal Leadership in Language Planning. Alice Springs, February 16–20, 1981.* Alice Springs: Institute for Aboriginal Development.

5 Towards evaluating the Aboriginal bilingual education program in the Northern Territory

WILLIAM G. EGGINGTON and RICHARD B. BALDAUF, JR

Introduction

There are times when language planning occurs as an almost spontaneous reaction to a particular social situation where there is a need or desire for language change. In such cases formal language planning procedures are not followed; rather, a vague, unarticulated notion of 'what should be' determines the specific direction. As this variety of language planning evolves, the government education sector often takes, or has thrust upon it, major responsibility for the implementation of the plan. This process fosters a subset of language planning: namely, language-in-education planning (see Baldauf, Chapter 1, this volume). Having been included in the formal education structure of the state, the language-in-education plan frequently is evaluated in terms of educational criteria. In such cases where the language plan has developed with no formal planning, there is little likelihood of a structured evaluation procedure for the whole language plan. Thus, the evaluation developed for the language-in-education planning subset fills the void, becoming the evaluation procedure for the broader plan.

One instance where this has occurred is the Aboriginal bilingual program in the Northern Territory of Australia where a language planning process developed without a formal language planning framework (Russo & Baldauf, 1986). The major responsibility for the implementation of the plan was given to the Northern Territory Department of Education (Northern Territory Department of Education, 1986) which, as one might expect, has interpreted its scope as a language-in-education program and has subjected the plan to language-in-education evaluation procedures. It is the purpose of this chapter to show that such a development results in significant harm to the overall objectives of the language plan as well as to suggest language planning evaluation procedures which might remedy the situation. Preliminary to this task, however, a review of the concept of evaluation in language planning is in order.

Evaluation in Language Planning

In the seminal work on language planning, *Can Language Be Planned?* (Rubin & Jernudd, 1971), evaluation is recognized as an important component in the language planning process. Two basic views of evaluation emerge from that book. First, evaluation is seen as a practice derived from the economic models that were used to develop language planning concepts. In particular, cost-benefit analysis is seen as an appropriate evaluative tool. Both Thorburn (1971) and Jernudd (1971) have discussed how cost-benefit analysis can be applied to language planning. Thorburn says the 'cost-benefit analysis in language planning is, in principle, an attempt to state the difference in consequences between two exactly defined alternatives in language planning' (1971: 256).

The basic idea behind cost-benefit analysis is that the language behaviour of people is a national or regional resource. As with any resource, language can be developed and used to achieve certain results and these results can be quantified. Language planning normally involves the selection and evaluation from among several methods and alternatives to meeting a particular language goal. The essential consequence of these different methods for reaching a language planning goal can be compared primarily in monetary terms. This comparison serves as the basis for selecting language planning alternatives which provide the greatest benefit for the least cost. The major benefit of this procedure is that:

> a cost-benefit calculation ought to assemble all relevant scientific knowledge pertaining to the problem in question (description and relations), which ought to be presented to the politicians in an impartial and clear way. How to weigh the advantages and dis-advantages and to judge the uncertainties is up to the politician.
>
> (Thorburn, 1971: 257)

Fasold (1984) discusses some of the limitations of cost-benefit analysis, focusing particularly on the problem of quantification. Some things can be quantified, but their impact cannot be defined in monetary terms. Consider, for example, the publication of Aboriginal language texts. In other cases more consequences can be identified than quantified; for example, the restoration of an Aboriginal language could stabilize and unify the community. Fasold points out that while cost-benefit analysis has its limitations, it may have some advantages if used in the preparatory phases of language planning. He notes however that there have not been many published reports of its application to language planning problems and he cites only three examples of its use.

The second approach to evaluation in language planning focuses more on the implementation phases of a language plan, rather than on the planning process itself. Rubin's (1971) *Evaluation and Language Planning* is the first attempt to define the role of evaluation in the language planning process. The acceptance of this argument for a major role for evaluation in the language planning process has resulted in its inclusion in Haugen's (1983) revised model of language planning. He argues for the need for evaluation procedures as an integral part of the implementation of any good language plan. The degree to which language spread has occurred due to some intervention in the language teaching process can only be assessed if proper evaluation procedures are instituted.

After reviewing the literature of the time, Rubin defines evaluation 'as a process through which information might be provided to help determine which kinds of decisions seem to be the best of several alternatives' (1971: 221). She indicates that there are four ways in which an evaluator can be of help to the language planner. In summary they are:

(1) to help the planner identify and construct alternative goals, strategies and outcomes;
(2) to help the planner to formulate or identify criteria (measures and values) through which to judge (weigh) the effects of pursuing different goals, employing various strategies, and preferring certain outcomes;
(3) to help the planner to establish an order of priority for alternative goals, strategies, and predicted outcomes; and
(4) to help investigate the logical inconsistencies of goals with strategies, of strategies with predicted outcomes, and goals with predicted outcomes (Rubin, 1971: 223–27).

Rubin also recognized that there are limits to the amount and kind of evaluation that can or should be built into any planning process. Some of the limitations identified include:

(1) Political limitations. Formal evaluation may not always be welcome. Policy makers may not wish to face the consequences of their actions.
(2) Uncertainty of environment. It is difficult to predict the best course of action in a changing world.
(3) Importance of decisions. Some types of decisions are more important than others.
(4) Intellectual limitations. It is difficult to collect, store and utilize all the information available.
(5) Difficulties in relating behaviour outcomes to particular strategies. In a multi-variable situation it is often difficult to attribute change to particular planned strategies.
(6) Incorporation of non-measured criteria. How can important non-measured variables be incorporated into the evaluation?
(7) Universal *versus* specific criteria for evaluation. Evaluation must be based on local rather than universal criteria. Universal criteria can only take on meaning within the local context (Rubin, 1971: 230–33).

In summary Rubin suggests:

> the evaluation process must be conceived as a continuing one that is constantly providing new and relevant information that is to be incorporated into planning. It should provide a technique both for continuous and systematic assessment of variables as well as for unpredicted *ad hoc* information that emerges as time goes on (1971: 233).

The evaluation process appropriate for language planning as defined by Rubin does not differ markedly from that which is used in education program evaluation. This should not be surprising as early papers by well known evaluators Guba and Stufflebeam feature in her work. The listing of limitations of evaluations is, however, unusual. Perhaps this feature is related to the scale of the evaluation assessment normally being undertaken in language planning as opposed to that usually found in educational evaluations. (See Smith, 1987.) Because the scale of the treatment in a language planning situation is so much broader than that normally found in a typical educational setting, the need to state the limitations of language planning evaluations is perhaps more obvious, even necessary. It may also be that in situations where educational systems become the *de facto* language planners, educational rather than language planning terms of scale are applied. This would account for the fact that some bilingual programs, which are really an attempt to implement language plans, are evaluated on a narrow set of educational criteria, rather than on the broader scale appropriate for a language plan.

Sociolinguistic Surveys as Planning Tools

In his discussion of the initial fact-finding element of language planning, Grabe (1980) shows how the rising need for empirical data as a basis in language planning can be met by the concurrently developed sociolinguistic field survey. The reliance on sociolinguistic survey techniques by language planners has resulted in a partnership between sociolinguistic surveys and language planning that Grabe describes as the *'modus operandi* for all language planning'. Kaplan (1980) describes a language planning program as one which begins with pre-survey planning, progresses through survey development and the actual survey implementation to the survey report which lays the foundation for policy decisions, policy implementation planning, policy execution and evaluation, once again through the use of survey data. In this context the sociolinguistic survey then becomes the 'pivotal activity' in any language planning work and an essential activity for an evaluation process. Indeed, Cooper (1975) lists evaluation of language policy as one of the five motivations for conducting a survey.

Cooper also describes a survey 'in terms of the generalizability of its results to a specified population', and a sociolinguistic survey as a means to 'gather information about the social organization of language behavior toward language in specified populations' (1975: 114). The distinction between these two major categories of assessment is developed by dividing language behaviour assessment into three types: proficiency, acquisition and usage, and behaviour towards language assessment into two types: attitudinal and implementational. This five-celled model is then doubled into a ten-cell model by Cooper's distinction between micro (concerning individual linguistic performance) and macro (concerning widespread linguistic performance) levels of observation. Figure 1 depicts Cooper's model.

It is suggested that these five behavioural categories can be applied to the processes of evaluation of a language policy to provide an *interactive* assessment of the effectiveness of the policy. By so doing, the types of evaluation by Thorburn, Jernudd, Rubin and Haugen can be integrated into a broad model for assessment which allows funding agencies to determine the whole impact of a language policy. With this model in mind we will now turn to the Northern Territory Bilingual Education Program (NTDE, 1984–1986) to investigate whether these evaluation procedures are presently being applied to the current program, and, if not, what steps would need to be taken for these criteria to be applied.

Behavior	Level of Observation	
	Micro	Macro
Language Behavior		
Proficiency		
Acquisition		
Usage		
Behavior toward language		
Attitudinal		
Implementational		

FIGURE 1   *Cooper's (1975) Model for Sociolinguistic Surveys*

Bilingual Education in the Northern Territory

From a detached language planning point of view, the introduction and development of the Bilingual Education Program in the Northern Territory was, and is, fraught with errors and inconsistencies (Russo & Baldauf, 1986). However, considering the severe social, linguistic, educational, financial and geographical constraints imposed upon the program as it has attempted to operate in the real world of 'outback' Australia, the program remains one of the most effective approaches towards assisting Aboriginal people to retain key elements of their culture and to gain more control over their present and future lives (House of Representatives Select Committee on Aboriginal Education, 1985: 112). One contributing factor to overcoming many of these challenges has been the considerable dedication of the Aboriginal and non-Aboriginal Education Department and various missionary group personnel involved in the program (Robertson, 1987: 31). The program consists of sixteen Aboriginal community schools scattered throughout the Northern Territory offering bilingual education in English and one or two of sixteen Aboriginal languages per school.

It is not the intent of this paper to review the development, present status and future of the program. Somewhat conflicting evidence and opinion on these matters is available in numerous works such as those by Harris (1975; 1980; 1982), Gale *et al.* (1981), Russo & Baldauf (1986), Urvet *et al.* (1980), Robertson (1987), and Devlin (forthcoming). Likewise government reports such as *Aboriginal Education* (House of Representatives Select Committee on Aboriginal Education, 1985) and *Handbook for Aboriginal Education in the Northern Territory* (Northern Territory Department of Education, 1986) give indications of a program which at first struggled to gain social legitimacy and which is now attempting to retain financial viability. Indeed Devlin (forthcoming) reports that the 'context of bilingual education in the Northern Territory is, at the macro-level, one of continuing official support coupled with severe budgetary constraints'. This view is reinforced by a former Northern Territory member of the Federal Senate, Ted Robertson (1987), who quotes a reply directed to him from the Federal Minister for Education given in the Federal Senate as:

> It would be my judgment that if the Northern Territory Government is as committed to the program as it assured me that it is, it needs to give a higher allocation of specialist resources.
>
> (Senate Hansard, 1986: 876)

One rationale often hinted at for this dichotomy of intent *versus* action is the thought that those holding power in the Northern Territory Government believe that the bilingual education program has not fulfilled its purposes (*Four Corners*, 1986). Such an opinion is not ill-founded if one relies on information gleaned from the official evaluations of the program which have shown that only three out of sixteen bilingual school programs have performed at a level to gain official accreditation as bilingual programs. Standardized test results in English and mathematics, as well as attendance comparisons, from many evaluation reports indicate that students from only a few bilingual schools perform or attend significantly better than students from non-bilingual schools (e.g. Northern Territory Department of Education, 1984). However, it may be that the Northern Territory bilingual education program is an example of the implementation of a language plan which has been evaluated on a narrow set of educational criteria rather than on the broader scale appropriate for a language plan. This point of view can be verified by the following brief overview of the present evaluation process.

Present Evaluation of the Bilingual Education Program

Individual components of the bilingual program are formally evaluated through an accreditation process which must occur after seven years of operation so that students in the upper primary levels who have been exposed to bilingual education through all grades can be tested. Richards (1986: 10) suggests that:

> The accreditation involves a school's achievement of the aims of bilingual education. As the same aims cover a total philosophy underlying bilingual education, they range from those which are very specific and which can be evaluated objectively . . . to those which are philosophical and which can be evaluated subjectively.

The evaluation objectives are seen as:

(1) *Academic*: measuring bilingual school pupils' performance in English and mathematics and making comparisons of these performances against progress of children in a reference group of non-bilingual schools. In addition a subjective evaluation of vernacular literacy as assessed by teachers in the schools is undertaken.

(2) *Social/psychological*: examining attitudes towards the program held by pupils, Aboriginal and non-Aboriginal staff, parents and community members as well as documenting benefits derived by the community from the implementation of the program.

(3) *Operational*: examining the implementation of school department rules, philosophies, programs and curricula together with staffing conditions and facilities.

Data are collected through a series of visits to schools by the Education Officer, Evaluation Unit, Northern Territory Department of Education. Social/psychological and operational data are collected through interviews with school staff and community leaders. Schools records are examined to gather information concerning attendance and health problems. Academic data are collected through the administration of individual mathematics and oral English tests to each child. All testing is done in English using outside evaluators.

Evaluating the evaluation

Most Aboriginal adults in the Northern Territory assume that the bilingual program exists to maintain traditional Aboriginal languages and culture (Graham & Harris, forthcoming). They see schooling as a 'two way' phenomenon, in so far as what is happening in the school classroom should be a reflection of both Aboriginal and non-Aboriginal ways.

This was indeed the original intent of the program, although, as noted, the focus has changed to one more closely aligned with the educational values held by the dominant English speaking culture (Russo & Baldauf, 1986). This redefinition of the program is underlined when Cooper's five sociolinguistic survey evaluation criteria are applied to the present evaluation procedures. Thus:

(1) Language Proficiency is measured objectively only in terms of the dominant English language. These results are then compared to a reference group of English-only Aboriginal schools. Accreditation is denied if the results from a bilingual program are significantly below the English-only standard. Only a subjective evaluation of the Aboriginal language proficiency of students is made by the bilingual Aboriginal teacher.

(2) Language Acquisition is measured objectively only in terms of English. First language acquisition is measured through subjective evaluation of the language performance of the children by an Aboriginal teacher. No longitudinal studies are conducted to evaluate the impact of the bilingual program on first language acquisition.

(3) Language Use is only measured indirectly. No attempts are made to ascertain the rate or type of English and vernacular usage in either the school or broader speech community. While some theoretical and empirical work has been undertaken towards investigating the language domains, code-switching, the spread of Kriol and Aboriginal English, Aboriginal community languages of wider communication (Graham & Harris, forthcoming; Baarda, forthcoming; Devlin, 1986; Sandefur, 1984), these findings have not been included in the official evaluation process.

(4) Attitudes Towards Language are measured through interviews with school staff, parents and community leaders. It is interesting to note that in a review of a number of accreditation reports, an average of 21 pages in each report is devoted to the English language and mathematics proficiency criteria with only eight pages devoted to the social/psychological area. The attention devoted to the quantifiable objective criteria is understandable given the emphasis placed upon quantifiable objectivity in Western society. However, the present language proficiency assessment virtually ignores one half of the proficiency aspect of the evaluation and treats the other areas of the program superficially. Thus the objective quantifiable data (English language proficiency and Western culture mathematical ability) are given much more weight in the overall assessment of the program than the other equally important data.

(5) Language Planning Implementation is measured through an examination of school policies and procedures. Accreditation reports

concerning the operational aspect of the program reveal data which allow one to understand more clearly the difficulties faced by the program. A review of the operational evaluation in two accreditation reports shows that there have been continual inadequacies in the programs caused by:

(a) high staff turnover (one half of the staff being replaced every year);
(b) lack of sufficient in-service provision;
(c) difficulty in payment of staff and Aboriginal workers; and
(d) lack of general departmental support for the programs as exemplified by numerous appeals for assistance from staff at these schools. (NTDE, 1984; 1985).

These inadequacies are also common in non-bilingual Aboriginal schools. However they cannot simply be ignored by saying they are the rule rather than the exception. In contrast, St Theresa's School, which had its bilingual program successfully evaluated, appears to have a much healthier operational report with a more stable staffing situation, adequate in-service programs, sufficient equipment and a more positive attitude towards operational support. This seems to indicate that strong operational support is a key factor in determining the success of a bilingual program (NTDE, 1984).

(6) In each operational report reviewed, the operational assessment was localized to that particular context and no attempt was made to generalize the findings to the implementation of the whole policy or to a whole program level. Indeed, this is a characteristic of the current evaluation process. Individual school programs are evaluated but no effort is made to collate the information so that an integrated evaluation of the program can be made. Such an integrated approach could well reveal those factors which contribute to a successful local program and which could be adapted to fit the needs of less successful programs. Finally the operational reports contained in the accreditation documents make no attempt to address the cost-effectiveness or cost-benefit issues.

This brief review has shown that the present evaluation process examines the effectiveness of bilingual programs from a narrow perspective only paying scant attention to language acquisition, language use and attitudinal issues. In addition, the evaluation reports give priority to English language proficiency and mathematical abilities which, as Graham suggests, are closely linked since the type of mathematics taught in Aboriginal schools is 'a context embedded language activity' focusing on Western mathematical meanings (Graham, 1986: 16). This narrow evaluation of programs results in the readers of the reports (government policy makers) gaining the impression that bilingual programs are expensive to operate and difficult to manage (the general view of the operations sections of the accreditation reports), while at the same time they are not educationally effective (the general view of the academic sections). It is our opinion that this form of evaluation has contributed to the aforementioned attitude where the Northern Territory Government supports the program publicly, as a political response, but does not see the program as being sufficiently successful to warrant additional funding and eventual expansion into other communities (a legitimate fiscal response based upon information derived from the formal educational evaluation of the program).

Recommendations for an Interactive Evaluation of Language Policy

As the data presented in this chapter have shown, the present narrow evaluation procedure based on virtual monolingual educational criteria, results in a predominantly non-positive interpretation of the effectiveness of the program. Yet, if the broader, interactive evaluation measures derived from Cooper's language planning model are fully utilized, an evaluation could be made which is more attuned to the real nature of the program. This would entail an evaluation procedure using the following criteria and methods.

Language proficiency

Obviously language proficiency needs to be measured in both languages in a bilingual program necessitating the development of tests in Aboriginal languages. Such an undertaking is possible if Aboriginal teachers are involved in all phases of test development, trialling, administration and analysis of results. This involvement would contribute significantly to the professional development and commitment of Aboriginal staff.

Language acquisition

Studies need to be conducted which attempt to measure the rate of acquisition of both first and second languages. Information of this kind can assist the language planner, teacher, curriculum and materials developer to highlight areas of strength and weakness in the language development of Aboriginal children.

Language usage

Language use could be measured by conducting participant observer sociolinguistic surveys within Aboriginal communities. Devlin (1986) undertook such a survey for the Galiwin'ku community and was able to isolate language types and domains for Gupapuyngu, Djambarrpuyngy and English. His research has allowed the bilingual program at Galiwin'ku to aim its policy directly at the language needs of the community. Since one stated aim of bilingual education is literacy development in both languages, the extent of literacy usage in communities can be ascertained through a language use survey. A survey procedure could be designed which would allow Aboriginal and non-Aboriginal staff to contribute extensively to the data collection and analysis. This process would also ensure that a language survey was conducted frequently in those communities where cross-generational language shift is occurring. Aboriginal students attending Batchelor College have researched Aboriginal languages, Aboriginal English and standard English usage in various communities and have demonstrated skills and interest in this vital aspect of the evaluation of a language plan (Hampton, forthcoming; Singh & Djayhgurrnga, forthcoming; Djayhgurrnga, forthcoming; Singh, forthcoming).

Another aspect which can be addressed in this language use context involves the relationship between a language plan and a language-in-education policy. As Bendor-Samuel (forthcoming) points out, a language must 'fill a hole' in the speech community for the teaching of that language to be viable and meaningful. Historical, cultural and geographic factors have combined in some Aboriginal communities to produce a situation where English adequately fulfils all the literacy needs of the community. In these communities, Aboriginal language-literacy instruction contributes to the preservation of the language, but does little to assist the language in meeting a communicative literacy role. Thus literacy in the Aboriginal language may only have the school as its domain of use. Gonzalez (Chapter 18, this volume) suggests that situations of this kind are examples of 'bottom-up' bilingual education where the 'education in a language' policy attempts to create an artificial purpose for certain aspects of the language. Gonzalez advocates a language plan where, as Kaplan (forthcoming) states, the broader speech community-based language plan drives the language-in-education policy. In such a top-down, bottom-up process, a language plan creates a need for the language to fill which can then be met by the language-in-education policy.

In contrast to Aboriginal communities where English literacy has come to meet all literacy needs, there are other Aboriginal communities where English has not gained such dominance. Here literacy in an Aboriginal language fulfils a meaningful, viable communicative need. However, a policy is still required to ensure that the role of Aboriginal language literacy is maintained or even expanded. In both situations described above, attempts have been made to strengthen the need for Aboriginal literacy through an overall comprehensive language plan which acts as an umbrella for the language-in-education policy. Once again, information needed to develop such a policy can only be gained by conducting a language use survey as previously suggested.

Language attitudes

Language acquisition theories abound with reference to the importance of attitudinal factors contributing to the acquisition process (Krashen, 1982), but as Oller (1979) points out, it is difficult to construct valid measures of attitudes. It is necessary, however, for those evaluating bilingual education programs to understand how a community feels about the languages involved in those programs. These data can be collected in the Aboriginal community context by conducting interviews with community members. Mention has been made previously of 'two way' schooling. This concept appears to have gained significant popularity among Aboriginal parents, teachers and community leaders and perhaps reflects an attempt to 'Aboriginalize' bilingual education. Only through the conduct of attitudinal surveys can concerns of this nature be measured and the results applied to bilingual programs.

Language policy implementation

One suspects the conduct of an in-depth evaluation of the operational aspects of the bilingual education program has been overlooked since the program appears expensive in comparison with non-bilingual Aboriginal schools. Obviously bilingual programs are expensive, more expensive than non-bilingual programs when judged against narrow Education Department annual budget criteria. However, consideration needs to be given to the real total costs and to long-term cost benefits. For example, bilingual schools employ many more local Aboriginal people than non-Aboriginal schools. This employment represents a reduction in teacher turnover costs (since community staff members are more stable); a flow of wages into the community rather than government assistance funds; the establishment of a core of 'two way' educated adults who can assist the whole community in bridging the gaps between Aboriginal and non-Aboriginal cultures; significant role models for children (and adults) to follow; and a general involvement and sense of community responsibility for the education of Aboriginal children. If these issues are included in a cost-benefit analysis, a realization may emerge that the bilingual program is not expensive, but rather a cost-effective method for Aboriginal social, political and economic community development. Such findings may contribute to the expansion of the program rather than its present less positive future.

Conclusion

The application of language policy theory to the bilingual education program in the Northern Territory has shown that some of the problems within the program are not due to the ineffectiveness of bilingual education, but rather are the result of the narrow educational measures used to evaluate the program. Just as language-in-education policy is a subset of a language plan, educational program evaluation is a subset of, and not a substitute for, language planning evaluation. In the Northern Territory's Aboriginal communities there appears to be a growing sense of involvement in and responsibility for the education of their own children as a result of the bilingual education program. We believe this process can be furthered if the program were to be evaluated in its language planning context rather than just as a language-in-education program.

References

BAARDA, W. (Forthcoming), Cultural differences in schools. Paper presented at the AILA Pre-congress Conference on Cross-cultural Issues in Educational Linguistics, Batchelor College, Northern Territory, Australia, 9–11 August, 1987. In W. EGGINGTON & C. WALTON (eds), *Cross-cultural Issues in Educational Linguistics*. Darwin: DIT Press.

BENDOR-SAMUEL, D. (Forthcoming), Factors affecting the successful development of spoken languages into written ones. Plenary Address to the AILA Pre-congress Conference on Cross-cultural Issues in Educational Linguistics, Batchelor College, Northern Territory, Australia, 9–11 August, 1987. In W. EGGINGTON & C. WALTON (eds), *Cross-cultural Issues in Educational Linguistics*. Darwin: DIT Press.

COOPER, R. (1975), Sociolinguistic surveys: the state of the art. *Applied Linguistics* 1, 113–27.

DEVLIN, B. C. (Forthcoming), Some issues relating to vernacular language maintenance: A Northern Territory view. Plenary Address to the

AILA Pre-congress Conference on Cross-cultural Issues in Educational Linguistics, Batchelor College, Northern Territory, Australia, 9–11 August, 1987. In W. EGGINGTON & C. WALTON (eds), *Cross-cultural Issues in Educational Linguistics*. Darwin: DIT Press.

— (1986), Language maintenance in a Northeast Arnhemland settlement. Ed.D. Dissertation, Columbia University.

DJAYHGURRNGA, E. (Forthcoming), Using standard English, Aboriginal English and Kunwinjku languages at Gunbalanya. Paper presented at the AILA Pre-congress Conference on Cross-cultural Issues in Educational Linguistics, Batchelor College, Northern Territory, Australia, 9–11 August, 1987. In W. EGGINGTON & C. WALTON (eds), *Cross-cultural Issues in Educational Linguistics*. Darwin: DIT Press.

FASOLD, R. (1984), *The Sociolinguistics of Society*. Oxford: Blackwell.

Four Corners (1986), Aboriginal languages: Their preservation, their role in the preservation of Aboriginal culture and bilingual education for Aborigines. Transcript of televised program, 17 March 1986. Darwin: Australian Broadcasting Commission.

GALE, K., McCLAY, D., CHRISTIE, M. & HARRIS, S. (1981), Academic achievement in the Milingimbi bilingual education program. *TESOL Quarterly* 15: 3, 297–314.

GRABE, W. (1980), The wider perspective of language planning for the 1980s. In W. GRABE & R. KAPLAN (eds), *Prospect and Retrospect: An Introduction to Language Planning*. In mimeo.

GRAHAM, B. (1986), Language and mathematics in the Aboriginal context: A study of classroom interactions about addition in the early years. M.Ed. thesis, Deakin University.

GRAHAM, B. & HARRIS, S. (Forthcoming), Bilingual education and the maintenance of Aboriginal languages: The Northern Territory experience. In P. McCONVELL (ed.), *Can Aboriginal Languages Survive*? Darwin: University College of the Northern Territory.

HAMPTON, E. (Forthcoming), Aboriginal English/Standard English dialects. Paper presented at the AILA Pre-congress Conference on Cross-cultural Issues in Educational Linguistics, Batchelor College, Northern Territory, Australia, 9–11 August, 1987. In W. EGGINGTON & C. WALTON (eds), *Cross-cultural Issues in Educational Linguistics*. Darwin: DIT Press.

HARRIS, S. (1975), Beyond common sense in bilingual education. *The Aboriginal Child at School* 3: 4, 3–27.

— (1980), *Culture and Learning: Tradition and Education in Northeast Arnhem Land*. Darwin: Northern Territory Department of Education.

— (1982), Towards a sociology of Aboriginal literacy. In D. BARNES, A.

CAMPBELL & R. JONES (eds), *Reading, Writing and Multiculturalism*. Adelaide: Australian Reading Association.

HAUGEN, E. (1983), The implementation of corpus planning: Theory and practice. In J. COBARRUBIAS & J. A. FISHMAN (eds), *Progress in Language Planning: International Perspectives*. Berlin: Mouton.

House of Representatives Select Committee on Aboriginal Education (1985), *Aboriginal Education*. Canberra: Australian Government Publishing Service.

JERNUDD, B. (1971), Notes on economic analysis for solving language problems. In J. RUBIN & B. H. JERNUDD (eds), *Can Language Be Planned?* Honolulu: The University Press of Hawaii.

KAPLAN, R. (Forthcoming), Conference summary. Plenary address to the AILA Pre-congress Conference on Cross-cultural Issues in Educational Linguistics, Batchelor College, Northern Territory, Australia, 9–11 August, 1987. In W. EGGINGTON & C. WALTON (eds), *Cross-cultural Issues in Educational Linguistics*. Darwin: DIT Press.

— (1980), The practice of language planning. In W. GRABE & R. KAPLAN (eds), *Prospect and Retrospect: An Introduction to Language Planning*. In mimeo.

KRASHEN, S. (1982), *Principles and Practices in Second Language Acquisition*. New York: Pergamon.

NTDE (Northern Territory Department of Education) (1984), *Bilingual Accreditation Ongoing Report – St Therese's School*. Darwin: Northern Territory Department of Education.

— (1984), *Report on the Bilingual Education Program at Oenpelli School*. Darwin: Northern Territory Department of Education.

— (1985), *Report on the Bilingual Education Program at Milingimbi School*. Darwin: Northern Territory Department of Education.

— (1986), *Handbook for Aboriginal Bilingual Education in the Northern Territory*. Darwin: Northern Territory Department of Education.

OLLER, J. (1979), *Language Tests at School*. London: Longman.

RICHARDS, A. (1986), Bilingual accreditation — Description and situation in 1986. In *NT Bilingual Education Newsletter* No. 86–2. Darwin: Northern Territory Department of Education.

ROBERTSON, T. (1987), History of bilingual education in the Northern Territory. In C. WALTON (ed.), *Linguistics for Language Teachers*. Darwin: Darwin Institute of Technology.

RUBIN, J. (1971), Evaluation and language planning. In J. RUBIN & B. H. JERNUDD (eds), *Can Language Be Planned?* Honolulu: The University Press of Hawaii.

RUBIN, J. & JERNUDD, B. (eds) (1971), *Can Language Be Planned?* Honolulu: The University Press of Hawaii.

Russo, C. & Baldauf, R. B. Jr (1986), Language development without planning. *Journal of Multilingual and Multicultural Development* 7:4, 301–317.

Sandefur, J. (1984), *A Language Coming of Age: Kriol of North Australia*. Darwin: Summer Institute of Linguistics.

Singh, J. (Forthcoming), Aboriginal teacher and non-Aboriginal teacher language in the classroom. Paper presented at the AILA Pre-congress Conference on Cross-cultural Issues in Educational Linguistics, Batchelor College, Northern Territory, Australia, 9–11 August (Forthcoming). In W. Eggington & C. Walton (eds), *Cross-cultural Issues in Educational Linguistics*. Darwin: DIT Press.

Singh, J. & Djayhgurrnga, E. (Forthcoming), Language register in and out of the classroom. Paper presented at the AILA Pre-congress Conference on Cross-cultural Issues in Educational Linguistics, Batchelor College, Northern Territory, Australia, 9–11 August, 1987. In W. Eggington & C. Walton (eds), *Cross-cultural Issues in Educational Linguistics*. Darwin: DIT Press.

Smith, K. (1987), A needs assessment model for classroom and system-wide curriculum development. Ph.D. dissertation, James Cook University of North Queensland.

Thorburn, T. (1971), Cost-benefit analysis in language planning. In J. Rubin & B. H. Jernudd (eds), *Can Language Be Planned?* Honolulu: The University Press of Hawaii.

Urvet, M., Heatley, A. & Alcorta, F. (1980), Case study II: The introduction of bilingual education in the Northern Territory. In *A Study in Transition: Education and Policy Making in the Northern Territory*. Monograph 8. Centre for the Study of Higher Education. Melbourne: University of Melbourne.

6 Controllers or victims: Language and education in the Torres Strait

JOAN KALE

Introduction

This chapter seeks to contribute to the continuing discussion concerning language and education in the Torres Strait. Throughout the era of colonial intervention in Straits affairs, English has been the official language of instruction in school. Speakers of the languages on the many islands of the Strait region have been trying for some time to juggle their loyalties to their linguistic heritage and their links to their cultural past, with the needs and demands of the neo-colonial, socio-economic and political structures which have been imposed on them. Some Islander leaders are becoming dissatisfied with this situation, and are asking that the traditional languages of the area receive formal consideration in the education of Islander children.

For many decades the people of the western Torres Strait area, for example, have sought to valorize and protect their ancestral language and to validate its role in their modernizing society. There have been a number of moves in this direction, including increased linguistic research, more frequent and extensive community meetings concerning the role of that language in educating their children, and the development of the expertise of native speakers through higher education. While this chapter elaborates a proposal for bilingual education with Torres Strait Creole (hereafter, TSC) as a medium of instruction, the argument for the first language as medium of instruction is equally valid for other community languages — with the caution that if a language is to be a medium of instruction in an educational program it is a necessary prerequisite that the language be the first and preferred language of the children attending school. It is not the role of an education program to be responsible for language revival: that is the prerogative of a community. There is ample evidence that schools may support and help sustain such a move, but are not sufficient of themselves to bring about the revival of a language which is not already spoken by the children as a first language and supported by a community of adult speakers. For to see educational policy and schooling as a primary means of language preservation may be to overestimate the role of education in cultural preservation (see Luke *et al.*, Chapter 2, this volume; Edwards, 1985).

In view of the recent moves by Torres Strait Islanders to secede from Australia, or at least to win concessions from the federal government, it may be timely to reconsider the issues of language in education, and of what will count as an education system relevant to the needs and aspirations of Torres Strait Islanders.

In what follows, it is first argued that pidgins and creoles are, linguistically speaking, languages with equal status to other languages and not merely broken forms or second-rate varieties of some other language. Then it is proposed that there is no well-founded reason why a pidgin/creole could not be part of a school program, and that there are probably very sound reasons why in some instances much is to be gained educationally by its inclusion. Next, information is presented about the specialized nature of classroom language required by the academic processes of mainstream schooling. Further, it is proposed that there are valid reasons why English and only English as the language of instruction in Torres Strait schools may not be an appropriate response to the intellectual and educational needs of Torres Strait children. Finally, it is argued that on the basis of all the evidence, a well-planned program of bilingual education incorporating English and TSC would be feasible for Strait schools.

The Torres Strait region is characterized by many small islands, only fifteen of which have permanent populations. In the Western group of islands, a language related to the Australian Aboriginal family of languages is spoken. This is Kala Lagaw Ya, with the related dialect Kala Kawaw Ya. In the Eastern group of islands a language (Meriam Mir) related to the non-Austronesian family of languages of Papua New Guinea is spoken by an aging population, along with TSC. The latter functions as a *lingua franca* throughout the whole area. Further to this, TSC is spoken in some communities as a first language and in others as a second language, and varies in functional importance according to attachment to and usage of one or the other of the traditional languages.

Throughout the area shown in Figure 1, English is spoken mainly as a language of administration and is used as a medium of instruction in schools.

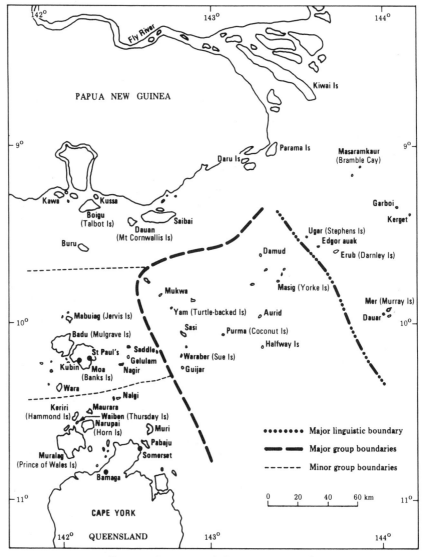

FIGURE 1   *Map of the Torres Strait*[1]

The dismal figures for students graduating from school in the Strait (cf. McGarvie, 1986) would appear to indicate that although advances are continually being made to provide quality education for the children of these island communities, there is still room for improvement. In these circumstances it seems reasonable to ask whether what needs to be done is 'more of the same' — that is, English-only language instruction, but 'of better quality' — or whether a more radical departure is warranted. This chapter suggests one such alternative: that TSC be used as a medium of instruction in a well-planned bilingual education program in which English functions as a second language and a medium of instruction.

Currently there is a surge of interest in bilingual education in Torres Strait. Some communities are proposing that their traditional language be considered a language of instruction in a bilingual program and this, of course, is one option to be explored. However, in communities where TSC is spoken as the first language of children of educable age, there is nothing inherently backward about proposing a former pidgin as one of the languages of instruction, and in fact there may be definite and measurable educational gains for doing so.

Torres Strait Creole: the *Lingua Franca* of the Strait

Shnukal suggests that the ancestor of TSC was Pacific Pidgin English (also known as Sandalwood English and Beach-la-mar), spoken by South Sea Islanders and imported by them into the Strait area during the first half of the nineteenth century (1983b: 173). TSC, also referred to in the literature as Ap-ne-ap, Big Thap, Torres Strait Broken, Pizin and Torres Strait Informal English, is an English-based creole which has acquired features of phonology, syntax, semantics and pragmatics from the Strait indigenous languages. It is now spoken either as a first or second language by almost all Islanders. In effect it has become a *lingua franca*, 'used between Islanders who speak different traditional languages' (Shnukal, 1983b: 175).

Shnukal's historical account of the relatively recent arrival and diffusion of TSC includes an examination of the factors which she considers crucial in its progression from the non-prestigious language of a relatively few 'marginal men' (1983a: 27), to that of a language of greater prestige, to its adoption as a functional *lingua franca* and increasingly the language of Islander identity. According to Shnukal (1982: 1) the language is now spoken:

as a first or second language by most Torres Strait Islanders of whom about 5,000 still live in Torres Strait itself, and perhaps another 18,000 on the mainland. On at least eleven of the fifteen predominantly Islander communities in the Strait, 'Broken' is the first language or mother tongue of the two generations born since the end of World War 2.

She comments on the irony that:

at a time when the creole is decreolising . . . [it] is being rediscovered as a marker of ethnicity and separateness from Europeans by Islander children who are bilingual in TSC and English,

and refers to the support the language is receiving, not the least of which is the 'increasing pride in the language shown by influential Islanders' (1983a: 31). It would appear then that TSC has come of age and, given its widespread institutional status and cultural capital, there is a firm basis for advocating its adoption as a language of instruction in Strait schools.

The Case for TSC as a Language of Instruction

There would appear to be no well-founded reason why a pidgin/creole could not be part of a school program. However, TSC has shared with pidgins and creoles in other places the uninformed disdain of the members of a dominant culture who speak another language (see Keesing, Chapter 8, this volume). Until linguists deemed these varieties to be 'languages' as such and worthy of study, pidgins and creoles were 'dismissed as marginal, inadequate and improper' (Harris & Sandefur, 1984: 17). Among the pejorative epithets bestowed on them historically were: 'argot', 'primitive', 'bastard jargon', 'compromise', 'contact', 'makeshift' or 'hybrid' language, 'broken English', 'mongrel lingo', 'grammarless', 'gibberish', to name a few (Adler, 1977: 4). A number of Australian researchers in the 1960s evaluated Australian pidgins and creoles thus: 'A collection of disjointed elements of corrupt English and native words' (Turner, 1966: 202); 'English perverted and mangled . . . ridiculous gibberish . . . childish babbling' (Strehlow, 1966: 80); 'lingual bastardiza- tion' (Baker, 1966: 316).

TSC has shared this disdain. It also shares the Australian continent with at least one other creole language. Throughout Northern Australia there stretches a language which had its genesis in the language needs of the multilingual inhabitants of the Roper Valley of the Northern Territory.

Its speakers are now located in areas as widespread as Western Queensland, the Barkly Tablelands, throughout the northern part of the Northern Territory and into the North West of Western Australia, where there are now upwards of 10,000 speakers in the Kimberleys alone. 'Ngukurr (Roper), Bamyili and the Kimberleys ... have clearly recognisable regional dialects but they are sufficiently mutually comprehensible for all to be unarguably Kriol' (Harris & Sandefur, 1984: 17).

Immediately to the north of Australia, Tok Pisin, a creole language of Papua New Guinea is going from strength to strength, not only as a *lingua franca* in that multilingual nation but also as the first language of increasing numbers of young citizens and as the preferred language of national identity and social cohesion (see Swan & Lewis, Chapter 12, this volume).

The circumstances in which pidgins and creoles arose and the manner in which they developed could have led to the belief, however erroneous, that they were deserving of the pejoratives. A knowledge of the processes of functional elaboration which distinguish creoles from trade jargons has only developed over the past 30 years. However, it would appear to be the layperson's knowledge about the supposed limitations of pidgins which has perpetrated the unfortunate and inaccurate belief that these languages are simple and unsystematic forms of some other language — in this case, of English. For a person who holds that point of view, it is not a great conceptual leap to believe that, at worst, speakers of such a language are of limited intellect, or that, at best, confinement to such a language may over time negatively influence cognitive development. This may account in part for educationalists' adamant opposition to the use of creoles as languages of education. However, if a creole is recognized as a rule-governed and systematic language, and viewed as a powerful linguistic resource in the community then the argument for the limited intellectual capacity of its speakers may be in fundamental error.

Torres Strait Island leaders, while recognizing the 'inevitability' of English as a language of instruction in schools, and its economic and strategic importance, would nevertheless 'like to see, within a decade, the introduction of a local language as the language of instruction in formal schooling' (Orr, 1982: 49). As previously stated, it is likely that some communities may opt for an indigenous language as their first choice; on the other hand the already widespread use of TSC would appear to make it a viable alternative as a language of education in several Strait community schools.

Although there are around 80 known creole language areas in the world (Hancock in Harris & Sandefur, 1984: 17), there is very little literature on their use as languages of instruction. It appears that educational planners around the world have shared the uncertainty about creoles as fit vehicles for the cognitive development which occurs in the formal settings of mainstream schooling.

To date the only information readily available of a language program which incorporates a creole as a medium of instruction is that of the Kriol language program of the Northern Territory. Following government approval for the establishment of bilingual education in that state, in 1977 the Bamyili (now Barunga) community school established a program for children whose primary language was Kriol. This was a maintenance program: initial literacy and the foundation for the type of cognitive competency required by the schooling process are established first in Kriol, with oral English taught as a subject. Transfer to English literacy and with it, to the language demands of higher levels of mainstream education, occurs gradually from Grade 4 onwards. Simultaneously, Kriol is maintained in specific culturally functional contexts throughout the remainder of schooling.

Evaluation of the effectiveness of the Bamyili program on the children's oral language development indicated:

> very definite trends towards the superiority of bilingual schooling over monolingual schooling for Creole-speaking students. With regard to oral language proficiency in both the mother-tongue, Creole (*sic*) and the second language English ... students schooled bilingually show progressively greater success at separating the two languages than their counterparts schooled monolingually. This increasing ability to sep-arate the two languages (English and Creole), which bilingually schooled students have shown and which appears to be explainable only in terms of the two languages being taught as separate entities in the classroom, constitutes a powerful argument for the introduction of bilingual education to other schools where similar conditions obtain.
>
> (Murtagh, 1979: 98)

In the light of these positive results in oral language development it was anticipated that Bamyili children's literacy development would follow a similar trend. Unfortunately, there are no data available at this stage to indicate whether the optimism concerning the effectiveness of the biliteracy program was well-founded.

Although not definitive, the Murtagh study indicates the viability of a creole as a language of instruction. Further, it would appear to be significant in light of Shnukal's (1983a: 30) suggestion that TSC is already decreolizing. While there is a limit to what the schools can accomplish in relation to language maintenance, a well-planned program of bilingual education might contribute toward stabilizing and standardizing TSC as a result of the domain separation and code specificity learned by the young speakers.

The First Language as the Medium of Instruction in Torres Strait Classrooms

In order to set the perspective for first-language education in Strait schools it is necessary to discuss the manner in which children learn their first language, and to compare that learning with the nature of the language required for formal schooling in mainstream contexts. Of course, the education of mainstream Australian children has predominantly been through the medium of English, their first language. But even within mainstream schooling the causes and concomitants of educational success or failure have been the focus of often conflicting research. Many factors have been examined in attempts to isolate the reasons for school success or failure. However, the body of research into the nature of the language of classroom learning contributes most to present concerns about quality education for all children. It also appears to be relevant to the discussion of quality education for Islander children.

In order to set the perspective for first-language education in Strait schools it is necessary briefly to digress to a discussion of the manner in which children learn their first language, and to compare that learning with the nature of the language required for formal schooling in mainstream contexts.

Children learning their first language do so in social situations. The young child engages in interaction with the significant persons of her/his immediate environment by means of language, which reciprocally shapes and interprets experience (Wells, 1981). The interaction which occurs early on in the child's development is firmly located in the present; child and parent talk about the here-and-now and this situational specificity both supports the parent's understanding of the child's messages and promotes and supports the child's understanding of the parent's messages (Wells, 1981). With increasing maturation and widening experience children are able to free themselves from dependence on the present, to develop the language to refer to the past, and to project as well to future experience. Thus the child — maturing cognitively, socially and in the development of motor skills — is developing the ability to employ language which is increasingly abstract and remote from the here-and-now. In addition, the child beginning school has developed ways of thinking and reasoning, and of encoding these processes in language, facilitated by previous experience and mediated through language by significant persons in his or her environment.

It is not possible to speak with certainty about the relationship between language and thought, nor of the way in which language functions to promote learning, but there is a broad consensus among linguists and psychologists that language is crucial to the learning process. Snow (1983) and Donaldson (1978) argue that the nature of the language used in classrooms is significantly different from that of the language of the child's everyday life. Classroom language becomes progressively more abstract and devoid of context as the child progresses through the system: 'disembedded' (Donaldson, 1978: 76), 'decontextualised' (Snow, 1983: 175) or 'context-reduced' (Cummins, 1984: 139). In Western cultures this tends to be the kind of language through which more abstract cognitive processes are realized, the language of a particular kind of logic which is highly valued by middle-class society and which requires that children reason not from common-sense knowledge based on personal experience and their own reality, but strictly from given premises specific to that logic. The 'shared reality' (Cummins, 1984: 139) of situation-specific, home-based language learning is replaced by context-reduced communication where shared reality cannot be assumed and much greater linguistic elaboration is required to ensure that misinterpretation does not occur.

In short: the language of the classroom fosters and shapes that mode of cognition required by the schooling process. This variety of language is not the language of everyday experience but rather an elaborated variety specific to the domains of formal education. It supports, and acts as the vehicle for, the expression of cognitive concepts which may be largely divorced from the real-life experiences of the child.

Snow (1983) and Heath (1982) indicate that growth in the decontextualized language of the classroom is valued and therefore deliberately encouraged by some parents, and that identifiable parent behaviours assist their children to develop a firm basis for moving into the text-related learning tasks of the classroom even before the beginning of the children's school careers. With such a good fit between the home-based language and that of the classroom, it is not surprising therefore that the children of these homes are advantaged in the race for academic honours. But what of those children for whom the fit is less than complementary?

Controllers or Victims? English in the Torres Strait

The relationship between language learning in home, community and school environments would appear to be of fundamental significance to matters of language and education in Strait schools. First-language English-speaking children — especially those from middle and upper middle classes — learn to be thinkers in ways valued by their culture, to be 'controllers' rather than 'victims' (Bruner, 1971: 158). Because they develop a range of cognitive competence attained through mastery of strategies and skills in their home-based (English) language, they are subsequently enabled to a large degree to control educational outcomes for themselves. However, there are a number of reasons why the policy of English-only as the medium of instruction in Torres Strait schools may not facilitate the development of the specialized literate behaviours and cognitive competencies which would enable Islander children to proceed to the high levels of academic expertise necessary for secondary and tertiary education. Also, and just as importantly, they might not gain the opportunity to continue to be well-informed and productive decision-makers within their communities without the need to give up something of themselves, specifically their language and their culture in the process of becoming 'educated'.

First, as with mainstream children, Islander children come to school with levels of language sufficient for interaction with their environment, and with the intellectual competencies for coping as participants within a particular sociocultural milieu. However, for these children the classroom modelled on mainstream English-only content and processes introduces a double discontinuity. It is likely that they will be expected to spend a significant part of each day learning the language through which education is mediated; and, that language will be increasingly embedded in speech and literary events divorced from their real-life experiences. Hence, many encounter not only an alien language but also alien ways with language. A notion of just how problematic that language may be to the child is indicated in the following:

> Teachers made sure we followed this 'golden rule' by forever shouting at us, 'Hey, you, speak in English' . . . I remember being completely

inhibited during my first years at school. I could no longer chat idly with my mates. I could no longer make fun through speech. My quick wit was no use to me. I was like a vegetable. I was controlled by the limits of my vocabulary. My days were spent listening to my teacher. Many questions I wanted to ask remained unasked because I did not have the ability to express them in English. Eventually, I found it much easier just to sit and listen rather than attempt to speak, so I sat and listened.

(Giraure, 1974: 101)

Second, the language the children are now learning may be functionally relevant only within the classroom or school, for in Islander communities it is probable that there will be few English role models. Any purpose for learning English may be restricted to the need to speak to the teacher and, perhaps, other more or less permanent native English speakers. In some cases the teacher may also be a second-language speaker of English. Further, until very recently there was no curriculum for the teaching of English specifically for Islander schools, and little if any training in cross-cultural education or methodology of teaching English as a second language for either mainstream or Islander teachers. It is also worth noting that much of the research and development currently underway on teaching Torres Strait children is centered on learning styles and cultural difference rather than on linguistic difference (e.g. Osborne & Coombs, 1987). It is not really surprising then, that the standards of English achieved by the children have not been adequate to support the complex register demands of higher education.

Finally, of no little importance is the question of how the child is to develop the intellectual capability sufficient to manipulate the systems of logic and reasoning integral to mainstream education when his/her knowledge of the language is initially so limited. It is not only that the child needs to learn the code. This in itself is difficult enough in the situational vacuum where English is in reality a 'foreign' language. But, as noted, the child also has to learn how to manipulate the language to facilitate the development of more complex cognitive processes. It is probable that the child may not be able to learn the language quickly enough to keep up with the rate of conceptual/cognitive development required for advanced academic achievement. It is difficult to imagine how the child, or for that matter the teacher, can hope to meet the demands of this intellectual development via what is the child's weaker language. If initial learning of the language is in some ways inefficient, faulty or limited this inevitably has consequences for the ability to use language to support thinking. Lewis (1970: 27), describing the dilemmas faced by children being educated through English in Papua New Guinea, suggested that students appeared to reach 'a plateau where so many accumulated inaccuracies and substitutions based on false analogies have been internalized that further progress in any case becomes more difficult'.

An idea of the nature of the difficulties experienced by students attempting formal schooling in a second language may be gleaned from studies of tertiary-level students in Papua New Guinea. Following the establishment of the University at Port Moresby, a compelling observation was that:

> probably the greatest problem facing students in a tertiary institution is having to study difficult and complex concepts in a foreign language. No matter how proficient they may be as English speakers, readers and writers, the level of English used in these institutions is considerably more difficult than is conversational English and students find difficulty in reading text books and understanding tutors and lecturers who have a propensity for using big words and idiomatic phrases.
>
> (Lewis, 1974: 58)

The notion of 'level of English' has been displaced by the insights gained from studies of register in speech, early literacy development, and classroom texts and genres. However, the point holds that even advanced lexico-grammatical knowledge of a language and verbal fluency may not be adequate preparation for the academic demands of higher education. This contribution foreshadows the theoretical framework proposed by Cummins (1981) in a different context, that of Canadian bilingual education. It is to that theory that we will now turn.

When Less Equals More

In view of the difficulties experienced by children faced with the formidable task of education in and through a second language, the discussion turns to a justification of the first language as the medium of instruction for Torres Strait children speaking Creole as their first language. What is being suggested is not an education solely in the first language, for that would not necessarily serve the needs of Islanders better than the English-only option. What is being proposed is education in the first language first, and a gradual introduction to the second language so that cognitive development is not impeded by the need to learn a language while simultaneously having that language as the medium of instruction.

There appears little doubt that in the past, up to the present day, Islander parents have asked for education in English — although one researcher (Shnukal, 1983a: 27) has suggested that what Islanders thought was English was in fact Pidgin English. It appears that this request may have been based on incomplete information: they may have been presented with an 'either–or' alternative — choose either an indigenous language *or* English as the language of instruction. It is also possible that a choice was never offered. It is in fact viable for both a community language *and* English to function as media of instruction with little if any cost to either in terms of competence, and with the likelihood of demonstrable educational gains. Furthermore, there is a groundswell of opinion from Islanders themselves that they now want bilingual/bicultural education for their children (Policy Statement, 1985: 7). Note, however, that children in Strait schools are already being educated bilingually. That is, they come to school speaking one language and through the process of schooling they learn another, to varying degrees of fluency and empowerment. This type of program, Krashen's 'submersion' model (1981: 53), is one in which the second language is the medium of instruction with little or no consideration given to the language or culture of linguistic minority members.

It would appear that the choices, or lack of choices, offered to Strait parents were well-motivated, based as they were on available research on effects of children's bilingualism on cognition. It was believed that bilingual children suffered cognitive or intellectual retardation, achieved lower levels of content mastery and unacceptable levels of native language or target language skills, and that in the main they became alienated from both cultural groups, existing in a wilderness of intellectual poverty (Mills, 1982: 26).

Many educationalists argue that children need English to survive in mainstream schools and society (see Stubbs, 1988, for a summary of the 'Standard English' debate), that minority children need more English, not less of it, and certainly not in competition with a minority language of supposedly limited potential. It furthermore seems obvious to advocates of this kind of 'linguistic mainstreaming' that deficiencies in English should be remedied by more, not less, instruction in English. To them, the alternative argument that teaching in the first language first would in fact promote the learning of English did not appear logical. To go part way toward answering this apparent anomaly, Cummins (1984) has attempted to develop a theoretical framework to illustrate the manner in which second-language learning is related to first-language learning.

It has already been noted that the nature of language proficiency required by the formal schooling process is qualitatively different from the nature of the language proficiency required for interaction in informal settings. Building on this notion, Cummins (1979: 233) suggests that:

> the level of second-language competence which a bilingual child attains is partially a function of the type of competence the child has developed in the first language at the time intensive exposure to the second language begins.

This is to say that, if the child has already begun to develop in the first language that kind of language essential to conceptual/cognitive growth and which is considered integral to the formal schooling process, then there is every likelihood that, given adequate exposure to the second language and sufficient motivation to use- it, the child will develop a commensurately high level of competence in that language. This, Cummins (1981: 23f) further argues, is because there is a 'common underlying proficiency' in language-learning: that is, 'aspects of a bilingual's proficiency in first language and second language are inter-dependent across languages'.

This hypothesis suggests that there are sound reasons for developing and maintaining the child's mother tongue within the school program (Mills, 1982: 34) based on cognitive and motivational considerations, as well as sociocultural justifications which have not been touched on in this chapter. The available research includes the findings of Skutnabb-Kangas & Toukumaa (1976) on the language development and academic progress of Finnish immigrant children in Sweden. Finnish children who immigrated to Sweden at age nine to ten after beginning their initial schooling in Finland in the Finnish language, maintained their competency in Finnish on a similar level with students in Finland. At the same time they achieved at an academic level and developed Swedish language skills comparable with those of Swedish children. By contrast, those Finnish children who migrated to Sweden at or before school age, i.e. before developing the abstract cognitive strategies and skills necessary to the processes of schooling, experienced great difficulty in maintaining educational progress. Another study (Hebert in Mills, 1982: 33) detailed the progress of a group of minority French students in Canada who received 80% instruction in French and 20% in English but performed as well in English as English-speaking children in bilingual or regular English-only programs.

In conclusion, education, rather than being solely a language-learning process as it often appears to be in second-language contexts, might more relevantly be thought of as a process of cognitive enrichment and academic empowerment. Since it now appears probable that cognitive and academic competence in the first language supports and promotes second-language development, there appears to be far less justification for insisting that children be subjected to the submersion experience of schooling and far more reason for promoting those programs which build on children's early learning in their first language as the foundation for learning in and through a second language.

An Agenda for a Bilingual Education Program for the Torres Strait

On the basis of the foregoing, I would argue that a well-planned program of bilingual education utilizing Torres Strait Creole, where it is the first language of the child, and English as languages of instruction in schools of the Torres Strait is a sound course of educational intervention. In what follows I want to outline an agenda for further research and development.

First, consultation with Islander leaders and parents is needed to determine what Islanders expect from education; how much of their expectations are achievable; what approaches would best serve their needs and aspirations; and what alternatives are possible. Any educational program which assumes that the needs of Islander children are identical to those of mainstream children may perpetuate the inadequacies of past educational enterprise.

Second, before such a program is established, forward planning is essential. Alcorta (n.d.:9), writing of the implementation of the bilingual education program in the Northern Territory suggests that:

> bilingual education ... was not only established in a vacuum, the program lacked any precise aims and goals and it was bedevilled from the start with infrastructural weaknesses ... there was no proper planning, no adequate logistics, not enough trained teachers.

It is surprising, given the factors working against the success of that program, that it has achieved even the modicum of success that it has, and that communities are still asking for the establishment of bilingual programs.

Third, a sociolinguistic survey of the whole area to determine the community's language-use patterns is a necessary prerequisite. This would include the nature and extent of language maintenance and shift, and the extent of domains of use. Further, research appears to indicate that 'it would be a mistake to overestimate what any school can accomplish' (Kjolseth, 1971: 95) by way of language maintenance. For this reason, in a community where the parents are not using the language proposed as a medium of instruction in everyday interaction with their children, there may not be much purpose in setting up an educational program using that language as one of the mainstays of the program. The survey would need to analyse attitudes to the languages in the area, bearing in mind that 'there is no necessary, invariable or universal correlation between attitudes toward a language ... and actual patterns of linguistic use ... within a speech community' (Kjolseth, 1971: 95). It has also now become apparent that a knowledge of community 'ways of talking' may provide insights of considerable significance to schooling (Heath, 1983).

Fourth, a thorough linguistic analysis of the language(s) to be incorporated in the program needs to be carried out. Essentials include a grammar and dictionary and an orthography acceptable to the speakers of the language.

Fifth, it would be necessary to understand and identify any possible changes which might occur in the socio-economic status of community members, and of the manner in which social mobility and access to mainstream culture is influenced as a result of the introduction of bilingual education. It is likely that the school itself will become an employer of community people, and that graduates may be employed in various capacities both within the community and in the wider national community. That is, the nature and extent of a possible 'brain drain', and of the effects on Islander communities, would need to be considered.

Sixth, strategies need to be developed to provide the appropriately trained specialist staffing for such a program which would include linguists, teacher-linguists, principals and classroom teachers with advanced knowledge of matters relating to language in educational contexts, such as knowledge of teaching English as a second language, teaching/learning across cultural and language boundaries, and knowledge of curriculum development in non-mainstream classrooms. Mainstream teachers need to be given time and opportunity, if not to become fluent in the local language, then to become knowledgeable about features of the language important to the educational process. Principals need to be well-informed, active proponents of bilingual education, since educational leaders unconvinced of the value of a program can effectively neutralize its effectiveness.

Next, decisions need to be made about teachers. One of the strengths of the Northern Territory program has been the personal empowering of Aboriginal teachers, who at the commencement of the program were aides without responsibility other than helping to keep order in the classroom. Through a program of gradual upgrading there are now accredited Aboriginal teachers in their own classrooms. Who will be the teachers of the future in Strait classrooms? Will they be speakers of English as a first language who will act as role models? Will they be already-competent speakers of Torres Strait Creole and English who may have only limited teaching experience and/or training? Will there be Creole-as-a-first-language and English-as-a-first-language teachers assigned to individual classrooms as teaching teams? Islanders themselves are asking that the teachers be as well-trained and qualified as teachers in mainstream schools (Policy Statement, 1985). Plans to bring this about need to be sensitive to the status of Islander teachers already in classrooms while keeping in mind long-term community educational goals. One powerful argument for promoting the development of a trained pool of local teachers is that the Strait is generally their home, and they are likely to remain if not in the one school, then possibly in the Strait for a considerable portion of their teaching career. This provides the essential element of program continuity which is lacking in community schools throughout large sections of Aboriginal Australia.

Further, the preparation of literature in the first language of the students is necessary. The production of materials specifically designed for the program requires thought and planning. In the past in other contexts this topic seems often to have generated more heat than light (Dutton, 1976: 27). However, given the current strategies for language teaching/learning in mainstream classrooms, there is less emphasis on the production of large quantities of pre-printed materials, and more on the development of classroom-initiated texts negotiated between teacher and pupils and based on the language and experiences of the children. The aim is to familiarize children with a range of literacy experiences that will introduce them to registers of language and academic processes which are prerequisite for more complex classroom learning. This approach reduces some of the pressure on the storing of large quantities of prepared materials but assumes a high level of teacher expertise. While that is so, it is still necessary to have a range of literature of differing genres that will engage the children's interest and attention as they learn to read. For this purpose, a survey of the functions of literacy in the community is indicated, along with general community consensus about what ought to remain in the orate culture and what can acceptably become part of the literate culture. The development of a body of literature in the languages of the Strait would generate reading materials for emergent literates as well as providing an audience for creative writers. It is unfortunate that the lack of analysis/orthography, and the prevailing attitudes to TSC and the other indigenous languages, until recently has worked against the emergence of a body of indigenous literature. It is to be noted that teacher education students in the James Cook University Aboriginal and Islander programs readily write poetry and prose, and prepare enlarged print books in those languages when given the opportunity to do so, as do students at the School of Australian Linguistics at Batchelor and the Batchelor Teacher Training College.

The mechanisms for the development of literacy-related materials are already in place. The Far Northern Schools Development Unit has been engaged in producing excellent materials for the teaching of English as a foreign/second language. The appointment of specialist staff in materials preparation in the local languages, and the availability of additional equipment, would increase the potential of that Unit.

In the Northern Territory programs, critical issues of curriculum development were determined 'at the work-face', but this placed unwarranted strains on relatively inexperienced mainstream and Aboriginal teachers. Curriculum documents published and disseminated were out of date almost before the printers' ink dried. There are important lessons to be learned from that context, the most relevant of which would seem to be that elements of curriculum content and process must be worked out well in advance of beginning any program of bilingual education.

It is difficult to predict very far into the future the possible effects of various models, but an in-depth survey of the experience of other bilingual communities and programs may provide the parameters within which particular models will support the aspirations of Islander communities.

Finally, as several other contributors to this volume have suggested, language planning and maintenance and the provision of education are intricately interwoven with larger questions of social identity and organization, and economic and political power. It is clear that tackling the issues of language in education should be a matter of high priority for community leaders and educators before and during social and political change, rather than as an afterthought. Recent developments in the Torres Strait bode well, then, for the resolution of some of these matters. Now, perhaps more than ever before, the opportunity exists for Torres Strait children to be the arbiters of their own destiny.

Note

1. I wish to express my thanks to John Ngai of the James Cook University Department of Cartography for preparation of the map of Torres Strait.

References

ADLER, M. K. (1977), *Pidgins, Creoles and Lingua Francas: A Sociolinguistic Study*. Hamburg: Helmut Buske Verlag.

ALCORTA, F. (n. d.), Case study: The introduction of bilingual education in the Northern Territory. Mimeo.

BAKER, S. J. (1966), *The Australian Language*. Sydney: Currawong Publishing.

BRUNER, J. R. (1971), *The Relevance of Education*. New York: Norton.

CUMMINS, J. R. (1979), Linguistic interdependence and the educational development of bilingual children. *Review of Educational Research* 49:2, 222–51.

— (1981), The role of primary language development in promoting educational success for language minority students. In *Schooling and Language Minority Students: A Theoretical Framework*. Sacramento, CA: California State Department of Education.

— (1984), *Bilingualism and Special Education: Issues in Assessment and Pedagogy*. Clevedon, Avon: Multilingual Matters.

DONALDSON, M. (1978), *Children's Minds*. Glasgow: Fontana/Collins.

— (ed.) (1983), *Early Childhood Development and Education*. Oxford: Blackwell.

DUTTON, T. E. (1976), Language and national development: Long wanem rot? In B. MCDONALD (ed.), *Language and National Development: The Public Debate*. Occasional Paper No. 11. Port Moresby: University of Papua New Guinea.

EDWARDS, J. (1985), *Language, Society and Identity*. Oxford: Blackwell.

GIRAURE, N. (1974), The need for a cultural program. In *Proceedings of the Eighth Waigani Seminar*. Port Moresby: University of Papua New Guinea.

HARRIS, J. & SANDEFUR, J. (1984), The creole language debate and the use of creoles in Australian schools. *Aboriginal Child at School* 12:1, 8–29.

HEATH, S. B. (1982), What no bedtime story means: Narrative skills at home and school. *Language in Society* 11:1, 49–75.

— (1983), *Ways with Words: Language, Life and Work in Communities and Classrooms*. Cambridge: Cambridge University Press.

KJOLSETH, R. (1971), Bilingual education programs in the United States: For assimilation or pluralism? In B. SPOLSKY (ed.), *The Language Education of Minority Children*. Rowley, Mass: Newbury House.

KRASHEN, S. (1981), Bilingual education and second language acquisition theory. In *Schooling and Language Minority Students: A Theoretical Framework*. Sacramento, CA: California State Department of Education.

LEWIS, D. (1970), Problems of bilingualism in Papua New Guinea. *Kivung* 4:1, 21–29.

LEWIS, N. R. (1974), An investigation of the difficulties experienced by students at a tertiary institution in Papua New Guinea. *Papua New Guinea Journal of Education* 10:2, 50–67.

McGARVIE, N. J. (1986), The influence of language in the education of Aboriginal students in urban and rural schools in Queensland. Unpublished manuscript, James Cook University of North Queensland.

MILLS, J. (1982), *Bilingual Education in Australian Schools*. Australian Education Review No. 18. Hawthorn, Vic: A.C.E.R.

MURTAGH, E. J. (1979), *Creole and English Used as Languages of Instruction with Aboriginal Australians*. Unpublished Ph.D. thesis, Stanford University.

ORR, G. M. (1982), Language instruction in Torres Strait Islander schools: Preliminary considerations for school-based curriculum development. *Aboriginal Child at School* 10:3, 48–59.

OSBORNE, B. & COOMBS, G. (1987), Setting up an intercultural encounter: Study of 'settling down' a Thursday Island class. Torres Strait Working Papers No. 6. Townsville James Cook University of North Queensland.

Policy Statement on Education in Torres Strait (1985), Torres Strait Islander Regional Education Committee. Brisbane: Queensland Department of Education.

SHNUKAL, A. (1982), Why Torres Strait 'broken English' is not English. *Proceedings of the Second Annual Workshop of the Aboriginal Languages Association*. Batchelor, Northern Territory.

— (1983a), Blaikman Tok: Changing attitudes towards Torres Strait Creole. *Australian Aboriginal Studies* 2, 25–33.

— (1983b), Torres Strait Creole: The growth of a new Torres Strait language. *Aboriginal History* 7:2, 175–185.

SKUTNABB-KANGAS, T. & TOUKUMAA, P. (1976), *Teaching Migrant Children's Mother Tongue and Learning the Language of the Host Country in the Context of the Socio-Cultural Situation of the Migrant Family*. Helsinki: The Finnish National Commission for UNESCO.

SNOW, C. (1983), Literacy and language: Relationships during the preschool years. *Harvard Educational Review* 53: 2, 165–189.

STREHLOW, T. G. H. (1966), On Aranda traditions. In D. HYMES (ed.), *Language in Culture and Society*. New York: Harper International.

STUBBS, M. (1988), *Educational Linguistics*. Oxford: Blackwell.

TURNER, G. W. (1966), *The English Language in Australia and New Zealand*. London: Longmans.

WELLS, G. (1981), *Learning Through Interaction: The Study of Language Development*. Cambridge: Cambridge University Press.

7 Language planning in Australian Aboriginal and Islander contexts: An annotated bibliography

ALLAN LUKE and JOAN KALE

Introduction

The official demise in the early 1970s of what was known as the 'White Australia Policy' had ramifications for research, policy and practice relating to languages and education which continue to this day. Prior to that time, most policy makers and educationists conceived of Australia as a monolingual, monocultural country. Following the longstanding traditions established by missionary linguists, much of the research on Aboriginal languages was descriptive in character. Since the entry of Aboriginal and Islander children into mainstream educational settings, and correlative attempts by successive governments to develop ameliorative social policies towards indigenous peoples, there has been an increasing concern with language and cultural maintenance, and with the development of educational policies and programs which aim towards bilingualism and the preservation of vernaculars.

Since the early 1970s, then, governmental recognition of and academic inquiry into the statuses of Aboriginal languages and migrant languages have evolved, however sporadically and gradually (see Lo Bianco, Chapter 3, this volume; cf Walsh, 1982). Indeed, one of the problems which has arisen is the tendency of policy makers to conflate the two under the sometimes confusing appellation of 'multiculturalism'. There is now a significant body of literature on migrant languages, language diversity and maintenance, English as a Second Language and community language programs (cf Clyne, 1982; Pauwels, 1986; Baldauf, 1986; Smolicz, 1983). As for the study of Aboriginal languages and related educational matters, much of the available literature focuses on the development, implementation and consequences of bilingual educational programs in the Northern Territory.

For this bibliography we have selected materials published since 1980 which are representative of three themes:

(1) planning and policy which attempts to develop or maintain Aboriginal and Torres Strait Islander languages and creoles;
(2) bilingual and vernacular language education programs; and
(3) general language-related educational problems encountered by Aboriginal and Torres Strait Islander children in schools (for pre-1980 references, see Walsh, 1982; Wafer, 1981; Black, 1982).

We have limited citation of those descriptive and sociolinguistic studies which do not bear directly upon these matters. We have chosen only some representative works in the third category. This latter decision is due in part to the multitude of non-research articles in specialist teachers' journals which relate classroom anecdotes, methods and techniques. The resultant bibliography, then, is not exhaustive. Throughout we have tried where possible to review materials accessible to overseas readers. Hence, we also have omitted some relevant articles which are unlikely to be readily available.

Applied and descriptive research on Aboriginal languages has flourished in large part due to support from: the School of Australian Linguistics (Batchelor); the Australian Institute of Aboriginal Studies; the Australian National University's School of Pacific Studies and Department of Linguistics (Canberra), the latter under the leadership of R. M. W. Dixon: the Summer Institute of Linguistics (Darwin); scholarly organizations like the Applied Linguistics Association of Australia (ALAA). The aforementioned themes, however, have assumed only a marginal location in the larger discourses of Australian educational research. In the period from 1980 to 1988, for instance, the *Australian Journal of Education* — the country's leading educational research journal — did not feature a single article which addressed in any depth Aboriginal language education, bilingual and vernacular programs. Further, the dispersion of research findings has been confined mainly to national and regional specialist publications, as the paucity of international journal and book article citations below suggests.

Several notes about sources are in order for overseas researchers. The

Pacific Linguistics series cited below and throughout articles in this volume is available from the Australian National University School of Pacific Studies. Materials published by ALAA can be obtained from the Treasurer, ALAA, Department of European Languages, University of Wollongong, New South Wales. Other Australian publications can be borrowed via interlibrary loans from the National Library of Australia in Canberra.

While the present volume goes to press, five important works on issues related to language planning and language education in Aboriginal contexts are in final preparation (McConvell, in press/1988; Eggington & Walton, in press/1989; Rigsby and Romaine, in press/1989; Harris, in preparation; Shnukal, in press/1988). The McConvell volume includes articles on language domains, maintenance and education by McConvell, Hasokawa, Shnukal, Avery, Black, Graham and Harris and others. The Eggington and Walton anthology includes papers by Baarda, Bendor-Samuel, Martin, Kaplan, Devlin and others, originally presented at the 1987 Australian Institute of Applied Linguistics Conference held at Batchelor College, Northern Territory. The Rigsby and Romaine collection, at this stage still in preparation, promises an overview on Australian languages.

The Harris monograph, a synthesis of his work on bilingual programs in the Northern Territory, discusses educational strategies for language maintenance and the development of literacy. In addition, Shnukal is finalizing a monograph which will provide a comprehensive sociolinguistic overview on Torres Strait Creole. These latter two works should have significant implications for the future of bilingual education in, respectively, the Northern Territory and the Torres Strait. Previous work by McConvell, Eggington, Harris and Shnukal is included in this bibliography.

Acknowledgement

We wish to thank Stephen Harris, Richard Baldauf, Anna Shnukal and staff of the Summer Institute of Linguistics for their advice and suggestions.

References

BALDAUF, R. B. (1986), Linguistic minorities and bilingual communities: Australia. In R. B. KAPLAN et al. (eds.) *Annual Review of Applied Linguistics* Vol. 6. Cambridge: Cambridge University Press.

CLYNE, M. (1982), *Multilingual Australia*. Melbourne: River Seine.
EGGINGTON, W. & WALTON, C. (eds.) (in press/1989), *Cross-cultural Issues in Educational Linguistics*. Darwin: Darwin Institute of Technology Press.
HARRIS, S. (in preparation), *Two-Way Aboriginal Schooling*.
McCONVELL, P. (ed.) (in press/1988), *Can Aboriginal Languages Survive?* Brisbane: University of Queensland Press.
PAUWELS, A. (1986), Australia as a multilingual nation. In R. B. KAPLAN, *et al*. (eds.) *Annual Review of Applied Linguistics*, Vol. 6. Cambridge: Cambridge University Press.
RIGSBY, B. & ROMAINE, S. (eds.) (in press/1989), *Language in Australia*. Cambridge/Melbourne: Cambridge University Press.
SHNUKAL, A. (in press/1988), *Broken: An Introduction to the Creole Language of the Torres Strait*. Canberra: ANU Pacific Linguistics D.
SMOLICZ, J. J. (1983), Linguistic diversity in Australia: Changing attitudes and policies. *Polycom* 35, 14–20.
WALSH, M. (1982), Language policy — Australia. In R. B. KAPLAN *et al*. (eds.) *Annual Review of Applied Linguistics* Vol. 2. Rowley, MA: Newbury House.

Annotated Bibliography

BALDAUF, R. B., Jr & EGGINGTON, W. G. (1988), Language reform in Australian languages. In I. FODOR & C. HEGÈGE (eds.) *Language Reform and Future* Vol. 4. Hamburg: Helmut Buske.

This article begins with a review of the historical treatment of the indigenous Australians and their languages since white settlement (cf. Russo & Baldauf, 1986). It then examines language reform and change under the general categories of unplanned change and planned change in both the pre-European and post-European periods. Implications for the survival of Australian languages are discussed.

BARLOW, A. & TRIFFET, G. (1987), Aboriginal languages in education. *Australian Aboriginal Studies* 2, 90–2.

This article begins with a commentary on the National Policy on Languages. The authors then review three preconditions for the expansion of the role of Aboriginal languages in mainstream Australian education: the inclusion of Aboriginal studies in teacher education; the inclusion of Aboriginal studies in the school curriculum; the provision of teaching resources and materials to enable teachers to teach Aboriginal languages. They also provide an overview of existing resources, noting appropriateness, location and accessibility for teachers.

BAVIN, E. & SHOPEN, T. (1985), Warlpiri and English: languages in contact. In M. CLYNE (ed.) *Australia, Meeting Place of Languages.* Canberra: ANU Pacific Linguistics C–92.

This article examines the influence of English on Warlpiri spoken by children in Yuendumu, a small town northwest of Alice Springs. It is of particular interest because since 1974 Yuendumu school has featured a 'transition' bilingual program. Domains of use of oracy and literacy are noted, as are diglossic situations. The case studies of individual children document how the borrowing from English is not restricted to lexicon, but also influences word order in the vernacular. This, it is argued, has implications for children's discourse style.

BLACK, P. (1982), Languages. In M. HILL & A. BARLOW (eds.) *Black Australia 2.* Canberra: Australian Institute of Aboriginal Studies.

Black provides an accessible introduction to the historical and current situation of Australian Aboriginal languages. A brief annotated bibliography for teachers is included (cf. Wafer, 1981).

BLACK, P. (1981), Why and how languages change. In J. BELL (ed) *Language Planning for Australian Aboriginal Languages.* Alice Springs: Institute for Aboriginal Development.

This article discusses how languages change without deliberate intervention. Examples from various Aboriginal languages are cited. Examining Koko-Bera and Kok-Paponk in the Cape York Peninsula, Black identifies what he calls 'normal' change, 'change due to contact', and language death. The paper concludes with a call for bilingual education as an important means for the preservation of traditional languages.

BUSCHENHOFEN, P. (1983), Current emphases in the Northern Territory Department of Education's bilingual education program for Aboriginal children. *Journal of Intercultural Studies* 4 (2), 9–22.

This article examines the priorities in policy and planning of the Northern Territory bilingual program. These include: assessment and evaluation of program outcomes; recruitment of adequately qualified specialist staff; recruitment and training of Aboriginal staff; curriculum development; development of teaching manuals. A brief resumé of the perceived strengths and weaknesses of the program is undertaken.

CHRISTIE, M. J. (with articles by D. Eades, A. Shnukal & B. Gray) (1985), *Aboriginal Perspectives on Experience and Learning: The Role of Language in Aboriginal Education.* Geelong, Vic.: Deakin University Press.

This volume is an overview of the field of Aboriginal education in Australia, with particular reference to the language-related issues which arise when Aboriginal children enter mainstream schooling. Christie begins with an introduction to the historical and current socio-economic contexts of Aboriginal society, linking these to the identification of a distinctive 'Aboriginal world-view'. This is a prelude to a brief review of aspects of Aboriginal languages which might affect education; this section is enhanced by essays by Eades on English as an Aboriginal language and Shnukal on Torres Strait Creole. Christie argues from this that Aboriginal/Islander children enter mainstream schooling with differing senses of what counts as 'thinking', 'knowledge' and 'learning'. This is attributed to both cultural and linguistic difference. Hence, the rituals, conventions and language of Western 'formal schooling' are seen to lead to 'communication breakdown in the classroom' (see Christie & Harris, 1985). As an alternative, Christie proposes classroom programs which attempt to consider the differences between Aboriginal and mainstream 'learning styles'. This short, useful book concludes with an article by Gray on the potential of naturalistic classroom strategies to enhance successful English language learning by Aboriginal children.

CHRISTIE, M. & HARRIS, S. (1985), Communication breakdown in the Aboriginal classroom. In J. B. PRIDE (ed.) *Cross Cultural Encounters: Communication and Mis-communication.* Melbourne: River Seine.

Christie & Harris classify three areas of 'difference' which lead to mis-communication between Aboriginal students and Australian teachers: the 'phenomenological', linguistic and 'learning styles'. All three are seen to generate problems in the mainstream classroom and hence to hinder effective teaching and learning.

DIXON, R. M. W. (1980), *The Languages of Australia.* Cambridge: Cambridge University Press.

This monograph is one of the most comprehensive and widely cited resources on Australian Aboriginal languages. Chapters 1–4 of this work contain a broad 'account of the anthropological, sociolinguistic and historical background' of these languages. Chapters 5–13 are technical and descriptive, covering lexicon, phonology and syntax. Of particular interest to language planners is Chapter 8, a classification and subgrouping of Australian languages.

DUTTON, T. E. (1983), The origins and spread of Aboriginal Pidgin English in Queensland: a preliminary account. *Aboriginal History* 7 (1) 90–122.

Dutton has collated data on Pidgin falling into 'five sets according to time and geographical location'. From this he traces the origin and development of the earliest *lingue franche* in Queensland. The socio-economic conditions leading to culture contact are noted; these in turn are seen as catalysts for language variation.

DUTTON, T. E. & MÜHLHAÜSLER, P. (1984), Queensland Kanaka English. *English World-Wide* 4 (2), 231–263.

The authors describe the origin and development of Queensland Kanaka English in terms of the continuous interaction between the demands of Queensland plantation industries and the 'jargonized and pidginized varieties of English' of the Pacific area.

EADES, D. (1981), 'That's our way of talking': Aborigines in Southeast Queensland. *Social Alternatives* 2 (8), 11–14.

For many minority groups, the variety of language spoken is symbolic of cultural distinctiveness. Eades argues that the language variety of Southeastern Queensland Aborigines functions as a significant marker of identity for the group which, while no longer speaking a traditional Aboriginal language, nevertheless retains 'a strong identity ... social organization and culture'.

EAGLESON, R. D., KALDOR, S. & MALCOLM, I. G. (1982), *English and the Aboriginal Child*. Canberra: Curriculum Development Centre.

Parts 1 and 2 of this volume are descriptive. Following a broad introduction to linguistic theory, an overview of linguistic aspects of traditional, rural and urban languages of Aborigines is provided. Unique here is the detailing of non-standard English dialects spoken by Aborigines in urban settings, aspects of which have been contested by Christie (see *The Aboriginal Child at School* 12 (2), 1986). Beginning from a recognition of the classroom as a speech community, Part 3 discusses theoretical and practical implications for the teaching of Aboriginal children. This useful, well-documented volume effectively connects descriptive research with educational implications.

ELWELL, V. M. R. (1982), Some social factors affecting multilingualism among Aboriginal Australians: a case study of Maningrida. *International Journal of the Sociology of Language* 36, 83–103.

This article outlines social factors affecting multilingualism among Aborigines in and around Maningrida, a settlement community in the Northern Territory, where approximately 100 speakers speak at least 11 different languages. Elwell describes historical and contemporary aspects of the demographics and social organization of this linguistically and tribally diverse area, also noting language uses and attitudes. She reports that the main social variables were:

> first language and linguistic repertoire (competence) of both speaker and interlocutor, leading to reciprocity (code switching and two-way conversations) in friend/equal interactions and the use of the dominant party's language . . . .

Interestingly, she also found that in many situations there appeared to be no 'preferred language', despite the importance of 'linguistic and social attitudes' in the community.

FESL, E. (1981), Literacy: an Aboriginal sociolinguistic view. In B. MENARY (ed.) *Aborigines and Schooling*. Adelaide: Adelaide College of the Arts and Education.

Fesl examines literacy from an Aboriginal perspective, asking 'for what purpose' and 'in what language' Aborigines should become literate. She maintains that much research and development is based on premature assumptions about Aborigines' needs for and attitudes towards literacy. Accordingly, Fesl argues for research by Aboriginal researchers and for direct community involvement in literacy-related educational decision-making and planning. She concludes that 'literacy is not the panacea of all Aboriginal ills, but it may be of assistance to some Aboriginal people'.

FESL, E. (1982), Australian Aboriginal languages. *Australian Review of Applied Linguistics* 5 (2), 100–115.

As Fesl notes, 'no large scale research project has attempted to determine the expressed needs of the Aboriginal population or the overall linguistic situation in regard to language use. . .'. This paper is a preliminary attempt to outline terminology, assumptions and directions for such an analysis. Fesl reviews the history of language 'annihilation' in Australia, observing that by the early 1980s 114 languages were in danger of extinction, in part because of the low priority assigned to language preservation in government policy. Fesl concludes with recommendations for the National Language Policy. She stresses the need that 'Aboriginal people be consulted and involved'.

FESL, E. (1985), Language death and language maintenance: action needed to save Aboriginal languages. *Aboriginal Child at School* 13 (5), 45–50.

As the title suggests, this article considers criteria for ensuring the continuation and health of Aboriginal languages. A key element of maintenance, Fesl argues, is that of community involvement in the encouragement of language use in as many domains as possible. She further argues that strategies be developed to control the input of English in order to minimize overt and covert effects on the community's uses of traditional languages.

GALE, K., McCLAY, D., CHRISTIE, M. & HARRIS, S. (1981), Academic achievement in the Milingimbi bilingual education program. *TESOL Quarterly* 15(3), 297–314.

This article reports on a four-year comparative study of the achievement of bilingual and English-only classes at Milingimbi School, Northern Territory. That school, located on an island off the coast of North-East Arnhemland, is 'reasonably typical of larger bilingual schools'. The authors set out to test the hypothesis that bilingual education was advantageous 'especially for minority groups who do not have a strong schooling tradition'. By administering a range of standardized measures (e.g. Dolch Sight Words Test, Schonell Reading Age Test) and locally developed instruments (e.g. story-retelling tests), the researchers found that children from bilingual classes were performing better at the 7 year level than English-only children in seven of the ten tests. The difference was most marked on tests which demanded abstract cognitive skills. The authors conclude that, although students still scored considerably below national averages, the bilingual program had been successful in 'effecting an improvement in standards'.

GRABER, P. L. (1987), Kriol in the Barkly Tableland. *Australian Aboriginal Studies* 2, 14–19.

This article is the result of a linguistic survey carried out to ascertain the spread and functional significance of creole varieties in communities of the Barkly Tableland area of North Queensland. Similarities and differences between the Kriol of subject speakers and that of the Northern Territory communities are briefly described.

> GRAY, B. (1985), *Helping Children to Become Language Learners in the Classroom*. Darwin: Northern Territory Department of Education.
> — (1985), *Teaching Creative Writing to Aboriginal Children in Urban Primary Schools*. Darwin: Northern Territory Department of Education.

These short papers are practical outlines of theory and practice for teachers (cf. Gray in Christie, 1985). They are cited here because they are exemplary, well-grounded attempts to address the needs of urban Aboriginal children in terms of the larger developments in language education (e.g. the systemic linguistics of Halliday *et al.*, cognitive and psycholinguistic theories of reading, process approaches to writing, and research on second language learning and communicative competence). Gray draws upon his work with children at Traeger Park, Northern Territory to describe the kinds of 'transactional' environments and strategies which are conducive to language learning.

> HARRIS, J. (1986), *Northern Territory Pidgins and the Origin of Kriol*. Canberra: ANU Pacific Linguistics C–89.

This monograph examines in detail the history of Kriol, with particular emphasis on the 'linguistic consequences' of cultural contact in the Northern Territory. Harris describes the development of a number of *lingue franche* between Aboriginal people and non-European visitors prior to the emergence of English-based pidgins in the nineteenth century. Throughout he notes the influence of economic factors in the use and development of pidgins.

> HARRIS, J. & SANDEFUR, J. (1984), The creole language debate and the use of creoles in Australian schools. *Aboriginal Child at School* 12, 8–29.

This article outlines the 'extreme social and linguistic consequences of the brutal culture contact' which brought many Aboriginal groups together in the Roper River area of the Northern Territory. The authors discuss the controversy which surrounds the issue of the validity of creoles as languages of education, and they provide an overview of the use of creoles in Australian schools.

HARRIS, S. (1980), More haste less speed: time and timing for language programs in Northern Territory Aboriginal bilingual education. *Aboriginal Child at School* 8 (4), 23–43.

This article summarizes theoretical considerations for bilingual education programs and reviews theory on the use of vernacular languages in education. Other considerations concern the relationship of first language development and intelligence, the timing of the beginning of formal schooling and the introduction of a second language, and practical pedagogical decisions regarding the instructional balance between first and second languages.

HARRIS, S. (1982), Bilingual education in the Northern Territory: a sharp tool easily blunted? *Australian Review of Applied Linguistics* 5 (1), 25–57.

Harris outlines the extent and progress of the Northern Territory bilingual education program. He discusses the strengths of the program under four broad headings: 'educational', 'social/psychological', 'linguistic' and 'economic'. Throughout, such key issues as language domains and education, Aboriginal control over the processes of 'modernization', and the academic and cultural effects of bilingual education are noted. In Harris' estimation, 'probably the most important strength' of bilingual programs is the improved quality of Aboriginal education (see Gale *et al.*, 1981). He balances this perspective with a discussion of 'vulnerability' of the program and concludes with a prognosis for future developments.

HARRIS, S. (1982), Aboriginal learning styles and the teaching of reading. In J. SHERWOOD (ed.) *Aboriginal Education: Issues and Innovations*. Perth: Creative Research.

This article reviews psycholinguistic and cognitive models in the reading process, applying these to findings on Aboriginal learning styles and social contexts (see Christie & Harris, 1985). From this description, Harris forwards particular strategies likely to be productive in helping Aboriginal children to become readers.

HARRIS, S. & GRAHAM, B. (1985), Linguistic research and Aboriginal bilingual education. *Australian Review of Applied Linguistics* Series S (2), 117–139.

From their perspective as educators, Harris and Graham appraise the kind of applied linguistic research required to support bilingual education in the Northern Territory. They outline various areas of research and would have linguists involved in activities ranging from 'foundational research' on Aboriginal languages to more applied work in 'previewing' curriculum materials, monitoring language learning and assessing results. Of note here is the authors' debatable position that 'applied [linguistic] research does *not* involve teaching children *or* producing teaching materials . . .'. They conclude with a call for an increased reciprocity between linguists and teachers.

JOHNSON, S. (1987), The philosophy and politics of Aboriginal language maintenance. *Australian Aboriginal Studies* 2, 54–8.

This paper frames the basic issues of language maintenance, renewal and revival as they relate to the status of Australian Aboriginal languages. Johnson reviews problems of funding programs, and the politicization of the language preservation issue. He concludes with an educational agenda for language maintenance which includes provision for informal, family education and community-based courses for children and adults.

KOCH, H. (1985), Non-standard English in an Aboriginal land claim. In J. B. PRIDE (ed.) *Cross-cultural Encounters: Communication and Mis-Communication.* Melbourne: River Seine.

A key aspect of language planning is the specification of the statuses of languages in legal domains. This article is an analysis of the kinds of mis-communication and confusion which result in court proceedings when Aborigines speaking non-standard English must deal with English-speaking judges, barristers and transcribers. The article suggests ways of remedying the situation.

LIPSCOMBE, R. & BURNES, D. (eds) (1982), *Aboriginal Literacy: Bridging the Gap.* Adelaide: Australian Reading Association.

This anthology features a range of papers on the teaching of literacy in Aboriginal contexts. Chapter 1 is an abbreviated version of Gale *et al.* (1981) which compares the academic achievement of bilingual and English-only classes in Milingimbi, Northern Territory. Chapters 2 (Harris) and 6 (Gale, Mehan & Gale) offer practical advice on, respectively, the teaching of 'purposeful reading to Aboriginal children' and of vernacular literacy in bilingual programs.

Chapter 3 (Zorc) examines differing facets of current programs to develop Aboriginal and Islander expertise in education and linguistics. Zorc provides a broad overview on the history, goals, curriculum and methods of the School of Australian Linguistics, located in Batchelor, Northern Territory. Since its founding in the early 1970s, that institution has become instrumental in the development of research on Aboriginal languages and the training of Aboriginal teachers and language professionals.

Chapters 4 (Ward) and 5 (Russo and S. G. Harris) consider in practical terms the production of vernacular reading and resource materials in 'Bilingual Literature Production Centres'. Ward describes her experiences working with Aboriginal teachers in bilingual programs. Russo and Harris argue that the programs need more than 'basic reading materials', and conclude with guidelines for the further development of vernacular literature. Finally, Chapter 8 (Baarda) comments on the problems and approaches encountered in bilingual literacy teaching at Yuendumu, Northern Territory (see Bavin & Shopen, 1985).

Although intended for Australian teachers, this anthology provides interested researchers with a preliminary overview of some of the goals and contexts of bilingual education in the Northern Territory.

McCONVELL, P. (1981), Supporting the two way school. In J. BELL (ed.) *Language Planning for Australian Aboriginal Languages*. Alice Springs: Institute for Aboriginal Development.

McConvell proposes the 'two way school' as an alternative model to the 'bilingual/bicultural' model adopted in several jurisdictions. The 'two way' school, the term borrowed from Aboriginal English, embraces a form of language planning which occurs independently of white authorities. He describes his experience in Daguragu where Gurindji community leaders developed the concept of a school which was based on a 'two-way flow in reciprocity and exchange' between community members and teachers. This, in turn, led to vernacular curriculum development undertaken locally. The article makes a strong case for the preparation of Aboriginal teachers and Aboriginal teacher-linguists who are fluent in vernacular languages, and exemplifies the possibilities for locally developed curriculum which uses traditional knowledge and vernacular semantic structures as the bases for the organization of instruction.

MᴄCᴏɴᴠᴇʟʟ, P. (1985), Domains and code switching among bilingual Aborigines. In M. Cʟʏɴᴇ (ed.) *Australia, Meeting Place of Languages.* Canberra: ANU Pacific Linguistics C–92.

This article is a critical, theoretical and empirical reappraisal of some commonly accepted views on domains and code switching. On the basis of a study of the Gurindji people, it is argued that code switching — a social reality which depends on cultural differences — 'occurs between a traditional language and English or Kriol . . . in the same way as . . . between different traditional languages and dialects'. This finding further casts 'doubt on the strong form of the domain model'. McConvell concludes that 'stable bilingualism' is a hypothesis without supporting evidence, a finding with significant educational and social policy ramifications.

MᴄCᴏɴᴠᴇʟʟ, P. (1986), Aboriginal languages and language maintenance in the Kimberleys. *Australian Review of Applied Linguistics* Series S (3), 108–122.

In view of the 'rapid decline of nearly all Aboriginal languages in the Kimberleys', the author proposes that the language situation in each community should determine the 'form of educational programmes in languages' to be offered. Three program types are described: bilingual education, language maintenance and language renewal. McConvell then describes the language needs of the Kija speakers of the Warrman community, who wish to maintain their language in the face of rapid shift to creole and English. He stresses the importance of linking 'language function with language maintenance and cultural maintenance' in such a program.

MᴄKᴇᴏᴡɴ, G. & Fʀᴇᴇʙᴏᴅʏ, P. (1988), The language of Aboriginal and non-Aboriginal children and the texts they encounter in schools. *Australian Journal of Reading* 11(2), 115–26.
— (1988), Contrasting children's oral discourse and the texts they read in schools. In G. Dᴀᴠɪᴅsᴏɴ (ed.) *Ethnicity and Cognitive Assessment: Australian Perspectives.* Darwin: Darwin Institute of Technology.

These papers summarize a study which compares the spoken language of primary school Aboriginal and non-Aboriginal children with the language of mainstream textbooks. In an analysis of cohesion, macro-structural and micro-structural characteristics, the authors found no significant differences between the spoken narrative and expository discourse of Aboriginal and non-Aboriginal children. There were, however, significant differences between these children's spoken language and the language of textbooks: the 'literary/autonomous' style and specialized metalinguistic markers of the latter do not appear in the former. The authors conclude with a critique of 'language deficit' explanations of Aboriginal school children's achievement, arguing that while the 'surface features' of Aboriginal children's spoken language are *seen* to interfere with learning, there is little empirical evidence that these children are at any greater linguistic disadvantage than their non-Aboriginal counterparts.

MALCOLM, I. G. (1982), Communication dysfunction in Aboriginal classrooms. In J. SHERWOOD (ed.) *Aboriginal Education: Issues and Innovations*. Perth: Creative Research.

Malcolm outlines factors which contribute to 'communication dysfunction', noting interference between the code of the teacher and that of Aboriginal children (see Eagleson *et al.*, 1982, Part 3). He discusses sources of sociolinguistic interference and concludes with a section on 'self-monitoring' and mis-communication.

MARETT, M. (1987), Kriol and literacy. *Australian Aboriginal Studies* 2, 69–71.

Commenting on the history of literacy, Marett cites reasons for studying the relationship between oral and written Kriol and the implications of such study for other Aboriginal languages. She argues that, following Halliday, such study could reveal a great deal about how distinctive 'registers' and 'language functions' evolve. The article concludes that the study of the actual processes by which oral languages develop written forms could inform debate over the role and desirability of literacy in language maintenance.

MILLS, J. (1982), *Bilingual Education and Australian Schools*. Hawthorne, Vic.: Australian Council of Educational Research.

Mills reviews literature on bilingual education in the U.S.A., Canada and other countries. Although the stress throughout is on migrant community languages in Australia, Chapter 4 provides a brief history of policy development for and an overview of bilingual education in Northern Territory schools until 1981.

OZOLINS, V. (1985), The national language policy issue in Australia. In M. CLYNE (ed.) *Australia, Meeting Place of Languages*. Canberra: ANU Pacific Linguistics C-92.

This article is a critique of the 1984 Senate Committee Report on a national language policy (see Smolicz, 1986). Ozolins outlines historical and contemporary contexts for Australian language policy. He then takes up each of the chief concerns of the report. He concludes that what is needed is a 'setting out of priorities' which get confused and conflated under the auspices of a hastily developed policy for 'multiculturalism'.

RUSSO, C. P. (1983), Developing educational policies for traditionally oriented Aborigines. *Interchange* 14 (2), 1–24.

This paper examines claims that the existing education system fails to meet the needs and desires of 'traditionally oriented' Aborigines in Australia's Northern Territory. A composite literature review samples reported Aboriginal assessments of the educational system and prescriptions for change. Russo notes the consensus of traditionally oriented Aborigines over the need for bilingual/bicultural programs and instruction, and the need for more direct community control of schools. He concludes with an outline of possible policy avenues for effecting such change.

RUSSO, C. P. & BALDAUF, R. B. Jr (1986), Language development without planning: a case study of tribal Aborigines in the Northern Territory, Australia. *Journal of Multilingual and Multicultural Development* 17 (4), 301–17.

Beginning from Haugen's revised language planning model, this paper is an historical account of the effects of various governmental and educational policies on language development and change among tribal Aborigines in the Northern Territory. The authors argue that these policies have served as *de facto* language plans, serving the sociopolitical ends of first 'protection-segregation' and, later, 'assimilation-integration'. Since 1972, however, a range of policies which aim to maintain Aboriginal language have developed: these include bilingual programs in languages such as Gupapuyngu and Djambarrpuyngu. The paper concludes with an argument for a research-based language policy which reflects the patterns of use and the social needs of Aborigines.

SANDEFUR, J. (1985), Language planning and the development of an Australian Aboriginal creole. *Language Planning Newsletter* 11 (1), 1–14.

Sandefur here examines aspects of language planning and development as they relate to Kriol in the Roper River area (cf. Sandefur, 1986; Harris & Sandefur, 1984).

SANDEFUR, J. (1985), Kriol Kantri: the first of its kind. *Education News* 19 (2), 21–3.

Kriol Kantri is a series of videos produced for Kriol-speaking Aboriginal school children in the Northern Territory. Comprising 40 half-hour programs, it was developed on the *Playschool/Sesame Street* concept by Northern Territory educators. Its aims were: to build 'self-esteem' of Kriol-speaking children; to enhance their 'potential for success'; and to 'encourage and reinforce literacy'. The production and content of the series are described.

SANDEFUR, J. (1986), *Kriol of North Australia: a Language Coming of Age.* Working papers of the Summer Institute of Linguistics, Australian Aborigines Branch, Series A, Vol. 10. Darwin: Summer Institute of Linguistics.

Sandefur here addresses 'some of the critical debates which surround the origin, nature and use of Kriol', the creole language of northern Australia. He reviews in detail three main areas of research: the origin of Kriol, the relationship of Kriol to other creole languages of the Australian continent and beyond, and, finally, theoretical issues on the origins of pidgins and creoles. In the first section, he traces the interrelationships between the pidgins which developed, from the middle of the nineteenth century onward, within the increasingly multilingual Northern Territory context. In this analysis, he outlines the influence of the Macassans, Chinese, the mining camps and pastoral frontier, and the various pidgins which developed from such contacts. The manner in which they converged to become a 'widely understood' pidgin is detailed. Sandefur refers to the complex situation where, in some communities, Kriol is spoken as a pidgin, while in others it has creolized, and in yet others it has been adopted as a second language.

In the second section Sandefur demonstrates the feasibility of a connection between Kriol and Southeastern Australian Pidgin English. Yet he maintains that there is no demonstrable connection between Kriol and the pidgin of the Queensland sugar plantations, nor that of the Torres Strait region. The final section discusses theoretical issues concerning the origin of pidgins and creoles, and the significance of the study for research on pidginization and creolization.

Sandefur notes that in the absence of an explicit language policy, the Australian government has in effect engaged in *de facto* language planning. He provides a 'typology of educational alternatives' with an eye to the 'instrumentalization' of Kriol. This is followed by a discussion of the viability of Kriol in wider information domains. He concludes his discussion of language planning with the proposal that the planning of the future of Kriol should lie 'predominantly in the hands of "Kriol-speaking people"'.

SAYERS, B. J. (1983), Aurukun children's speech: language history and implications for bilingual education. In *Applications of Linguistics to Australian Aboriginal Contexts*. Applied Linguistics Association of Australia Occasional Papers No. 5, 47–67.

Sayers documents the socio-historical interaction of Aboriginal languages and English in Aurukun, North Queensland. She notes changes which have resulted from the return of residents speaking Aboriginal English, and from the establishment of a bilingual education program. Sayers suggests that the direction of future language change can only be speculated upon, but notes that the use of Wik-Munkan in the classroom has had a stabilizing effect on community use of the language and thus appears to be assisting in language maintenance.

SHNUKAL, A. (1983), Blaikman Tok: changing attitudes towards Torres Strait Creole. *Australian Aboriginal Studies* 2, 25–33.

— (1983), Torres Strait Creole: the growth of a new Torres Strait language. *Aboriginal History* 7 (2), 173–85.

— (1984), Torres Strait Islander students in Queensland mainland schools — Part 1: language background. *Aboriginal Child at School* 12(3), 27–33.

— (1984), Torres Strait Islander students in Queensland mainland schools — Part 2: language difficulties. *Aboriginal Child at School* 12 (5), 13–21.

— (1985), Multilingualism in the Eastern Torres Strait Islands. In M. CLYNE (ed.) *Australia, Meeting Place of Languages*. Canberra: ANU Pacific Linguistics, C–92.

— (1985), Torres Strait Creole: some non-linguistic constraints on dictionary making. *Australian Review of Applied Linguistics* Series S (2), 154–68.

— (1985), The spread of Torres Strait Creole to the Central Islands of the Torres Strait. *Aboriginal History* 9 (2), 220–34.

This series of articles reports on Shnukal's ongoing research into Torres Strait Creole (see Shnukal, in press/1988). They provide an historical perspective on the development, diffusion indigenization and present status of the language. The language's relationship to the traditional languages of the Strait region is described, with reference to language maintenance and language shift. Shnukal also describes its linguistic characteristics, as well as the attitudes of speakers and non-speakers towards the Creole. Shnukal argues that Torres Strait children attending mainland schools experience difficulties as the result of mainstream educators' negative attitudes towards Torres Strait Creole.

SMOLICZ, J. J. (1986), National policy on languages: a community language perspective. *Australian Journal of Education* 30 (1), 45–65.

A brief historical précis of Australian language policies before recent government action is undertaken. This is followed by a re-examination of the 1984 Senate Standing Committee Report in the light of Smolicz's ongoing research on language as a 'core value' for minority ethnic Australian groups (see Smolicz, 1983). Although Smolicz's research and discussion stresses migrant community languages, this paper provides a valuable review of policy statements and guidelines released by the States of Victoria and South Australia. It concludes with a call for further recognition of the need for and interest in the teaching of languages other than English.

VASZOLYI, E. (1982), Alphabet design for Aboriginal languages. In J. SHERWOOD (ed.) *Aboriginal Education: Issues and Innovations.* Perth: Creative Research.

This article discusses the inconsistencies in the spelling of Aboriginal words and place names in relation to the difficulties of matching the English phoneme system with those of Aboriginal languages. It further makes the case for consistency in the design of Aboriginal orthographies, especially for those languages and dialects which show close relationships.

WAFER, J. (1981), Planning for Australian Aboriginal languages: a preliminary guide to resources and concepts. In J. BELL (ed.) *Language Planning for Australian Aboriginal Languages.* Alice Springs: Institute for Aboriginal Development.

Wafer provides an extensive annotated bibliography of research literature up to 1980 relating to language planning in Australian contexts, with particular reference to Aboriginal language planning. He also lists key educational, government and academic institutions involved in linguistic research and planning.

WALSH, M. (1981), Remarks on a possible structure and policy for an Aboriginal language planning organization. In J. BELL (ed.) *Language*

Planning for Australian Aboriginal Languages. Alice Springs: Institute for Aboriginal Development.

Beginning from Rubin's classification of language planning aims, this
article is a preliminary attempt to outline a brief for an Aboriginal
language planning agency. Walsh describes some of the bureaucratic and
political problems which have arisen in the existing governmental infrastructure of Aboriginal organizations, which, he argues, have led to 'white
manipulation and desire to maintain control'. He concludes with a
statement of the need to avoid over-reliance on 'non-Aboriginal "experts"'
(see Fesl, 1982).

Part III:
Language Planning and Use in
Melanesia and Polynesia

8 Solomons Pijin: Colonial ideologies[1]

ROGER M. KEESING

Introduction

In Papua New Guinea and Vanuatu, dialects of Pidgin English are accorded a legitimate place as national languages. Tok Pisin and Bislama have conventional orthographies; their importance as media of grass roots communication and political life has been recognized. In contrast, in the former British Solomon Islands, Pidgin has never been accorded recognition, legitimacy, or a standard orthography. Solomons Pidgin remains, in government policy and in the dominant popular ideology, a 'bastardized' form of English, a holdover from the days of plantation labour, to be progressively replaced by English.

I will sketch the history of the ideology that views Pidgin as a debased form of English and an impediment to modernity: an ideology primarily a product of decades of British colonial rule. This in turn will underline how ironic is the perpetuation of this ideology in the postcolonial period. For the denigration and misunderstanding of Pidgin English in the Solomons continues despite a sociolinguistic situation where Pidgin has become the primary vehicle of an urban culture which increasingly reaches into the countryside (Jourdan, 1985). Some Solomon Islanders, and some expatriates, now realize that the colonial ideology was deeply flawed, both in misinterpreting the nature of Pidgin and in misjudging its place in the life of Solomons Islanders and its potential as a vehicle of communication in a young country: but theirs remains a minority view.

The History and Nature of Solomons Pidgin

In a recent book (Keesing, 1988) I examine the historical development of Pidgin English in the Pacific. In the latter chapters, I narrow the focus down to Solomons Pidgin. A brief summary of the points most relevant to the European ideology about Pidgin will provide a necessary background.

First, my research indicates that a Pacific Pidgin attained considerable complexity and stabilization earlier than the prevailing literature has suggested. The development of relatively expanded and stable Pidgin dialects out of an earlier unstable trade jargon has been attributed in the literature to the Labour Trade in the southwestern Pacific, in which labourers were taken under indenture to work on the plantations of Queensland, Fiji, Samoa and New Caledonia. Prior to the 1880s, Pidgin was supposed to be grammatically simple and unstable (see e.g. Mühlhäusler, 1980). My data suggest that many of the grammatical patterns and lexical usages characteristic of twentieth-century Melanesian Pidgin dialects had emerged by the 1870s; and indeed, many are attested from texts of the 1860s and even earlier — that is, from the 'sandalwood' period, prior to the Labour Trade.

Second, the impact of the Oceanic Austronesian languages of the central and southwestern Pacific on the grammar of a developing Pacific Pidgin appears to have been more strong and pervasive than has generally been recognized. Melanesian Pidgin dialects have been recognized by linguistic theorists as incorporating grammatical complexities — such as the marking of transitivity and elaboration of embedded clauses — not generally found in pidgins or creoles. I show in my book that these grammatical elaborations of Melanesian Pidgin closely follow structures common to the Oceanic Austronesian languages whose speakers were statistically preponderant in successive stages in its development. Such a strong 'substrate' influence is, I argue, an expectable concomitant of a sociolinguistic situation in which speakers of genetically related and grammatically similar languages are the primary agents in the formation of a pidgin. (In my book I deal at length with the interaction of such 'substrate modelling' with universal grammatical patterns and faculties of linguistic simplification; I argue that excavating underlying patterns common to genetically related languages and following universal pathways are complementary, not mutually exclusive, processes.)

Although the grammatical structures of Melanesian Pidgin are fundamentally those of Oceanic Austronesian, the lexicon is almost entirely derived from English, and from a nautical pidgin embodying centuries of cumulated traditions of how to talk to 'natives', such as 'savvy'. But the semantics of categories with English-derived labels such as 'die' and 'win' are strikingly Oceanic. Linguistic elements such as -*im* attached to verbs and *fella* quantifying nouns follow Oceanic grammatical patterns, and English-derived labels fit into Oceanic semantic slots.

In narrowing my focus to Solomons Pijin, I show that Pijin grammar parallels remarkably closely the grammars of the indigenous languages of the Solomons, particularly those of the southeastern Solomons (Malaita, Guadalcanal, Makira, Gela, etc.) — albeit with a somewhat simplified structure and lexicon. Thus older Solomon Islanders for whom Pijin was a second language learned in young adulthood, appear to map (calque) Pidgin very directly onto their native languages, grammatically and semantically. For fluent indigenous speakers of Pijin, able to draw on the discourse strategies and syntactic models of their (themselves closely related) native languages, Solomons Pijin has for decades approached in its communicative power the richness of a natural language, despite its relatively limited lexicon and the attendant imprecisions and/or need for paraphrase.

My research further indicates that it has been Islanders (in the Solomons and elsewhere in the southwest Pacific) who have, from the 1870s onwards, been the fluent, grammatical speakers of Pidgin; and that most Europeans have had a defective command of Pidgin, grammatically, lexically, and phonologically. Of course, Europeans bent on extending their sources of plantation labour, and later their administrative control, were continually encountering Islanders from peripheral and 'bush' areas with a limited command of Pidgin, who provided endless sources of anecdotal mirth. Moreover, those Islanders who were in sustained, regular communication with English speakers characteristically acquired anglicized registers that in various degrees resembled or approached English (although in addition they were fluent speakers of a pidgin they used with fellow Islanders). Both phenomena were instrumental in generating and sustaining an ideology that Pidgin was a bastardized form of English and that Europeans were the ones who spoke it properly, by adding to simple English a sprinkling of *fella*s, *save*s, etc., for the benefit of 'the natives'.

In the Solomons as elsewhere in the southwestern Pacific, then, a quite fully developed and grammatically elaborate pidgin of which Islanders were the most fluent speakers — the Pidgin English of the Labour Trade — existed prior to the imposition of colonial rule and the development of extensive internal plantation systems. This pidgin was grammatically not only elaborated, but closely modelled on the structures broadly common to indigenous languages. Yet the lexicon was almost entirely derived from English and from a worldwide nautical pidgin embodying cumulated centuries of ways of 'talking to natives'; it embodied what had become archaic (*gammon*) and vulgar (*bugger*) English forms. Europeans thought the Pidgin was a bastardized, simple and vulgar form of English; and since Pidgin was the medium used by Europeans to maintain capitalist control and colonial domination, and since most Islanders had little or no access to English, many Islanders thought Pidgin *was* the language of those who ruled them. We had, then, the ingredients for contradiction: a wide split between a European-created ideology and linguistic and sociolinguistic realities.

In what follows, I use 'Pijin' to refer to the Solomons dialect[2], except where reference is made to the interpretation of 'pidgin English' in colonial ideology; I use 'Pidgin' to refer to the several dialects of Melanesian Pidgin.

British Views of Pidgin: The Colonial Ideology

Abuses of the Labour Trade, attacks on ships and planters, and expansionist moves in the region by France and Germany, led the British to declare a Protectorate over the Solomons just prior to the turn of the century. By this time there was a small European planter community, mainly in the New Georgia group in the western Solomons. Until the first years of this century, the main plantation areas in the southwest Pacific were in Queensland, Fiji, Samoa and New Caledonia.

To understand the roots of a colonial ideology toward Pijin, we must distinguish three elements in the European community of the Solomons, with rather different interests in and attitudes toward the *lingua franca*.

First were the missionaries. Catholics of the Marist order, initially French, were active in the southeast Solomons well in advance of colonial rule. So too were Anglicans. Both of these missions, and particularly the latter, had a strong commitment to learning, preaching and publishing religious materials in indigenous languages. The French Marists chose particular languages — Ghari and Visale on Guadalcanal, for instance — for regional use. The Anglicans initially used Mota, a Banks Island language, as the vehicle for teaching within the New Hebrides and Solomons; later, missionary linguists, notably Codrington, Fox, and Ivens, made indigenous languages such as Bughotu, Arosi and Gela the bases for teaching and Bible translation. In the western Solomons, the Methodists used Roviana, and the Seventh Day Adventists Marovo, as regional languages of teaching and preaching. Pijin became the primary linguistic medium of the fundamentalist South Sea Evangelical Mission (SSEM), grown out of the Queensland Kanaka Mission, and most strongly based on Malaita. As the Adventists moved into the southeast Solomons, they too relied heavily on Pijin, although through the years they have been a conduit through which elements of the New Guinea dialect have entered the Solomons. Missionary attitudes toward Solomons Pijin range, accordingly, from the scorn of Anglicans such as Ivens to the pragmatism of the SSEM, which had a condescension toward the childlike 'natives' (reborn into Christianity from wild savagery) for whom a childlike version of English was apt. Florence Young's comments about the use of Pidgin in Queensland set the tone for what was to follow:

> Even Christians thought it was impossible to impart divine truths through the curious jargon of pidgin English, which . . . was our only medium of communication. The answer . . . we knew to be — *'With God* all things are possible'.

> (Young, 1926: 42)

Interestingly, one of the issues in the postwar anticolonial Maasina Rule movement was the way the SSEM had used Pijin as the vehicle for training catechists at the Bible School at Onepusu, hence withholding 'true' knowledge, education and literacy in English.

As an internal plantation system expanded, through the first three decades of this century, the planters became a dominant voice in the Protectorate. The planters learned Pijin, often relatively well, and used it as the medium of command. The dominant tone toward Pijin was of smug superiority: Pidgin English was a simple and childlike form of English of which they, the planters, were fluent speakers; it was a low register appropriate to command, and to the mental simplicity of 'the natives'. In the slick propaganda magazine *Planter's Gazette*, published by Solomon Islands Planter's Association to put political pressure on the colonial government, a regular column (*Cannibals and Coconuts*) reported what were supposed to be howlingly funny examples of linguistic misunderstandings and Pidgin absurdities on the part of unsophisticated 'natives'. Pidgin was a simple and droll medium for communicating about a superior culture and technology to savages, whose linguistic ineptitude was the mirror of their cultural backwardness and lower mental powers.

Government officers in the Solomons faced something of a contradiction on the linguistic front. They were heirs to traditions of colonialist Orientalism (Said, 1978), traditions pioneered in India and later Africa, where Gentlemen government officers learned local languages and did ethnological or epigraphic studies. The Pacific outposts of Empire, although low on the scale of Imperial prestige in comparison to India or Nigeria (Huessler, 1963), saw echoes of this in Fiji and the Gilberts. But in the Solomons there was not only little to romanticize about in local peoples or cultures, bereft as they were of copper skin or indigenous aristocracies. The 'natives' spoke so many languages and dialects — some sixty languages — that there seemed no point or possibility of trying to learn one of them. An early comment by the first police officer on Malaita, reported by a visiting entomologist in 1916, illustrates the sort of negative pragmatism that propelled the government into using Pijin:

'I don't know the dialects of these people,' he [Campbell] said. 'Neither does [District Officer] Bell. If someone swings on you with a tomahawk, who the hell could write notes to them?'

(Mann, 1948: 280)

The Anglican missionary C. E. Fox (1962: 137), looking back at some fifty years in the Solomons, observed that 'no Government officer has ever learnt a local language'. Pijin became, by default, the medium of colonial administration.

But although Pijin was a pragmatic necessity, as a medium of command for servants, police, boats-crews and other indigenous employees and as a medium for establishing colonial hegemony through local headmen, courts and head tax, it was — filtered through the ears of British Gentlemen — never a language that could be romanticized or even rendered respectable. Its *bugger-ups* and four letter words — or missionary derived euphemisms in place of them — as well as its laughable circumlocutions and childlike character, as perceived by English speakers, made it both disreputable and ridiculous. Horton (1965: 16) illustrates this with a conversation in Tulagi shortly after his arrival as a fledgling District Officer, in which his host queried a servant:

'Which way coffee im e no come?'
'Oh, Mastah — me sorry too much — arse piece bilong coffee pot im e bugger up finis . . .'
I sat up with a jerk, but my host took it calmly.

From fairly early in the history of the Protectorate, a division emerged between experienced field officers who used Pijin regularly in everyday administration (and hence tended to speak it relatively well, though virtually never with a grammaticality, semantic and lexical command, phonology and fluency approaching that of Islanders[3]) and senior officers based in Tulagi (and after World War II, Honiara), more preoccupied with the rituals, hierarchy and paper-shuffling of Empire than the pragmatics of using a *lingua franca* for everyday communication. There was thus a contradiction whereby for many years field officers had to pass oral tests of Pijin competence after an initial period of service; yet Pijin was never given a standard orthography, committed to writing, or codified with published dictionary or grammar. It was just something you 'picked up' and spoke, if your job required you to. The ambivalence field officers acquired toward this useful but vulgar medium is reflected in the comments of a District Officer serving in the 1920s:

> Pidgin English, an excellent if revolting (to nice minds) basic English in which some of the more lurid and picturesque cuss-words used by our ancestors do honest duty in conveying precise enough thought, offers a convenient *lingua franca*[4] (MacQuarrie, 1946: 70).

Official Attitudes Toward Pijin

Because through the pre-war years education was left entirely to the missions, there was no need for the Protectorate Government to formulate any clear policy regarding the status and use of Pijin in relation to local languages, and English. The missions had their own policies, as I have noted.

We get some glimpses of official attitudes in the 1929 report by Lieut–Col. Sir H. C. Moorehouse, appointed by the Secretary of State to the Colonies to investigate the assassination of a District Officer on Malaita (Keesing & Corris, 1980):

> Except in the central schools of the missions the education has scarcely got beyond the kindergarten stage, but . . . an advance in that direction is certain to take place and as it is the schools do some good in inculcating habits of cleanliness, discipline, and order.
>   Owing to the diversity of the languages spoken within the Group it seems essential that the teaching should be in some *lingua franca* which would become the common language outside the village, and I would strongly support what I believe to be the view to which the

majority of the missionary societies are coming that that language should be English. A short experience of the horrible variant of that language at present spoken leads one to encourage any attempt that may be made to obliterate it, but I do not think that this will be achieved by teaching English as a subject in the schools, but by teaching in English.

(Moorehouse, 1929: 25)

Another illustration of the attitude of the times comes from the unpublished memoirs of Major Eustace Sandars, who served (mainly on Malaita) from 1930 until 1948:

> The only *lingua franca* [is] pidgeon [*sic*] English which consists of the English word in the Melanesian context. It is a queer sounding garbled business and not in any way satisfactory.
>
> The Melanesian Mission at one time tried to introduce a language named Mota which was a very grievous mistake in my opinion as had they attempted to introduce pure English it would have been very much better. As the years go by English is becoming more and more spoken and it will be a very great help to everybody when it is accepted by all the people.

Another interesting text comes from Dick Horton, who as a District Officer in the second half of the 1930s acquired a relatively good command of Pijin. Having returned to the Solomons after the War, he reminisced that:

> One great drawback in trying to understand what the people were thinking and how they looked at life was caused by the very poor shades of meaning which could be derived from pidgin English. Unfortunately, until the Government started a proper educational system and there were more schools in the islands where English could be taught, Pidgin had to be used, for there were so many other dialects that it was impossible to find one that ran right through the islands.

(Horton, 1965: 46)

A fascinating set of texts on governmental attitudes towards Pijin is found in the annual and sometimes biennial reports of the Protectorate. The pattern was for a Government Officer, given the task of writing the annual report, to adopt the text from his predecessors, add some touches and comments of his own, and update the figures and facts where necessary. Once a decade or so, an industrious or ambitious officer would thoroughly rewrite the text, setting the pattern for the years to come. The paragraphs on language are fascinating, since so often the writer-of-the-year added some touch based on personal experience or point of view to a standard passage that was retained from year to year. Some extracts will illustrate the pattern and the views of successive authors:

> Pidgin is almost universally spoken by Solomon Island males, less often spoken by females, and is becoming noticeably more anglicised as time passes. Although at first somewhat distasteful to the ear of an English-speaking person, the language is nevertheless flexible and expressive, and a true *lingua franca*. It is used officially *faute de mieux*, but is not encouraged and efforts are made to use simple English rather than Pidgin, whenever there is a likelihood of English being understood.
>
> (BSIP, 1948)

The aim of shifting progressively towards English is already clear. The author the next year added at the end 'Basic English may well be the answer to this problem.' (BSIP, 1949–50). The latter sentence was removed in the 1951–52 report, and this form was preserved in 1953–54, except that 'somewhat curious' was substituted for 'somewhat distasteful'. In the 1955–56 report, the author added 'but Pidgin remains indispensable for the time being'.

In the 1957–58 report, and through 1965, the following passage was to remain unchanged:

> Pidgin is almost universally spoken by Solomon Island males, less often by females, and is becoming noticeably more anglicised as time passes. Although still useful as a *lingua franca*, Pidgin is a bar to progress in the modern world and its day is passing. English is now compulsory in all registered schools and, in a simple form, is replacing Pidgin in the main centres.
>
> (BSIP, 1959)

In 1971, another general overhaul was done, by an author who evidently had some interest in and understanding of local languages and cultures, and some insight regarding Pidgin:

> Public communication is possible only in English and informally in Pidgin English — a form of language invented by the Islanders themselves with a vocabulary derived from English and a typically Melanesian syntax . . . Pidgin English has not been given an orthography, but is universally spoken between people of different languages, forming, at the present, the most effective *lingua franca*. It differs slightly from the Pidgin English of New Guinea and the New Hebrides, in the former case in having a more anglicized vocabulary.

. . . English, however, is the official language and is widely spoken and taught in all the schools.

(BSIP, 1972)

This generally sensible view, clearly deriving from experience in the field, had little impact on the policy-makers in Honiara who were planning the country's destiny with independence on the horizon, who regarded Pijin as nothing more than a residual nuisance and an obstacle to progress. Long since, even the practice of requiring field officers to pass practical examinations in spoken Pijin had been abandoned.

Pijin and Élitist Education

When in the 1950s the Protectorate Government had begun to pay attention to education, primary attention was devoted to creating an élite to whom greater responsibility could gradually be passed. The majority of senior Solomons leaders of the post-colonial period, including the country's first two Prime Ministers and first Governor General, were classmates at King George VI Secondary School when it was located outside Auki, on Malaita. Most of this first élite generation, including many of the country's senior public servants as well as political leaders, had received their initial training at mission schools; many had gone on to study at overseas tertiary institutions.

The policy of the Education Department in the 1960s was squarely élitist, with token attention paid to education outside the few government centres.[5] English was the medium of instruction and a major subject of study. In the élite schools, once students were supposed to be able to speak English, they were forbidden to use Pijin on school premises (although doubtless most indulged in this 'forbidden vice'). In any case, the whole system was predicated on creating a first generation of fluent English speakers, who would eventually be the heirs to the colonial state and teachers of the next generation. The sense of destiny inculcated in this first élite was built around a command of English: a linguistic capacity that would distinguish them from the parental generation, many of whom were leaders in mission work or government functionaries in the police or administration.

It was assumed that these first élite students were the vanguards of a new linguistic order in the Solomons, whereby Pijin progressively gave way to English, as adequately·trained teachers and successful role models emerged. They, the élite speakers of 'pure' English, were to lead and oversee the metamorphosis of the Solomons from a Pijin-speaking country into an English-speaking country. At first, the English the less advantaged would manage would be 'simple'. 'Simple English', widely used in Government publications and news media, was to supersede Pijin. Indeed, it was imagined by many in the British community that through progressive anglicization, Pijin would progressively turn into 'simple English'; if Pijin had originally developed through Melanesians attempting clumsily to speak the vulgar English to which they were exposed, what they needed was more exposure to better English. Eventually, 'simple' English would be transformed into 'proper' English, once primary education was broadened and teachers were properly educated.

The 1963–64 report for the BSIP defined the interim goals of education policy[6] as:

> to produce a system which will ensure a flow of educated Solomon Islands leaders into the main stream of the territory's life, including an adequate supply of teachers upon which the eventual extension of primary education to all can be based.
>
> (BSIP, 1965:1)

The Keesing–Payne debate

When I was in the Solomons in late 1969, after hearing a series of radio broadcasts on adult education in the Solomons which illustrated both the disdain of the Adult Education Officer for Pijin and his inability to speak the language when attempting to communicate in village settings, I was moved to write an open letter to him, which I distributed relatively widely within the Protectorate Administration and among Solomons leaders. I shall quote some extracts from my letter:

> Pidgin is not debased or simplified English. It is a language ... governed by rules as neat as those of English. ... Melanesians speak it fluently and grammatically, and very few Europeans do ...
>
> A view of Pidgin as a simplified or debased form of English, rather than as a Melanesian language with English-derived labels for Melanesian categories, leads to misunderstanding of the relationship (in educational terms) of Pidgin-speaking to English-speaking. Far too often in the Solomons the view has been held that Pidgin is a 'stepping stone' to English. By taking a person's Pidgin, and modifying it, one could thus teach him to speak English. ...
>
> [But] Pidgin does not provide either a means or a motivation for

learning English. Melanesians know Pidgin, or learn it very quickly
... [To learn] English, [they] must struggle to master a new
grammatical structure. ... Pidgin scarcely helps at all in this learning
process. ...

For educational purposes, the notion of choosing between Pidgin
or English as languages to be learned by Solomon Islanders is
unrealistic. They are different languages, they serve complementary
functions. The choice is never, for a Melanesian, whether to learn
Pidgin *or* English; it is always whether to learn English *as well as*
Pidgin.. . .

Hence the idea of Pidgin dying out in the Solomons some day,
and being replaced by English, is absurd. No matter how many
Solomon Islanders learn English, they will still speak Pidgin — about
different things, in different settings, and for different reasons. ...

To make English the only legitimate language as a matter of
policy would be to restrict news and information to a privileged élite.
... I think that English, not Pidgin, will increasingly become the
language of news broadcasts, political discourse, education, and of the
public and official sectors of Solomon Island life. Hence English will
be an avenue to prestige, privilege, knowledge, and earning power.
However, I do not believe that English will replace Pidgin as the
language in which Melanesians informally talk to Melanesians about
things Melanesian. ... Thus I believe that it is insidious, unrealistic
and ultimately self-defeating to suppose — as has so often been
supposed here — that by weakening Pidgin or demeaning its use or
'diluting' it by Anglicizing its grammar, one is in fact strengthening
English. If one perceives that their nature and functions in the
Solomons are complementary, ... both Pidgin and English can be
strengthened and given the position of dignity and legitimacy they
deserve ...

I went on to urge the development of a standardized orthography for Pijin,
which would allow it to serve more effectively as a medium of grass-roots
communication.

The reply by the Adult Education Officer, Keith Payne, was again
widely distributed. Among other things, he argued that Pijin was changing
so rapidly that any codification, even in the form of an orthography, would
hinder its natural evolution and would be incompatible with diverse local
pronunciations. (Did Payne imagine that having written forms of English,
German or French prevents these languages from changing? Did he
imagine, in spite of the diverse English phonologies in the British Isles,
that a standard written form entails a standardization of pronunciation?)

Payne went on to add some predictions about the future:

> I personally, would surmise that Pidgin as we know it now will phase itself out in the years to come and that something that is neither strictly Pidgin nor English will become the language of the people, whilst true English will become the mark of the educated Solomon Islander.
>
> If Pidgin can be allowed to evolve, it will become heavily Anglicised in the natural course of events. ... If the people themselves want to perpetuate Pidgin, then they will. But the whole trend is towards Anglicisation. ...
>
> In thirty years, I shall probably be as dead as the Pidgin we are talking today. But English ... will still be marching on.

My letter stirred a lively correspondence in early 1970 among various government departments, with senior officers in Lands and Surveys, Agriculture and the Geological Survey — the ones who knew Pijin and used it in their work in village contexts — endorsing my views about the need to legitimize use of Pijin and develop a written form for grass-roots communication. After several such letters critical of education policy, the Secretary for Protectorate Affairs circulated a memorandum ordering Government officers not to comment further on the issue.

I do not know whether Payne has survived as well as Pijin. The Solomons *lingua franca* continues to change[7] — as English does — but his other forecasts are not, so far, being realized. Payne had responded to my observations that Honiara nurses used Pijin, not English, in the workplace, by commenting that this was 'because they have never had the opportunity to practise the little formal English that was imparted to them by indifferently qualified teachers in the past (this state of affairs is changing)'. Payne might be surprised, seventeen years later, to see the Prime Minister and his Parliamentary colleagues — most of them university educated — shifting into Pijin in contexts of everyday informal conversation, and even using it in Parliament for rhetorical purposes. Pijin remains the main language of everyday urban social life, even among children 'officially' being schooled in English (Jourdan, 1985).

Solomon Island élites and the colonial ideology

In retrospect, it is not surprising that those Solomon Islanders who went off to become the first generation of leaders and teachers well-educated in English inherited very directly the prejudices toward Pijin articulated by their own teachers and incorporated into the rules and orientations that had governed their own schooling. For them, using Pijin at school had been a forbidden temptation, tantamount to a sin: it was to be the same for the students in an independent Solomons.

It is these first well-trained teachers who became, by and large, the senior figures in education in the post-colonial government. In 1984, for example, the Minister of Education was a former secondary school teacher; his Permanent Secretary had been the Headmaster of the same school. For these and other members of the first élite generation, English had been the medium of advancement and opportunity and status. Pijin, the language of the functionaries of their parents' generation, locked in colonial subservience to missionaries and government, was a symbol of subordination and the past.

It is perhaps surprising — since Pijin so directly mirrors the syntactic and semantic structures of the languages they speak natively — that so many Solomon Islanders have accepted uncritically an ideology depicting Pijin as a bastardized form of English, and a language of domination primarily created by Europeans rather than as a language of survival and solidarity primarily created by Melanesians. Many well educated Solomon Islanders echo the colonial view that Pijin has 'no grammar', even though in speaking and understanding Pijin, those who express this view use (unconsciously) a grammar so complex and intricate and powerful that (like the grammars of all languages) it defies formal description.

Yet we know from other parts of the world that attitudes speakers have toward the languages they (and others) speak need have little to do with, and may be completely disconnected from and incompatible with, linguistic realities. Speakers of minority languages, regional dialects or lower-class registers may accept and endorse the hegemonic ideologies of dominant ethnic groups or social strata, which depict their speech as primitive, subhuman or deviant. The meaning and valence of a language as a *symbol*, in relation to status and identity, need have little to do with its structure, its linguistic history, or the sociolinguistics of its actual use.

Another significant element in the opposition to Pijin by Solomon Islanders has lain in the different historical experiences of different parts of the Solomons. It is primarily Malaitans (and secondarily Guadalcanal men) who have comprised the plantation labour force in the Solomons; and as we have seen, it has primarily been on Malaita that missions used Pijin. In the more prosperous and developed western Solomons, missions used Roviana and Marovo, and had long taught English as well; and Pijin was the language of the hated and feared Malaitan underclass. Similarly,

Pijin has acquired negative overtones on Makira, Isabel and Gela. Given the statistical domination of Malaitans within the Solomons population, and the lack of development and education in large bush zones of Malaita, negative attitudes toward Pijin, fear of Malaita domination, and class interests and prejudices among a neo-colonial élite have been intricately intertwined.

Questioning the Ideology

In the mid-1970s, a cluster of young Solomon Islanders, mainly educated at the University of Papua New Guinea and University of the South Pacific and imbued with ideologies of cultural nationalism and liberation from colonialism, began to question the prevailing view of Pijin. In the pages of the nationalist and often radical *Kakamora Reporter*, privately published weekly, a view of Pijin as a Melanesian language and as a potential vehicle of indigenous nationalism and populism began to emerge. Two Solomon Islanders later to achieve recognition in international arenas, Francis Bugotu[8] and Francis Saemala[9], initiated a programme to teach Pijin to expatriates. Some works of literature began to be produced in Pijin. Finally, first steps were taken that have led toward a creation of a standard orthography, dictionaries and the production of religious materials in Pijin. In the last decade, much of the impetus in this direction has come from the Solomon Islands Christian Association, with a strong input from the Summer Institute of Linguistics, which has viewed Pijin as an under-utilized medium of religious instruction. These forces seeking to expand the usefulness of Pijin for religious purposes have added strength to and complemented the minority nationalist ideology regarding Pijin. Some significant gains have been made, including the acceptance of Pijin as a second language of parliamentary debate (along with English); but even here, in the absence of a widely known and used standard written form of Pijin, contradictions arise at every turn. In view of the regional differences in historical orientations toward Pijin, it is not surprising that the strongest pro-Pijin voices have come from Malaita and Guadalcanal; and the strongest opposition has come from leaders from other areas. Pijin is part of the 'Malaita Menace'; and its political uses smack of dangerous populism.

Despite the emergence of a substantial counter-ideology, nationalist and populist, supporting the legitimation of Pijin and its codification as a medium of grass-roots communication and national political life, the institutions of education and government remain squarely predicated on the replacement of Pijin by English. The dominant ideology continues to denigrate Pidgin as a bastardized form of English, created by Europeans as a form of domination and to be replaced as soon and as efficiently as possible by a language less demeaning and vulgar with which it is in direct competition for the minds and habits of the young — 'proper' English.

Notes

1. I am grateful to Richard Baldauf, Christine Jourdan, Allan Luke and Darrell Tryon for helpful comments and suggestions.
2. The label 'Pijin' has become current in the writings of the Solomon Islands Christian Association and among Solomon Islanders who have sought to gain recognition for the Solomons dialect of Pidgin as a legitimate national language (a movement I discuss at the end of the paper).
3. Even those Government Officers most fluent in Pijin were massively subject to code interference, in using English-derived forms according to English rather than Melanesian phonology; thus they have rendered Pijin *olgeta* (the plural marker and 'they' pronoun) as 'altogether' and *wanem* (the interrogative 'what?') as 'what name'.
4. Although his own texts show him to have spoken Pijin very badly.
5. A sum of £16,000 was spent, in the 1960s, on the buildings for the Government Primary School in Auki (the administrative headquarters on Malaita), as a showplace for visiting dignitaries inspecting progress toward decolonization, while insignificant amounts were spent on schools and teachers in rural areas.
6. As set out in the 1963 White Paper on Educational Policy.
7. As Jourdan's Ph.D. thesis (1985) indicates, some of the changes (especially lexical changes) represent 'anglicization', but many represent processes of grammatical streamlining as a pidgin learned as a second language in adulthood has become the primary language of an urban population (a process of 'creolization', if we mean by this a phenomenon broader than the acquisition of a pidgin as a native language, as Jourdan urges that we should).
8. He did postgraduate study in linguistics at the University of York and later became Secretary General of the South Pacific Commission.
9. He served as Solomons' Ambassador to the United Nations.

References

BSIP (British Solomon Islands Protectorate) (1949), *British Solomon Islands 1948*. Honiara.
— (1951), *British Solomon Islands 1949 and 1950*. Honiara.
— (1953), *British Solomon Islands 1951 and 1952*. Honiara.
— (1955), *British Solomon Islands 1953 and 1954*. Honiara.

— (1959), *British Solomon Islands 1957 and 1958*. Honiara.

— (1965), *British Solomon Islands 1963 and 1964*. Honiara.

— (1972), *British Solomon Islands 1971*. Honiara.

Fox, C. E. (1962), *Kakamora*. London: Hodder and Stoughton.

Horton, D. C. (1965), *The Happy Isles*. London: Heinemann.

Huessler, R. (1963), *Yesterday's Rulers: The Making of the British Colonial Service*. Syracuse: Syracuse University Press.

Jourdan, C. (1985), *Sapos Iumi Mitim Iumi: Urbanization and Creolization in the Solomon Islands*. Unpublished Ph.D. thesis, Departments of Anthropology and Linguistics, The Australian National University.

Keesing, R. M. (1988), *Melanesian Pidgin and the Oceanic Substrate*. Stanford: Stanford University Press.

Keesing, R. M. & Corris, P. (1980), *Lightning Meets the West Wind*. Melbourne: Melbourne University Press.

MacQuarrie, H. (1946), *Vouza and the Solomon Islands*. Sydney, London: Angus and Robertson.

Mann, W. T. (1948), *Ant Hill Odyssey*. Boston: Little, Brown and Co.

Moorehouse, H. C. (1929), Report of Commissioner Appointed by the Secretary of State for the Colonies to Inquire into the Circumstances in which Murderous Attacks Took Place in 1927 on Government Officials on Guadalcanal and Malaita. London: H. M. Stationery Office.

Mühlhäusler, P. (1980), Structural expansion and the process of creolization. In A. Valdman & H. Highfield (eds.) *Theoretical Orientations in Creole Studies*. New York: Academic Press.

Said, E. (1978), *Orientalism*. New York: Pantheon.

Young, F. (1926), *Pearls from the Pacific*. London: Marshall Bros.

9   Solomons Pijin: An unrecognized national language

CHRISTINE JOURDAN

In his article, Roger Keesing (this volume, Chapter 8) has discussed the historical and ideological pressures brought to bear on Solomon Islands Pijin (hereinafter SIP) during the colonial period, and the resulting duality in which English became the prestigious medium of élite communication and Pijin the devalued medium of practical communication. This duality lives on today, but has been amplified by the fact that Pijin is nowadays spoken throughout the archipelago. In many respects this duality reminds us of a great number of similar situations found currently in the Third World; a foreign language imposed on the local population by way of the administration and education systems serves as the official language of the country as well as the language of social advancement. This situation is reflected, for instance, in the role played by French in West Africa and by English in India.

The history of colonization throughout the world has shown us that where settlement colonies developed, the local vernaculars met the fate of their speakers: they have either disappeared or been relegated to the social and geographical fringes of the colonies. The Americas, North Africa, New Zealand, Australia and of course New Caledonia are the examples that spring to mind. However, when colonization was 'limited' to commercial exploitation without large scale population settlement, vernaculars had a better chance to survive the onslaught of colonial enterprise. But ironically, their survival was due, in many instances, to the Europeans' lack of interest in the local population beyond the head tax that could be collected from them and the potential labour force they represented.

The Solomon Islands fall into the latter group. Seen by the then administration as a backwater of the British Empire, the Solomon Islands were never, before the Second World War, the locus of European interest, in terms of development at a grass-roots level. Except for some missionaries, the odd traders or planters, vernacular languages were not spoken by Europeans — least of all members of the British administration. Prolonged contact with the local population took place, not in the realm of vernacular usage, i.e. the villages, but rather on plantations and trading and administrative posts where multilingualism rendered the use of Pijin almost obligatory. Because they were spoken in areas that were of no interest to Europeans, the vernaculars never became, to the same extent as Pijin had, the target of British criticism and denigration (to the point of wanting to eliminate them). Moreover, because these languages were totally unintelligible to them, the Europeans could not apply in the same manner, to the vernaculars, the linguisticocentric value judgements that they were applying to Pijin. On the other hand Pijin was spoken in areas that were important to the colonial enterprise: Europeans had to speak that *lingua franca* in order to interact with the Melanesians who were their servants, workers, and petty functionaries (such as police). Since lexically Pijin bore some resemblances to English (due to the history of its formation and development), this led to three reactions on the part of the British:

(1) they considered it as a debased and bastardized English language that had no structure;
(2) they never thought it necessary to learn it in a serious way, as they would have with another foreign language, in order to speak it properly; and
(3) they never considered it as a real language but rather as a bad variety of English that was in competition with standard English, and thus had to disappear (Jourdan, 1985; Keesing, this volume, Chapter 8).

Ironically, the very fact that the Europeans were using Pijin (albeit badly) with the Melanesian population reinforced the idea amongst Solomon Islanders that this was the language that had to be mastered if one was to have access to European organized economic activities. It is obvious that during the colonial period, very few Solomon Islanders had access to English in a sustained enough fashion to allow them to realize how different the two languages were. This contributed to and reinforced the Islanders' impression that the language they were using with the Europeans was indeed the Europeans' language — that is, English.[1]

However, what was seminal in the development of Pijin as the *lingua franca* of the archipelago was not so much the symbolic and social value of the language as its practical value. As the country became increasingly incorporated into a cash economy and as opportunities for travel and education increased, intertribal and inter-island contacts escalated to levels well beyond those of the pre-war period. Urbanization developed, inter-island migration expanded, and as a result the use of Pijin expanded geographically and socially, overflowing the limits previously constraining the uses to which the language had been put. All this exposed Solomon Islanders to multilingualism on a grand scale. More and more people found themselves in social contexts and sociolinguistic intercourse so diverse ethnically and linguistically, that they had to have recourse to Pijin to overcome the communication gap. Those who had had previous knowledge of Pijin (see Jourdan, 1985; Keesing, 1988) naturally resorted to it; the others learned it very quickly, *sur le tas*, at work or in daily casual contacts with Pijin speakers (through schools, neighbourhood and church ties, etc.). Very early in the history of the Protectorate, SIP had become the *lingua franca* amongst the Melanesians on plantations and in other multilingual contexts, as it had been amongst 'Kanakas' during the Labour Trade: it had never been primarily a *lingua franca* used between Europeans and Melanesians. It is as a *lingua franca* through which Melanesians communicated with one another over the years, that Pijin gradually became the most widespread language of the archipelago.

I have explained elsewhere (Jourdan, 1985) the social history of SIP, and will not therefore go into details here. I shall focus rather on domains of the contemporary social role of SIP — education, media, town life, family life — to show that despite the fact that English is the *de jure* official language of the country, Pijin is its *de facto* national language. However, we shall see that the two languages are not mutually exclusive, as they fill complementary niches in the sociocultural life of the Solomon Islands. This situation is, however, exacerbated and perpetuated by Pijin's major handicap: its lack of legitimacy. I shall move on to address the concept of Melanesian Pidginophony as a way for the pidgin-speaking countries of the South West Pacific to strengthen their cultural bonds and to maximize financial resources allocated to communication and education in a way that would be their own.

Education

One of the peculiarities of education in the Solomon Islands lies in the fact that except for the first two years of primary schooling, the official teaching medium is English. This follows the recommendation made by the 1972 British Solomon Islands Protectorate Education Conference (BSIP, 1972: 68), namely that English should become the medium of instruction full-time in Standard Three (i.e. the third year of primary education) onwards. It is a peculiarity on three grounds. First, despite the fact that Pijin is the most widely spread language of the archipelago, and certainly the main language of urban centres, it is not recognized as being an asset in the education process. Second, English is not the mother tongue or the main language of the children who are nevertheless taught in that language. Third, it is not a language to which most of the children have a great amount of exposure in everyday life (other than in listening to the odd radio program and popular music). In that sense, English is not at all a 'natural' and familiar language to most Solomon Islands children. As there is not as yet, after almost 90 years of British rule, a natural Melanesian English-speaking speech community,[2] English is perceived as the technical language of education that has no reality of its own in the daily activities of the students outside of the classroom. The children know, however, that English plays an important role in other realms of the Solomon Islands' life: in the public service and in the world of commerce, for instance. As they grow older, they realize only too well that English is the key to social advancement through secondary schooling or well paid employment. But the absence of natural exposure to English in daily life is a barrier to good language proficiency. In some cases, and for the same reasons, the teachers themselves do not master the language very well. Indeed who could blame them? As with the students, English is for many teachers a language limited to the domain of the classroom. Watson-Gegeo (1987) notes that the quality of English instruction, particularly in rural schools, has declined over the years, and that this decline is concomitant

> with the rapid expansion of primary schools to meet development goals. Since independence, expatriate teachers have increasingly been replaced by local teachers, many of whom do not have a command of standard English.
>
> (1987: 25)

Note that I do not write here 'the domain of the school' but rather the 'domain of the classrooom'. For it is obvious to anyone who has observed children at play in the schools of the Solomon Islands that English does not belong in the schoolyard — in the same way that it does not belong in the streets or in casual meetings with friends or inside the home. In urban schools (be they primary or secondary schools) and in the provincial secondary schools of the country, Pijin is the natural medium of communication that allows pupils and teachers alike to overcome the linguistic diversity found in such multilingual settings. In the rural primary schools, the local vernacular takes over the school life as soon as classes have ended.

With regard to the teaching medium in school, the 1972 Education conference made another recommendation. It was a far-sighted recommendation which showed how aware some members of the Education Conference were of the difficulties of implementing recommendation No. 1. Recommendation No. 2 was:

> Where the teacher finds that children meet difficulties in understanding, he should use the vernacular. When pupils find it difficult to ask questions in English, the vernacular can again be used.
>
> (BSIP, 1972: 68)

More than ten years later, this recommendation still proves to be appropriate, with the difference that Pijin is now used in lieu of vernaculars in schools where the students are from various ethnolinguistic backgrounds. This is particularly the case in urban schools or provincial secondary schools. For instance, I had a sample of 70 pupils of the Vura primary school in Honiara, who included speakers of 40 different vernaculars. To all these children, Pijin proved to be the only medium of interaction they shared at school. During my two months residency in the Vura school, I never witnessed any conversation held in English amongst the children outside of the classroom. Even within the classroom, English was never used amongst the children for casual conversations, and it was seldom used to address or answer the teacher, except in formal teaching interactions such as the English language class. Whenever possible, teachers were following Recommendation No. 1. But more often than not, noticing the blank looks that appeared on the children's faces following their utterances in English, the teachers had to resort to Recommendation No. 2 and translate into Pijin whatever English questions or explanations they had just given. Vernaculars were almost excluded as well, as it was very uncommon that children would find a friend sharing the same vernacular. Of course, some vernaculars were, statistically, more represented in that school than others, and it is possible that children selected as friends students belonging to their language group and therefore sometimes used vernaculars. It was, however, obvious that Pijin, and not English or vernaculars, was the natural medium of communication used in that school, by teachers and students alike.

It is not my intention to advocate that English should disappear from the classrooms simply because students and teachers would rather use Pijin instead of English whenever they have a chance. Nor is it my intention to advocate the use of English across the board, simply because Solomon Islanders need to communicate with the rest of the world, or because the financial resources of the country are too limited to allow the government to produce its own teaching material in the language of its choice. After all, Swedes, Danes, Portuguese and other citizens of small European countries are not isolated from the rest of the world simply because they keep on using their own national languages in the various realms of the country's life.[3]

A balance should be struck here. It should be a balance between practical realities and economic and national needs, and between the realities of individuals' daily lives and their need for cognitive, cultural and material 'blossoming'. It is a problem that all nations facing, or dealing with, language planning know well. Furthermore, it is a problem that the literature dealing with language planning and the sociocultural problems it entails has covered extensively: studies have shown repeatedly how difficult it is to reconcile the interests of the individuals with the interests of the nation. The Solomon Islands will be no exception whenever they decide to face the thorny language planning problem. Meanwhile the country is still living in a linguistic situation it inherited from the British administration.

Lack of standardization and the limited and very recent existence of a written literature are two of Pijin's main problems with regard to its becoming a useful language of education for young Solomon Islanders. However, Pijin presents one advantage over English: it is the language that all the children raised in multilingual settings such as towns and plantations know by the time they enter school at the age of seven. It is the main daily language of most of these children. From a cognitive point of view, this is a formidable educational advantage for such a plurilingual society. How widespread a fluent command of Pijin is among contemporary urban children is illustrated by the fact that in the same sample of 70 children mentioned earlier, only one child did not know Pijin by the time she entered school: she had just arrived from an outer-Polynesian atoll where she had been raised exclusively in the vernacular. Moreover, owing to an increasing movement of population between the rural and urban areas, more and more rural children have exposure to Pijin on a regular basis even if there is no need for a *lingua franca* in the daily life of the villages.

Pijin and Family Life

Pijin has not yet penetrated on a wide scale into family life in the rural areas of the country. In the villages, people still tend to marry within their language group and raise their children in vernacular languages. There is no need for a *lingua franca* in the everyday life of the villager. It might happen that some villagers marry outside their language group but in most cases, the spouse will tend to learn the local language rapidly. If the spouses met and lived in town and moved back to the village of one of them, and if they do not belong to the same language group, it is likely that they used Pijin together while in town, and might still be doing so in the village. However, as the vernacular is a *sine qua non* condition of a social life in the village, the spouse will very quickly learn the local language.

Even in the most remote areas of the country, most men have some knowledge of Pijin which they have learned in plantation settings or during sojourns in town. Traditionally, women were not incorporated into Pijin-speaking communities, and had hence no need or incentive to learn that language. Therefore, it is still possible to find old women in remote parts of the archipelago who do not know Pijin or at best have a poor passive knowledge of it. This is changing, however. Increasing movements of population, expanding education, and the media (principally radio) nowadays allow Pijin to find its way to the village. Where before only men had gone to work on plantations, both men and women now move to and from the towns. Villages located close to multilingual centres such as towns, mission stations, provincial secondary schools, and plantations have more exposure to Pijin due to contacts with members of these centres. One hears Pijin being spoken more often in those areas than is the case in the remote villages. It is true, however, that any villager who has some knowledge of Pijin will try to accommodate linguistically any visitor who does not know the local vernacular. This is an old pattern. In the colonial period, even in Queensland days, Pijin had been used with European visitors, and Pijin was the language of tax-collection, missionary visits, and police patrols.

The linguistic landscape of the town is very different, and so is the linguistic praxis of urban families. In a country where 225,000 people speak some 63 different languages plus many dialects (Tryon & Hackman, 1983), a town is by definition a multilingual centre. In that respect Honiara, the capital city of the country, is the epitome of multilingualism. Almost all of the languages and dialects of the country are represented in this town of roughly 25,000 people, in various degrees of course (SIG, 1980). Even though the town is very recent (40 years), Pijin has become very quickly the *lingua franca* of its residents.

With the increasing number of inter-ethnic marriages taking place in town (more than 50% of all urban marriages of my 1983 sample), Pijin has found its way into urban homes. Spouses naturally use Pijin to overcome the linguistic barrier facing them and very often raise their children in Pijin. For many parents, this is a deliberate choice. For others, it is just a natural extension of the sociolinguistic situation they live in. It is true, of course, that the attitudes of parents towards using Pijin at home are correlated with their attitudes towards urban life, with the amount of time spent in town, with their age at migration, and most of all with their intention of settling in town permanently or not.

Whereas Pijin used to be for the Solomon Islanders a second and secondary language, contextually bound to work places, commerce or intercourse with speakers of other languages, it is now becoming the predominant language of a growing urban population. It used to be a male prerogative, learned in young adulthood in sociolinguistic contexts to which women and children had no access. It is now being used in town and other multilingual centres as the main medium of communication, irrespective of age, gender, activities and social status. Pijin permeates the life of the town. If it is possible for Solomon Islanders to arrive in town without any knowledge of Pijin, it is virtually impossible for them to leave the town, even after a short stay, without any knowledge of it. As soon as urbanites leave the family circle and the 'wantok system',[4] they enter a Pijin-speaking world: Pijin at the clinic with the nurse from Isabel; Pijin at the Co-op shop with the salesman from Choiseul; in the bus with the driver from To'abaita; at the pharmacy with the cashier from Santa Cruz; with the neighbours; at church; at work, etc . . .

Not only has Pijin become the main language of the urban adult population, but it is becoming the mother tongue,[5] solely or in conjunction with a vernacular, of an expanding generation of children raised in town.

This has far-reaching implications for the linguistic and social development of the language. With regard to the linguistic development, I have shown elsewhere (Jourdan, 1985) that the contribution of the urban children to Pijin so far is not one of creation but of streamlining and reduction of the linguistic variation found in their parents' speech. Moreover, as the children form a speech community unto themselves, they produce a variety of Pijin that is very homogeneous, be they unilingual or bilingual Pijin speakers. Of course this growing generation is still very young and it is impossible to predict whether the additional linguistic changes that will take place will be due to the nativization of the language, or to the social expansion and generational history of the language. My own studies of urban Pijin suggest that the changes which occur will be due to the latter kinds of influence. Differences which were found between the speech of rural and urban adults for whom Pijin was a second language were greater than differences between the speech of urban adults and urban children for whom Pijin was respectively a second language and a mother tongue. It therefore is reasonable to hypothesize that nativization *per se* is not the causal factor of linguistic change in the creolization process of Solomon Islands Pijin.

The social development of Pijin will be even more interesting to watch; it is most probable that it will be accompanied, *mutatis mutandis*, by the progressive disappearance of vernaculars from the linguistic register of the urban children, a process already underway (Jourdan, 1985). We may expect as well that as the pool of unilingual Pijin speakers increases, the chances of Pijin acquiring some social status may increase.

The Media

English is widely used in the media, both media of written communication and media of cultural transmission such as movies, video, libraries, and churches. The two weekly newspapers of the Solomons, published in Honiara, are written exclusively in English, except for Solomon Islands Christian Association Pijin translations of verses of Scriptures that appear in one of them. The circulation of these newspapers is limited to the urban centre. The readership includes civil servants, businessmen, members of the élite and educators. As the rate of literacy amongst adults is still rather low, frequently someone will read aloud, or translate orally into Pijin for neighbours or friends, the content of the newspaper. Reading newspapers or books is not yet a common activity in the country. Whatever is printed or imported into the country is in English.

The radio programs, on the other hand, have a much wider audience and reach even the remotest areas of the country. Without any doubt, they contribute to the ongoing expansion of Pijin in the country. It is, however, the urban variety of Pijin that reaches out to the rural areas, thus contributing to the increasing influence of that particular variety of Pijin over the rural varieties. The favourite programs, according to a survey questionnaire I circulated in town, are the evening news in Pijin, popular music in English, or sometimes in Pijin, that is being played on the air during a large part of the day, and the weekly program of custom stories, as told in Pijin by a very gifted story teller. The news broadcasts are read first in Pijin and then in English. Very often people turn off the radio after the Pijin news. Many listeners complained bitterly about the anglicization of the variety of Pijin used in most of the radio programs (except for the custom stories) and about what they referred to as the poor standard of Pijin in the news broadcasts. Tryon (1979:42) noted that the anglicization of Pijin was on account of the fact:

> that the broadcasters are usually fluent English speakers and tend to be heavily influenced by this when they speak Pidgin, resulting in a 'sophisticated' Pidgin which the bulk of the population finds difficult to follow.

The most powerful media for cultural transmission used to be the Churches. However, the various missions had different policies as to the languages used for religious instruction and worship (Keesing, this volume, Chapter 8). Presently, the modern media of culture transmission have invaded the country: videos, movies and popular culture that are coming in from the West and are bombarding the urban scene are predominantly English-speaking. What impact this will have on the urban way of life remains to be seen, as it is still a very new phenomenon. It would be naive, however, not to recognize the potential impact of English and through it of Western culture on the urban population through the encroachment of a popular foreign culture in the Solomons. Such an impact might in the end prove to be more efficient in spreading the knowledge of English in the population than insisting on using English as the medium of education has been so far.

Pijin and English Complementarity

It should be obvious from the preceding discussion that Pijin and English occupy complementary sociolinguistic niches in the life of the Solomon Islands. This complementarity is in many cases a contrast between oral and written realms of communication. Pijin is the predominant medium of oral communication in multilingual settings throughout the country, while English is the predominant medium of written communication in the realms of activity that make the country part of a wider world.

Despite the fact that Pijin is still only a language of oral com- munication, it has a much wider distribution in the country, socially and geographically, than English has ever had. Practically, it is the language that serves to bridge the cultural and linguistic diversity of the archipelago and to unite it. If ever a sense of nationhood appears in the Solomon

Islands, Pijin will play a very important unifying role. Moreover, as the language is Austronesian in its basic structure, it is learned very quickly and very easily by Solomon Islanders. These two positive aspects of Pijin in the Solomons represent a big practical advantage over English. This is the kind of advantage that should be looked for and capitalized on by language planners.

Standardization would of course be a problem. First, standardization would have to make allowances for the linguistic diversity of contemporary Pijin. This diversity, however, is primarily phonological. Speakers, especially those from rural areas who have acquired Pijin in adulthood, tend to apply to Pijin the phonetic, and in some cases, syntactic rules that govern their own vernaculars. The biggest difficulty would be to deal with the increasing differences found between rural and urban varieties of Pijin. Second, in order to avoid possible negative comparisons with English, orthographic standardization and media usage would have to stress the phonological and semantic independence of Pijin forms from the English ones from which they ultimately derive. Black (this volume, Chapter 4) has suggested that in the Australian Aboriginal Kriol context, standardization should be a non-problem. That is, speakers of a language should have the possibility of writing it down according to their own rules. In the Solomon Islands, however, there are a totally different set of circumstances which lead to very different solutions to the basic question: standardization for what? Will standardization meet the cultural needs of a linguistically and culturally homogeneous group of speakers, or will it meet the educational needs of a developing nation, rich with the diversity of some 64 different languages and concomitant cultural differences?

English, on the other hand, is the language that allows access to the outside world, and so far, to the written media of communication and culture transmission. It definitely has its place at school in the form of a strong program of second language education, so that Solomon Islanders in general are given the opportunity to have access to this outside world. I think, however, that for the sake of cognition and learning, English should not be the language in which primary school children are taught mathematics, or social or natural sciences. Nor do I think that this language should remain, in all fairness to the children and to the country itself, one of the two criteria for selection to secondary schooling, along with mathematics. In a country where children outside of the élite have very little or no regular exposure to this foreign language, the selection procedures, as they are now, have to do more with the social background of the students than with their real abilities. The system is biased even before it starts. However, one has to remember that English is the language spoken by the élite of the country. It is an élite trained and educated abroad in English-speaking universities, who attach a very great importance to the education of their own children, and who have imbibed many of the British attitudes towards English and Pijin. They are already caught up in a system of class symbols of which English is an important part. In that light, it is not surprising that 10 years after independence, English remains the language used as a criterion of selection for further schooling and for entry into the Public Service.

Pijin's Legitimacy

From no one's language to everybody's language, Pijin has become in town and in some rural areas, the symbol and cradle of new Melanesian aspirations and identities. This recent development is linked to the speakers' new sets of attitudes and expectations towards the speech community, the new forms of social relations, and the language itself. A consensus of belief in its legitimacy and permanency is important in the processes of legitimation of a language, as it is through such commitment that successful reproduction of the language will be achieved.

Legitimation of Pijin, or of any other language for that matter, lies primarily in the realms of politics and ideology. Clearly, any legislation, or absence of legislation, aiming at promoting, or condoning, the socio-economic or sociocultural position of a language is a political statement. It is a form of legitimation of the dominant language that is intimately related to class interests. Any effort to justify such statements as answers to economic necessities or cultural realities represents mystification. Habermas' (1979: 181) discussion of the legitimation problems in the modern state can equally, and usefully, be applied to legitimation of languages. For languages do not live *in vacuo*. They are intimately associated with the lives and socio-economic positions of their speakers. If the speakers are powerful, the language they speak will be recognized as valuable. This language will become the criterion (cf. Bourdieu's [1982] concept of *'etalon linguistique'*) against which all other languages, or varieties of languages, will be measured, provided that speakers of the non-valued languages, or non-valued varieties of language, believe in the legitimacy of such a measure. Habermas has stressed how 'the legitimacy of an order of domination is measured against the belief in its legitimacy on the part of those subject to the domination' (1979: 199). In the Solomon Islands, Pijin speakers have been bombarded by British negative attitudes and prejudices towards their language. This has led them to consider English as the legitimate language of the country. It was the language spoken by the people who held the power and had a material wealth many hoped to enjoy eventually.

The other problem faced by Pijin is its absence of cultural legitimacy. Until very recently, Pijin was a language limited to what I have elsewhere called 'artificial cultures' such as those of plantations (Jourdan, 1985) and had no cultural reality in the traditional Solomon Islands' 'natural cultures'.[6] Moreover, Pijin has in the past always existed in parallel with other languages. There was no speech community speaking Pijin natively, nor was there any speech community for which Pijin was the natural language. Except for the world of the plantations, Pijin was not a language that could be identified with a permanent and particular culture in the country. Urbanization, however, has changed all that: urban life in the Solomons is based on multilingual sociolinguistic networks. Pijin has become, perforce, the major element of social life and the linguistic medium of a new Solomon Islands culture centred around Honiara. No one who has spent time in Honiara could dissociate the life in town from Pijin; both are intermingled in day-to-day activities of the capital. Is the town what it is because of Pijin? Is Pijin what it is because of the town? Each serves as a support and context for the other. Each lives and breeds on the other in a symbiotic relationship. At last Pijin has acquired not only native speakers through creolization, but a natural and permanent culture of which it is the medium. As Honiara is in the process of becoming the cultural core of the country, Pijin's cultural legitimacy is being established. The growing generation of urban children having Pijin as a mother tongue might very well contribute to Pijin acquiring this legitimacy.

Pidginophony

By analogy with Francophony, Pidginophony refers to a group of countries having cultural and economic ties through the medium of Pidgin. No such network exists anywhere in the world,[7] despite the great numbers of pidgin languages which are to be found. There are some good reasons for this. First, wherever pidgins are found, they co-exist with a more powerful language, sociologically, economically and culturally. It is through this language, usually the language of the former colonial power, that contacts with the outside world are established. Second, pidgin languages come in an array of varieties: they are languages that are lexically and structurally very different from one another, even where the superstrate language — English or French or Portuguese — is the same.

No unity, even artificially created, could be found that would not mean building a whole new language from scratch.

In Melanesia, however, the situation is rather different, in the sense that the three varieties of pidgins spoken in that area are very similar to one another. Tok Pisin, Bislama and Solomons Pijin, share initially a common history. Bislama and Solomons Pijin are very similar and mutually intelligible, once the phonetics and idiosyncracies of both have been worked out. Tok Pisin presents a slight problem in the sense that it differs slightly from the other two with regard to lexicon and syntax. However, speakers of SIP claim to understand Tok Pisin, and make themselves understood very well, once the initial surprise has passed. To build on this substantial degree of mutual intelligibility through a genuine accommodation of the three dialects would pose difficult practical and political challenges. Given the regional dominance of Papua New Guinea in terms of population, wealth and political power, Solomon Islanders and Ni-Vanuatu have good reason to be concerned about issues of hegemony in the region. The domain of Pidgin could become a cultural battleground.

What would be the advantages of pidginophony in Melanesia? Initially it could not be more than the symbolic proclamation of the cultural and linguistic homogeneity of this region of the Pacific. Practically, it could prove to be useful for these countries, small in terms of inhabitants and resources, to share a medium of communication that would not be a language foreign to most of their citizens. Through pidgin, cultural contacts could be enhanced, educational materials and radio programs could be created or exchanged: all of these contacts in a language that would not be a foreign one but would be an indigenous creation. (Belated recognition that historically, Melanesian Pidgin dialects *are* indigenous creations, rather than bastardized forms of English, is of course a necessary precondition.)

Whether pidginophony can be a more than symbolic step toward Melanesian unity and regional cultural and political consciousness, whether it could — through mutual accommodation of dialectal differences and mutual sharing of resources — become a means to create useful educational materials and a body of literature, is a challenge for language planners.

To move in this direction would require not only an expansion and reinforcement of the efforts underway in recent years to create a standard orthography, a dictionary, and useful written materials. It would require commitment by Solomon Islands Government and individual Solomon Islanders to overcome the residual power of the colonial ideology toward

Pijin. Such a development, then, lies squarely in the realm of politics, a realm in which outsiders — specialists in Pijin and its history though they may be — must tread with great caution. Whatever cultural glosses are placed on questions of language planning, in the end they relate to political issues, and appropriately, they should be decided by those whose lives and countries are shaped by them. In the meantime, Pijin retains its role of unofficial national language of the Solomon Islands.

Notes

1. This *quid pro quo* is quite common nowadays amongst some old Solomon Islanders, who claim that the language they used with me during interviews and many conversations, was English, when we were actually speaking Pijin.
2. And for good reasons! The colonial social (and geographical) distribution of the population in the Protectorate never allowed the Solomon Islanders to have an effective exposure to English in a regular and socially meaningful way. Nor were the British interested in organizing formal schooling for the young Solomon Islanders during the first 50 years of the Protectorate.
3. Obviously, history provided these European languages and Pijin with very different social and cultural backgrounds. Moreover, European languages have established social and cultural roots over the centuries of their existence that give them a legitimacy nobody will challenge. This is not yet the case with Pijin.
4. Wantok: Pijin word from English origin 'one talk' meaning literally 'someone who speaks the same language'. The word seems now to be encapsulating notions of group identity as well as of linguistic boundary. By extension, the 'wantok system' refers to an *ad hoc* and informal organization of wantoks outside of the village, based on reciprocity and exchange.
5. In multilingual societies such as Honiara, the concept of 'mother tongue' has to be expanded. Many children learn two and sometimes three languages concurrently, which they speak natively and with the same fluency.
6. I mean 'artificial' in the special sense that they are cultures developed within structures of domination such that they are shaped by, and respond to the constraints of, the institutions within which their 'users' live: the cultures of prisons and mental hospitals — or plantations.
7. With the partial exception of Swahili in parts of East Africa.

References

BOURDIEU, P. (1982), *Ce que parler veut dire: L'economie des echanges linguistiques*. Paris: Fayard.

B.S.I.P. (1972), *Report on the British Solomon Islands Protectorate Education Conference*. Honiara. Mimeo.

HABERMAS, J. (1979), *Communication and the Evolution of Society*. Boston: Beacon Press.

JOURDAN, C. (1985), *Sapos Iumi Mitim Iumi: Urbanization and Creolization in the Solomon Islands*. Ph.D. thesis. Australian National University.

KEESING, R. M. (1988), *Melanesian Pidgin and the Oceanic Substrate*. Stanford: Stanford University Press.

TRYON, D. (1979), Remarks on the language situation in the Solomon Islands. In S. A. WURM (ed.) *New Guinea and the Neighbouring Areas: A Sociolinguistic Laboratory*. The Hague: Mouton.

TRYON, D. & HACKMAN, B. (1983), *The Languages of the Solomon Islands: An Internal Classification*. Canberra: Pacific Linguistics C-77.

Solomon Islands Government (1980), *Report on the Census of Population*. Vol.1. Statistics Division, Ministry of Finance, Honiara.

WATSON-GEGEO, K. A. (1987), English in the Solomon Islands. *World Englishes* 6 (1), 21–32.

10 Language planning and the language of education in Papua New Guinea

JOAN KALE

Historical and Political Background

Papua New Guinea is an independent nation of upward of three million people. Its territory comprises a large mountainous island and numerous offshore islands. It is located to the north of the eastern tip of Australia, and just below the equator. It was colonised by the British and Australians in the south (Papua) and Germany in the north of the island (New Guinea). At the conclusion of World War I Germany ceded New Guinea to Australia under a League of Nations Mandate which gave Australia the freedom to administer New Guinea much as it saw fit. The economy of the Mandated Territory was much healthier than that of Papua due to the discovery of gold, and to the productivity of the annexed German plantations. This economic imbalance was to some extent the cause of long-lasting rivalry between the two territories which persisted up to and beyond their fusion into one nation at Independence. The period between the wars, that is from World War I when Australia accepted responsibility for New Guinea until World War II was:

> notable for official Australian indifference so long as no enemy approached, of white enclaves vociferously demanding that the black be kept in his place; and of the blacks themselves, rarely considered except as units of labour, owners of land, and a shadowy threat to privilege — blacks bewildered and mute.
>
> (Woolford, 1976: 3)

The Second World War was in some respects fortuitous for Papua

New Guineans. It effectively caused Australia to recognise the indis-pensability of Papua New Guinea for national security, which in turn led to a commitment for the development of an infrastructure of health and education services, and of an economic plan which would serve Papua New Guinea at a hitherto undreamt of national independence. At the end of 1946 Australia entered into a Trusteeship agreement with the United Nations which ensured a more realistic approach to a national develop-ment plan than the previous undertaking with the League of Nations. Australia was finally committed to preparing Papua New Guinea for independent nationhood, sooner rather than later.

In 1962 a visiting United Nations Mission recommended the im-mediate establishment of a university, a national parliament and a national plan for economic development. Just two years later, in 1964, the population of Papua New Guinea went to the polls to elect the members of their first House of Assembly. 'There were no political parties and virtually no issues. Tribal or religious affiliation and customary status were usually the main determinants' in the voting (Woolford, 1976: 11). Thus within a very short period of time Papua New Guineans were to think of themselves not as numerous tribal groups living more or less for their own interests, but as nationals of a united country dependent on its own human resources. They were responsible not only for internal self-government, but were implicated by the policies of the former colonial power in international politics. The task of keeping the ship of state afloat and on course was complicated by the country's extreme geographic and linguistic fragmentation.

The Linguistic Context

Papua New Guinea is linguistically very diverse, having over 700 languages on the mainland and offshore islands. The major linguistic groupings are as follows:

Non-Austronesian (also Papuan)

These occupy most of the mainland and some offshore islands. Research has established that the majority of these languages exhibit deep-level relationships, and are members of the Trans-New Guinea Phylum (Wurm, 1975: 14–18). Speech communities tend to be small, with up to a couple of hundred speakers. Some, however, have many thousands of speakers, the largest being Enga in the Western Highlands Province with upwards of 150,000 speakers shared among a number of dialects.

Austronesian

These are located mostly in the island regions, the coastal areas and slightly inland. It is believed that the speakers of these languages, which also show close relationships with one another, were part of relatively recent migrations from the West from about 5,000 years ago (Wurm, 1975: 14–18). There are approximately 250 languages spoken around the island, but none constitutes a very large speech community. The largest and most prestigious are: the Tolai language of New Britain with 65,000 speakers; and Motu with over 10,000 speakers. This language gained its prestige from its selection and diffusion as a church language and its proximity to the administrative centre of Papua.

Mission lingue franche

These may be classified, following McElhanon (1979: 277), as either 'major' or 'minor'. The major grouping included Kate, Yabem, Dobu, and Kuanua. The minor grouping included Motu, Suau, Wedau, Toaripi, Gedaged, Gogodala, Boiken and Kiwai. It is interesting that the existence of some of these languages as functional *lingue franche* predated mission contact; it is not difficult to understand why mission personnel would have utilised them, often promoting their spread over areas where there were as many as 50 different languages. The decline in their influence was brought about mainly by the administration decision to withdraw funding for schools not using English as the medium of instruction.

Hiri Motu

This is the principal *lingua franca* of that part of Papua New Guinea which was originally named Papua. It is a pidgin wholly derived from indigenous languages. Its earlier name of Police Motu was possibly a reflection of its role in pacification. In Papua the language was preferred above the English-based pidgin which was becoming widely used in New Guinea because it was thought to sound less like a 'deprived' form of English.

Tok Pisin

This is an English-based creole which has been for a long time the *lingua franca* of the previous Territory of New Guinea. It is extending into new domains in Papua notably within the multi-racial administrative capital of Port Moresby.

English

Once the language of the colonial administration, it is also the language of education and national government. As well, it has functional significance within the upper echelons of the political, economic, educational and administrative affairs of the nation.

Language Choice — How to Decide

In common with leaders of emerging nations elsewhere, as independence approached, Papua New Guinea's leaders decided to select markers of identity which could symbolise the country's national image. Selecting a design for a distinctive flag and deciding on a name for the country were fairly straightforward procedures. Controversy, however, surrounded the possible candidates for selection of a language capable of embodying the evolving national ethos. Some thought it advisable to consider the adoption of an indigenous language which offered the possibility of sloughing off the stigma of the colonial era. Others considered the promotion of a wholly indigenous language to the rank of national language as potentially divisive and disruptive internally. Further, international politics and economics could also have been somewhat disrupted by such a choice. In the interests of building constructive internal management policies, and of breaking down communication barriers and old rivalries, it made sense to nominate a language which was widely spoken and widely acceptable.

There are general guidelines which assist in the selection of a language to act as the focus of a population's national identity and loyalties. The main criteria include:

(1) Political neutrality: the choice of a language which promotes the interests of one group and gives unequal access to the 'national cake' is likely to revive old rivalries, create jealousy and prove nationally divisive.
(2) Dominance: a language which is numerically superior is a possible choice. So is a language which is functionally diverse and can readily be learned as a second language by speakers of other languages.
(3) Prestige: the prestige factor relates to access to goods and services not available to speakers of other varieties. This would include access to education and the opportunity for employment and general social mobility.
(4) A great tradition: the ability to associate a language with a cultural

'great tradition' providing continuity with the past is another significant factor.

(5) Areal affinity: a language which is related semantically and lexically to other languages in the region and based on similar cultural systems is favoured over one showing few such relationships. This affinity generally indicates that the language could be learned relatively easily and used creatively by speakers of other languages.

The following section contains an analysis of possible choices for national language, based on these selection criteria.

No wholly indigenous language was clearly identifiable as one which could serve as a focus for national aspirations. The most numerous language group is Enga. As with most vernaculars it is only marginally transportable to the urban areas, and is learned as a second language by few if any speakers of other languages. Motu, prestigious because of its proximity to the administrative capital of Port Moresby, has little credibility outside of the former Territory of Papua. With the high level of mobility among the employed, Motu has been transported to the urban areas of New Guinea without becoming popular as the second language of significant numbers of speakers. In Papua, official Administration policy was that education should be through the medium of English, but even until as late as the 1950s many missions utilised the vernacular languages of the area in which they were located. Even so, this did not lead to any significant gain in prestige — not surprisingly in view of official antagonism to their continued use in education.

None of the mission *lingue franche* appear to be contenders for selection, mainly because of association with a particular mission. In a country where missionary enterprise was parcelled out geographically, they maintain regional importance only, even where their sphere of influence has been extended to other groups. The evidence of time is that none has taken on the characteristics of a national language.

Hiri Motu (also Police Motu) is a wholly indigenous pidgin language, the antecedents of which are still being argued (e.g. Mühlhäusler & Dutton, 1979; Dutton, 1978). The Australian administration of Papua used it as a language of pacification and control, and one result is that it maintains its parochialism at the national level. It is ironic that prior to 1906 there was a Papuan variety of the pidgin used in New Guinea. One of the first administrators was firmly opposed to the use of that pidgin and actively and consistently discouraged its use and promoted the use of the pidgin Hiri Motu. By 1941 he had succeeded almost completely in eliminating the language from the Papuan linguistic scene — unfortunately so, in view of current concerns (Johnson, 1977a: 431). The Papua Besena separatist movement selected Hiri Motu as a symbol of identity and as the rallying point of the group. This resulted in a rise in its prestige and number of speakers (Wurm, 1968b: 339). In becoming a focal point for the aspirations of many Papuans, the regional connotations became quite sharply defined. With the high level of mobility of educated Papuans, many speakers of Hiri Motu learn Tok Pisin when posted to the New Guinea coastal towns. The reverse is also the case.

Since the annexation of New Guinea from Germany, the English language has been the language of higher levels of administration, of economics, of politics and of education throughout the combined Territories. It has high prestige as the language of the white administration. Further, only a relatively small number of Papua New Guineans achieve high educational levels and they do so through English. This facilitates social mobility and provides routes to professional status and economic and political power. It is possible that some social dislocation may occur as this group seeks to maintain entrenched privileges at the cost of free communication with more remote and less favoured countrymen. The high prestige associated with English and its undoubted usefulness in the urban areas as well as its utilisation in international affairs have decided its role as the national language and promoted and maintained its favoured position within national life.

Tok Pisin: The *de facto* National Language?

The language which appears to meet most of the criteria for selection is Tok Pisin. The history of its development has been described in detail by Mühlhäusler (1979) and in summary by Kale (1979: 24–32) and will not be further described here. Likewise, attitudes to Tok Pisin of the various administrations and of private citizens which are summarised elsewhere (Mühlhäusler, 1979) will not be included. What follows is an account of the diversification of Tok Pisin even as, and to some degree because, it was expanding as a useful language. In the very early days of its history, indigenous speakers may have been motivated to acquire the language because of a recognised need for communication with whites. Further, there was a pressing need for communication across language boundaries where members of many speech communities found themselves in proximity, for example on the copra plantations. At this stage of its growth, indigenes may have believed that Tok Pisin was the white man's language, and that ability to communicate with whites and with fellow-nationals would bring access to power. This may have been related to the fact that fluent Tok Pisin speakers often held positions of secondary power within the colonial system and appeared close to those who held real power. Along with the ability to speak the language came a resistance to mission and government efforts to promote the use of German and later of English.

The older generation of males resisted the spread of Tok Pisin into vernacular domains, perhaps because of a perceived threat to traditional leadership roles maintained through the vernacular languages. Even after the growth of a general awareness that Tok Pisin was not the magical language of the whites there was no lessening of its popularity, but it became obvious to speakers that its usefulness was limited in relation to access to mobility within white society. That could only be achieved through a knowledge of English. Still, the overall increase in the numbers of speakers indicates that its usefulness as a bridge across language barriers has not abated. In 1966 the number of speakers was quoted as 300,000 (Wurm, 1966: 49); in 1971 the Census figures indicated 750,000 speakers and 10,000 creole speakers; in 1977 there were one million people who claimed some knowledge of the language (Wurm, 1977: 511). Speakers of varying degrees of competence now number over half the total population and the numbers continue to rise. Such increase does not occur at the expense of traditional languages, for Papua New Guineans share with members of other multilingual communities an aptitude and tolerance for learning other languages. It is likely that high mobility will continue to be a feature of national life. This will ensure a continuing place for Tok Pisin and will be the means of extending its functional significance while maintaining a pool of competent language models.

Tok Pisin does not appear to show evidence of dialects as such; however, sociolects which have been identified (Mühlhäusler, 1979: 142–153) carry some of the characteristics of dialects. Differentiation appears to be the result of social factors such as speaker's race, urbanisation, the age at which Tok Pisin is learned and its mode of transmission, speaker's sex, level of education and professional status. Some of these factors obviously interrelate with others. One apparent reason for the absence of clear regional dialects lies within: Tok Pisin is the means of communication across linguistic and geographical regions, and the degree of mobility associated with its use, and demand for intelligibility, results in a large amount of internal levelling.

The four principal social varieties include two which are marginal: 'Tok Masta' and 'Tok Bush'. The first refers to that type of jargon commonly used between non-speakers mainly speaking English as a first language, and their domestic servants. In a sense, this variety recapitulates the earliest stage of a pidgin. It is grammatically unstable, and heavily dependent on English lexically. It is characterised mostly by *ad hoc* solutions to communication needs, with the burden being on the fluent speaker to interpret the idiosyncratic usage of the English speaker. This variety carries the potential for high levels of misunderstanding. In the very recent colonial past it fulfilled two functions: maintenance of non-intimacy between servant and master, and social control.

Bush pidgin, collectively those varieties spoken in the very remote areas which until recently had little contact with the administration, is heavily influenced by the sound systems of the local substratum language. It has a very simple syntax and limited vocabulary. Once again, high levels of misunderstanding and misinterpretation of the language of fluent speakers may occur. As the infrastructure of the country improves and increased contact with neighbouring and more distant areas is effected, it is expected that this transitional variety will undergo gradual shift toward standard Tok Pisin.

One further variety contains the potential for the breakdown of communication between urban and rural areas. This is that variety spoken by immigrants to the towns and by speakers who have had the benefit of acquiring a reasonable educational status leading to professional employment and access to ideas outside of the traditional way of life. Speakers of this variety attempt to approximate the English language phonologically, syntactically and lexically. It is probable that speakers believe this strategy enhances their prestige: their language identifies them as people having access to the urban areas, or as those who have acquired a reasonable standard of education and social and professional status. Mühlhäusler comments (1979: 151):

> . . . the development of a separate variety of Urban Pidgin may have undesirable effects on nationwide communication. Already, complaints have come from the rural areas that they are unable to cope with the massive amounts of innovations entering NGP (*sic*) via its urban varieties.

Indeed, this variety is becoming so different from the standard that a separate speech community identifying as urban dwellers may be in the process of development (Mühlhäusler, 1979). Educated persons speak

English to others whom they know to speak the language, but on occasion, as an indicator of solidarity they speak in Tok Pisin (see Swan and Lewis, Chapter 12, this volume, for discussion of current developments). As well, they use Tok Pisin to express social solidarity with working class people. Thus English and Tok Pisin are in a diglossic relationship in these urban contexts. Mühlhäusler states:

> Since the two systems are alike at some levels of grammar, structural fusion is encouraged and there is a real possibility that the two linguistic systems will not be kept apart.
>
> (1977: 535)

As a result, a pidgin–English continuum may already be evolving, as has occurred in other places where speakers have ready access to the superstrate language. Further, the day may come when the two varieties — urban pidgin and rural pidgin — may be mutually unintelligible, creating distance between the governing and the governed, and potentially isolating the rural areas from the process of government.

Finally, 'rural pidgin', characterised as 'fluent but unsophisticated, coastal rather than Highlands, Melanesian rather than English' (Laycock, 1969: 12), is the standard form spoken by the majority of users of Tok Pisin. It is the most stable variety and its grammar shows little influence from English. Several linguists have made this variety the subject of grammars and dictionaries. Its functional significance has been strengthened through use as the recognised norm for printed materials, such as the translation of the New Testament, the Wantok newspaper and many Government booklets, especially those targeted for the rural areas. It is also widely used in national and regional broadcasting. Its social setting is the rural community, outside the ambit of the towns but not uninfluenced by them. Contact with missions and administration has ensured familiarity with Western ideas and influences, and the variety functions as a vehicle of cultural change.

At the national level, Tok Pisin suffers from the early decision to eradicate it from Papua. The strongly regional conflict between speakers of Hiri Motu and Motu on the one hand, and Tok Pisin on the other, may only be resolved over time. A case could be made for legislating for their peaceful co-existence as 'national languages', as suggested by Nekitel (1984: 7).

Tok Pisin is now firmly rooted within the Papua New Guinean cultural milieu. It has both shaped and been shaped by the cultural complexity of the country. It is easier to learn than English for two reasons: by definition a pidgin is a syntactically more simple language; and having grown to maturity within those borders, it reflects and embodies the way of life of Papua New Guineans. It has developed the semantics, structure and vocabulary to reflect contemporary culture, capturing a wide variation in life styles in a way that the English language has not been able to emulate. It is easily learned as a second or even a third language without risk to the first language and culture. For some time a nationalistic pride in the language has been evolving.

> With increasing frequency one hears natives (*sic*) refer to Pidgin as 'our language' (*tok bilong mipela*) in contrast to the white man's language, i.e. English . . .
>
> (Wurm, 1968a: 14)

Tok Pisin speakers have become less tolerant and more openly critical of Europeans who do not have mastery of the language, with the result that a reasonable command of Tok Pisin or Hiri Motu was made one of the prerequisites for citizenship.

By many of the criteria, then, Tok Pisin appears already to be functioning as a national language, serving as a vehicle for the expression of national aspirations, promoting national unity as it provides a viable interface between the traditional culture and that of the former coloniser. It grew to maturity on Papua New Guinean soil; it was developed and spread by indigenous speakers and is now their property and their language (Laycock, 1969: 15). It has survived the virulent opinions and opposition of whites, government fiats and continuing cultural change. It is not bounded by geographical limitations but thrives in many situations far removed from those which provided the original stimulus for its emergence.

> Pidgin, the real success story among the languages of Papua New Guinea, was condemned outright by almost every language planner who was consulted or who offered an opinion on the subject until very recently. It flourishes in spite of them.
>
> (Johnson, 1977a: 459)

To summarise: Tok Pisin already has wide functional relevance nationally. Even so, its potential as a unifying force, as a symbol of national identity, as a part-way solution to the economics of education has been recognised by only a few, and never fully utilised. What follows is an attempt to justify its place as a language of instruction in school, along with that of English which to date is unassailable as the sole medium of instruction.

Language Planning Through Educational Policies

Up until the end of the decade of the 1940s the missions bore the brunt of education which they carried out largely through the medium of the indigenous languages. Toward the end of that decade major shifts occurred as a result of the changing tide of political opinion which now stipulated the need, not for universal primary education, but for the production of an educated élite capable of running the country's institutions at independence. The criteria for this change in policy were clearly not educational but rather political, economic and logistic (Johnson, 1977a: 442). In 1955 universal literacy through the medium of English became the goal of education and vernaculars were abandoned by all except missions not wholly reliant on grants for the maintenance of their education programs.

By the late 1960s despite the vigorous pursuit of that policy and despite a very real rise in the standard and amount of English being taught it was becoming increasingly apparent not only that the aim of universal literacy in and through English was proving difficult to attain, but also that for many children it was in any case inappropriate or even irrelevant. More than 80% of the population was rural. There was little support or need for the hard-won limited English skills of children destined, by education policies which drastically weeded them out of the schooling process, to return to the rural areas. These children were left with a language only partially learned, and had learned in some measure to despise or at least to mistrust the village origins which they perceived were responsible for holding them back from reaching their goals. Attitudinally, they were thus unfitted to return to what they sometimes considered to be the stultifying effects of village life. That attitude was also reflected in the observations of some parents that their children were often 'good for nothing now' (Johnson, 1977a: 447).

With a comprehensive policy of universal education through the medium of English and the availability of funding and materials specifically designed for second language teaching, by 1972 it was possible for the Education Department to recommend 'the allocation of between two-fifths and one-half of school time to various subskills under the heading of English, and teaching English became the main aim of primary education' (Johnson, 1977b: 814). However, despite a general unease induced by research reports which indicated that even the children who were relatively successful in learning English were not achieving academic flexibility, the policy of English and only English was continued throughout the 1970s.

In 1974 the Five-Year Education Plan sought to re-route the direction of education from one that was increasingly perceived as contributing in no small way to community disruption and discord to one that sought to promote the development of communities. The bureaucratic position was that the school was to be an agent of integration rather than an alienating institution. Primary-level education now became 'essentially for life in a village community' (Johnson, 1977a: 450) and major curriculum changes occurred to reflect such supposed redirection. As well, a language policy was formulated proposing as a medium of instruction the language of the community in which the school was situated. The awful irony of this purported new direction was that the Plan was accepted in its entirety except for the language policy which was rejected, and English and only English was re-affirmed as the sole medium of instruction. Indigenous languages could be introduced only under stringent conditions which were almost impossible for communities to meet.

By this time Papua New Guineans were entering the national language-in-education debate. Innovations which they may have considered necessary were controlled by three factors. First, the educated élite no doubt attributed their privileged position and economic advantage to English and sought no less for their own children. Second, there was no uncontroversial contender in the unlikely event that English was displaced. In favour of English was its political neutrality. Finally, regional rivalry was such that those regions which had not had access to education in English for as long as others, were justifiably anxious that their children might be locked into an educational and thus an economic backwater with little prospect of redress, with the result they would then be denied their share of the national economic pie. Through all of these vicissitudes English to date maintains its favoured position.

The English Only Option: To Be Reconsidered

It may now be time to reconsider the English-only alternative in education, and in the light of further research into and knowledge of bilingual education and its results, to re-examine the direction of education, particularly as it pertains to the language(s) of instruction.

For mainstream children, schooling ideally is an extension of the cognitive and language development which has occurred prior to commencing school. Even so, it has been proposed elsewhere (Kale, Chapter 6, this volume) that the language demands of the schooling process are quite complex, even for a child able to function exclusively in the first language. For the child being educated in a second language, understanding of what is going on, and development of the cognitive processes required by schooling, must often be suspended until such time as the child is sufficiently fluent in the second language to be able to learn through that language. In Papua New Guinea a large amount of program time is allocated to the teaching of English, and it is debatable whether the majority of children are being 'educated', or merely half-learning a language of dubious usefulness to them in the immediate future or the long run.

Current research appears to indicate that under certain conditions, educational programs which make provision for the development of the first language of the child alongside of the second language are more likely to promote that cognitive growth which will facilitate higher-level learning than educational programs which create discontinuity between the child's early conceptual development and the new learning experiences of the classroom through the sole use of a second language as the medium of instruction. Furthermore, contemporary indigenous educationists are themselves arguing for a reconsideration of community languages as media of instruction, at least in the early years of schooling (e.g. Ahai, 1984; Maladede, 1987).

Alongside of the proposal for the use of vernacular languages in education, it has been proposed elsewhere (Kale, Chapter 6, this volume) that there is no well-founded reason why a pidgin/creole language cannot be utilised as a medium of instruction in bilingual education programs, and that in fact there may be very good reasons for doing so.

For Papua New Guinean children, learning in English involves a conflict of cultures:

> for we must also face the fact that in moving from one language to another in an educational system we are not simply changing the medium through which facts about geography or arithmetic are conveyed; we are, however imperfectly, presenting a new Weltanschauung ... in discussing a language policy ... the deeper psychological and sociological problems raised are the important ones for the educationist, and, in the long run, the results on the national life of a country may be very far-reaching.
>
> (Maw, 1971)

A new generation of Papua New Guinean children now speak Tok Pisin as a first language. It has thrived in the unique sociocultural milieu of the country, and has entered every domain of national life. In effect, it could be considered a 'home-grown' language along with the vernaculars. Given the particular conflation of a unique set of historical, political, economic, linguistic and educational factors in national development, it would therefore seem appropriate for vernacular languages and for Tok Pisin to become functionally relevant as languages of instruction in the education system alongside of teaching in and through English.

References

AHAI, N. (1984), A case for vernacular education in Papua New Guinea. *Yagl–Ambu* 11 (2), 25–38.

DUTTON, T. (1978), Tracing the Pidgin origin of Hiri (or Police) Motu: Issues and problems. In S. A. WURM & L. CARRINGTON (eds.) *Proceedings of the Second International Conference on Austronesian Linguistics*. Canberra: Australian National University. Pacific Linguistics C61.

JOHNSON, R. K. (1977a), Administration and language policy in Papua New Guinea. In S. A. WURM (ed.) *New Guinea Area Languages and Language Study. Vol. 3*. Canberra: Australian National University. Pacific Linguistics Series C140.

— (1977b) English in Papua New Guinea. In S. A. WURM (ed.) *New Guinea Area Languages and Language Study. Vol. 3*. Canberra: Australian National University. Pacific Linguistics C140.

KALE, J. (1979), Papua New Guinea: the language issue. Unpublished M.A. thesis, Sydney University.

LAYCOCK, D. (1969), Pidgin's Progress. *New Guinea and Australia, the Pacific and South-East Asia* 10, 8–15.

MALADEDE, M. (1987), Vernacular literacy in Papua New Guinea. Unpublished manuscript, James Cook University of North Queensland.

MAW, J. (1971), Sociolinguistic problems and potentialities of education. In W. H. WHITELEY (ed.) *Language Use and Social Change*. London: Oxford University Press.

McELHANON, K. A. (1979), Some mission lingue franche and their sociolinguistic role. In S. A. WURM (ed.) *New Guinea and Neighbouring Areas: A Sociolinguistic Laboratory*. The Hague: Mouton.

MÜHLHÄUSLER, P. (1979), *Growth and Structure of the Lexicon of New Guinea Pidgin*. Canberra: Australian National University. Pacific Linguistics C52.

— (1977), The social role of Pidgin in Papua New Guinea today. In S. A. WURM (ed.) *New Guinea Area Languages and Language Study*.

Canberra: Australian National University. Pacific Linguistics C140.

MÜHLHÄUSLER, P. & DUTTON, T. (1979), Papuan Pidgin English and Hiri Motu. In S. A. WURM (ed.) *New Guinea and Neighbouring Areas: A Sociolinguistic Laboratory*. The Hague: Mouton.

NEKITEL, O. M. (1984), Language planning in Papua New Guinea: A nationalist viewpoint. *Yagl-Ambu* 11 (1), 1–24.

WOOLFORD, D. (1976), *Papua New Guinea: Initiation and Independence*. Brisbane: University of Queensland Press.

WURM, S. A. (1966), Pidgin — A national language. *New Guinea, the Pacific and South-East Asia* 7, 49–54.

— (1968a), Papua New Guinea nationhood: The problem of a national language. In J. A. FISHMAN, C. A. FERGUSON & J. DAS GUPTA (eds.) *Language Problems of Developing Nations*. New York: Wiley.

— (1968b), Pidgins, Creoles, Lingue Franche, and national development. In J. A. FISHMAN (ed.) *Readings in the Sociology of Language*. The Hague: Mouton.

— (1975), Language distribution in the New Guinea area. In S. A. WURM (ed.) *New Guinea Area Languages and Language Study*. Vol. 1. Canberra: Australian National University. Pacific Linguistics C38.

— (1977), Future outlooks and standardisation of Pidgin. In S. A. WURM (ed.) *New Guinea Area Languages and Language Study. Vol. 3.* Canberra: Australian National University. Pacific Linguistics C140.

— (1979), The language situation in the New Guinea Area. In S. A. WURM (ed.) *New Guinea and Neighbouring Areas: A Sociolinguistic Laboratory*. The Hague: Mouton.

11 Creolized Tok Pisin: Uniformity and variation

GEOFF P. SMITH

The purpose of this paper is to look at the use of Tok Pisin by first language speakers in Papua New Guinea. The emerging national character of the creolized language is examined, and some of the social and linguistic factors which give rise to variation, and the constraints which limit this variability are considered. Questions related to language policy are briefly addressed.

Introduction

Tok Pisin is the name given by its speakers to Papua New Guinea's largest language. It has also been known by a number of other names including New Guinea Pidgin, Melanesian Pidgin and Neo-Melanesian. As its name suggests, Tok Pisin arose as a pidgin language, and is somewhat over 100 years old. Like other pidgin languages, Tok Pisin arose to meet communication needs where no common language existed, in this case on the plantations of Western Samoa and other areas of the Pacific (Mühlhäusler, 1978). A nautical jargon developing even earlier has also been suggested as a significant influence on its formation (see Keesing, this volume, Chapter 8). Labourers from a variety of Melanesian home areas faced the problem of communicating with one another and with the overseeing expatriate planters, who largely spoke a simplified or pidgin English to the labourers. On their return to Melanesian homelands, the pidgin which developed and stabilized still served a useful role in the diverse linguistic situation characteristic of the area. Since New Britain appears to have been a centre of recruitment, this became the new focus of the later development of New Guinea Pidgin. The language has received a great deal of attention from linguists such as Sankoff (1977), Mühlhäusler (1979), Wurm (1971), Laycock (1970), Dutton (1973), Hall (1966) and Romaine (1987), and its history and development are relatively well documented (see also Kale, this volume, Chapter 10).

Attitudes towards Tok Pisin by those in authority have changed dramatically. While the language suffered almost universal condemnation by English-speaking expatriates during its earlier years, Hall (1966), recognizing its legitimacy and critical social role, began a counter movement which is still continuing. Although officially there are two other national languages — English (the language of education) and Hiri Motu (the former *lingua franca* of the Papuan region) — the rapidly changing social situation saw a great increase in Tok Pisin's use, and it has grown to the point where it is now P.N.G.'s *de facto* national language. Since Independence, Tok Pisin has continued to spread and is now making inroads both in the Papuan provinces and the more remote areas of what was formerly the territory of New Guinea. While vernacular languages have an influence on the type of Tok Pisin spoken, Tok Pisin similarly is affecting vernaculars in many areas.

Tok Pisin as a Creole

According to classical definitions of pidgin and creole languages, a pidgin has a simplified grammar and lexicon, is used in a restricted range of situations, and is the first language of no one. This would clearly be an accurate description of Tok Pisin during its early development. If this pidgin becomes a first language, it then becomes a creole, and undergoes a characteristic expansion determined at least partially by the needs of first language speakers. This situation is found in many of today's urban households.

These definitions, however, are not without their problems when considering Tok Pisin in P.N.G. The study of creole languages in other parts of the world has generally featured social contexts where more drastic linguistic change has resulted (e.g. Bickerton, 1975: 195). Typically, the linguistic input to children of parents with no language in common has been severely limited, and a first language has developed from this in a short period. This expansion from such apparently limited input has given rise to the 'bioprogram' theory, which postulates innate devices as a means to restore an adequate linguistic repertoire (Bickerton, 1981). Tok Pisin, on the other hand, expanded and stabilized over a considerable period of time before there was a significant number of second language speakers. Even quite recently, Mühlhäusler (1977: 574) was able to describe the use of Tok Pisin as a native language as 'marginal'.

Tok Pisin today exists in a number of varieties, including what may be termed the creolized form. While people in the remoter areas are acquiring a first shaky command of the language, an increasing number of first language speakers are appearing both in urban and rural settings. The main use of the language, however, remains as a *lingua franca* between people of different language backgrounds, and this tempers the more drastic changes which might result from uninhibited creole developments. Another problem concerns the nature of 'first' and 'second' languages. Multilingualism in P.N.G. is extremely widespread (Sankoff, 1977), and it is not always easy to determine which language is spoken with the greatest degree of fluency and competence. Even 'second language' speakers of Tok Pisin may have a competence almost as complete as first language speakers, and, as Jourdan (1985) has also noted for Solomon Islands Pijin, the line between creolized and second language use is often somewhat vague. The concept of a primary language, in which the speakers have a native-like fluency and competence may be useful in this regard.

It is clear that Tok Pisin, like other pidgin languages, had a number of practical limitations in its earlier forms. It is these 'inadequacies' that stimulate the developments which take place in creoles. However, a considerable development has taken place both in the lexicon and syntax of Tok Pisin while spoken as a second language. A comprehensive account of development of the lexicon appears in Mühlhäusler (1979). As well as English borrowings, considerable use is made of the internal resource of the language to overcome referential inadequacy and come to terms with new semantic fields. A number of syntactic developments are also appearing, such as in the area of number and tense distinctions. Creolization appears to be associated with the emergence of obligatory categories of number and tense, and greater redundancy (Mühlhäusler, 1977).

One possible fate of an expanded pidgin language is the development of degrees of mixture with the superstrate language to form a post-creole continuum. Whether this will happen in the case of Tok Pisin and English has yet to be seen. English is an official language and while it exists side-by-side with Tok Pisin, a post-creole continuum is a distinct possibility. A number of unknown factors will determine this outcome, such as official language planning and policies and unofficial attitudes towards the languages.

This review makes reference to the author's investigation of young first language speakers in a number of areas in Papua New Guinea. Young people who claimed to have grown up speaking Tok Pisin as their main language were interviewed in Lae, Goroka, Kundiawa, Kimbe, Rabaul, Arawa and Buka. A full analysis is not yet available, and the following comments represent preliminary indications only.

Sources of Variation

A number of varieties of Tok Pisin have been described. Mühlhäusler (1975) identified four sociolects, and regional differences have been widely commented upon. Different styles and registers add further dimensions to this variability.

Social variation

Mühlhäusler's four sociolects, which he names bush pidgin, rural pidgin, urban pidgin and Tok Masta, can be found today among various Tok Pisin speakers. However, the two marginal varieties, bush pidgin and Tok Masta are by definition of little direct relevance to the majority of first language speakers.

Urban Tok Pisin is the variety most likely to influence the growing population of urban creolized speakers. The situation described by Sankoff and Laberge (1973: 34) is perhaps typical of this group. Here, children of parents speaking different languages grow up speaking Tok Pisin and have no more than a passive understanding of any other language. Borrowing of English words is especially common among this group for two reasons. Firstly, ready-made expressions from the English-speaking world of commerce and administration are convenient props for handling burgeoning urban phenomena. Hence expressions such as *ol spea pats* (spare parts), *go long men wof* (main wharf), *kaunsil chembas* (Council Chambers) and *laisens* (license) are widespread. Secondly, the primary schools use English as a medium of instruction, and this also provides a prolific source of borrowing. This is also the case for rural areas, but the chances of a primary education are generally greater in towns than in many rural districts. Examples from Lae children include words such as *frenldi*, *em fil taed*, *trastim* (to trust), *jaiant*, and *jamp* instead of adequate standard alternatives.

The extent of variation among first language urban speakers is not clear. There were children in the primary school in Arawa, for example, who appeared to have a poor command of Tok Pisin, especially recent arrivals from provinces where Tok Pisin is not widespread, or those whose parents spoke English at home. Among those who were apparently first language speakers, samples from the different provincial centres did show considerable variation in the degree of English borrowing. Some tended to use the 'standard' lexicon and phonology, while others pronounced words using an expanded phoneme repertoire more typical of English, and used English borrowings in many places where adequate Tok Pisin terms could have been used. It thus appears that the extent of borrowing from English is a significant variable in the speech of urban first-language speakers.

Creolization is largely an urban phenomenon, but not exclusively so. Mühlhäusler's observations of rural communities in Manus and Sepik where creolized varieties are spoken provide examples of non-urban creolized speakers (1977). These communities comprise speakers of a variety of languages in resettlement areas or plantations. My observations in minor language groups close to Lae such as Musom and Yalu with a more homogeneous language composition also suggest that Tok Pisin is the overwhelming choice of the emerging generation.

Rural Pidgin represents the variety spoken by the majority of Papua New Guineans for whom pidgin is not a primary language. Even though there may be those who have a native-like command of the language, the extensive use of Tok Pisin as a *lingua franca* appears to prevent the more drastic developments which might otherwise have resulted from creolization. Even so, it is possible that the gap between rural and urban Tok Pisin could widen, possibly to the point of incomprehensibility.

The phenomenon of deliberate exaggeration of speech differences to promote distinctive group identities has been commented on with respect to a number of P.N.G. languages. Sankoff (1977: 284) sums this up as 'local pride in difference, coupled with a rather thorough knowledge of the differences'. The role of Tok Pisin as a *lingua franca* would appear to preclude its use as a source of group identity. However, Dutton and Bourke (1987) have drawn attention to particular syntactic structures used by Tok Pisin speakers in parts of Southern Highlands which could be explained in this way. The adoption of secret uses of words for specific purposes has been noted (Mühlhäusler, 1985: 268) but again, there are a multiplicity of other resources which could be used to obscure meaning without jeopardizing the second language role of Tok Pisin. Urban children growing up with only Tok Pisin are in a slightly different situation, and it is possible that a distinctive 'street argot' may emerge to reinforce group identity such as membership of a gang or other social circle. However, no examples of this have been observed in the data available.

Regional variation

The extent of regional variation in Tok Pisin is still rather uncertain. Many Tok Pisin speakers claim to be able to distinguish regional differences in speech, but the extent of these perceived differences is not easy to assess. Wurm (1971) and Laycock (1970) published course materials which refer specifically to Highlands and Lowlands Tok Pisin respectively, while other writers have commented on general differences (e.g. Chowning, 1983; Mühlhäusler, 1985).

One continually present influence on the nature of Tok Pisin in different areas is the substratum of other vernacular languages spoken. The question of the influence of substrate languages on the phonology, syntax and semantics of Tok Pisin is a complex one. In the case of second language speakers, a number of studies indicate a variety of substrate phenomena. Bee (1971) has described in detail phonological interference from Usarufa. However, these are not speakers of Tok Pisin as a primary language, and the variations recorded may be considered more as learners' 'interlanguage' than standard area varieties. Laycock (1985) also comments on substrate features in phonology in a variety of areas. A variety of studies of substratum influences have been made, but two recent examples are worthy of note. Reesink (1987) demonstrated certain distinctive grammatical features among speakers of Tok Pisin from some language groups in Madang, Siassi and the Highlands, while Faraclas (1987) in a monumental analysis describes numerous phonological and syntactic substrate influences from a wide variety of languages. The debate over the role of the substrate languages on Tok Pisin's development and its relationship to the 'bioprogram' theory are likely to continue for some time.

Whatever the differences among adult second language speakers, the situation among young urban speakers in different areas is not clear. A number of observations taken from Smith (1986) are mentioned here as relevant to the question of regional variation. Young first language speakers in all the locations investigated appeared to differ significantly from their parents' generation in the speed of delivery of their speech, with associated reduction in number of syllables receiving primary stress. This 'allegro' characteristic of the children's speech was the most striking feature observed. It was less noticeable in the Goroka children interviewed, but these particular children perhaps spoke a greater amount of their parents' language (Usarufa) than others interviewed in the other centres.

A notable example of convergent patterns of syllable reduction was observed for the expression *em i kirap na em i tok olsem* (he got up and said), which commonly introduces direct quotations. The following reductions of the nominally 10-syllable expression appear from different centres:

Lae: *em kira to em*; *em kra to sem*, *em ka tose*
Rabaul: *em kra tok sem*; *em krat sem*

Certain reductions appeared to be almost universal among first language speakers, such as *bilong* to *blong*, *bilong em* to *blem*, *-pela* to *-pla*, *dispela* to *disla*, *save* to *sa* and other examples (cf. Lynch, 1979).

Pronunciation did appear to be subject to some variation according to region among these children. For example the tendency to omit initial 'h' was marked in Rabaul, not so much in Lae. There were cases in Kimbe of the substitution of 't' for 's', for example *tapos* for *sapos*, while this was not observed in other areas. Buka children tended to pronounce certain words differently, for example *pitchin* for *pisin* (bird) and *divai* for *diwai* (tree). The Goroka children tended to pronounce *bilongen* as *blogen* or *bloken*, which did not appear elsewhere. There were cases of r/l alternation among Lae children. It seems from these few examples, and others which could be cited, that here is a fair amount of regional variation in pronunciation which persists among first language speakers.

Similarly, there were differences in the range of meanings of certain words. Goroka children used the pronoun *yumi* in contexts which clearly indicated its exclusive nature. Normally, the first person plural pronoun *yumi* indicates that the person addressed is included, while the alternative form *mipela* is used to exclude the addressee. For example, in conversation with the investigator who was previously unknown, one informant began as follows:

Wanpla taim ia, yumi sa stap long ples bilong yumi nau, yumi sa go, yumi wantaim brata bilong yumi, yumi go hukim fis ...

Wurm (1971) has noted the opposite tendency, the use of *mipla* as an inclusive pronoun. Other writers have commented on differences in semantic range for lexical items in different regions (e.g. Mühlhäusler,

1985: 258; Chowning, 1983: 191), but these are not always easy to determine from a brief acquaintance.

Regional variations in syntax have also been described. It is commonly suggested that the use of the predicate marker *i* is less frequent in the Highlands than in Islands provinces. An analysis of data available to the author would tend to support this. In a sample of speech from the Goroka children, no occurrence of the predicate marker was recorded out of 100 possible occurrences, while the corresponding figure for Rabaul was 44%. Although a more detailed analysis is needed, it appears that there are regional variations, coupled with an overall trend towards a reduction in the occurrence of the predicate marker among first language speakers.

The use of the redundant *ol* as a plural marker with *planti* and *sampla* was also briefly investigated, but the number of occurrences was too small to permit detailed analysis. However, *ol* was used in this way in the Kimbe and Kundiawa samples. In Kundiawa, for example *ol sampla mangki* (some boys) and *sampla ol skul mangki* were recorded, and *ol disla* appeared to be reduced to the form *olsla* (these) on some occasions. The similarly redundant *tupla* after a dual subject also occurred in Rabaul, Lae and Goroka, for example *tupela brata, tupela go* (two brothers, two went).

There appear to be competing tendencies towards regional differentiation and national conformity. The underlying substrate influences of parents and second language speakers undoubtedly have an effect on pronunciation, phonology and semantics, and also probably some influence on syntax. However, there is a high degree of regional mobility which brings speakers from different areas into contact. Plantation labour schemes have been responsible for bringing large numbers of people from the Highlands and Sepik provinces to work on the copra and cocoa production in the Islands province. Similarly, administration workers are posted throughout the country and this has led to highly heterogeneous urban communities in all parts of the country. Even in rural villages, intermarriage, migrant labour and increased travel opportunities have led to increased mobility. It is common for people to refer to themselves as *hapkas Sepik na Morobe* (half-cast Sepik and Morobe) or one or other of an increasing number of parental combinations. The rapid increase in the extent of the national road network has made travel cheaper and easier, and the proposed construction of a trans-national highway will no doubt increase this trend. Some parts of the country are in fact planned as resettlement areas, notably the oil palm schemes in West New Britain and Oro Provinces.

Idiomatic and stylistic variation

In its earlier stages of development, Tok Pisin appears to have been somewhat limited in its expressive flexibility. However, a number of stylistic resources have made present day Tok Pisin remarkably expressive and flexible, whether as a first or second language. Brash's (1971) account of various special registers was later supplemented by Wurm & Mühlhäusler's (1982) more comprehensive treatment. Smith (1987) further amplifies the role of idiomatic expressions in developing increased stylistic flexibility.

The phenomenon known as *tok pilai* is the stimulus for a great deal of innovation. It involves the use of extended metaphors, often alluding to taboo or risqué topics, and is typically accompanied by a good deal of hilarity. The activity generates so much good humour and well-being that it appears that certain phrases gain currency as hilarity prompts before any generally accepted meaning is assigned to them. Eventually, the catch phrase may fade out of fashion, or may become a normal phrase with a conventional meaning. An example of the latter is the development of the catch phrase *draiva, givim siksti* (driver, go 60 mph). The term *siksti* has now become interchangeable with the more common word *spid* (fast) among some speakers.

The Influence of Standards

The variability of Tok Pisin is limited by a number of constraints which include standards and prescriptive norms. The prescriptive force of Tok Pisin is generally considered to be fairly low, and a great deal of tolerance of aberrant forms is typically exercised, although Chowning (1983: 193) mentions an old Kove man in West New Britain who was ridiculed because of his poor knowledge of Tok Pisin. This, however, refers to incomplete acquisition, and the novel varieties of fluent speakers are also subject to constraints. Generally, innovation is held back due to the over-riding need to communicate across language boundaries. As Mühlhäusler (1977b: 574) puts it:

> The use of Tok Pisin as a *lingua franca* is operative in filtering out drastic changes such as may have occurred during the creolization of other varieties in other social contexts.

However, changes are nevertheless taking place, and creolization is one source of these changes. It is tempting to think that as the number of first language speakers increases, the complexity and variation in Tok Pisin will increase proportionally. This appears not to be the case for a number of reasons. Even though Tok Pisin is fairly simple in its grammatical rules and has a modest lexicon, the adequacy of the language for fulfilling everyday needs can be greatly underestimated. The gradual expansion of the language has produced something which can scarcely be thought of as impoverished, and is therefore not subject to the drastic repairs apparently needed in more catastrophic situations. It is more likely to be the stylistic potential of the language which first language speakers will expand. As Sankoff & Laberge (1973: 45) note in an often quoted statement:

> ... native speakers appear to be carrying further tendencies which were already present in the language. We are not arguing that the presence of native speakers creates sudden and dramatic changes in a language, but rather that their presence may be one factor in influencing directions in language change.

Conscious attempts, of course, have also been made to standardize Tok Pisin. The translations of the New Testament and Mihalic's *Dictionary and Grammar* (1971) are notable examples. Mihalic's standard, based on the language as spoken around Madang, is being continued in the media through Word Publishing, of which the main Tok Pisin organ is *Wantok Niuspepa*. As the circulation of this weekly increases, the influence of its style sheet reaches further into the population. Provincial radio stations also broadcast a good deal in Tok Pisin, and this too has a unifying effect. Media Tok Pisin has its innovations too. The stylistic creativity of reporters and journalists, and the need for novel and interesting language provide a constant force for change. These innovations are not always successful. For example, direct translations of English may be quite unacceptable to conservative rural Tok Pisin speakers. Siegel (1983: 84) uses a translated advertisement for 'Aerogard' to illustrate this. The cartoon strip, headed *Hao mipela painim gutpela pren* (how we found a good friend) concludes *Mipela bin hevim gutpela piknik tru. Inogat ol natnat i kaikaim mipela. Tenks long niupela pren* aerogard. (We had a really good picnic. Mosquitoes didn't bite us. Thanks to our new friend *Aerogard*.) Such translations are reminiscent of the semi-comprehensible utterances of Mühlhäusler's *Tok Masta* exponents, but it is not clear whether this is merely bad translation, or a conscious attempt to project a high-prestige variety of the language.

Government policy could have dramatic effects on the direction of Tok Pisin's development, but the government has so far kept an exceedingly low profile with regard to planning. Were a national language planning institute to be established, or Tok Pisin to be adopted as the medium of education, it is evident that new and unexpected changes could result. Although Tok Pisin has occasionally been tried as a medium of education — it is not officially sanctioned in many schools — it appears to be increasingly used both in informal situations and 'unofficial' explanations. Such use appears to make good educational sense. The problems faced by young children attempting to acquire literacy and learn a new language at the same time must surely prompt some changes in the 'English-only' policy before long.

Although Tok Pisin is clearly gaining ground in a wide range of social and educational contexts, there is a reluctance to recognize this formally and to abandon the English language, which has for so long been associated with economic success. If Tok Pisin were to be formally sanctioned, the question of regional variety, standardization of spelling, and related problems would have to be addressed. This could lead to dissatisfaction with the standard adopted, and possibly a more active differentiation of regional varieties. It appears that the policy of as little interference as possible may be a wise one for the time being.

Conclusion

Tok Pisin's dramatic growth as the most popular language in Papua New Guinea has brought it to a position where a number of competing tendencies are influencing its development. The rise of urban first language speakers and their heavily Anglicized speech could lead to a post-creole continuum or even a new hybrid language developing in these areas. Distinctive regional varieties could emerge on account of rapid innovations or feelings of group identity, but this is tempered by social and regional mobility, the unifying effect of the media and the role of Tok Pisin as a *lingua franca*. More active government involvement in language planning or the formal adoption of Tok Pisin in the education system could dramatically influence the direction of change.

References

BEE, D. (1971), Phonological interference between Usarufa and Pidgin Englis. *Kivung* 5 (2), 69–95.

BICKERTON, D. (1975), *Dynamics of a Creole System*. Cambridge: Cambridge University Press.

— (1981), *Roots of Language*. Ann Arbor: Karoma.

BRASH, E. (1971), Tok Pilai, Tok Piksa na Tok Bokis, Imaginative dimensions in Melanesian Pidgin. *Kivung*, 4 (1), 12–20.

CHOWNING, A. (1983), Interaction between Pidgin and three West New Britain languages. *Papers in Pidgin and Creole Linguistics* No 3. Canberra: ANU, Pacific Linguistics A65.

DUTTON, T. E. (1973), *Conversational New Guinea Pidgin*. Canberra: ANU, Pacific Linguistics D12.

DUTTON, T. & BOURKE, R. M. (1987), *Taim* in Tok Pisin: An interesting variation in use from the Southern Highlands of Papua New Guinea. Paper presented to International Tok Pisin Conference, Madang, Papua New Guinea, July 1987.

FARACLAS, N. (1987), From Old Guinea to Papua New Guinea: A comparative study of Nigerian Pidgin and Tok Pisin. Paper presented to International Tok Pisin Conference, Madang, Papua New Guinea, July 1987.

HALL, R. A. Jr (1966), *Pidgin and Creole Languages*. Ithaca: Cornell University Press.

JOURDAN, C. (1985), Creolisation, nativisation or substrate influence: What is happening to *bae* in Solomon Islands Pidjin. *Papers in Pidgin and Creole Linguistics* No 4. Canberra: ANU, Pacific Linguistics A72.

LAYCOCK, D. (1970), *Materials in New Guinea Pidgin (Central and Lowlands)*. Canberra: ANU, Pacific Linguistics D5.

— (1985), Phonology: substratum elements in Tok Pisin. In S. A. WURM & P. MÜHLHÄUSLER (eds.) *Handbook of Tok Pisin*. Canberra: ANU, Pacific Linguistics C70.

LYNCH, J. (1979), Changes in Tok Pisin morphology. Paper presented at 13th PNG Linguistic Society Congress, Port Moresby.

MIHALIC, F. (1971), *The Jacaranda Dictionary and Grammar of Melanesian Pidgin*. Milton: Jacaranda.

MÜHLHÄUSLER, P. (1975), Sociolects in New Guinea Pidgin. In K. A. MCELHANON (ed.) *Tok Pisin i go we? Kivung Special Pub. No 1*. Port Moresby: Linguistic Society of PNG.

— (1977), Creolisation of New Guinea Pidgin. In S. A. WURM (ed.) *New Guinea Area Languages and Language Studies* No 3. Canberra: ANU, Pacific Linguistics C40.

— (1978), Samoan plantation Pidgin and the origin of New Guinea Pidgin. *Papers in Pidgin and Creole Linguistics No 1*. Canberra: ANU, Pacific Linguistics A54.

— (1979), *Growth and Structure of the Lexicon of New Guinea Pidgin*.

Canberra: ANU, Pacific Linguistics C52.

— (1985), Variation in Tok Pisin. In S. A. WURM & P. MÜHLHÄUSLER (eds.) *Handbook of Tok Pisin*. Canberra: ANU, Pacific Linguistics C70.

REESINK, G. (1987), Mother tongue and Tok Pisin. Paper presented to International Tok Pisin Conference, Madang, Papua New Guinea, July.

ROMAINE, S. (1987), Change and variation in the use of *bai* in young children's creolized Tok Pisin in Morobe Province. Paper presented to International Tok Pisin Conference, Madang, Papua New Guinea, July.

SANKOFF, G. (1977), Multilingualism in PNG. In S. A. WURM (ed.) *New Guinea Area Languages and Language Studies No 3*. Canberra: ANU, Pacific Linguistics C40.

SANKOFF, G. & LABERGE, S. (1973), On the acquisition of native speakers by a language. *Kivung* 6 (1), 32–47.

SIEGEL, J. (1983), Media Tok Pisin. *Papers in Pidgin and Creole Linguistics No 3*. Canberra: ANU, Pacific Linguistics A65.

SMITH, G. P. (1986), A preliminary investigation of the spoken Tok Pisin of some urban children in Lae and Goroka. Lae: University of Technology, Language Departmental Report No 10.

— (1987), Idiomatic Tok Pisin and Referential Adequacy. Paper presented to International Tok Pisin Conference, Madang, Papua New Guinea, July.

WURM, S. A. (ed.) (1971), *New Guinea Highlands Pidgin: Course Materials*. Canberra: ANU, Pacific Linguistics D3.

WURM, S. A. & MÜHLHÄUSLER, P. (1982), Registers in New Guinea Pidgin. *International Journal of the Sociology of Language* 35, 69–8.

12 Tok Pisin at university: An educational and language planning dilemma in Papua New Guinea?

JOHN SWAN and DON J. LEWIS

Introduction

As can be seen from Chapters 10 and 11 (this volume) by Kale and Smith, the language situation in Papua New Guinea is one of the most complex in the world. A dozen years after Independence it remains in a state of considerable flux. In such circumstances it is by no means easy (and perhaps even a little foolhardy) to make predictions as to the likely outcomes of the present interplay between the country's 700 vernaculars, two main *lingue franche* — Tok Pisin and Hiri Motu — and, of course, English. Nevertheless the present and future status of Tok Pisin within this sociolinguistic melting-pot is a matter of such fascination to linguists and of such importance to the development of the nation that most commentators have found it impossible to resist a little crystal ball gazing.

In 1979, Wurm & Mühlhäusler asserted that: 'New Guinea Pidgin and English are undoubtedly the two most important languages in Papua New Guinea today' (1979: 247). Probably no one would dispute that this still holds true. Yet oddly enough there are doubts as to the future of both. Since well before Independence, the dominant language of education has been English. Despite this, the country is nowhere near achieving universal literacy or even oracy in English. Lynch (1983) estimated that only 10–20% of the population would understand radio broadcasts in English (including the one he was then making). Primary schooling (in English) is now more widely available throughout the country than ever before, yet drop-out rates are high — about one third overall — between Grade One and Grade Six. Only about 25% of ex-Grade Six pupils move on to Grade Seven (Weeks, 1986). Those who drop out are unlikely to have any further use for English. They join the 30 to 40% of primary school-age-children who have never been to primary school at all (Annual Education Report, 1983). It is not clear that these figures are likely to improve dramatically in the foreseeable future, especially as there is growing evidence of parental disenchantment with the English-based educational system. One possible scenario then is that English will remain the preserve of a small educated élite while Tok Pisin continues to develop as the effective national language for the majority.

One commentator who disputes this scenario is Laycock. He argues that: 'Tok Pisin may be very close to reaching its maximum expansion'. He sees Tok Pisin in the long term as essentially a temporary expedient. Tok Pisin, he concludes:

> will decline because, however appropriate it may seem as a solution to linguistic problems on a *national* level, there are other ways of solving the linguistic dilemma at *regional* levels. In a modified form, what we are likely to see is a return to the local solutions of the pre-contact era — at least until such time as English is widespread enough to serve as a truly national language.
>
> (Laycock, 1982: 267)

There do seem to be barriers to the further development of Tok Pisin. Despite numerous calls for its official introduction, there is so far little evidence of government support for its use within the educational system except in the most marginal way. The inevitable consequence of this is that the vast majority of those who speak Tok Pisin rarely or never read or write it. Yet without literacy, there will be little chance of standardization of the language. As Smith (Chapter 11, this volume) shows, there are already significant differences between speakers from different areas of the country and Mühlhäusler (1984: 458) has indicated that divergence between Rural and Urban Tok Pisin *could* become so great as to render the two mutually unintelligible. Since the Conference on the Future of Tok Pisin (1973), various scholars have called for officially backed efforts at language engineering ('pidgineering') to assist speakers in expanding the lexicon in ways that are consistent with the 'genius' of the language rather than submitting to the massive borrowing of the '*lo na oda*' (law and order) variety. The cartoon reproduced in Figure 1 vividly illustrates the dilemma. There is, however, little sign so far of any official intervention. Laycock indeed is rather pessimistic. He argues that expatriate scholars have failed to take into account:

> Melanesian attitudes — especially the pragmatic tendency to let problems find their own solutions. A dramatic new policy on the part of the Papua New Guinea government *could* upset these predictions — but, in view of the Melanesian tolerance, even preference, for diversity, this seems unlikely.

(Laycock, 1982: 268)

FIGURE 1 (Department of Language, 1981: 241)

There can be no question that Laycock is right to emphasize that the ultimate fate of English and Tok Pisin lies with Papua New Guineans themselves and not with foreign linguists. Though they would probably disagree with Laycock's predictions, other scholars have argued that the views of Papua New Guineans have been insufficiently considered and that the evidence as to their attitudes to the two languages is fragmentary and 'impressionistic' (Wurm & Mühlhäusler, 1979: 260).

It is against this background of uncertainty about the trends among Papua New Guinean speakers in their use of Tok Pisin and English that the present authors have been conducting an ongoing inquiry among students at the country's two universities. The first stage of the inquiry took place in 1984 and was confined to the University of Technology (UOT). The second stage in 1986 involved students at the University of Papua New Guinea (UPNG) as well. We are currently (1988) carrying out a third stage investigation at both universities.

Prior to entering university, the students concerned had come through a schooling which lasted either 10 or 12 years. Their school education was, at least in theory, totally English medium. Yet this schooling had taken place during a period when observers (e.g. Mühlhäusler, 1984: 454) seem generally agreed that the status of Tok Pisin within the country at large was on the rise and its use was certainly spreading. It virtually monopolized Parliamentary debating, some of which was broadcast; it could be heard in some other broadcasting; it was used in some pop songs. It appeared to a certain extent in print, notably in the weekly *Wantok* newspaper; in dramatic productions, both in towns and in villages, by such companies as Raun Raun Theatre and Dua Dua Theatre Group; in two popular full-length feature films; and generally in on-the-job communication in offices, shops, factories, and other worksites where Papua New Guineans from different mother tongue speech communities were thrown together. A recent investigation of post-university professional language use in Papua New Guinea indicates that fully 75% of UOT graduates of the 1978 and 1979 cohorts use Tok Pisin, to some extent, on the job (Swan, 1986: 14).

Undoubtedly, it is their ability to use English in an academic context which has opened the door to membership of the educated élite for Papua New Guinea's current undergraduate population. But how far does this 'instrumental' valuation spill over into the adoption of a more 'integrative' approach? (Lambert, 1956). Will they, as with certain of the intelligentsia in India, for instance, adopt English as their 'language of preference', rejecting Tok Pisin and thus isolating themselves from what appears to be a strong contrary trend within the country as a whole?

A full account of Stages One and Two of our investigations has been given in Swan & Lewis (1987a; 1987b). For present purposes we shall concentrate on those data which cast light on students' language use in relation to trends in the use of English and Tok Pisin nationwide. We shall call attention in particular to one trend which points to a possible language planning and educational dilemma for the future.

The student sample

Whatever their future or concurrent subject specialism, students at both universities take an English course in their first year. At UOT some students take a further English course or courses in later years. In the first stage of the inquiry, though the vast majority of students in the sample were in their first year (72%), we canvassed a number of second to fourth year students as well. In 1986 we confined our attention to Year One students at both universities and propose to do so again in 1988. Table 1 summarizes student numbers for both stages.

TABLE 1 *Number of students in the sample*

| | Stage One (1984) (Years 1–4 combined) | Stage Two (1986) (Year 1 only) | | |
	UOT	UOT	UPNG	TOTAL
Male students	390 (90%)	220 (88%)	297 (82%)	517 (85%)
Female students	41 (10%)	30 (12%)	63 (18%)	93 (15%)
	431	250	360	610

As shown in Table 1, over the two samplings, we have obtained information from somewhat in excess of 1000 students. The sample for 1984 represents just under half the entire student body at UOT (excluding non-Papua New Guineans) at the start of that academic year. The sample for 1986 constitutes over 90% of all students in their first year at UPNG. We can be confident therefore that results obtained are representative of the views of the population in question.

Methodology

The inquiry was questionnaire-based. Version One of the questionnaire, used in 1984, was fairly hastily put together and proved less than satisfactory as some questions were interpreted differently by different students. The two versions appear as Appendix A and B respectively to this chapter and should provide readers with a clear picture of the scope of the inquiry.

The validity of the questionnaire approach in obtaining data on language use depends to some extent on how accurately respondents are able to introspect. In this case we asked them *inter alia* to give a percentage estimate of the amount of each language they used either overall or — in Version Two — both overall and in select circumstances (for socializing and for study). We were encouraged to believe that students could make such an estimate in the light of a statement by Wurm (1980: 240):

It is usually assumed that speakers of two different dialects or sociolects have difficulty in keeping them apart, with resulting interference phenomena. What I have said suggests that Papua New Guineans have an unusual ability or inclination for keeping lectal forms of a language apart from each other. This is in fact a traditional cultural feature in Papua New Guinea. Much of the tribal and clan structure in Papua New Guinea is associated with linguistic differences, often of a very minute nature, which are jealously preserved. This principle is easily translated into use of the two forms of Tok Pisin [Bush Pidgin and Urban] and of English, by Papua New Guineans, and speakers are very conscious indeed of which lect and which language they use in a given speech act.

Our data also proved encouraging in that they met a number of built-in consistency checks. We accept that there is a considerable amount of code-switching even in mid-sentence in educated Papua New Guinean speech and that percentages can be only a rough estimate. Nevertheless our results on both occasions seemed eminently reasonable. Moreover we asked just over half the sample for a second estimate after a gap of between five and six months. Results were remarkably consistent and therefore, we believe, a reliable estimate of their use of various languages had been obtained.

Of course, our evidence on student attitudes to English and Tok Pisin is indirect and quantitative. We did not, in either version of the questionnaire, explicitly invite attitudinal comments either in an open-ended way or by use of an attitudinal scale. However, it seems reasonable to infer that a relatively high estimated percentage use of Tok Pisin indicates a favourable attitude to the language, especially in a learning environment where all the pressures, in terms of lectures, seminars, tutorials, textbook reading and academic writing are in the direction of English. In such a situation, of course, the converse would not necessarily hold true: in an English medium learning environment a relatively low estimated use of Tok Pisin would not necessarily indicate an unfavourable attitude; it might simply mean that opportunities to use Tok Pisin rather than English were few and far between. Equally, a high estimated use of English in such an environment might merely reflect the exigencies of the situation rather than favourable student attitudes to that language.

Results and Discussion

Data from UOT in 1984 could be seen as establishing benchmarks for later inquiries at that institution and as providing a reference point for comparisons in 1986 with UPNG. While it is probably premature on the basis of just two samplings at UOT to speak of an established trend towards an increased use of Tok Pisin among students there, the increases shown in Table 2 which have been subjected to a t-test are considered to be statistically strongly significant.

TABLE 2 *UOT students' mean relative self-estimated percentage use of various languages in all circumstances of use combined*

	UOT (1984) (Years 1–4 combined but 72% Year 1) (%)	UOT (1986) (Year 1 only) (%)
English	63	54
Tok Pisin	28	35
Hiri Motu	—	3
Vernacular	9	8

One unfortunate oversight in Version One of the questionnaire was that it did not include Hiri Motu in the question in which students were asked to make estimates of relative percentage use of their various languages. It will be noted, however, from the 1986 figures that the overall mean percentage self-estimated use of Hiri Motu is very low and we presume it would have been similar in 1984. Since only 9% of our 1984 UOT sample claimed to be fluent in Hiri Motu and the mean percentage Tok Pisin use for the Hiri Motu speakers was only 18%, the general effect of the inclusion of a figure for Hiri Motu in the 1984 data would presumably be to lower the percentage for Tok Pisin a little (and at the same time slightly raise the figure for English). In terms of our *comparison* between 1984 and 1986, the net effect would in fact be to underline the significance of the increase in Tok Pisin at UOT over the two year period.

In 1984 the questionnaire was administered to UOT students early on in Semester One. In 1986 it was administered in both universities about the middle of Semester One. We believe the latter figures are more reliable, as students would have been long enough at their respective institutions to have established a pattern of language use typical of their new situation whereas this might not have been so in 1984. Table 3 shows second estimates for UOT for 1984 taken in the middle of Semester Two.

TABLE 3 *Comparison of UOT Year One students' mean relative self-estimates of percentage use of various languages (all circumstances combined) made early in Semester One and in the middle of Semester Two*

| | UOT (1984) (Year 1 students only) | |
	First estimate (%)	Second estimate (%)
English	60	51
Tok Pisin	29	37
Vernacular	11	12

Though second estimates were obtained for only 153 (i.e. 55%) of the Year One students, this increase in the use of Tok Pisin is considered on the basis of a matched pair t-test to be highly significant statistically ($p < 0.01$).

Second estimates were also obtained about the middle of Semester Two at both institutions in 1986. For the purposes of simplicity we shall simply record the results for Tok Pisin use here (Table 4). In both cases the proportion of second estimates obtained was relatively small (about one-third for UOT and only one-fifth for UPNG).

TABLE 4 *Comparison of students' mean relative self-estimates of percentage use of Tok Pisin (all circumstances) made in mid-Semester One and mid-Semester Two (both universities)*

| | 1986 | |
	First estimate (%)	Second estimate (%)
UOT	35	33
UPNG	30	33

These differences are *not* considered to be statistically significant. Instead we see a levelling out at both universities over the period from mid-Semester One to mid-Semester Two. Since the 1986 first estimate for UOT is much closer to the second estimate for 1984 (see Table 3), we would suggest that we must have set the questionnaire to UOT students in 1984 before they had established their relative levels of language use in the university environment.

Table 5 shows a breakdown for use of all languages at both universities in 1986 both overall and in two specific domains: study and socializing. Since the exact wording of this part of the questionnaire may be considered crucial, the reader is directed to Part C of Version 2 of the questionnaire (see Appendix B). Note that the term Tok Ples was used to refer to vernacular as it was expected to be a more familiar term for students. Question 1 takes account of the fact that English (unlike the other languages) is used not only in speech but writing and reading, whereas in Question 2 we wished to focus on the amount of Tok Pisin used in talking about study matters with fellow-students. (It may be taken for granted that little writing and almost no reading takes place in Tok Pisin or any language other than English so far as study is concerned, especially at UOT.) Question 3 self-evidently restricts itself to speech.

As can be seen at a glance from Table 5, relative percentages for both Hiri Motu and vernacular are virtually identical at both universities for all uses. There is, however, a statistically significant difference in the use of Tok Pisin and English for all uses combined and in the two specific domains. In all cases UPNG students use significantly less Tok Pisin and significantly more English.

TABLE 5 *Students' 1986 mean relative self-estimated percentage use of various languages at both universities (all circumstances combined and in study and social domain)*

	All circumstances		Study		Social	
	UOT	*UPNG*	*UOT*	*UPNG*	*UOT*	*UPNG*
English	54	58	67	72	44	50
Tok Pisin	35	31	28	23	45	39
Hiri Motu	3	2	1	1	3	3
Vernacular	8	9	3	4	8	9

Four possible explanations of the above findings occurred to us:

(1) UPNG is situated in the capital, Port Moresby, which has traditionally been the heartland of Hiri Motu speakers, whereas UOT is in Lae in Morobe Province which is known to have a very high number of Tok Pisin speakers.
(2) UPNG might have a significantly higher proportion of Papuan Hiri Motu-speaking students (some of whom speak little or no Tok Pisin).
(3) A sex difference might be involved. UPNG has about twice as many female students proportionally as UOT.
(4) The two institutions are rather different in terms of fields of study and might attract different types of students requiring different types of language use.

For present purposes it is unnecessary to go into a full statistical analysis of the above factors. Suffice it to make the following comments:

(1) Our data do not allow us to measure the effect of the difference of location, but since busy students spend most of their time on the university campus in relative isolation from the city communities, we doubt if this factor has a significant influence.
(2) Our data show that the percentage of Papuan students at both universities is almost identical (about 25%). This factor can therefore be discounted.
(3) Our data for UOT in 1984 indicated no significant variation in estimated overall Tok Pisin use by sex. Strangely enough, for 1986 the reverse was true. Female students at both universities gave lower estimates of Tok Pisin use than their male counterparts. However, this pattern was even *more* marked for UOT than for UPNG female

students and would therefore tend to influence statistics in the opposite direction.

(4) There is a significant statistical correlation between students' subject area and the percentage of Tok Pisin they use. Overall, technical students at UOT (i.e. those other than Accountancy/Business Studies students) use an estimated 38% Tok Pisin. All other students in our study — Arts and Science students as well as Preliminary Year students at UPNG together with Accountancy/Business Studies students at UOT — use 28–30% Tok Pisin overall.

From the above discussion we can conclude that the main explanation for the difference in results between the two universities is the nature of the field of study.

This result may seem surprising in view of the widespread view that at its present stage of development Tok Pisin lacks a full technical register. Independent testimony as to what is going on at UOT indicates that at least some students of technology find it helpful to translate technological concepts and problems into Tok Pisin for discussion and analysis. Walsh (1987), one of our colleagues at UOT, has obtained evidence to this effect.

Our own data, however, show another factor to be at work. Students in the study were asked to estimate their relative competence (both speaking and comprehension) in the languages they use. Again, we need not go into the full statistical analysis here, but there is clear correlational evidence along the following lines:

(1) In general, a higher than average percentage use of Tok Pisin correlates significantly with a relatively low self-rating in English competence.

(2) Since students of technological subjects at UOT are among the highest users of Tok Pisin we find, not surprisingly, that they show significantly less confidence in their use of English than other students. (For example, 36% of technical students rate their spoken English 'fair' or 'poor' as against only 19% of UPNG Arts students so rating themselves; 26% of technical students rate their comprehension of English as 'fair' or 'poor', whereas only 13% of UPNG Arts students do so.)

We can conclude therefore that the tendency among UOT technical students to use a lot of Tok Pisin, including for study purposes, is less on account of a faith in Tok Pisin but more a lack of confidence in their command of English.

It should be emphasized that technical students are not unique in this respect — merely extreme. Though only 23% of our sample in 1986 consider themselves to be L1 Tok Pisin speakers (with a slightly higher number — 26% — claiming to use Tok Pisin as 'first choice' language nowadays at home), the vast majority of students rate themselves significantly better at speaking and comprehending Tok Pisin than English. The two main exceptions to this are the 6% of students for whom English is 'first choice' language at home; and the 4% for whom Hiri Motu is the main home language. It is surely a pointer to the prevailing strength of Tok Pisin in present-day Papua New Guinea that the country's educational élite, after twelve years of English medium education, feel less confident in English than in Tok Pisin, a language virtually excluded from the formal education system.

It seems clear from the above evidence that there is little sign of the present undergraduates adopting English by preference. To the contrary, the indications are that, given the constraints within their English-medium academic environment, these students use a remarkable amount of Tok Pisin — in the case of technological students even for study purposes.

At this point it may be in order to summarize other significant findings of our inquiry. We shall then go on to consider an aspect of our study, which is as yet tentative, but, if true, could prove to be a somewhat disturbing factor for the future of language planning and education in the country.

Stage One of our inquiry provided evidence that the amount of Tok Pisin used by UOT students varied significantly according to the student's origin. New Guinea Islands and New Guinea Coastal students were found to use significantly more Tok Pisin than Highlands students who in turn used significantly more than Papuan students. This pattern was clearly confirmed by second estimates in 1984. Exactly the same pattern emerged at both universities in Stage Two of the inquiry with a low of 11% use for all circumstances by Papuan students at UPNG and a high of 46% for New Guinea Coastal students at UOT.

We also found evidence in 1984 of significant variation in use of Tok Pisin according to father's occupation. Fifty-six per cent of our sample came from a rural subsistence background and used significantly more Tok Pisin at university than those from a rural (non-subsistence) background (24% of our sample) or from an urban background (9%). (There were 11% 'nil' responses to this question for some reason.) If we define as 'urban', students from the main towns (specified in the questionnaire as Port Moresby, Lae, Goroka, Wewak, Madang and Rabaul) or from villages close enough to large towns to have been heavily influenced by town lifestyle and presumably also linguistic patterns, we find significant differences overall, and also in the study and social domains, for use of Tok Pisin at university. Those from the urban areas use less Tok Pisin than those from rural areas (i.e. villages in the bush, small towns and villages close to small towns). This result is perhaps surprising as Tok Pisin might have been expected to be particularly strong in urban areas in its capacity as a *lingua franca*. By contrast, students from rural backgrounds might be expected to — and apparently do — make greater use of the vernacular in the home context. It must, however, be borne in mind that our student population would to a large extent have been boarders at school and therefore have been detached from their home background during their four years at High School and two at National High School prior to entering university. This would be especially true among rural students who might well have found themselves using a great deal of Tok Pisin during these six years because of a lack of fellow students with whom they shared a vernacular and this pattern might well have carried over into university life.

It should be emphasized that, whatever the students' place of origin — urban or rural — they are on average using a substantial amount of Tok Pisin for social purposes: 37% in the case of urban, and 44% in the case of rural students. Bearing in mind that social occasions are also the most likely circumstances for employing vernacular and/or Hiri Motu, this would seem to indicate that the vast majority of present Papua New Guinean undergraduates use English for social purposes less than half the time.

One further finding which may be mentioned here is that both in 1984 at UOT and in 1986 at both universities, our data showed that use of Tok Pisin varied significantly according to which one of the country's four National High Schools students had previously attended. We believe this to be due to a combination of two factors. First, the National High Schools do not have an equal mix of students from all parts of the country. Some 60% of intake in each case is from the more immediate catchment area, with obvious implications for the amount of Tok Pisin one might expect such students to use. The second factor is school policy on language use. At least one National High School is known to put fairly strong pressure on students to use their English outside the classroom and this is reflected in decidedly lower use of Tok Pisin by its ex-pupils when they move on to university. This latter influence surely highlights the considerable volatility of the language situation in present-day Papua New Guinea. If pressure in a certain direction from largely expatriate school staff in National High School can significantly influence language choice of ex-pupils, could not decisive intervention in favour of Tok Pisin in the educational system by central government influence it even more? Our suspicion, based on the data we have collected from undergraduates, is that any move toward sanctioning the wider use of Tok Pisin at school or even university level would have a very decisive effect indeed on the fate of both English and Tok Pisin in Papua New Guinea. Perhaps it is for this very reason that the authorities remain so silent!

We have earlier alluded to the positive correlation between high use of Tok Pisin and relatively low self-confidence in the use of English. In an English-medium university context, one might wonder whether a high use of Tok Pisin might also therefore be coupled with a greater chance of failure. We did not investigate this possibility in 1984 and for 1986 we collected data only for UOT. Our evidence is therefore less comprehensive than we would have liked. We hope to be able to make a special study of this important possible correlation during the third stage of our investigations at both universities. Despite the limited data, there is indeed some reason to believe that such a relationship does exist. Table 6 summarizes the data from UOT (1986).

TABLE 6 *Mean estimated percentage use of Tok Pisin (all circumstances) by UOT technical and business students according to course result (1986)*

	Tok Pisin use in all circumstances (%)	No. of students (%)
Technical Students		
Passed	38	82
Failed	43	35
Deferred	32	14
Withdrew	—	22
Total		153
Accountancy/Business		
Studies students		
Passed	31	49
Failed	32	10
Deferred	24	6
Withdrew	—	1
Total		66

As can be seen we have usable information on 219 of the 250 students in our UOT sample. A number of factors need to be borne in mind. The term 'deferred' refers to students who were considered borderline and had to take a re-sit examination in at least one of their subjects. The term 'withdrew' covers a multitude of circumstances ranging from recognition by the student of inevitable imminent failure to ill-health or problems, such as an outbreak of tribal fighting, at home. For this reason there is no point in giving percentage use of Tok Pisin for such students.

It is clear that technical students who failed their Year One course used significantly more Tok Pisin than those who passed. However, this pattern does not hold true for Accountancy/Business Studies students. Results for the borderline students in both groups are anomalous, indicating that they used significantly less Tok Pisin than those who failed. Numbers in this category are, of course, small. Nevertheless we would have felt more confidence in our hypothesis had our results conformed to the pattern in terms of Tok Pisin use:

Passes < Deferred < Failed

There is enough evidence, however, to prompt further study. If such a pattern does emerge during Stage Three of our inquiry, then Papua New Guinea is faced with something of a language planning and educational dilemma, with particularly serious consequences for students of technology on whom the country relies rather heavily for its future development.

Conclusions and Indications for the Future

Our investigations to date lead us quite firmly to the conclusion that there is widespread use of Tok Pisin by students at Papua New Guinea's two universities. Tok Pisin is used widely not only for social purposes, but also to some extent for study purposes, particularly by students of technology. Ironically, it may be these students who are at greatest risk of jeopardizing their chances of success in an English-medium university environment.

There is no sign that present undergraduates are adopting English as their 'language of preference' (whether for prestige or purely practical reasons) and thereby creating the possibility of the development of an educated élite cut off linguistically from the rest of the community. If the educated élite are not adopting English in this way, it seems extremely unlikely that others lower down the educational ladder are doing so.

There is no sign of antipathy to Tok Pisin among present under-graduates. This is in contrast to the position some 10 years ago when Mühlhäusler could speak of 'opposition against Pidgin . . . commonly found among more educated Papua New Guineans' (1977: 554). Interestingly enough, university students may from the outset have been more favourably disposed towards Tok Pisin than other educated Papua New Guineans. Forty-five per cent of a group of 392 students canvassed by UPNG's Educational Research Group in 1976 favoured the use of Tok Pisin (and/or Hiri Motu) 'at least in some classes' (Shea & Still, 1976: 44–5).

A recent report by the Commission for Higher Education pinpoints the long-term significance of the influential Foot Report (commissioned by the UN in 1962) as being that: 'it lent support to an élitist, manpower-oriented approach to education [which] has dominated the development of higher education in Papua New Guinea ever since' (Commission for Higher Education, 1984: 6). But perhaps there are signs that factors other than simply highly trained manpower are coming to be re-appraised. In 1987 the Wingti government proposed cutting funding to the tertiary sector and redirecting money to primary school level and despite outcries from both universities the government is enforcing this policy. The National High Schools may well also feel the squeeze in future, as they are no longer looked after by a separate body (National Institutions Division) but must vie with other areas of the secondary system for funding. In 1987 there appeared the report of the Committee on the Philosophy of Education for Papua New Guinea, chaired by the elder statesman, Sir Paulias Matane. Not unexpectedly this placed stress on matters of traditional value, including the nation's vernaculars and *lingue franche*.

The educational system at primary school level has been fully localized for some time. This is largely true also of the High Schools (Grades 7–10) and increasingly true of the National High Schools (Grades 11–12), though there is still quite a long way to go here. Hearsay evidence indicates that where national staff are involved quite a lot of Tok Pisin is used unofficially even in the classroom. Given the favourable disposition of present-day undergraduates, it seems likely that as more national staff come on stream at the two universities, more and more Tok Pisin will come to be used both for social and study purposes there too. This might even serve to neutralize the possibly disadvantageous effect of high Tok Pisin use on examination results in an English-medium system.

Looking further into the future, one might foresee a decline in the standard of English among the student body along the lines indicated for

Malaysia by Ożóg (see Chapter 17, this volume). Already one hears criticisms from students regarding the quality of English teaching in the schools.

However, as we have indicated, the Papua New Guinea linguistic scene is exceedingly complex and volatile. There are factors operating in the opposite direction against Tok Pisin and in favour of English. Here we may note just two things. Female university students use significantly less Tok Pisin than their male counterparts. Will they pass this predilection onto their children? Secondly, there is the imponderable influence of television; live broadcasting, as distinct from Australian programmes via satellite, is confined currently to Port Moresby, but is scheduled to spread to Lae and later to other centres. It is quite likely that developments in the use of solar power could make television available virtually nationwide by the turn of the century. Of course, if a significant proportion of programmes were to be in Tok Pisin the reinforcing effect on the spread of Tok Pisin would be tremendous. However, the cost of local television production almost certainly precludes this. Far more likely is the transmission of a host of English language programmes from Australia, U.K. and U.S.A. If television fever grips Papua New Guinea, this factor alone might swing the balance decisively back in favour of English — particularly among university students who, like many of the urban population, are already 'hooked' on video.

The one thing we can be sure of in the midst of such continuing uncertainties is that the next twelve years of the post-colonial era are likely to be just as fascinating from the linguistic and language planning point of view in Papua New Guinea as the first twelve.

References

Annual Education Report (1983), Port Moresby: Papua New Guinea Department of Education.

Commission for Higher Education (1984), *Higher Education: A Review of Trends in Papua New Guinea*. Port Moresby: Commission for Higher Education.

Department of Language (1981), *Readings in Communication and Language*. Port Moresby: University of Papua New Guinea.

LAMBERT, W. E. (1956), Developmental aspects of second language acquisition. *Journal of Social Psychology* 63, 83–110.

LAYCOCK, D. C. (1982), Tok Pisin: A Melanesian solution to the problem of Melanesian linguistic diversity. In R. J. MAY & H. NELSON (eds.) *Melanesia: Beyond Diversity*. Canberra: ANU.

LYNCH, J. (1983), Text of Broadcast on Papua New Guinea National Broadcasting Commission radio programme. *The Times of Papua New Guinea* 1st June.

MATANE, Sir Paulius (1987), *Report of Inquiry into the Philosophy of Education for Papua New Guinea*.

MÜHLHÄUSLER, P. (1977), The social role of Pidgin in Papua New Guinea today. In S. A. WURM (ed.) *New Guinea Area Languages and Language Study, Vol. 3, Language, Culture, Society and the Modern World*. Canberra: ANU, Pacific Linguistics C40.

— (1984), Tok Pisin in Papua New Guinea. In R. W. BAILEY & M. GÖRLACH (eds.) *English as a World Language*. Cambridge: Cambridge University Press.

SHEA, J. & STILL, K. (1976), *Student Opinions about Teaching and Learning in the University*. Port Moresby: University of Papua New Guinea (Educational Research Unit Report No. 18).

SWAN, J. (1986), *Looking Beyond Unitech: Report of an Investigation of Employer Satisfaction with the Professional Communicative Competence of Graduates of the Papua New Guinea University of Technology*. Lae: Papua New Guinea University of Technology (Report Series No. 52.86).

SWAN, J. & LEWIS, D. J. (1987a), There's a lot of it about: Self-estimates of their use of Tok Pisin by students of the Papua New Guinea University of Technology. In D. C. LAYCOCK & W. WINTER (eds.) *A World of Language: Papers Presented to Professor S. A. Wurm on his 65th birthday*. Canberra: ANU, Pacific Linguistics C100.

— (1987b), It's only a matter of time: The advance of Tok Pisin at university in Papua New Guinea. Paper presented to the Annual Conference of the Papua New Guinea Linguistic Society, Lae, July.

WALSH, R. (1987), Personal communication relative to interview material collected in connection with M. A. Thesis (in preparation).

WEEKS, S. G. (1986), School time is back again but with a difference. *The Times of Papua New Guinea*, Feb. 1.

WURM, S. A. (1980), Standardisation and instrumentalisation in Tok Pisin. In A. VALDMAN & A. HIGHFIELD (eds.) *Theoretical Orientations in Creole Studies*. New York: Academic Press.

WURM, S. A. & MÜHLHÄUSLER, P. (1979), Attitudes towards New Guinea Pidgin and English. In S. A. WURM (ed.) *New Guinea and Neighbouring Areas: A Sociolinguistic Laboratory*. The Hague: Mouton.

Appendix A: 1984 Version of Questionnaire

PAPUA NEW GUINEA UNIVERSITY OF TECHNOLOGY
Department of Language and Social Science

STUDENT INFORMATION FORM

Personal Information

FULL NAME: _____ DATE OF BIRTH: _____
          (underline surname)

SEX: ☐ Male ☐ Female   MARITAL STATUS: ☐ Single ☐ Married

COURSE: _____ GROUP: _____

YEAR YOU FIRST ENTERED THE UNIVERSITY: _____

RESIDENTIAL ADDRESS: Hall/Lodge: _____ Room No: _____
   Other (if not hall or lodge): _____

POSTAL ADDRESS IN LAE: _____

Background Information

PLACE OF ORIGIN:

   Village: _____ District: _____

   Province: _____ Country: _____

FATHER'S OCCUPATION: _____

Where does your family live now (if different from place of origin)?

_____

YOUR EDUCATION:

	Name	Location	Grade Reached
High School	_____	_____	_____
Technical School	_____	_____	_____
National High School	_____	_____	_____

ACTIVITIES AND LEADERSHIP POSITIONS IN HIGH SCHOOL AND THE COMMUNITY.

_____

_____

WORK EXPERIENCE: _____
(if any)   _____

Language Information

Name of the language you first spoke as a child: _____

Name of the language your mother first spoke as a child: _____

Name of the language your father first spoke as a child: _____

What languages do you now mostly speak
when at home with your family? _____

How well can you speak and understand the following languages?

	ENGLISH		TOK PISIN		HIRI MOTU	
	speak	understand	speak	understand	speak	understand
very well	☐	☐	☐	☐	☐	☐
well	☐	☐	☐	☐	☐	☐
fairly	☐	☐	☐	☐	☐	☐
poorly	☐	☐	☐	☐	☐	☐
not at all	☐	☐	☐	☐	☐	☐

What other languages do you speak? _____
_____
_____

For Tok Pisin Speakers Only
(Please tick as appropriate)

1. I *first* learned TP from:
   - (i) my father ☐ my mother ☐ both parents ☐
     in the village
   - (ii) people other than my parents in the village
     — relatives ☐ other children ☐
   - (iii) my father ☐ my mother ☐ both parents ☐
     in town

(iv)   people other than my parents in town

    — relatives ☐   other children ☐

(v)   my teacher(s) in community school ☐

(vi)   my teacher(s) ☐   fellow-pupils ☐   in High School

(vii) fellow-students in NHS ☐

(viii) fellow-students at Unitech ☐

(ix)   elsewhere (please state: _____

_____

2. I now use TP (at least sometimes) when speaking to:

(i)   my mother ☐   my father ☐   both parents ☐

    in the village

(ii)   relatives ☐   children ☐   people my own age ☐

    adults (not parents or relatives) ☐   in the village

(iii) my mother ☐   my father ☐   both parents ☐   in town

(iv)   relatives ☐   children ☐   people my own age ☐

    adults (not parents or relatives) ☐   in town

(v)   fellow-students at Unitech ☐

(vi)   expatriates ☐   (Please specify: _____

_____)

3. Did you use TP (at least sometimes) when speaking to fellow-students at NHS?

Yes ☐   No ☐

4. Estimate the relative amounts of TP, English and Tokples you use(d) in each of the following situations. Use a % age.

(TP   English   Tokples)

(e.g., in the village   20   10   70)

		TP	English	Tokples
(i)	in the village			
(ii)	in town			
(iii)	in community school			
(iv)	in High School			
(v)	in NHS			
(vi)	at Unitech			

5. Would you say you use more or less TP at present than say:

	More	Less	
5 years ago	☐	☐	
10 years ago	☐	☐	?

Appendix B: 1986 Questionnaire

QUESTIONNAIRE ON YOUR USE OF TOK PISIN AT UNIVERSITY

What happens to Tok Pisin and where and how it is used is of considerable interest and importance to PNG. The Language Departments of both Universities would appreciate your help in collecting information. Please fill in this questionnaire fully and carefully. Thank you.

A. YOUR PERSONAL BACKGROUND

Course you are studying: . . . . Year (tick one)

Preliminary ☐

First Year ☐

Did you do a Preliminary Year either at UPNG or Unitech last year?

(Please tick) ☐ Yes ☐ No

Did you attend National High School before coming to university?

(Please tick one) ☐ Yes ☐ No

If so, which National High School? . . . .

Your name (please underline surname): . . . .

Sex (tick M or F)   M ☐   F ☐

Age: . . . . years . . . . months

Province you were born in: . . . .

Where your family lives now (please tick *one* only):

      in a large town (eg. POM, Lae, Gka, Wwk, Madang, Rabaul) ☐

      in a small town (eg. Popondetta, Wau, Wabag) ☐

      in a village close to a large town ☐

      in a village close to a small town ☐

      in a village *not* close to a town ☐

B. *LANGUAGE BACKGROUND*

1. What language did you first learn as a child? (Please tick *one* only):

   English   ☐
   Tok Pisin   ☐
   Hiri Motu   ☐
   Tok Ples   ☐

   If you have ticked Tok Ples, please give the name of the language:

   . . . .

2. What language is *most frequently* spoken in your family *at home* now?
   (please tick *one* only):

   English   ☐
   Tok Pisin   ☐
   Hiri Motu   ☐
   Tok Ples   ☐

C. *THE LANGUAGES YOU USE AT UNIVERSITY?*

Please estimate the amount of Tok Pisin, Hiri Motu, English and Tok Ples you use currently for each of the situations described below. Use a percentage.

Example:

Tok Pisin	Hiri Motu	English	Tok Ples
25%	5%	60%	10%

(Note that the percentages should add up to 100!)

1. How much of each language do you use at the university, taking *all* your use of language *in all circumstances*?:

Tok Pisin	Hiri Motu	English	Tok Ples
%	%	%	%

2. How much of each language do you use at university *when talking about your studies with fellow students*? :

Tok Pisin	Hiri Motu	English	Tok Ples
%	%	%	%

3. How much of each language do you use at university when talking socially to friends? :

Tok Pisin	Hiri Motu	English	Tok Ples
%	%	%	%

4. Compared with 5 years ago do you use more or less Tok Pisin nowadays?
   (Please tick one only):

   I use more Tok Pisin than 5 years ago ☐

   I use less Tok Pisin than 5 years ago ☐

   I use about the same amount of Tok Pisin ☐

5. Compared with 10 years ago do you use more or less Tok Pisin nowadays?
   (Please tick one only):

   I use more Tok Pisin than 10 years ago ☐

   I use less Tok Pisin than 10 years ago ☐

   I use about the same amount of Tok Pisin ☐

D. HOW WELL YOU KNOW CERTAIN LANGUAGES

How well do you *speak* and *understand* the following languages now? (Put only *one tick* in each column):

	English		Tok Pisin		Hiri Motu		Your Mother's Tok Ples		Your Father's Tok Ples	
	Speak	Understand	Speak	Understand	Speak	Understand	Speak	Understand	Speak	Understand
Very Well	☐	☐	☐	☐	☐	☐	☐	☐	☐	☐
Well	☐	☐	☐	☐	☐	☐	☐	☐	☐	☐
Fairly Well	☐	☐	☐	☐	☐	☐	☐	☐	☐	☐
Poorly	☐	☐	☐	☐	☐	☐	☐	☐	☐	☐
Not At All	☐	☐	☐	☐	☐	☐	☐	☐	☐	☐

Thank you very much for your help in this inquiry. Your answers are a valuable source of information.

13 Language planning in Vanuatu

ANDREW THOMAS

Introduction

Vanuatu is a nation of immense linguistic diversity. Its estimated 135,000 inhabitants speak 105 indigenous languages (Tryon, 1979). Few of these languages have more than 3,000 speakers. As social situations arose in which there was a need for communication across language boundaries, so the contact vernacular, Bislama, emerged and expanded. French and English were introduced by white settlers and missionaries in the nineteenth century, and these two metropolitan languages were used by the colonial administrators during the period of Condominium rule, from 1906 to 1980. The need for migrant labour resulted in the growth of small speech communities of Vietnamese, Chinese (Hakka), Wallisian, Gilbertese, Fijian and other Pacific island languages. No other country in the region can rival Vanuatu's dubious reputation of being the 'Babel of the Pacific'. Whereas no visionary plan has yet emerged to resolve the considerable difficulties faced by language planners in Vanuatu, there are indications that the sociocultural climate now exists for a re-appraisal of the language policies inherited from the Condominium government at Independence in 1980.

In this chapter, I shall outline recent developments in Bislama, and its rise to the dominant position it now holds *vis-à-vis* other languages in the archipelago. The ascendancy of Bislama over indigenous and exogenous languages is not complete. In the domains of education and the legal system, Bislama is still waiting at the gate. The evidence I shall adduce in support of the introduction of Bislama as a language of instruction is based on observations made while I was a language teacher in Vanuatu, between 1977 and 1984. Data collected on a subsequent visit in November/December 1986 have reinforced my contention that, without Bislama, the existing language-in-education policy is consonant neither with the sociopolitical importance of the language in the past, nor with the needs of Ni-Vanuatu today or in the future.

Vanuatu Pidgin: from Beach-la-mar to Bislama

Well-documented accounts of the origins of Bislama can be found in Clark (1979) and Charpentier (1979). An early description of Beach-la-mar is provided by Schuchardt, in his studies of Melanesian English (1883 and 1889, in Gilbert, 1980). Other early observers subsumed the different pidginised varieties of English used in the South West Pacific under various labels derived from *bicho do mar*. This is the Portuguese term for *Holothuria edulis*, a marine animal, known also as *trepang* (a Malay word), and sea-cucumber or sea-slug, on account of its shape. Clark (1977) lists twelve versions of the term Beach-la-mar, recorded between 1783 and 1851. However, it is uncertain at what stage the meaning was extended to include both sea-slug and pidgin. A number of observers have ascribed the derivation of Bislama to the French *bêche de mer* or *biche de mer*. Charpentier (1979: 40) rejects this etymology, asserting that these terms have only recently come to denote a 'sea-slug', which has commonly been called *concombre de mer*. Both Charpentier, and Guy (1974: 57), believe that a derivation from the Portuguese *bicho do mar* is more plausible. They suggest that a Portuguese term could have remained in use after the relexification of the *lingua franca* which became the China Coast Pidgin English (CCPE). It is now widely accepted that CCPE influenced varieties of pidgin in the South West Pacific. To attribute the origin of the term 'Bislama' to an early Gallicised form of *bicho do mar* would appear unwarranted, as trepang fishing, trading with the Chinese and the use of related trade jargons considerably predate any continuous French presence in this part of the Pacific.

Charpentier ascribes the Gallicised forms of the term used by nineteenth century Anglophone observers to the 'universality' of French as perceived by such writers, 'for whom it was their only foreign language'. He suggests that *bêche de mer* was a preferable alternative to the 'Latin-sounding' *bicho do mar*. It may, nevertheless, be true to say that the increasingly strong French influence in the area later in the century, following France's annexation of New Caledonia in 1853, led to the sound shift from Beach-la-mar to 'Bichelamar'. Schuchardt (1883, in Gilbert, 1980) quotes the French writer Louise Michel, as referring to

'Bichelamar'. She describes it as 'the very serviceable language spoken in New Caledonia, in which English is predominant'. This was the case even after over 30 years of French administration. ʰThe absence of [ʃ] in local vernaculars has resulted in 'Bichelamar' becoming 'Bislama'. French-speakers in Vanuatu still sometimes refer to the language as 'Bichlamar'. Another variant is 'Bislaman', though this is an old form, which is dying out. To Ni-Vanuatu (as inhabitants of the country are known) 'Bislama' denotes both the language and the trepang. Significantly, perhaps, for proponents of a Pan-Melanesian Pidgin, 'Bislama' also designates the pidgin languages of Papua New Guinea and the Solomon Islands; hence, *Bislama blong Solomon* means 'Solomon Islands Pijin', and *Bislama blong Nyugini* refers to 'Tok Pisin'. It is worth noting that the term 'Beach-la-mar', which had previously been in widespread use throughout the South West Pacific, became restricted this century to denoting the contact vernaculars of New Caledonia and Vanuatu. Hollyman (1976) documents the decline of Bichelamar in the French colony, where a relexified French form survived into this century. French influence in the then Anglo-French Condominium of the New Hebrides would appear to have assured the continued use of the term in Vanuatu.

After France had taken possession of New Caledonia in 1853, the French government showed an increasing desire to annex the neighbouring group of islands, Vanuatu. French traders and settlers arrived there in considerable force, creating a predominantly French atmosphere in the archipelago. We can reasonably assume that the French community in Vanuatu chose to refer to the English-based vernacular spoken there by the same term as was formerly used in New Caledonia. Indeed, they may have expected a relexification of the language, along the lines of Bichelamar in their nearby colony. History was not to repeat itself, however. A number of French words were added to the lexicon, but a variety of sociopolitical factors ensured the survival of a stabilised, predominantly English-based pidgin in Vanuatu. The decisive factor was the return to the islands from the plantations of Queensland, Samoa and Fiji of pidgin-speaking indentured labourers (Mühlhäusler, 1978).

The period of French economic domination, then, effectively cut off Bislama from its lexifier language. The plantation economy was in the hands of French-speaking settlers, who, unlike their British counterparts, were given both moral and financial metropolitan support. However, whereas the German presence in parts of New Guinea led to a significant German influence on the lexicon of Tok Pisin (see Kale, Chapter 10; Smith, Chapter 11, this volume), the result of linguistic isolation in Vanuatu was a heavier reliance on the substrate languages for expansion.

This took the form of borrowing and calquing. The development of regional varieties was most pronounced in the period up to the outbreak of war in the Pacific in 1941. Regionalects only started to wane as inter-island contact increased in the 1960s.

The Post-War Expansion of Bislama

The period since the war has seen a gradual shift in language attitudes in Vanuatu, culminating in the 1980 declaration of Bislama as the national language of the Republic. Hopes by the joint colonial rulers of a bilingualism in the metropolitan link languages of English and French have been proved unrealistic. Bislama has strengthened its traditional role as principal *lingua franca*, for horizontal inter-tribal or inter-island communication among the indigenous population. A consideration of any aspect of language planning in Vanuatu today requires that we understand the socioeconomic and cultural factors which have brought about the enhanced status and currency of Bislama.

Six main factors account for the recent expansion of Bislama. Firstly, improved inter-island communications led to greater mobility, and a consequent need for a medium of communication between people having different mother-tongues. A second factor in the growth of Bislama was the urbanisation which came to Vanuatu in the late 1960s. Young people from all over the archipelago were attracted to the urban centres of Port Vila and Santo during the building boom which lasted through the early 1970s. The number of banks in Port Vila rose from one to twelve in just three years, and Trust companies mushroomed as overseas businessmen began to exploit the tax-free status of Vanuatu. With the completion of the deep-sea wharf in 1972 the tourist industry expanded rapidly, further increasing the opportunities for employment open to Ni-Vanuatu in the urban centres. This wide-scale migration brought people from diverse linguistic backgrounds together in new social and occupational situations. The larger multilingual communities which resulted created ideal conditions for the propagation of Bislama. Marriages between couples of differing speech communities led to increasing use of the *lingua franca*, and Bislama became the first language of a small, yet growing number of children of such marriages.

The third factor in the expansion and increased acceptability of Bislama was the impetus given it by the Church from the late 1960s. From its use for taking the minutes of the Presbyterian Church Assembly, Bislama advanced in strides to the publication in 1971 of a translation of the Four Gospels. Hitherto, local vernaculars had been widely used as the languages of evangelism, and extensive scripture translations had been made. Certain languages had been elevated to the position of *lingua franca*, such as the Banks Island language of Mota by the Anglican Melanesian Mission. Other missions had adopted vernaculars for liturgical purposes outside their traditional speech communities. The *volte-face* on Bislama brought to a close the period in which the Church considered it a pariah among vernaculars, 'a plantation language, not fit for worship' (cited in Tryon, 1979). Psychologically, then, a major hurdle was negotiated with the publication of this translation, which was followed in 1980 by a translation of the New Testament, *Nyutesteman long Bislama*. Although not all linguists have viewed such translations as proof of the adequacy of Bislama as a medium of sophisticated communication (e.g. Charpentier, 1984: 54), Ni-Vanuatu were more impressed. All concerned were, however, ready to concede that these translations were a step in the direction of a standardised form of Bislama.

A further factor in the expansion of Bislama was the establishment of boarding schools at certain centres, once the British and French Residencies took over responsibility for education from the missions. Although Bislama was not used as either a medium or subject, the presence together of pupils from different islands ensured its use outside the classroom. The New Hebrides Biennial Report for 1971 and 1972 rules out language teaching in the vernacular on account of the large number of local languages spoken in limited areas by small populations. The teaching of Bislama is rejected out of hand. 'The lingua franca Pidgin (Bichelamar) is not considered suitable for the purposes of formal education' (p. 63). The spread of Bislama through the developing educational system can thus be seen as both unintended and undesired.

A fifth factor was the political role which Bislama fulfilled during the two decades leading to Independence in 1980. It was used to maintain solidarity among the members of disparate indigenous movements, notably the John Frum cargo cult on Tanna and the southern islands, and the Nagriamel movement of Chief Buluk and Jimmy Stephens on Santo and the islands of the north. But it was the New Hebrides National Party (renamed the Vanuaaku Pati in 1977) which realised the potential of Bislama as a unifying force, and a focus for anti-colonial discontent. Leaders of the party made speeches in Bislama, encouraging its members to view the language as unique to their country, embodying the history of Ni-Vanuatu. The party faithful were exhorted to see Bislama not as the language of domination created by Europeans, but as the language of survival and solidarity created by Melanesians. As such, it was proclaimed a viable alternative to the two colonial languages. Political news-sheets and manifestos to air grievances against the Condominium administration were published in Bislama. It succeeded in creating a feeling of nationalism among the inhabitants of these scattered islands who had traditionally lacked a sense of national identity, and who had shown allegiance to their island rather than their country of birth. Against this background, the first ever Municipal Council elections were held in August 1975, while the first Representative Assembly elections took place in mid-November. Bislama received semi-official recognition when it was voted one of the three languages for use in the Assembly proceedings.

A final, but crucial factor in both the currency and standardisation of Bislama was the opening, in 1966, of Radio Vila. Jointly controlled by the two Residencies, the station accorded equal broadcasting time to Bislama, English and French. This in itself was indicative of an attitudinal change. Party political broadcasts in Bislama were permitted on the radio before the 1975 elections. Since 1978, Bislama has been the most frequently used language on the station, which was renamed Radio New Hebrides, and became Radio Vanuatu at Independence. Programmes about current affairs, health, agriculture, music or local culture are all broadcast in Bislama. The transistor radio has ensured that these broadcasts are received throughout the islands, exposing Ni-Vanuatu to an increasingly standardised form of Bislama. The radio has played a key role in transforming the position of earlier years, when Bislama was seldom heard in the villages, and even then only among the men.

In administration, Bislama grew unofficially in the lower ranks, where there was a need to converse with the population outside the two Residencies, particularly in the police and health service. Increasing numbers of Ni-Vanuatu were recruited by the two National Services, as clerical positions were localised. Although the process of localisation was more rapid in the British National Service, the attitude of the French towards Bislama was arguably less censorious. Many English-speakers still tended to regard Bislama as 'garbled English', and resorted to *ad hoc* simplification of their own language, rather than treating Bislama as a language to be learned. This is reminiscent of the situation with Tok Masta in New Guinea described by Mühlhäusler (1981: 93–113).

Clearly, the colonial governments had no coherent language policy for Vanuatu. A few token gestures towards the principle of English/French bilingualism were made when the days of the Condominium were already numbered. One of these was the exchange of language teachers between the Lycée and the English-medium High School in which I took part.

Another was the United Nations Development Project to fund intensive teaching of French to key personnel in the English-medium education service. This was attended by some officers from other Government Departments. Similarly, an English language course was arranged by the French Education Department for Francophone education officers. Few of the staff were able to complete the course, which caused objections to be raised about officers' frequent absence from districts.

The eventual elevation of Bislama to the status of both the national and an official language of the Republic was foreshadowed by a British Foreign Office minister in September 1978, in a statement placing Bislama on a seemingly equal footing with English and French (*Nabanga*, 1978).

Language Use in Post-Independence Vanuatu

Because of its implications for future policies, the declaration regarding languages in the Vanuatu Constitution is worth further examination. The political circumstances in which the Constitution was agreed upon are also worth noting. The French Government, which had always insisted on the establishment of a constitution as a pre-condition for elections leading to Independence, had sent Paul Dijoud, the Minister for Overseas Territories, to Port Vila, to try to break the stalemate within the constitutional committee. With Dijoud anxious to return to Paris, agreement was finally reached after an all-night session of the weary committee, attended by Dijoud himself. Cynics might wish to add at this point that the French Government had made it clear that economic aid to the new Republic would be directly tied to the maintenance of French-medium education in Vanuatu. Thus, Article 3 of the Constitution states that:

(1) The national language of the Republic is Bislama. The official languages are Bislama, English and French. The principal languages of education are English and French.
(2) The Republic shall protect the different local languages which are part of the national heritage, and may declare one of them as a national language.

The Bislama version appears to admit the possibility of the future replacement of Bislama as national language, by a local language, whereas the English allows for the elevation of a local language to the status of national language alongside Bislama:

Sipos gavman ya i wantem mekem olsem, bambae hem i save jusumaot wan long ol lanwis ya blong i jenisem Bislama, i kam lanwis blong Ripablik blong Nyuhebredis.

(Should the Government think fit, one of the local languages may be chosen to replace Bislama as national language of the New Hebrides Republic.)

The point seems academic, however. On the eve of Independence, when the Constitution was drawn up, some may have thought that Bislama, the language of political protest and Melanesian solidarity, had reached its zenith, and would go into decline once the political goal of Independence had been achieved. Certainly there were those who predicted that the acrolect and some of the mesolects of what they saw as an incipient post-creole continuum would evolve into a nativised form of New English. This was predicted as being the inevitable consequence of closer ties with English-speaking neighbours in the Pacific, such as Australia and New Zealand. Yet eight years after Independence no rival has yet displaced Bislama from its pre-eminent position. Nor is there a candidate likely to do so in the foreseeable future.

But what of those critics of the Constitution who are dismissive of the status of Bislama as national language? Topping (1982: 2), for example suggests that mandating Bislama as national language is on a par with appointing a national flower! He makes the point that Bislama is not the language used where it counts, namely in education and law. Rather than applauding the pragmatic wisdom of declaring a pidgin *lingua franca* the national language (a unique phenomenon), Topping points to the divisiveness of continuing to conduct education and law in English and French, languages which he views as alien to the Pacific. If, then, the legacy of polarisation in politics, religion and language is to be tackled, a language-in-education policy free from the stranglehold of English and French would seem an imperative. Before discussing my specific proposal, however, more needs to be said about the background to the debate on language in education.

Education was a field virtually ignored by the Condominium powers until the 1960s. It was left to the missions to finance and run their own elementary schools. Most people viewed these mission schools as 'bible bible sing sing, no more' (MacClancy, 1980: 115). Conscious of the poor image which the low level of education in Vanuatu created, the national administrations of Britain and France finally stepped in to the educational patchwork which had developed under the missions. If the missions could be said to have put up schools in a haphazard fashion, governed by no overall plan, then the same criticisms can be levelled at the colonial governments. Acting separately, and more in a spirit of competition than concern for the appropriate educational needs of the country, Britain, and later France, embarked on programmes of building or rebuilding schools. France, in particular, sensing that it was losing the race in the language stakes, injected massive amounts of cash and manpower into its educational programme. The Lycée d'Enseignement Professionnel (later renamed the Vanuatu National Institute of Technology) was just one of the French administrations's prestige projects. Lavishly equipped, it was capable of training numbers of students far in excess of the country's limited manpower needs.

The failure of the Condominium to achieve even French/English bilingualism is aptly described by Charpentier (1979: 136) when he castigates the joint administration for its policy of 'back-to-back monolingualism'. Although the English and French systems could be said to co-exist, they do so more back-to-back, than side-by-side. The inevitable consequence is that pupils end up either 'English-educated' or 'French-educated'. Historically this has been the case ever since education was in the hands of the missions. To achieve English/French bilingualism, an individual would have had to undergo a religious conversion, thus permitting a schooling at both Protestant and Catholic missions. Despite Independence and the 'unification' of the two systems, English/French bilingualism still exists only at an official, national level, rather than at the level of individual speakers.

Any suggestion of changing the *status quo* before Independence met with a hostile response. In June 1977, after its Sixth Annual Congress, the Vanuaaku Pati issued a statement to the effect that, if elected to power, it would legislate for English to be the main European language of instruction in the schools. The horrified outcry culminated in the largest ever demonstration in Port Vila, when thousands of teachers, parents and children marched in favour of 'francophonie', the maintenance of the French language in Vanuatu. Although the demonstration was in part orchestrated by expatriate teachers, there was no denying the strength of feeling which existed among French-speaking Melanesians. According to statistics published before Independence, enrolments at French-medium schools had caught up with, and indeed just overtaken, those at English-medium schools. It would be cynical to suggest that enrolments soared purely because parents were attracted to the new French-medium schools because they were free, unlike the fee-paying English-medium schools. It was not uncommon for children from the same family to be enrolled in schools with differing languages of instruction, possibly in the hope that they would pool their language knowledge.

It is debatable whether the maintenance of French-medium schooling stems from a genuine desire on the part of Vanuatu's post-Independence Anglophone leaders to pursue the chimera of English/French bilingualism, or from apathy which allows the existing system to continue intact. The level of provision of French has been a bargaining point between Vanuatu and France ever since Independence. Threats and counter-threats concerning 'francophonie' have accompanied every incident in the history of diplomatic relations between the two countries since Independence. Feelings between them have run high on numerous occasions since 1980, in what could be called the 'Francophony War'! Vanuatu's opposition to French nuclear testing in the Pacific, and its alleged support for independence movements in New Caledonia have resulted in an, at times, stormy relationship between the two. Early in 1981, barely six months after Independence, the French Ambassador was expelled, causing the postponement of an aid agreement. On that occasion, the (British) Technical Adviser to the Minister of Education was asked to draw up a contingency plan in the event of large numbers of expatriate French teachers being withdrawn in protest. Late in 1986, a Chirac government less conciliatory than the socialist administration of Laurent Fabius ordered the withdrawal of a score of French 'co-opérants' (teachers and advisers) as a retaliatory measure. Again, late in 1987, the French Ambassador was expelled, for allegedly giving support to the Francophone opposition party prior to the November elections. The French government's response was to withdraw further personnel from the Lycée and Institute of Technology. Early in 1988, the Vanuatu Ministry of Education recruited eleven Tunisian teachers to make up the shortfall of Francophone staff at the two institutions.

Given the continuing uncertainty surrounding future French aid and political relations with Vanuatu it would be unrealistic purely in economic terms to attempt to prolong the *status quo* in the education system. A golden opportunity to address the whole issue of language in education was missed in the early 1980s, when an education commission, headed by J. Maraj, Vice Chancellor of the University of the South Pacific, was set up to report on all aspects of education in Vanuatu. The Maraj Commission's findings were never made public, though a Ministry of Education 'Policy Document' released late in 1982 was said to incorporate the Commission's recommendations. This document demonstrates that the Ministry's implicit objective at that time remained the discredited English/French bilingualism of the former colonial rulers. It refers to the need for 'a common curriculum in the English and French language media', with research to begin into 'the advisability and means of introducing a second metropolitan language at a suitable stage in the primary school' (1982: 3). Bislama and the indigenous vernaculars are given short shrift, in a single paragraph of the document:

> Bislama will be used to enable pupils to gain a clearer understanding in practical activities where it is necessary to have assistance from local craftsmen and specialists. Vernacular languages will be better suited to areas concerned with custom (story, legends, history of the country, etc.) and with traditional and artistic activities.
>
> (Vanuatu Ministry of Education, 1982: 4)

The limited role in the education system accorded to Bislama in this document is surprising in the light of views expressed both in Parliament and at the first Vanuatu Language Planning Conference held in 1981. During a debate on the question of Bislama in schools, in April 1982, a majority of members of parliament favoured the introduction of Bislama as either a medium of instruction or as a subject. Support for the teaching of Bislama in schools came from government and opposition members alike. This uncharacteristic consensus bears witness to the reluctance of politicians, so soon after Independence, to be seen questioning the unifying role of Bislama in the decolonising process in Vanuatu. The Minister of Education admitted that children were 'set back by having to learn subjects in a language foreign to them'. He went on to call for 'a system with a single language as the main language of education'.

The seeds for the 1981 Vanuatu Language Planning Conference were sown in 1978, by Rodney Moag of the University of the South Pacific. His proposal that a regional conference should be held in Port Vila to examine the whole question of language in Melanesia fell on stony ground. In the wake of the previous year's language demonstrations and the political stalemate at that time, it was adjudged too sensitive an issue. The conference was eventually jointly organised and run in July 1981, by the Pacific Churches Research Centre, and the University of the South Pacific Extension Centre. Participants at this conference were predominantly Ni-Vanuatu in key positions in education, the legal system and the media. A small number of overseas linguists also attended as 'observers' and 'resource people'. Topping (1982: 1–4) summarises the conference from a participant's viewpoint, affirming that Bislama is 'an adequate language for conducting complex, and often abstract discussions involving education, law, the media, and politics'.

The prime concern of the conference participants was to define the appropriate role of local languages and Bislama in the future life of the country. The Vanuatu National Council of Chiefs argued strongly in favour of the use of vernacular languages in the early primary school years as a means of developing a strong local identity among Ni-Vanuatu. The importance of Bislama in forging a strong national identity was emphasised by the Prime Minister and many other delegates. In particular, the Bislama Bible Translation Team advocated further work in standardising Bislama spelling and usage, to permit its more widespread use in written texts. A call was made for the production of a monolingual Bislama dictionary as a necessary step in this regard. This call was to be echoed in the following year's parliamentary debate.

One of the most common fears concerning the introduction of Bislama as a language of education is that, owing to lexical similarities, negative transfer occurs when pupils subsequently learn English. This fear was also expressed at the conference, when it was claimed that when children learn Bislama at an early age 'it tends to interfere with their learning of English' (see Pacific Languages Unit Report, 1981). However, no study has ever been carried out in Vanuatu to investigate this claim. Moreover, there is evidence from Papua New Guinea which suggests that achievement in English is not impaired by Tok Pisin (Crowley & Lynch, 1986). Papua New Guineans' levels of acquisition of English were comparable, irrespective of their Hiri Motu or Tok Pisin-speaking backgrounds.

The final resolution which the Language Planning Conference adopted showed strong support for the use of Bislama. It recommended that Bislama should be taught at least as a subject in the first four years of primary school and used as the medium of instruction for classes five and six. It was recommended that, in the overall education system, priority should be given first to the teaching of local languages, then Bislama, and then English and French. Further recommendations related to language use in the media, Parliament and the legal system. The Bislama of news reporting and debating was said to be redolent of 'translationese', and calls were made for greater efforts to improve the quality of Bislama texts and speeches. It was also proposed that the laws of Vanuatu be translated into Bislama, and that, when necessary, the language of the courts should be Bislama.

More general recommendations concerning language use, not just in Vanuatu, but throughout the Pacific region, were made at the conference held in Port Vila in August 1984. Entitled 'Pacific Languages: Directions for the Future', it was hosted by the Pacific Languages Unit of the University of the South Pacific. (See Crowley, 1984, for a more detailed account of the conference.) Intended not merely to be a forum for academics to express their own views on the future of Pacific languages, the conference brought together Pacific Islanders involved in the formulation of policy relating to language. What emerged from discussions was a consensus that there was little in the way of language policy in the region, except what had been conveniently inherited from the former, or still present, colonial powers. Despite the lip-service paid by Vanuatu's acting Prime Minister to the status of Bislama and the local vernaculars as enshrined in his country's constitution, a more ambivalent note was introduced by another prominent figure in the Vanuatu government. Commenting on the diagnosis of language problems in Vanuatu Grace Molisa, from the Prime Minister's Office, said, 'It is rather like silent diseases — you do not know you are sick until it is too late' (Pacific Languages Unit, USP report, 1984: 12). She went on to explain that, given Vanuatu's painful emergence as an independent country, the government saw other areas as having higher priority than language.

It became evident at this conference that, of the education systems of the Pacific, the Melanesian systems gave least recognition to vernaculars. Vanuatu was just one of the countries where mistrust of local languages as media of instruction has led to the pursuance of policies designed to maintain the hegemony of European languages. The Melanesian delegates called for vernacular pilot-projects to be set up, as a necessary step towards multilingual education in Melanesia. They also moved a resolution that:

> The various Pidgin languages of Melanesia should be given official status by introducing and encouraging them in school curricula; using them widely in the mass media; and attempting to have internal standardisation in each country, with the view to eventually having external standardisation of a variety to be used throughout the Melanesian region.
>
> (Pacific Languages Unit Report, 1984: 32)

Towards a More Standardised Bislama?

I have here discussed some of the sociopolitical and sociolinguistic developments before and after Independence that have led to the rise in status of Bislama. The need for continued status planning has been a rallying cry in all discussions about the future of Bislama and, indeed, of the other local languages. The relatively low social status of these languages in the eyes of their speakers is symptomatic of the absence of any degree of public or governmental education. Clearly, academic institutions such as the University of the South Pacific, need to work with government departments in order to break down resistance to the introduction of Bislama into the domains where it is still shunned. Before looking at a specific proposal for a language-in-education policy in Vanuatu, I shall refer briefly to certain developments which have directly affected the status and corpus planning of Bislama. These developments together have promoted a climate in which Bislama could take its rightful place in the community, being used for educational and legal purposes.

In the first part of this section I shall recall the political events surrounding Vanuatu's Independence in 1980, in so far as language change is caused by the need for the expression of social identity. The process of maturation or expansion of a pidgin can be described as the development of a language which can satisfy the communicative function, in response to the requirement also that it fulfil a reflexive or identifying function. The progressive disappearance of regionalects of Bislama in Vanuatu, and the concomitant emergence of sociolects to replace the non-referential dimension of the language has been a potent force in the standardisation of Bislama. Here I shall limit discussion to the case of the decline of the Santo Island regionalect, which illustrates linguistic changes stemming from a shift in perspective regarding the reflexive function of the language. This relates to the ideologically driven manipulation of Bislama by the Vanuaaku Party to promote first, anti-colonialist, and later, anti-separatist goals.

As we have seen, the concept of 'national identity' is comparatively new to Ni-Vanuatu. Allegiance was traditionally felt with one's home island rather than to the country as a whole. This reflected the political reality of the Condominium, which effectively denied the right of nationality to the indigenous inhabitants of the archipelago. The importance of this loyalty at island level was manifest in the retention of a higher degree of substrate influence in the regional varieties of Bislama. This situation prevailed into the 1970s when Guy produced his *Handbook of Bichelamar — Manuel de Bichelamar* (1974). His somewhat idiosyncratic description of Bislama (see the review article of Lynch, 1975, for a corrective) is based on a variety spoken on the northern island of Santo. Speakers from other islands recognise the localised nature of the variety, which they refer to as '*Bislama blong man Santo*'.

The existence of this regional variant may be accounted for by sociopolitical factors. Mühlhäusler (1986: 19) suggests that a form of regional dialect may be indicative of the fact that: 'indigenes from different parts of the archipelago traditionally went to work on different plantations'. Another factor was the French influence on the island, particularly in the administrative and economic centre, Luganville. This contributed to the intensely regional and separatist outlook which developed, with the growth of Jimmy Stephens' Nagriamel Movement in the 1970s. Before Independence, its opposition to the central government in the capital, Port Vila, grew. Then as now, the government was dominated by English-educated Anglicans and Presbyterians. This regional defiance found an expression in the dialect of Bislama spoken on Santo. The movement culminated in the 1980 Santo Rebellion, which dominated the months preceding Independence in Vanuatu in July of that year.

Ironic portents of changes in the country's language policy can be seen in the *dénouement* of the Santo crisis. The combined force of French and British marines, whose responsibility it had been to re-impose law and order on the island, failed to quell the rebellion. It was left to (pidgin-speaking) troops of the Papua New Guinea Defence Force to suppress the insurrection.

The unsuccessful outcome of the secessionist revolt resulted in considerable demographic changes on Santo. Supporters of Nagriamel from neighbouring islands who had congregated round their leader on Santo were repatriated, and many French residents were deported. Civil servants loyal to the central government took over administrative control of Luganville, which was increasingly referred to as 'Santo Town'. These changes, combined with a substantial increase in Bislama radio transmissions from Port Vila and the disappearance of privately-run newspapers (removing the Santo 'platform') are reflected in the progressively less distinctive nature of the Santo regionalect of Bislama. My own recent findings, based on fieldwork in South Santo in late 1986, suggest that substrate lexical features have been rapidly eroded since Independence. This, then, would appear to be a case of a post-colonial government seeking to eradicate regional language variation in the name of national unity. Mühlhäusler (n.d.) describes the decline in the diversity of languages in the Pacific region during the colonial period, as a result of pressure from colonial governments. In Vanuatu, however, we find an example of a decline in diversity under a post-colonial government, which has sought to supplant a politically marked variety of Bislama by an ideologically more acceptable form.

Speakers from the island, in common with those from other islands, often still betray their island of origin through certain phonological features of their Bislama. It should be stressed that regional forms were not restricted to Santo, only that the Santo variety was, perhaps, the most clear-cut example of a Bislama regionalect. Bislama, as we have seen, came to symbolise national unity. The use of Bislama by leaders of the Independence movement was calculated to act as a unifying force in the country, aimed at instilling feelings of nationalism which would transcend the traditional island loyalties of the populace. In the changed circumstances of the post-Independence period, the reflexive force of the language was channelled by the leaders of the young nation into ironing out regional differences. The dialect of the Port Vila area (home of the educated élite), and more particularly of the north of Efate (a Vanuaaku Pati stronghold), has become the predominant variety. The point could be made that a feature of creolisation is the degree to which a pidgin has come to represent and symbolise the aspirations of its users, not at an individual or regional level, but at a national level. This is not to deny the identifying function of a pidgin at a social level. However, when the function of the use of Bislama is to demonstrate the users' *national* identity, to express solidarity with speakers from their home country, not just their home island, then, perhaps, we can talk of the creolisation of Bislama.

Little research has been carried out into the social diversification of Bislama. However, unlike Mühlhäusler's findings in Papua New Guinea (1982: 439–66) my own observations would suggest a narrowing of the gap between 'rural' and 'urban' Bislama. It is undeniable that the better educated social group uses a more Anglicised form of Bislama, but it would be an over-simplification to assume that increasing contact with English will make Bislama more like English. The presence in Vanuatu of a significant minority of Bislama/French bilinguals should ensure that the conditions required for the development of a post-creole Bislama/English continuum are not met. It is arguable whether the mixing of Bislama and English should ever lead to the replacement of one language system by another. This can be demonstrated by a historical analysis of contact situations elsewhere in the Pacific. In Papua New Guinea and the Solomon Islands can be found examples of language genesis, where the speakers' goal was the creation of a contact medium, not the learning of any particular existing language. Fiji, on the other hand, illustrates another type of contact situation. In this case, a target language (English) clearly existed, which, in a non-native context, both socially and culturally, has undergone certain changes, which can be referred to as indigenisation or nativisation. This involves adopting carry-over features from the local languages without, however, leading to a radical reduction or restructuring of English in the process.

This, then, is a case of language change, rather than language genesis. In the absence of reliable research, the question of whether increased contact between Bislama and English (in either a native or nativised form) can be said to lead to a 'linguistic encounter of a third kind', or merely an urban sociolect, must be left open.

Opinions differ as to the intelligibility of the Anglicised urban sociolect in rural areas, that is, outside the capital, Port Vila. If the gap between rural and urban Bislama has indeed narrowed, it has mainly been the result of the rural population's ability to assimilate the rapid influx of new terms and concepts. Although Clark's description of the urban Bislama speakers' dilemma is sound, his conclusion may no longer be valid:

> The educated élite, faced with the task of translating these into Bislama, has often been content with mere transliteration or calquing, so that newspapers, radio broadcasts, and political speeches are typically larded with lexical and syntactic Anglicisms (occasionally Gallicisms) mainly unintelligible to unsophisticated village people.
>
> (1983: 540–41)

While agreeing with Clark that fuller use could be made of the existing resources of Bislama for lexical and idiomatic innovation, my own findings lead me to the conclusion that the rural population is remarkably receptive to the new terms. Proceedings in Parliament are broadcast live on the radio, which suspends its normal programmes. The debates may be punctuated with unfamiliar terms such as *amenmen* (amendment) and *ekseketif* (executive), but these are usually embedded in familiar Bislama in such a way that their meaning becomes clear. Non-urban speakers may initially have difficulty, but the majority of Ni-Vanuatu soon develop at least a passive understanding of these borrowings.

In addition to the usual agents of language spread, such as radio broadcasts, there is also the widespread practice of young people from the islands moving to the capital for short periods. These 'birds of passage' gain experience of urban life, and sometimes employment, for a few months, then return to their villages, acting as 'carriers' of the new Pidgin. Neologisms first heard at the Port Vila night-clubs soon gain currency in the islands, as the returning migrants spread the word. Bennett (1979: 69), reporting a similar phenomenon in the Solomon Islands, states that 'their input on return to their villages provides village youth with an age-group argot'.

In a paper based on a brief return visit to Vanuatu in April, 1983 Charpentier (1984) professes astonishment at what he terms the rapid 'depidginisation' of Bislama since Independence. He gloomily predicts that this will result in a kind of 'Bislamarenglish', or heavily nativised English, incomprehensible to English-speakers elsewhere. Charpentier rightly expresses concern at what he sees as Anglicisation of Bislama at a morphological and syntactic level. However, the examples he quotes are evidently instances of careless 'translationese', found in the Government newspaper, *Tam Tam*. He is also critical of lexical borrowings from political, diplomatic and administrative domains, which he regards as incomprehensible to most Ni-Vanuatu. However, his examples are presented in isolation, extracted from their full context. In late 1986, I carried out a small project with speakers of rural Bislama. They were given articles to read from the Bislama section of the trilingual *Vanuatu Weekly/Hebdomadaire* (as the Government newspaper has been renamed). Their subject matter resembled that of Charpentier's earlier survey. I ascertained that by using standard reading strategies, such as bottom-up and top-down processing, or inferencing, the readers succeeded in achieving a high level of comprehension. Whereas Charpentier expresses dismay at the inclusion of borrowings such as *kredensial* in Bislama texts, my own informants seemed unconcerned by the language of the following news item from the *Vanuatu Weekly* (No. 120:2):

> *Niufala Ambasada blong Sweden long Vanuatu emi presentem Kredensial mo Leta blong Rikol blong Ambasada blong bifo we emi tekem ples blong hem, i go long Hed blong State.*

The article concerns the newly accredited Ambassador of Sweden to Vanuatu, who presented his credentials and a letter of recall of his predecessor to the Head of State.

Most of my informants glanced at the headline '*Niufala Ambasada blong Sweden long Vanuatu*' and moved on to another article. The reaction of a passenger on the Clapham omnibus or Melbourne tram to similar reports of such diplomatic niceties would scarcely be different. Without labouring the point further, there are universals of language behaviour, which enable us to derive the appropriate level of meaning from a text; in this case the reading techniques of skimming and scanning.

A survey of the functions of Bislama was carried out by Charpentier shortly before Independence in 1980. Evidence showing the questionable nature of the survey's design which throws into doubt Charpentier's claims about the exact extent and use of Bislama can be found in

Thomas (1986: 48–51). Charpentier & Tryon (1982: 159), in a discussion of the results of this survey, recognise that Bislama will continue to flourish, but predict a bleak future (*fiutja, fuja, fiuja, fyuja, fija, fiutsa,* etc.) for the language (*languis, lanwis, lanwits, langwis,* etc.) in the educational domain: 'It is unlikely to become the language of education, for there are many practical obstacles in that direction'. These 'practical obstacles' must be assumed to include issues relating to corpus planning, such as the establishment of a superimposed standard variety, and the provision of standard spelling.

I have already sought to demonstrate that considerable progress towards the standardisation of Bislama has been made in recent years. Since Charpentier & Tryon's (1982) analysis, further steps have been taken in the direction of a standardised orthography of the language. In 1984, for example, the Bislama Bible Translation Team published its *Fasin blong Raetem Bislama*. The standard word list which it contained was a monolingual extension of Camden's well-received *Descriptive Dictionary — Bislama to English* (1977). The word list has been widely disseminated through government departments in Vanuatu, and should contribute to the creation of an orthographic norm for educational purposes, and for more extensive publishing in Bislama. A measure towards an improved Bislama in the media has been the running of workshops in Bislama translation techniques by the Pacific Languages Unit of the University of the South Pacific in Port Vila. Tryon's *Tok Tok Bislama* (1988) will provide newcomers to the language with the most detailed introductory course yet to conversational Bislama. The existence of such a course should be ample proof to non-speakers of Bislama that, far from being a 'bastardised English', the language has a distinct and separate identity.

Early in 1986, further discussions were held in Port Vila, aimed at ensuring the preservation and development of the Pidgin and vernacular languages of Melanesia. The meeting, described as a 'linguistics think-tank' (Crowley, 1986: 49), led Melanesian education policy-makers, administrators and academics to produce for Melanesian governments a series of recommendations to consider as options for official language policies in each country. The position of Melanesian languages in the education systems of the region provided the pivot for these discussions. One suggestion made at this meeting was that Bislama should be taught as an optional subject at high schools in New Caledonia. Given the historical importance of 'Bichelamar' in that territory, Bislama justly can be said to form a significant part of the heritage of the Kanak people.

A major landmark for Bislama in both status and corpus planning was the establishment in 1987 of a university-accredited course in Bislama, for Bislama speakers. Entitled *Introdaksen long Stadi blong Bislama*, the course includes materials designed exclusively in Bislama by the Pacific Languages Unit of the University of the South Pacific. Its *Grama blong Bislama* is the most comprehensive description of the grammar of Bislama so far undertaken.

The orthography for the course is substantially that of the 1984 word list. The materials include a paper by Crowley & Lynch dealing with the aspect of language-engineering relating to the modernisation of Bislama. This contains recommendations on what Laycock (1975) termed 'pidgineering' i.e. using the internal word-formation potential of a pidgin, rather than borrowing, so that the character of the language remains intact.

Another important development was the setting up in 1986 of the 'Komiti Blong Bislama'. This committee comprises representatives from the media, Department of Language, and the University of the South Pacific. Its aim is to examine ways of arriving at accepted norms for Bislama, in areas such as graphisation, standardisation and modernisation. The first issue of its publication, entitled *Olsem wanem bae yumi raetem Bislama* (n.d.), makes proposals regarding a standardised orthography. The committee is ideally placed as a clearing-house for proposals from all sources relating to the above issues, such as Camden's (n.d.) recent paper on the written forms of /i/ and /u/ in Bislama.

A Proposed Language-in-Education Policy for Vanuatu

The 'practical obstacles' to change in language policies should not be minimised. Political uncertainty in Fiji could undermine work presently being undertaken by the Pacific Languages Unit of the University of the South Pacific in Port Vila in the areas of both status and corpus planning. Even natural disasters such as cyclone Uma in January, 1987 seem to have conspired to delay progress towards change. However, there appears to be a new willingness on the part of Ni-Vanuatu to assume a greater responsibility for the direction which their education system will take in the future.

My own proposals regarding a language-in-education policy for Vanuatu are summarised in Table 1.

TABLE 1 *Proposed language-in-education plan for Vanuatu*

Class	Language as medium	Language as subject
Primary		
1	Bislama (+vernacular)	(vernacular)
2	Bislama (+vernacular)	(vernacular)
3	Bislama	EFL/FFL (+vernacular)
4	Bislama	EFL/FFL (+vernacular)
5	Bislama + ESL/FSL	FFL/EFL (+vernacular)
6	Bislama + ESL/FSL	FFL/EFL (+vernacular)
Junior High		
7		
8	Bislama + ESL/FSL	FFL/EFL
9		
Senior High		
10→	ESL/FSL	Bislama + FFL/EFL

The complex nature of the table merely reflects the complexity of the language situation in the country. However, during the period of compulsory education (nine years is the goal of the present Ministry of Education) there is only one important transition.

Looking more closely at the proposals, the following points should be made:

(1) In the first two years of primary school, Bislama would be a medium of instruction in all state schools. However, in schools with homogeneous speech communities, where teachers were in a position to use the local vernacular, this language could also serve as a medium for teaching initial literacy. Failing this, suitably qualified members of the local community could be made responsible for providing instruction in matters relating to traditional culture. In this case, the vernacular would enjoy subject status. Hence the inclusion of the vernacular in both columns.

(2) English or French would be taught as a foreign language (EFL/FFL) in the third and fourth years. The vernacular would remain in the curriculum as a subject, where this was feasible.

(3) The major transition would occur in the fifth year, when English or French would join Bislama as a medium of instruction, hence ESL/FSL. The other European language would be introduced as a

subject. For example, in a school staffed predominantly by teachers trained in English, English (ESL) would be a medium in Classes Five and Six, with French being taught as a subject (FFL) by a French-trained teacher. A vernacular would continue as a subject, depending on local circumstances.

(4) The same arrangement would apply to the three years of junior high school. The teaching of any one vernacular would be impracticable, as pupils from different language backgrounds would be grouped together at the still limited number of boarding schools.

(5) English or French would become the sole medium of instruction only after the period of compulsory education, namely at the beginning of senior high school. The present proportion of Ni-Vanuatu for whom places at this level are available is still relatively low.

A significant advantage of the above scheme over the existing system is the flexibility it would provide. The present system effectively commits children to an education in the language in which they first set foot on the educational ladder. Introducing both 'foreign' languages in primary school opens the door to a possible switch if the parents so choose, or if a change in their circumstances requires them to move to a district where the local school favours the other language. The question of which schools would be designated ESL + FFL, and which ones FSL + EFL would be a matter for negotiation between the Ministry and local communities.

The above plan may appear unduly complicated to those who argue for the maintenance of the *status quo*. The cost resulting from the re-training of teachers and preparation of new materials would also be seen as a deterrent to change. However, my seven-year experience of the present system has convinced me of the need for change. Inevitably teachers will express reservations about teaching in the languages they have been conditioned to shun (at least, officially) in the classroom. They will need encouragement to be more self-reliant in the area of syllabus design and the development of teaching resources.

Paradoxically, the existence of Bislama to perform the function of link language in the community should preclude the development of highly nativised forms of the European languages. Use-oriented variety has already been noted in the form of English spoken in Vanuatu, with speech variants in certain registers which result from the use of English in non-native contexts (Thomas, 1986: 78). User-oriented variety, a function of the indicative or reflexive force of language, is minimally present in the local form of English. The same can be said for the variety of French spoken locally. It is Bislama that serves as a vehicle for Ni-Vanuatu to express their identity, or to show their solidarity with a particular group or groups.

It is to be hoped, then, that the negative attitudes and inherited prejudices which have so far proved insurmountable obstacles to a reappraisal of language policy in Vanuatu are being dispelled. Doubts about the viability of Bislama and the vernacular languages as media of instruction have, hitherto, led to feelings of language insecurity. In the post-colonial period, there is likely to be less pressure on parents to regard English or French as the sole key to wealth and economic progress. Some would go so far as to claim that in present-day Vanuatu a knowledge of English or French is almost totally irrelevant for many school leavers.

A variety of factors have led to a questioning of the view which has so far prevailed, namely that Bislama and the island vernaculars were unsuitable for educational purposes. In arguing the case for reform, I have sought to identify and describe the events and agents which have contributed to the changed mood in which such reform should be possible. This reform must take into account the new language realities in Vanuatu. English, and to a lesser degree French, will increasingly be used only for international communication, with Bislama assuming the role of language of intra-national communication. The renewed interest in local languages will be maintained, as it is more widely perceived that they are essential for the preservation of indigenous custom and culture. But there must be recognition that Bislama fulfils an over-arching role, not so much caught in the middle between the traditional and the modern, between Melanesian vernacular and metropolitan importation, but astride the two, having a foot in both camps.

References

BENNETT, J. A. (1979), Solomon Islands Pidgin. In S. A. WURM (ed.) *New Guinea and Neighbouring Areas: A Sociolinguistic Laboratory*. The Hague: Mouton.

Bislama Bible Translation Team (1984), *Fasin Blong Raetem Bislama*. Canberra: Australian National University Research School of Pacific Studies.

CAMDEN, W. G. (1977), *A Descriptive Dictionary: Bislama to English*. Port Vila.

— (n.d.), *Fasin Blong Raetem Tufala Saon Ya i mo u Long Bislama*. Unpublished MS.

CHARPENTIER, J.-M. (1979), *Le Pidgin Bislama(n) et le Multilinguisme aux Nouvelles-Hébrides*. Paris: SELAF.

— (1984), Le pidgin Bichelamar avant et après l'indépendance de Vanuatu. In R. B. LEPAGE (ed.) *York Papers in Linguistics* 11, 51–61.

CHARPENTIER, J.-M. & TRYON, D. T. (1982), Functions of Bislama in the New Hebrides and independent Vanuatu. *English World Wide* (3) 2, 146–60.

CLARK, R. (1977), On the origin and usage of the term 'Beach-la-Mar'. *Te Reo* 20, 71–82.

— (1979), In search of Beach-la-Mar. *Te Reo* 22, 3–64.

— (1983), Review of *Le Pidgin Bislama(n) et le Multilinguisme aux Nouvelles-Hébrides* by J.-M. CHARPENTIER (1979). *Language in Society* 12, 539–42.

CROWLEY, T. (1984), Pacific languages: directions for the future. *Language Planning Newsletter* 10 (4), 1–2.

— (1986), Minding your language. *Islands Business* 12 (3), 49–52.

CROWLEY, T. & LYNCH, J. (1986), *Language Development in Melanesia*. Suva: Pacific Languages Unit (USP) and Department of Language and Literature (UPNG).

GUY, J. B. M. (1974), *Handbook of Bichelamar, Manuel de Bichelamar*. Canberra: ANU, Pacific Linguistics C34.

HOLLYMAN, K. J. (1976), Les pidgins européens de la région calédonienne. *Te Reo* 19, 25–65.

KOMITI BLONG BISLAMA (n.d.), *Olsem Wanem Bae Yumi Raetem Bislama*. No. 1. Port Vila.

LAYCOCK, D. C. (1975), Pidgineering. In K. A. MCELHANON (ed.) *Tok Pisin I Go We: Kivung Special Publication* No. 1. Port Moresby.

LYNCH, J. (1975), Bislama phonology and grammar: a review article. *Kivung* 8 (2).

MACCLANCY, J. V. (1980), *To Kill a Bird with Two Stones: A Short History of Vanuatu*. Vanuatu Cultural Centre Publications No. 1.

MÜHLHÄUSLER, P. (1978), Samoan plantation Pidgin English and the origin of New Guinea Pidgin. *Papers in Pidgin and Creole Linguistics* No. 1. Canberra: ANU, Pacific Linguistics. A–54, 67–120.

— (1981), Foreigner Talk: Tok Masta in New Guinea. *International Journal of the Sociology of Language* 28, 98–113.

— (1982), Tok Pisin in Papua New Guinea. In R. W. BAILEY & M. GORLACH (eds.) *English as a World Language*. Ann Arbor: University of Michigan Press.

— (1986), *Pidgin and Creole Linguistics*. Oxford: Basil Blackwell.

— (n.d.), *The Politics of Small Languages in Australia and the Pacific*. Oxford University: Linacre College.

Nabanga (1978), Publication of the French Residency No. 88, 2. Port Vila.

New Hebrides Biennial Report 1971 and 1972 (1973), British Service of the New Hebrides, for H.M.S.O.

Pacific Churches Research Centre and USP Centre (1981), *Report of the Vanuatu Language Planning Conference*. Port Vila.

Pacific Languages Unit, USP (1984), *Report on the Conference 'Pacific Languages: Directions for the Future'*. Port Vila.

SCHUCHARDT, H. (1883 and 1889/1980). In G. G. GILBERT, ed., *Pidgin and Creole Languages: Selected Essays by Hugo Schuchardt*. Cambridge: Cambridge University Press.

THOMAS, A. E. (1986), *English Language in Contact; Contact Literature in English: Profiles from the South Pacific*. Unpublished M.A. Dissertation. University of London Institute of Education.

TOPPING, D.M. (1982), Language planning issues in Vanuatu. *Language Planning Newsletter* 8 (2), 1–4.

TRYON, D. T. (1979), The language situation in the New Hebrides. In S. A. WURM (ed.) *New Guinea and Neighbouring Areas: A Sociolinguistic Laboratory*. The Hague: Mouton.

— (1988), *Tok Tok Bislama*. Canberra: Australian National University Research School of Pacific Studies.

Vanuatu Ministry of Education (1982), *Education in Vanuatu: Policy Document*.

14 Education and language planning in the Samoas[1]

RICHARD B. BALDAUF, JR

Introduction

The Samoan Islands are a culturally and linguistically homogeneous island group which has been politically divided since 1900. Eastern or American Samoa is a small (197 sq. km in area, with a population of about 34,500) mountainous American territory with a magnificent harbour which originally served as a naval station. Its relatively high per capita income is largely due to employment generated by United States Government programs and services. Western Samoa, which is much larger (2,934 sq. km in area, with a population of about 163,000), is economically self-sufficient, but at a subsistence level. It was a German colonial possession until 1914 when New Zealand took over its administration. It has been an independent country since 1962. Western Samoan families have traditionally held most of the social status and political power in the islands. Given the unequal distribution of social/political status and wealth which divides the islands, a politically divided Samoa seems likely for the foreseeable future.

Samoa still retains a strong common cultural and linguistic heritage, including the common colonial language of English. However, since 1900 the colonial powers have created not only different economic and political situations in the two Samoas, but have introduced Westernization and language change. These changes, particularly as they relate to education and language development, are the major focus of this chapter.

The Language Situation

Samoan language speakers, together with speakers of Fijian, now comprise the largest indigenous language communities in Oceania.

Samoan is a homogeneous language which has almost no regional variation. It is characterized instead by social variation (i.e. chiefly versus ordinary Samoan) which reflects the highly stratified and ceremonially-orientated nature of traditional Samoan culture. The Samoan language also has two distinct phonological styles, the 'T' or dental style and the 'K' or velar style, which are independent of the lexical variation found in honorific speech. The T style has greater prestige and is generally used in formal situations or when writing. The Samoan language literacy rate is estimated to be over 97% for adult Samoans (Pawley, 1981).[2]

English is spoken as a first language by a few hundred expatriates in each of the Samoas and by a growing number of returning Samoans who were raised either in the United States or in New Zealand. In American Samoa most people under 35 have some English language fluency. In Western Samoa, the proportion of people with English language proficiency is much smaller.

Pressures for linguistic change have been greater in American Samoa than in Western Samoa. This may be due in part to the greater economic development and universal free education through to grade 12 which have been features of that society for nearly 25 years. Also, it is undoubtedly influenced by the fact that American Samoans are U.S.A. nationals and have unrestricted access to the U.S.A. It has been estimated that there are twice as many Samoans living in Hawaii and the mainland U.S.A. as in American Samoa (Lewthwaite *et al.*, 1973). This situation has created a need for many Samoans to acquire native-like English language skills to be able to compete on an equal basis with non-Samoans in American society for educational and employment opportunities. These perceived needs have in turn created one of the pressures for upgrading English in the Samoan educational system. For this and other reasons which have been argued more extensively elsewhere (Baldauf, 1981), the educational system has been a major focus for language planning developments in the American territory.

The Sociolinguistic Context

Although the Samoan language remains the major vehicle for oral communication, most Samoans — particularly those living in American Samoa — are to some degree bilingual, and can attend to media in both Samoan and English. English serves as an important vehicle for media communication in Samoan society. Television, broadcast by KZVK on two channels from American Samoa, is received in most parts of the islands. An examination of a television schedule for a week in August, 1981 revealed 97 hours of evening English language programming, while only 13 hours, mainly local news, were broadcast in Samoan. Anderson (1977) reports that viewers of Samoan language programs tend to be older than those for English language ones. Schramm *et al.* (1981) found that not only does television affect English proficiency but that the advertisements have created demand for previously unheard of commercial products. These observations suggest the increasing importance of English as the broadcast medium of communication.

The local newspapers provide another indication of language usage. In American Samoa a check by the author of 52 issues of the Government's *News Bulletin* from 1976 to 1981 located only 13 issues with items written in Samoan, which accounted for about 12% of the space in those issues; 22 issues of the Pago Pago weekly, the *Samoa News*, between 1977 and 1981 contained between 4 and 19% of items written in the Samoan language, with an average of about 8%. Many of the Samoan language items were translations of previously published English language materials. Thus, the print-media fosters English language usage by providing access to outside events through wire service news for its English language readers. Only local events and notices appear in both languages.

In Western Samoa, the Government produces two editions of *Savali*, one in English and one in Samoan. This fortnightly paper carries mainly government news and notices. Four newspapers, *The Samoa Times*, *The Observer*, *The Samoa Weekly* and the *South Seas Star* are published in Apia in both English and Samoan. *O le Tusitala Samoa* is a 12-page weekly that is published entirely in Samoan. Thus, while Western Samoan print-media is less English language oriented than its American Samoan counterpart, English remains an important communicative medium.

Each of the Samoas has its own radio station which can be heard throughout the islands. WVUV in American Samoa is a commercial station which operates 24 hours a day, broadcasting mainly popular music and news. In Western Samoa 2AP broadcasts a variety of news, entertainment and schools programmes. Both stations broadcast some programs in English and some in Samoan. The evening service of 2AP consists of two channels, one in English and the other in Samoan.

The predominance of English also appears in other media areas. Films, whose popularity has declined since the advent of TV, consist mainly of low standard English language productions. There are only three bookshops in Samoa, two in Apia and one in Pago Pago. They are run as part of missionary activities and sell mainly religious books and classics, almost all of which are in English. Both Samoas have central library services and mobile units to bring books to the people. These services are used most heavily by students and those people living in the capital 'city' areas. Most of the materials are in English. Despite recent commendable efforts by both Education Departments and by the missions to produce Samoan language print materials, only a relatively few items have been published to date and these are not always easily available.

Some extent of the use of the Samoan and English languages in other linguistic domains can be judged from figures which I collected in a survey done in May, 1973 from 300 of a total of 503 high school graduates in American Samoa. These figures indicate that in the extended family situation (parents, siblings, aunts and uncles, and the pastor) 69% of those responding spoke Samoan or mostly Samoan, 23% used both Samoan and English, while only 7% used English or mostly English. In interpersonal situations with best friends, classmates, teachers and storekeepers 20% had a Samoan orientation, 50% used both languages about equally while 29% favoured English. In situational usage of a personal nature (thinking, praying, teasing, and joking) 44% used Samoan or mostly Samoan, while only 8% used the Samoan language predominantly for impersonal uses such as writing, homework, listening to the radio or television (Baldauf, 1984).

These figures for graduates from an English language medium of instruction high school program indicate that Samoan is still the dominant language in the islands, especially in personal situations. Domains of high English language usage encompass mainly to school and media situations. There can be little doubt that if a comparable study had been carried out in Western Samoa, which does not have universal high school education, the Samoan language usage would have been found to be much higher.

Although more English is used in American Samoa, there remain many linguistic similarities in language use between the two parts of Samoa. English is the language used to conduct business in government departments and in the commercial sector. Yet an observer of Samoan society would note that much daily business is conducted in Samoan, with English used as necessary to include English-only speakers. Most official forms are available in Samoan and/or English, and both High Court proceedings are generally conducted in the two languages.

In the American Samoan *fono* (legislature) both the English and Samoan languages are used to set |out all| bills.| Legislation is usually introduced and debated in Samoan with bills later being translated into English. Where debates or bills are introduced in English, they must be translated immediately into Samoan for the understanding of the whole house. It is interesting to note in reading the legislative record that the required translation process often leads to the discussion of comparable meanings in English and Samoan. In the Western Samoan *fono* debates are conducted in Samoan with simultaneous English translation.

This summary of the sociolinguistic situation in Samoa indicates that English has become a major language in Samoan society. At the same time, John Kneubuhl (1981), a well-known Samoan writer, reported that the Samoan language remains 'in healthy condition' although other languages all have their influence on Samoan. Kneubuhl said he realizes Samoans are stronger in speaking Samoan than in writing it and that the Samoan written language should be standardized.

Church Sponsored Education[3]

The early missionaries came to Samoa to teach the gospel and to train pastors. Some time after 1836 they introduced formal education, which included Samoan literacy training, basic education with an emphasis on biblical studies, and some practical subjects, as a major way of reaching their religious goal. By 1854 it was claimed that 25% of the population were literate in their own language (Pitt, 1970: 21). By 1902, when the United States Navy took over administration of the eastern islands, there were 55 *faife'au* schools. This form of education has declined markedly in the last three decades with the coming of television and large-scale Westernization.

The teaching of the Samoan language in the *faife'au* schools and its use with religious materials represents a successful instance of planned vernacular literacy development (cf. Huebner, 1986). The missionaries wanted vernacular literacy so that Samoans could read the vernacular bible. However, Christianity spread so rapidly that the control of the churches soon passed from the missionaries to the Samoan *faife'au* and the desire for universal vernacular literacy gradually became a Samoan cultural institution. Only in recent years with the decline of the *faife'au* schools and the return of Samoans born in the U.S.A. has there been a decline in literacy standards.

Government Education to 1932

American Samoa is ruled by a governor, until 1951 a United States naval officer and subsequently, until 1978, a presidential political appointee. While naval officers in the early years had the ability to rule by fiat, this power was muted by lack of funds and staff, and by policy established by the first governor, Commander Tilly. He declared land ownership should be exclusively in government or Samoan hands, that Samoan laws and customs would be preserved, and that Samoans would run their own local affairs (Gray, 1960: 126). However, this directive did not seem to apply to the early policies and aims of the governmental educational system, which reflected colonial educational thinking of the time, and which implied United States educational practices could be transplanted to Samoa without any disadvantage at all (Reid, 1941). Early schools aimed to teach Samoans English to make Samoa 'an English speaking colony' (Stearns, 1914). The education regulation issued in 1914 was intended primarily '. . . to absolutely require English be taught in every school in American Samoa' (Sanchez: 1955: 84).

> The Governor in American Samoa believed that . . . in planning an educational system the first important question was the language in which education was to be imparted. . . . Since textbooks in Samoan language covered only primary subjects, it was necessary to adopt the English language in the schools . . . If the Samoan race is going to elevate itself to the standards of Western Civilization, it must be able to read the literature of the world and to pursue scientific studies. . .
>
> (Graham, 1928)

These English language teaching policies had some community support, as many Samoans realized there were advantages in learning English. However, there was a widespread dissatisfaction among the population because children were not being taught Samoan or Samoan customs (Sanchez, 1955). In 1932 one school superintendent stated:

> The effect of Americanism in our public schools and the life in the American colony has influenced the young natives to look upon the customs and habits of the American people as ideal; to believe that their elders are primitive and foolish.
>
> (Department of Education, 1932)

The early colonial administrators, then, steeped in a 'white man's burden' philosophy, introduced English into the educational domain as a first step to bringing 'culture' to Samoa. However, the learning of English, seen as the core of Samoan educational development, was imposed on the

Samoan educational system rather than integrated into it as the *faife'au* schools had been. Perhaps this was the reason that the schools were not very successful in creating many English-speaking Samoans. In general, these policies generated dissatisfaction with the educational system.

Government Education, 1933 to 1961

Beginning in 1933, a new educational policy based on discussions with village leaders was adopted. This new policy subscribed to the following two aims as listed in the 1938 Annual Report of the Department of Education:

(1) to give all children of American Samoa an elementary education in the language, which will open to them the vast field of knowledge which Samoan language at present cannot and perhaps never will touch, and
(2) to make them increasingly conscious and proud of their own Samoan heritage of arts, crafts, customs and culture, in the hope that these may not disintegrate under the influence of increasing contact with the world beyond (cited in Sanchez, 1955: 87).

These two principles remained the basis of educational policy until 1961. Although they seemed to differ from earlier policy, English language and American curriculum continued to dominate the school system. This continued lack of policy balance can be seen in a statement from the 1935 Annual Report of the Department of Education which stated that:

It is further recognized that the present practice of translating in the Samoan language is costly in time, and, of more serious consequence, a handicap to the learning of English. Therefore, no other language than English shall be used in public schools . . .
(cited in Sanchez, 1955: 173)

Although Department of Education reports in the early 1940s began to reflect a nascent recognition of the value of the Samoan language in the early grades, it was not until about 1949 that it was officially used extensively in the early primary grades. This policy continued throughout the 1950s, but neither the Samoan leaders nor visiting American educators were satisfied that the system was working well. Many pupils were not becoming literate in either Samoan or English (Long & Greuning, 1961: 147).

During this period language plans continued to be made and implemented by American government leaders; these yielded little planned language change. What emerged was a linguistic stalemate where Samoan flourished in the church and the community while English struggled in the schools for viability. Without consistent policy, staff continuity, physical resources, and community support, little real progress was made on plans to develop English language competence in the Samoan community.

Pressures for further language development

Despite the apparent linguistic stand-off which existed in the Samoan community, there were other important pressures for linguistic change which were developing in the community. Pitt (1970: 219) points out that besides literacy development 'missionaries usually thought the economic development of the native people to be a part of their task of propagating the gospel'. This was shown through the teaching of practical subjects in the *faife'au* schools and through projects to make the missions self-supporting.

The need to focus on economic issues became increasingly important in American Samoa because there was little arable land and because the population had increased 253% between 1900 and 1960. These population pressures forced a significant number of young people to migrate to Hawaii or the American mainland each year where they had to fit into an English-speaking economy. This in turn created pressures to improve drastically English language instruction in the schools (Schramm *et al.*, 1981). These pressures, along with a growing American awareness of their neglect of Samoa during the first 60 years of colonial rule, led to the creation of a new set of educational language plans, this time backed with money and technology.

Co-operative Education

When Governor H. Rex Lee arrived in Pago Pago in May, 1961, he was unprepared for what he found. Many children were not in school and many teachers who were supposed to teach all subjects in English were not fluent in it. Lee believed 'there was no time for waiting, . . . what was needed was a sudden and explosive upgrading' of the educational system (cited in Kaiser, 1965: 58). He believed this could best be accomplished through the creation of good school facilities and by using 'a co-operative system of instruction making maximum use of television' (Bronson, 1968: 9).

Lee had developed a plan, the aim of which was to educate Samoan children to a standard equivalent to their native-speaking counterparts in the U.S.A. With massive economic backing from the United States Congress, in 18 months he transformed the village school system into a modern television-centred one using American teachers. Although the designers of co-operative education felt the new curriculum was more relevant to the needs and situations of Samoan students, the central focus was on the ability to communicate in English. Teaching in Samoan was virtually eliminated from the curriculum except as a subject during the first two years of school.

While co-operative education undoubtedly had a massive impact on language usage in American Samoa, its success as a language planning exercise was limited. Although sufficient resources were made available to make it work, and Governor Lee was prepared to tolerate no opposition to the project, a review of the system by a variety of consultants in the early 1970s concluded that the system was not meeting its objectives of providing an education equivalent to that available in the United States. This was particularly true in the area of English language fluency. On the basis of these recommendations, the time devoted to English language instruction in high schools was doubled (Nelson, 1971).

Several reasons can be advanced to explain why co-operative education did not radically alter language use patterns in the Samoan society. First, it lacked support in the Samoan community and among many educators. Its implementation came from above without consultation with community leaders and depended for its survival upon a few key individuals who eventually left the project. As the Samoan community itself was alienated from the process, many Samoans actively discouraged English from being used as a community language (National Association of Educational Broadcasters, 1962: 11). Second, the plan tried to do too much too rapidly. Not only was a lot of waste created by trying to change the system overnight, but unrealistic expectations were generated. This relative failure of the system made it increasingly difficult to maintain support for the plan. Finally, although co-operative education had a feedback system built into it, this quickly broke down. Formal evaluation was not included in the design of the project because it was argued that only the progress of students who had been through the entire system could reasonably be judged. Without proper feedback or evaluation, planning as a process broke down and co-operative education became increasingly stagnant and irrelevant to the real language skills possessed by Samoan teachers and students. Eventually this failure to meet the changing situation turned many educators against the system (Schramm *et al.*, 1981).

The introduction of co-operative education had many unintended side effects, especially in the economic sphere. The massive inflow of capital created many new jobs and community facilities, not only in education but in other domains. Whereas the traditional economy was built around subsistence farming and fishing, the new economy was built around salaried employees, nearly half of whom were employed by the government. Transportation greatly improved, thereby increasing access to the U.S.A. As Samoans moved out of their traditional roles, the demand for them to be proficient in English increased.

Recent educational developments

In the early 1970s, a detailed survey of educational needs in the Samoan community concluded that the two most critical needs, out of ten listed were:

(1) *Command of English.* At all age levels, pupils need to read, speak, write and aurally comprehend English at a higher level of proficiency than is currently the case.
(2) *Mastery of Samoan language and knowledge of Samoan culture.* Students need to develop greater fluency in the Samoan language . . . (Thomas & Titiali'i, 1973: 59).

Under the leadership of Samoan Directors of Education steps towards these goals have gradually been implemented. English-as-a-second-language programs have been consolidated and refined. An English medium program has also been made available in five primary schools for those students who have a fluent command of English. Programs are now primarily delivered by classroom teachers, although televised oral English instruction continues to provide elementary students with native speaker language models.

Although Samoan language arts have been taught in elementary schools since 1965, the main function of Samoan language teaching has always been as a transitional program until English skills were learned. In 1979, this program was redesigned and expanded to include grades 1–4. In 1980, a Samoan language arts program was available for grades 1–8 along with two high school level Samoan language and culture electives.

The new program takes a maintenance approach to Samoan language development. A Samoan-as-a-second-language program was also started in a few schools in 1980 for those ethnic Samoans for whom English is a first language (Department of Education, 1980).

The development of these programs was made possible through Title 1 (Compensatory Education) and Bilingual Education grants from the U.S.A. Government. However, it has been the Samoans themselves, who now for the first time control their own educational system, who have taken the lead in re-ordering the system toward one with bilingual goals.

Thomas (1981) has suggested that the goal of true bilingualism creates unreasonable expectations about what can reasonably be achieved. As was the case with co-operative education, unrealistic expectations can undermine efforts to collect accurate evaluation information and to use it appropriately. As these language programs are still in their formative stages, it is too early to tell how they will affect community language use patterns.

Development of Education in Western Samoa[4]

Until the political division of Samoa in 1900, education throughout the islands was church sponsored and *faife'au* schools were part of every church (cf. Huebner, 1986). The London Missionary Society had the most extensive school network which included 'district' schools and higher schools. The Methodist, Roman Catholic and Mormon missions had similarly structured but much less extensive systems of religious training. In 1844 missionaries compiled and printed some Samoan language tracts and in the same year the largest mission, the London Missionary Society, opened a theological college at Malua for Samoan *faife'au*.

> By the first of (these events) the Native language took on a permanent form, and was no longer subject, without due sanction, to those changes incidental to all living tongues; the accumulated knowledge of one generation could be passed on to the next in a medium secure from interference ... In the last event the way was opened to the Samoan to receive systematic instruction in religious matters, which ever since have bulked so largely in his affairs.
>
> (*Handbook of Western Samoa*, 1925: 9)

For eighty years, little happened to change this order of things. The German Governor, Dr Solf, was interested mainly in commerce and keeping the peace and left education and language mainly to the missions, who were paid a small subsidy and were asked to stress practical skills. There was also a German private school near Apia which provided for the education of white and part-Samoan children. In 1904 the German administration took over this school and renamed it 'Ifi Ifi', thus marking the modest start of government sponsored education. Later a government high school was started at Malifa, near Apia, to train Samoans for government service. In terms of language planning, German aims were modest. The German language was taught at this government school, which had the aim of preparing government officials, and to a limited extent in the higher mission schools. In all other schools instruction continued to be in Samoan.

In 1920 New Zealand became the post-war ruling colonial power under a League of Nations mandate. Its initial proposals to upgrade the schools did not meet with much enthusiasm from either the missions or the local population who worried about the increased expense and the duplication of facilities which might result. In the mid-1920s a compromise was reached under which three grades of school were created. Grade I schools (Pastors' Mission Schools) enrolled children aged 5–10 years and provided basic instruction in Samoan in the 'three R's'. The schools were completely mission-controlled and continued the educational provisions already established. In the early 1930s there were about 300 of these schools enrolling 10,000 children.

Grade II schools (Mission Schools) were jointly supervised and funded 'district' schools. They had a standard curriculum which included English as a subject but which was taught by *faife'au* in Samoan. In 1931 there were 45 of these schools enrolling about 4,000 students.

Grade III schools included both the government schools, Malifa on Upolu, Vaipouli on Savai'i and the top school Avele, near Apia, and 16 higher mission boarding schools and three theological colleges. Total enrolment in these schools was about 1,850 students. The government schools were run using white teachers with the assistance of qualified Samoan helpers. Instruction in these schools was in English with an emphasis placed on practical and agricultural skills. The mission schools were more theological in content and placed less emphasis on English.

In 1924 government officials indicated that:

educational policy should not educate the Samoan child too much in advance of their surroundings and social conditions, but should have for its object the making of good citizens. A joint conference of government and mission educationalists agreed unanimously that 'Europeanising' the native was most undesirable, and proposed that the teaching of English be curtailed for the time being.

(Keesing, 1934: 420–421)

However, in 1929 the Chief Inspector of Primary Schools in New Zealand, after a visit to Samoa, reported that:

Above all, there is evident a desire to learn, and the one subject in which this 'urge' is most manifest is English. The schools . . . have now reached a point where I think that the desire for English should be more fully met . . .

(Keesing, 1934: 424)

These official statements are indicative of the debate of the period both among educationalists and among Samoans in Western Samoa. On the one hand, government education and English language instruction were seen as causing social disruption, maladjustment to village life, and the destruction of the *fa'a Samoa* (the Samoan way of life). On the other hand, it was argued that Samoans needed education and English language skills to open the way for wider opportunities and, ultimately, to make it possible for Samoans to rule their own affairs.

Thus, New Zealand's efforts during the mandate period can be seen as well-intentioned but extremely modest. The education provided was conducted mainly in Samoan and under the auspices of the missions. No clear cut language policy was developed and education was left to go on pretty much as it was. Hence, by 1945 there was:

an extreme shortage of schools, severe overcrowding in classrooms, teachers' lack of education and training and an almost complete absence of facilities for post-primary and technical education.

(Barrington, 1973: 256)

Educational development under the United Nations trusteeship

In 1945 New Zealand undertook to upgrade the educational system in Western Samoa consistent with the needs of self-government. A number of actions were taken to implement this. A section of the Education Department was created for islands education to provide professional support, teachers were seconded to aid educational development, facilities were improved, and scholarships were granted to Samoans to study in New Zealand. During this period the government replaced the missions as the major educating body, so that by 1956 about two thirds of all students were in government schools (Ma'ia'i, 1957). The reason for this shift was simple from the Samoan perspective:

> To the question, 'What is education?', the Islanders in the main would promptly reply, 'Knowing how to speak English'. . . Education is still a means of getting office work because this lends to prestige.
>
> (Ma'ia'i, 1957: 57)

Government schools provided an increased emphasis on English during this period enabling graduates to get jobs and thereby making government schools more attractive than the mission school alternative.

In terms of language policy, the Samoan language came to be seen as a bridge to English rather than as an acceptable medium of instruction. With the provision of more funds, it became possible to implement this as educational language policy. In the 1950s the bilingual model, featuring English as a second language, was held out as the model to follow (Benton, 1981).

Some of the educational changes during this period can be attributed to the United Nations Trusteeship Council missions which visited Samoa and made suggestions and recommendations. Barrington (1973) believes that much less would have been accomplished during this period had New Zealand not been put in the international spotlight by the Council's visits and deliberations.

Educational developments since independence

The years since independence in 1962 have been marked by further developments in the bilingual approach to education. The development and implementation of the Tate Oral English course in the schools in the 1960s has led to the widespread availability of basic English skills. At the same time recent Directors of Education have stressed the importance of vernacular education. A Samoan language and customs syllabus was introduced in 1966 and made subject to examination in 1971 (Amosa & Hanna, 1974). 'By the late 1970s consideration was being given to making Samoan the major language of instruction during at least the first four years of primary schooling' (Benton, 1981:89), as it was and continues to be in the remaining *faife'au* schools.[2]

Towards the end of the 1970s junior secondary schools were expanded to cater for an increasing proportion of primary school leavers. A secondary teacher training college was established in Apia, partly staffed and organized by Australians from Macquarie University. These developments intensified English language development at this level and affected many more individuals than in the past (Benton, 1981).

Thus, moves have been made in Western Samoa since independence to strengthen both the standard of English and Samoan, thereby lending some substance to the bilingual policy begun earlier. However, to develop a truly bilingual program, 'Samoan must develop both an indigenous literature and printed materials of academic worth' which are seen as equal to those available in English (Benton, 1981: 91). This process is under way, but proceeding slowly.

Conclusions

The planned introduction of English as a second language into the Samoas has proved to be much more difficult than anyone would have foreseen 70 years ago. Despite numerous attempted plans, English still has not gained the dominant position in the society that many of its proponents over the years have favoured. However, if English language planning has failed, it is due in part to the high standard of proficiency or goals which Samoans have set for themselves. Many Samoans speak English very well and the language is spoken widely throughout the islands.

The Samoan experience with English seems to have created ambivalent attitudes and 'language ideology'[5]. Samoans desire the benefits of English language competence, but at the same time are afraid it will destroy their traditional language and culture. These latter fears have in the past often been fuelled in American Samoa by expatriates who were plainly contemptuous of most things Samoan, and by the way many plans for English language development were created and implemented without local consultation. These conditions in turn led to the public espousal of the need for English, but the failure to create community conditions in which it could properly develop. Yet, despite all these problems, English is becoming more prominent across the range of language domains, especially among younger people.

The Samoan language has remained strong, especially in personal usage situations, and there is a growing recognition that it needs to be more formally developed within the community. However, the spread of early formal Samoan literacy programs may only come at a cost: the

Westernization of the forms of language available in the Samoan written register (Duranti & Ochs, 1986). This issue can perhaps be more readily dealt with in the current situation where Samoans have more control over their own educational destiny. With less fear and more mutual linguistic respect, and with the aid of bilingual school programs, there could well be a gradual improvement of skills in both languages across domains for the benefit of the Samoan community.

These conclusions are undoubtedly more applicable to American Samoa than to her Western neighbour. However, contact between the two Samoas is great, and a recent study by Schramm *et al.* (1981) indicates that values there appear to be following those in American Samoa. Thus, the language planning policies in both Samoas, despite some differences, appear to be taking Samoans towards a similar linguistic destination, albeit by different paths and at a different pace.

Notes

1. This research was supported in part by a James Cook University Research Grant and by the East–West Culture Learning Institute, Honolulu, Hawaii, which first published some of the American Samoan material in their *Language Planning Newsletter* 8 (1) (Baldauf, 1982). I would like to thank Björn Jernudd, Allan Luke and Joan Rubin for their encouragement and editorial assistance with parts of this chapter, and Ruth Horie and Martin Combs for help in locating reference materials.
2. For a discussion of Samoan language literacy development and its implications in contemporary Western Samoa see Duranti & Ochs (1986).
3. Those interested in a detailed historical discussion of education in American Samoa may wish to consult Thomas (1987). Thomas (1984) also provides a contemporary comparison of education in American and Western Samoa against their sociopolitical and historical backgrounds.
4. The material in this section is based on Keesing (1934) unless otherwise noted.
5. The term 'language ideology' is used by Ferguson (1986) to describe the composite set of beliefs and attitudes held by a community towards a given language.

References

AMOSA, A. & HANNA, G. S. (1974), A cart before a horse. *International Education* 4 (2), 27–31.
ANDERSON, J. A. (1977), Samoan TV: 13 years of change. *Pacific Islands Communication Newsletter* 7 (2), 1, 10.
BALDAUF, R. B., Jr (1981), Educational television, enculturation, and

acculturation: A study of change in American Samoa. *International Review of Education* 27 (3), 227–245.

— (1982), The language situation in American Samoa: Planners, plans, and planning. *Language Planning Newsletter* 8 (1), 1–6.

— (1984), Language policy and education in American Samoa. *International Education Journal* 1 (2), 133–150.

BARRINGTON, J. M. (1973), The United Nations and educational development in Western Samoa during the Trusteeship Period 1946–1961. *International Review of Education* 19, 299–261.

BENTON, R. A. (1981), *The Flight of the Amokura: Oceanic Language and Formal Education in the South Pacific*. Wellington: New Zealand Council for Educational Research.

BRONSON, V. A. (1968), *A System Manual for the Staff and Faculty*. Pago Pago: Department of Education.

Department of Education (1932), *Annual Report*. Pago Pago. (Cited in Sanchez, 1955: 122).

— (1980), *D.O.E. Instructional Program*. Pago Pago: Division of Instructional Development.

DURANTI, A. & OCHS, E. (1986), Literacy instruction in a Samoan village. In B. B. SCHIEFFELIN & P. GILMORE (eds.) *The Acquisition of Literacy: Ethnographic Perspectives*. Norwood, NJ: Ablex.

FERGUSON, C. (1986), Language planning: An introduction. Presentation to the Department of Language and Arts Studies in Education. Townsville: James Cook University.

GRAHAM, S. V. (Governor), 4th December 1928. Letter to Mrs Helen Wilson (Cited in Sanchez, 1955: 171).

GRAY, J. A. C. (1960), *Amerika Samoa*. Annapolis, MD: U.S. Naval Institute.

Handbook of Western Samoa (1925), Wellington, NZ: Government Printer.

HUEBNER, T. (1986), Vernacular literacy, English as a language of wider communication and language shift in American Samoa. *Journal of Multilingual and Multicultural Development* 7 (5), 393–411.

KAISER, T. (1965), Classroom TV comes to Samoa. *Saturday Review* 25, 58.

KEESING, F. M. (1934), *Modern Samoa*. London: George Allen & Unwin. (New York: AMS Press Reprint, 1978).

KNEUBUHL, J. (1981), ASSC increases Samoan classes. *News Bulletin*. Pago Pago: (Interviewee). 26th February, p. 1.

LEWTHWAITE, G. R., MAINZER, C. & HOLLAND, P. J. (1973), From Polynesia to California: Samoan migration and its sequel. *Journal of Pacific History* 8, 133–157.

LONG, O. E. & GRUENING, E. (1961), *Study Mission to Eastern (American) Samoa*. Washington, DC: U.S. Government Printing.

MA'IA'I, F. (1957), Education in New Zealand's Pacific dependencies. *Overseas Education* 29, 54–59.

National Association of Educational Broadcasters (1962), The uses of television to reorganize and upgrade the educational system of American Samoa. Report to the Governor H. Rex Lee. January. (Cited in Schramm *et al.*, 1981).

NELSON, L. M. (1971), *Report of the Educational Television Task Force*. Honolulu: University of Hawaii.

PAWLEY, A. (1981), Samoa: The linguistic situation in Samoa. In H. KLOSS & G. D. McCONNELL (eds.) *Linguistic Composition of the Nations of the World, Vol. 4. Oceania*. Quebec: les Presses de l'Universite Laval.

PITT, D. (1970), *Tradition and Economic Progress in Samoa*. Oxford: Clarendon Press.

REID, C. F. (1941), *Education in the Territories and Outlying Possessions of the United States*. New York: Teachers College Columbia University (Cited in Sanchez, 1955).

SANCHEZ, P. (1955), Education in American Samoa. Unpublished Doctoral Dissertation, Stanford University.

SCHRAMM, W., NELSON, L. M. & BETHAM, M. T. (1981), *Bold Experiment: The Story of Educational Television in American Samoa*. Stanford, CA: Stanford University Press.

STEARNS, C. D. (Governor) 14th April 1914. Letter to the Rev. Mr Houglo of the London Missionary Society. (Cited in Sanchez, 1955: 84.)

THOMAS, R. M. (1981), Evaluation consequences of unreasonable goals — the plight of education in American Samoa. *Educational Evaluation and Policy Analysis* 3 (2), 41–99.

— (1984), American Samoa and Western Samoa. In R. M. THOMAS & T. N. POSTLETHWAITE (eds.) *Schooling in the Pacific Islands: Colonies in Transition*. Oxford: Pergamon.

— (1987), From talking chiefs to videotapes: Education in American Samoa 1700s to 1980. Santa Barbara: University of California: ERIC ED 273 544.

THOMAS, R. M. & TITIALI'I, T. F. (1973), *Summary Report of a Study of Unmet Educational Needs in American Samoa 1971–1973*. Pago Pago: Department of Education.

15 Language planning and education in Melanesia and Polynesia: An annotated bibliography

VICKI TELENI

Melanesia and Polynesia are groups of linguistically and culturally diverse islands in the South Pacific. The Melanesian group includes Papua New Guinea, the Solomon Islands, Vanuatu and New Caledonia. Polynesia includes Fiji, Tonga, Western and American Samoa as well as the small island states of Niue, the Cook Islands and Kiribati. None of these countries have official language planning bodies. All except the French territories use English as at least one of their official languages.

The cultures of this region are linguistically rich, diverse and complex, a situation which has given rise to many language planning issues that require resolution by these independent nations and dependencies. Most have inherited English from British, Australian, New Zealand and American administrations. This situation has given rise to varieties of pidgin English in Melanesia, where over 1,000 indigenous languages are spoken. Multilingualism is the norm for many islanders. Linguistic loyalties to indigenous languages are strong. However, such small states, relatively dependent upon aid for development and outside advice and expertise, have left language planning issues mainly in the hands of expatriate advisers, funding bodies like the World Bank, UNESCO and the Australian Development Assistance Bureau, or to individual bureaucrats and Ministries of Education.

Dissatisfaction with the Western educational model, the failure of academic curricula and an insufficient knowledge of English to meet social and economic aspirations demonstrate a need for a reappraisal of *de facto* language policies in some countries. Furthermore, broadcast languages through radio and television and external languages for instruction are placing pressure upon indigenous languages, the local *lingue franche* and their established functions in these societies. Some of the pressing unresolved language planning issues in the societies in the region are: What language(s) should be used for what functions? What is/are the most appropriate language(s) for primary literacy — the vernacular, *lingue franche* or English? If and when should English be introduced? What are valid and reliable measures of competency in all languages? Who will be responsible for the standardisation of *lingue franche* (particularly pidgins) and for the development of teaching materials? What should be the languages of the media? What are the appropriate processes for the implementation of plans? How are scarce resources to be allocated to language-related research? Who will evaluate language plans? And, most importantly, who will ensure the development of policies and plans which accord with the wishes of the people and meet the development requirements of the countries? The advantages of national language planning bodies are self-evident. However, it is doubtful that these bodies will be created where militant nationalism is stirring, where potentially divisive issues like language selection are best avoided for political reasons, and where economic priorities are undergoing re-examination.

This annotated bibliography comments on a selection of monographs and papers published since 1980 related to language planning in this region. There are, however, many unpublished theses, conference papers and some interesting earlier publications worth reading which have not been included here because of difficulties of access. There are also other important documents such as administrative, World Bank and UNESCO reports which should be read by those who wish to pursue language planning issues in detail.

Annotated Bibliography

General

BENTON, R. A. (1981), *The Flight of the Amokura. Oceanic Languages and Formal Education in the South Pacific.* Wellington: New Zealand Council for Educational Research.

The first two parts of this monograph deal with language policy and bilingual education in New Zealand. Parts 3 and 4 however, provide a brief historical overview of language policies in education in most of the countries in Polynesia, Melanesia and Micronesia up to 1980. The author comments upon the nature of the language situations, some problems which various policies have encountered and then estimates the potential for bilingual education in each country. Part 5 summarises the discussion arising from the 1974 Bilingual Education Conference in Pago Pago and concludes that Pacific Islanders believe in their power to determine their own linguistic destiny and that they believe that world powers have moral obligations to help them achieve this. Chapters 14 and 15 examine the Pacific experience in relation to Fishman's typology of language policies. Benton predicts that the fate of the indigenous languages over the next 100 years will depend on two factors — the will of the people and institutional support. Finally, based on the Navajo Reading Study experience, Benton lists the various factors that language planners should consider and comments on each in relation to the New Zealand Maori/English bilingual policy. This is a superficial treatment of the Polynesian and Melanesian educational situations and their language planning dilemmas.

GONZALEZ, A. (1979), Language and social development in the Pacific Area. *Philippine Journal of Linguistics* 10 (1/2), 21–44.

Gonzalez attempts to develop a quantitative measure of language welfare based on seven language indicators that are rated on a 1 – 5 scale: the status of minority languages, language homogeneity, communicative efficiency, efficiency of the languages of education, mastery of the languages of government and trade, competence in a language of wider communication, and development of a national language of the state. In his model each factor is given an equal weighting. A numerical index is computed for all the countries bordering the Pacific Ocean. In order to test the validity of this scale, he correlated this index with other development indices such as *per capita* income, life expectancy, infant mortality rates, population and daily newspaper circulation resulting in a high correlation with other development indicators. Predictable however, was the finding that development of a national language correlated highly with competence in languages of government, trade and literacy. On the other hand, low inter-item correlations were found with linguistic homogeneity and status of minority languages. Once again, partitioning out *per capita* income he found that literacy correlated highly with his language welfare index. The tables he generates which allow some comparisons between countries (e.g. Fiji 2.0, Papua New Guinea 1.3, Samoa 3.0, Tonga 2.7) suggest some quantitative measures of non-economic aspects of development. However, the indicators upon which his model is based are Western industrial/social measures and a model should be developed which allocates a differential weighting to indicators appropriate for the situation in each country. The Pacific Islands, it could be argued, may generate indigenous models of development for which alternative, culturally and nationally appropriate indicators would have to be developed.

> HUEBNER, T. (1986), A socio-historical approach to literacy development: A comparative case study from the Pacific. In J. LANGER (ed.) *Literacy, Culture and Education*. Norwood, N.J.: Ablex.

Huebner examines the socio-historical developments in Hawaii and Samoa to explain the transition from pre-literate language learning, function and use in the vernacular to secular technological learning, function and use in a language of wider communication (LWC). He draws together political history, research on literacy, education, language shift and language maintenance, in order to identify the roles and status of oral languages in past and present Samoan and Hawaiian societies. He employs socio-historical analysis to explain the functions and domains of vernacular literacy and the shifts which have occurred in these functions and domains following literacy instruction in the LWC. This article synthesises wider disciplinary research with sociolinguistic theory. The resultant case study comparisons demonstrate the interpretive power of Huebner's socio-historical approach. They further demonstrate the importance of ethnographic, historical and survey studies for language planning theory and educational decision-making, a lack of which is inhibiting the development of informed language planning in many Pacific countries.

Papua New Guinea

> AHAI, N. (1984), A case for vernacular education in Papua New Guinea. *Yagl-Ambu* 11 (1), 25–38.

This author argues persuasively for education in the vernacular, particularly in the primary school. First an examination of the aims of community-based primary education in Papua New Guinea is made. Then educational, psychological, linguistic and socio-cultural reasons for vernacular languages for primary literacy in Papua New Guinea are identified. Papua New Guinea did experience a short-lived experiment in national vernacular education which was quickly abandoned in favour of English-based education in order to meet demands for a local bureaucracy and professional class. However, some experimental schemes are still operating successfully (see Delpit & Kemelfield, 1985).

BRAY, M. (1984), What crisis in educational planning? A perspective from Papua New Guinea. *International Review of Education* 30, 427–439.

This is an historical look at educational planning in Papua New Guinea in the 1970s and the 1980s which sets out to refute the view that educational planning is in the decline. The author enumerates the various educational plans developed in Papua New Guinea whose primary purpose, it seems, was to lay down economic training and manpower estimates so that funding could be secured from aid sources such as the World Bank. Although this paper does not deal specifically with language planning, it does offer an insight into the purpose of educational plans and the significant role of aid bodies in policy-making in countries like Papua New Guinea.

DELPIT, L. D. & KEMELFIELD, G. (1985), *An Evaluation of the Viles Tok Ples Skul Scheme in the North Solomon Province*. Port Moresby: University of Papua New Guinea ERU Report No. 51.

This is an invaluable document which describes the planning, implementation and evaluation of a unique experiment in vernacular elementary education in Papua New Guinea. Placing educational policy in the hands of provincial governments has provided an ideal opportunity for language planners to meet the development and educational needs of local communities. Strong communal involvement and support has led to a '...viable institution that has made considerable progress towards meeting its declared goals' (p. 122). The language and education solutions offered by this scheme are apparently realistic. The authors claim that '. . . it is a resolution of the colonial language versus mother language debate' (p. 123) by the implementation of serial multilingualism which has resulted in a synthesis of realities — traditional and modern. Questions about financial costs of such a solution are examined with hopeful optimism. Detailed reports on similar schemes should be made available publicly so that language planners, economists, development planners and government policy-makers have evidence about alternative language planning models for Melanesia.

GILLIAN, A. M. (1984), Language and development in Papua New Guinea. *Dialectical Anthropology* 8 (4), 303–318.

In this paper the writer interprets what is meant by development in Papua New Guinea and the implications of this for language use in Papua New Guinea where 'control of the English language is a virtual requirement for participation in national economic power' (p. 307). She argues that because vernacular languages (Tok Ples) are not encouraged, 'lexical arrest' can occur as a manifestation in speech of alienation. The author describes how the existing language policy in Papua New Guinea reinforces the externally responsive nature of national development in Papua New Guinea. She examines the status and roles of Tok Ples, Tok Pisin and English and explains how the present 'policy' reinforces the unequal distribution of wealth and development in Papua New Guinea. She questions the value of the Summer Institute of Linguistics, externally responsive scholarship and foreign researchers to national development in Papua New Guinea. This paper lifts the debate about language use from a narrow educational framework into the broader framework of the relationship between economic power and language use.

NEKITEL, O. M. (1984), Language planning in Papua New Guinea: A nationalist viewpoint. *Yagl-Ambu* 11 (1), 1–24.

Nekitel argues strongly for the establishment of a national language planning agency (LPA) in Papua New Guinea. He describes the present absence of a policy as 'a policy in disguise' (p. 7). Because language loyalties are strong and emotional attachments to the two national *lingue franche* (Tok Pisin and Hiri Motu) are potentially divisive, language issues have been deliberately avoided. He concludes that a fair and neutral language policy should be based on both *lingue franche*. He rejects English as irrelevant, and the present Western-based education model as a failure. The author then goes on to list some of the corpus planning issues which an LPA would need to consider. These include the functional roles of the languages, and issues of standardisation and spelling. In addition, he sees the prime responsibility of an LPA would be to control and engineer the borrowing of terms and the modernisation of the national languages (p. 19). A further integral part of its role would be ongoing evaluation. The author concludes that there is a need for nationwide language and attitude surveys and national consciousness-raising. Nekitel argues passionately for his view but more importantly, he pinpoints some of the major tasks confronting Papua New Guinea — tasks which will be decided either by historical and political forces in an *ad hoc* manner that may not satisfy the national aspirations of Papua New Guineans, or by national planning.

OLSSON, M. (1984), Merging formal with informal through vernacular education. *Yagl-Ambu* 11 (1), 39–51.

Olsson begins by stating the dual goals of education for development in Papua New Guinea: to provide the skills and knowledge for the top of the social pyramid and to provide those necessary for grassroots development. He presents a case for the development of dual systems of education, formal and informal, which could share resources and knowledge. The experimental vernacular schools would teach traditional knowledge and culture through the mother tongue, a critical base for teaching literacy. The formal schools based on the Western model would provide new knowledge from the outside where appropriate. Olsson suggests practical means by which this could occur with minimal expenditure. He emphasises the need for careful language planning assessments to be carried out in order to gauge the potential for vernacular schools. This author begins to propose some processes and solutions to language issues in Papua New Guinea.

TODD, L. (1984), *Modern Englishes: Pidgins and Creoles*. London: Basil Blackwell.

Chapter 4 of Todd's monograph is a case study of Papua New Guinea Tok Pisin (TP). Firstly, he provides an historical background to Papua New Guinea contact with Europeans and the development of TP as a trade language and *lingua franca*. Secondly, he provides a brief description of the sociolinguistic status of TP. A linguistic description of TP follows, including phonetic, lexical and syntactical information. From a simple vocabulary count, Todd hypothesises that TP is a variety of English rather than a new language. He concludes that TP is a 'vital, flexible language . . . well suited to expressing the unique way of life of the people of Papua New Guinea' (p. 209). This primarily descriptive work is useful as an introduction to the linguistic features of TP which also contributes comparative information about other pidgins, principally Cameroon pidgin.

SMITH, P. (1987), *Education and Colonial Control in Papua New Guinea: A Documentary History*. Melbourne: Longman Cheshire.

Smith chronologically documents a national experience familiar to Melanesians: colonial control in and through education. The documents are grouped into a number of educational themes: changing policies of the educating bodies; contrasting experiences of the various regions under German, missionary, Japanese and Australian control; competition between the various missions and the administrations; staffing and financial constraints; teacher training and school development. These are presented in the context of the expectations and reactions of the linguistically and culturally diverse people of Papua New Guinea.

Although the book does not focus solely on language issues in education, the underlying missionary and colonial assumption that education equals reading, writing and arithmetic and later manual skills emerges as a powerful theme. The Germans saw the teaching of German as the primary means of political control and economic exploitation. The Australian administrations under Murray extended this utilitarian policy of a single language to the belief that 'the superiority of English to any New Guinean language is so great that it is obviously to the advantage of the natives to acquire it' (p.57). Most missions, however, preferred the vernacular or a *lingua franca* as the most expedient means of appropriating primitive souls. These language policies are the hallmark of Melanesian education and Smith documents the issues, arguments and some of their effects in their historical contexts.

Smith's format combines the advantages of primary source documents with the chronology and commentary of more traditional histories. He documents a depressing history of neglect, paternalism and unsystematic cultural vandalism.

This is a superb text for teachers, those interested in colonial history, and especially Melanesians searching for explanations and answers to the dilemmas of language planning facing their nations today. The issues, the arguments and the results of previous language and education policies are evident. What remains is the need for studies of the effects of these language policies on Papua New Guinea society and other societies like it.

Fiji

> MILNER, G. B., ARMS, D. G. & GERAGHTY, P. (1984), *Duivosavosa Fiji's Languages: Their Use and Their Future*. Fiji Museum Bulletin No. 8. Suva: Oceania Printers Ltd.

This monograph is a collection of three papers. Milner's 'Language, culture and education in Fiji' is an examination of the 'Westernisation' philosophies, processes and their consequences for Fijian culture. He argues that the Fijian language is under threat from a misguided over-emphasis on English. This issue is central not only to Fiji but to most Pacific cultures and Milner approaches the issue with a well-argued case for elementary education in the vernacular. This is based on the assumption that what is at stake is in fact the survival of the language and therefore the culture of the Fijian people.

Arms' 'The Church and the Vernacular' is based on the notion that language is a system of communication and that no one language is inherently superior to any other. Therefore, for effective communication and instruction the vernaculars should be the languages of instruction in schools and the language of choice in the church. He addresses several questions: Can Fijian survive? Will Fijian survive? Should Fijian survive? His answer is that government and church institutions must provide the necessary institutional support to improve the status of the vernaculars and increase the domains of their uses. Next he outlines a number of ways in which the church can implement this through liturgy and instruction in the community and schools. He savagely attacks the 'English only on campus' policy as pedagogically unsound, counter-productive and culturally destructive. He recommends that the church take part in the shaping of official language policies in education and in the development of textbooks in the vernacular, and that the clergy learn the vernaculars. Since the time that this paper was originally written (1975) some of the changes he recommends have been implemented but not to the extent envisaged.

Geraghty's 'Language policy in Fiji and Rotuma' is a comprehensive outline of the historical development of language status and attitudes from pre-colonial time to the present. He provides a detailed description of current language status in Fiji and Rotuma supported by census and survey data and personal observations. Since independence there has been increasing pressure from the community, particularly through language use in the media, and from educational agencies, to improve the status of Fijian and encourage its wider use. Since no official corpus planning body exists and there is a shortage of trained language personnel, the Fijian Dictionary Project has become the *de facto* corpus planning body for Fijian. Despite the popular move towards the vernacular, official educational syllabi remain dominated by English language requirements. Geraghty highlights the ambivalent position of the Christian churches in their schools, liturgy and publications towards the English versus vernacular questions. He predicts no drastic changes in the language use and status, but some changes resulting from changes in ethnic composition may occur. He concludes that 'Fiji will perhaps resort to a novel expedient: informed language planning' when community pressure for change becomes strong. This stage may have been reached as a result of drastic changes brought about by the 1987 coup. The probability of the establishment of an official language planning agency appears unlikely in view of current economic constraints. Therefore, the language statuses of Hindi and Fijian will probably be changed, rather than that of English.

MANGUBHAI, F. (1987), Literacy in Fiji: Its origins and its development. *Interchange* 18 (1/2), 124–125.

Mangubhai traces the religious, political, linguistic, social and educational factors which have given rise to the ascendancy of English over the vernaculars in education and government in Fiji since early missionary contact. He then examines the narrow range of literate behaviours among Fijians during this period which ensured mission and colonial control over the Fijians. Based on newspaper data and locally operating linguistic constraints on vernacular literacy, the author hypothesises that language shift towards English literacy among Indo-Fijians has been more evident than among Fijians. However he acknowledges that reliable survey data on English and vernacular reading achievement have never been collected in Fiji. The author next outlines the results of a study of reading comprehension ability of Grade 6 pupils which led to the 'Book Flood Project'. This two-year experiment evaluated the effect of access to interesting and well-illustrated story books on the reading and writing proficiency of rural primary children. Mangubhai raises some dilemmas facing a traditional society which arise from the adoption of a foreign literature and language which embody foreign models and values. The challenge to develop local reading materials and local literature in all languages is one which Fiji shares with other countries in the region. Rather than attempt a national solution, perhaps regional solutions — at least for English materials — are more economically viable and more attractive to aid agencies. Mangubhai predicts a slow growth of literate behaviour within the community, and he touches on some of the social and cultural changes brought about by fostering literate behaviour in an oral society.

MANGUBHAI, F. (1987), Literacy in the South Pacific: some multilingual and multiethnic issues. In D. A. WAGNER (ed.) *The Future of Literacy in a Changing World*. London: Pergamon Press.

Mangubhai briefly outlines the history of literacy and schooling in the South Pacific. He uses Fiji as a case study to support his hypotheses that literacy in the vernacular is easier to achieve in linguistically homogeneous cultures based on small island states whereas literacy in a language of wider communication is more widespread and comes first in linguistically diverse countries with large populations and land masses. He predicts that these factors will result in differentiation of language uses and functions. These are reinforced by the differentiation in literacy schooling through the two agencies, the church and the state. Mangubhai then outlines the Fiji Book Flood Project in detail. His main hypotheses are attractive, but socio-historical case studies of several South Pacific countries need to be examined in order to test them. A further examination of historical and present factors operating on language shift and maintenance may provide information upon which confident deductions could be based.

Kingdom of Tonga

SPOLSKY, B., ENGELBRECHT, G. & ORTIZ, L. (1983), Religious, political and educational factors in the development of bi-literacy in the Kingdom of Tonga. *Journal of Multilingual and Multicultural Development* 4 (6), 459–469.

The authors describe the historical and current language situation in Tonga and indigenous sociolinguistic and politico-cultural pressures on language use in Tonga. Tonga has near universal literacy in Tongan and almost 50% literacy in English. The authors enumerate the various domains for oral language and conclude that most Tongans are orally monolingual. In domains of literacy, Tongan still dominates in religion, politics and the media whereas English predominates in commerce, administration and secondary education. The authors suggest that the high levels of literate behaviour in Tongan homes and society facilitate early Tongan literacy among children. In order to explain this development, the authors look to traditional Tongan culture, its political infrastructure and value system. A strong, cohesive culture that values 'control' was able to indigenise Western institutions such as religion, literacy, the education and political systems. This interpretation appears to have some explanatory power when compared to the American Samoan experience. The political history of Tonga is unique in the region and differences in economic developments must have exerted some pressures on language use — an aspect neglected by sociolinguists. Papers such as this are a movement away from a more 'Eurocentric' interpretation which often assumes European cultural dominance and portrays the traditional cultures as 'passive' in contact situations.

The Solomon Islands

WATSON-GEGEO, K. A. (1987), English in the Solomon Islands. *World Englishes* 6 (1), 21–32.

This paper attempts to explain the present role of English and pijin in the

Solomon Islands by examining some of the major English language influences during European contact from the early traders and missionaries to World War II. The second part of the paper outlines the socio-economic and educational roles of English in the society. The author acknowledges the role of broadcast languages and how pijin, the vernacular and the local English interact with each other. She hypothesises that urban pijin may be undergoing a decreolisation. Finally, the author briefly raises some of the important language planning problems to be resolved in the Solomons: which languages should be used for literacy teaching: for the language curriculum in school; for primary vernacular education. In a society where 'language functions as the gatekeeper to political and economic resources' (p. 27) these problems are central to national development. In small rural communities print media are not widely used, and the influence of broadcast languages has not been fully evaluated. Language planners in fact may be seriously underestimating these influences in linguistically complex situations where standardisation of all languages is not occurring through the education system. This author perceives these language questions as educational issues, but they are more properly national, political and language planning issues and must be examined in the wider cultural context.

Western Samoa

> DURANTI, A. & OCHS, E. (1986), Literacy instruction in a Samoan village. In B. B. SCHIEFFELIN & P. GILMORE (eds.) *The Acquisition of Literacy: Ethnographic Perspectives*. Norwood, N. J.: Ablex.

In the past, the relationship of language and identity has been neglected by language planners. Duranti and Ochs present ethnographic data on Samoan society to support their contention that a global effect of literacy instruction is a change in the social identity of the child. Traditional Samoan caregiver speech and socialisation through child–adult relationships are juxtaposed with literacy instruction in the school. The different behaviours, expectations, attitudes, values and instructional methods in the two processes provide persuasive evidence for their hypothesis. This paper points to possible unanticipated outcomes and concomitants to language and literacy educational programs. Such insights, yielded by ethnographic fieldwork, are of value to language planners.

American Samoa

BALDAUF, R. B. Jr (1981), Educational television, enculturation and acculturation: a study of change in American Samoa. *International Review of Education* 27 (3), 227–245.

Baldauf contrasts the traditional Samoan enculturation 'system' with the Western education 'system' of acculturation introduced in 1964 by co-operative education through television. He argues that these systems were so radically different that the Samoans 'compartmentalised' them. The Samoans had no control over the medium and the process. Although educational television was designed as co-operative education, that it could ever be viewed as co-operative from the Samoan perspective is doubtful. Television failed as a successful medium for education, but had the side-effect of creating a demand for television as a medium of entertainment with consequent social changes. The eventual rejection of educational television, however, has ironically returned control of education to Samoans. Electricity in every village and other technological changes in lifestyle may effect changes in the education system, and create demands for an increased level of competence in English which language planners will need to address. Such an 'experiment' needs to be continually re-examined in the light of further developments if other societies in the Pacific and language planners are able to take full advantage of the Samoan experience.

BALDAUF, R. B. Jr (1982), The language situation in American Samoa: planners, plans and planning. *Language Planning Newsletter* 8 (1), 1–6.

Baldauf first briefly outlines the current sociolinguistic situation in American Samoa, noting the domains of Samoan and English language use. Then he identifies what he sees as the two primary controlling agents of use: American institutions and indigenous institutions. Next, the author traces the historical events and the accompanying processes through which language policies were implemented. The policies have two stated aims: to teach English in order to provide access to Western knowledge, and to instil cultural identity through vernacular literacy. Baldauf hypothesises that failures of various attempts to meet these aims, particularly the massive injection of funds into English language education during the 1960s and 1970s, are primarily a result of imposition of policy without consultation. Two other possibilities arise however: that such conflicting aims are unachievable through one system, or that the implementation has been in practice something different from that which was planned. If indeed plans are formulated and implemented without consultation then the Samoan experience demonstrates the need for theories and models of language planning to incorporate such fundamental assumptions.

HUEBNER, T. (1986), Vernacular literacy, English as a language of wider communication and language shift in American Samoa. *Journal of Multilingual and Multicultural Development* 7 (5), 393–411.

Huebner traces the social, political, economic, linguistic and educational influences operating in Samoa in order to account for the success of vernacular literacy until World War II. He evaluates the effects of administration policy, Samoan employment patterns, emigration and specifically the introduction of television. These have created a shift towards English use since World War II. He outlines the correlative decline in Samoan language skills and a weakening of traditional institutions. This language shift has led to new demands on the educational system and to changes in the level of competency required in both languages. Huebner recommends that language and attitude surveys, and ethnographies be carried out and that new measures of language proficiency be developed so that new policy directions and language planning changes can be based upon valid and reliable information. Huebner's paper demonstrates the need for historical approaches to language planning. This approach calls for a broadening of perspective among language planners. The Samoan story is an example of planning which views language policy primarily as educational policy, divorcing it from its sociocultural environment.

SCHRAMM, W., NELSON, L. M. & BETHAM, M. T. (1981), *Bold Experiment: The Story of Educational Television in American Samoa.* Stanford: Stanford University Press.

This is a compulsory text for any language planner. This detailed study of the establishment of educational television in American Samoa describes and evaluates the project from its initial conception under the Governorship of Lee in 1964 to its virtual demise in 1979. The book is readable, the content fascinating and Chapter 10 features 'Lessons from the Samoan Experience'. Still, the focus is primarily educational. Papua New Guinea and Fiji are currently experimenting with non-educational television. Their language and educational planners might include this overview in their list of required reading.

THOMAS, R. M. (1981), Evaluation consequences of unreasonable goals — the plight of education in American Samoa. *Educational Evaluation and Policy Analysis* 3 (2), 41–49.

Thomas argues that the goal of the American education system in American Samoa, to prepare youths to compete successfully in both traditional Samoan society and stateside American society, is unreasonable. He traces the history of educational policy to 1932 when the goals were first introduced by progressive bicultural educators. Next he lists the means by which these goals are evaluated, both formal testing and informal opinion surveys. Based on the formal test results he concludes that Samoans are not prepared to compete on equal terms with their U.S.A. mainland counterparts because their academic and social skills are inadequate. This reflects adjustment difficulties and English competency shortcomings. Tests of Samoan language and culture achievement carried out in the 1960s and 1970s also showed results below those expected. He then states that neither the students nor the school system are congruent with the achievement of these goals. Thomas states that this has led to a drop in morale among Samoan educators who have become discouraged by constant criticism that they have been unable to achieve the unachievable. He suggests that the bicultural goals be dropped in favour of an Americanisation objective, but he acknowledges that this goal is politically unpalatable. Thomas finally proposes several possible solutions: modification of the goals themselves without abandoning them; determination of new priorities and objectives that would be achievable by the majority of students; or the development of criterion-referenced tests divided into academic, vocational and social domains. He hopes that politicians will develop the constitutional fortitude to adopt these plans and increase the staffing needed to implement these changes. This 'élitist' model of education is well ensconced in many other Pacific countries and does appear to meet some of the development needs of the country, but whether it will gain popular support in American Samoa where more egalitarian goals have been pursued is another question.

THOMAS, R. M. (1987), *From Talking Chiefs to Videotapes: Education in American Samoa — 1700s to 1980s*. ERIC Document. ED 273 544.

With the demise in educational television in Samoa, there has been a loss of interest in educational programs being developed there. Unfortunately this monograph ends at 1980 with a short list of some of the issues yet to be resolved, including the issue of language education. However, Thomas' history is a comprehensive and well-documented prelude to the study of the current broader issues of bicultural and bilingual education in American Samoa.

PART IV:
Language Planning and Use in Southeast Asia

16 How bilingualism is being integrated in Negara Brunei Darussalam

GARY JONES

Country and Background

Brunei Darussalam is a small country on the North-West coast of Borneo with a total area of 2,226 square miles, a coastline of about 100 miles and a population of 215,843. Malays constitute 138,783 or 65% of the population; other indigenous groups 17,974 or 8%; Chinese 43,708 or 20%; Europeans, Indians and other races 15,478 or 7%. Owing to a healthy oil-based economy this small population enjoys one of the highest living standards in the world, with annual per capita income in excess of $18,000 US.

The languages that can be heard spoken in Brunei are Malay, English, various Chinese languages and the languages of the different indigenous people — Dusun, Iban, Murut, Tutong and Belait. The types of schools within the country are representative of these different races. There are Chinese medium private schools, separate Ministry of Religious Affairs Arabic medium schools for boys and girls, and both English and Malay medium Education Department schools.

The private schools are outside of the government's jurisdiction and cater mainly for non-Bruneian citizens while the Ministry of Religious Affairs schools have only about 1,000 pupils out of a total school population of approximately 75,000. Therefore, the majority of Brunei's school children attend either Malay or English medium government schools. In English medium schools, however, some subjects are taught in Malay so the description of these schools as English or Malay medium can be misleading.

In early 1984, shortly after full independence from Britain, Brunei introduced a bilingual education plan that would replace the English/-Malay medium split with a single system of education. This system is known locally as *Dwibahasa* (two languages) and retains Malay as the country's official language while at the same time recognising the importance of English.

Those familiar with the situation in Malaysia might be forgiven for thinking that such a concept is nothing new. However, in Fishman's (1977) terms, Bahasa Melayu is the language given primary emphasis in the Malaysian education system while in Brunei's new education system English is the language given primary emphasis. In fact, what is happening in Brunei is almost a complete reversal of what has happened in Malaysia, even though Malaysia does not have a formal bilingual education system as such (see Ożóg, Chapter 17, this volume).

The Introduction of a Bilingual Education System

Brunei's adoption of a bilingual education system has its origins in the 1972 Report of the Brunei Education Commission. This Commission recommended that the country's paramount education aims should include:

(i) to make Malay the main medium of instruction in National Primary and Secondary schools as soon as possible in line with the requirement of the constitution.

(ii) to raise the standard of the usage of English in the primary and secondary schools in the country.

(Brunei Government Publication, 1972: 4)

Twelve years later, in 1984, the importance of English as an educational medium was realised and given more stress. To quote a 1984 document, *The Education System of Negara Brunei Darussalam*:

The concept of a bilingual system is a means of ensuring the sovereignty of the Malay language, while at the same time recognising the importance of the English Language.

(1984: 2)

The message is still the same as it was 12 years earlier, that is: Malay is the national language but the populace and government recognise the need to be able to use English. However, by 1984 there had been a change of emphasis and it was no longer stipulated that Malay be the main medium of instruction.

Between 1972 and independence in 1984, Brunei witnessed how other newly independent countries fared with, amongst other things, their language planning programmes. Within Brunei English has never been strongly perceived as an instrument of colonial rulers. Brunei was a protectorate with internal self-government and Britain did not interfere in the internal administration of the country. As a result in the post-colonial period there was no clamour to unburden the country of all things British, including the English language, as had been the case in some other countries in the region, most notably Malaysia (see Lim Kiat Boey, 1976). Instead, English was regarded as the key to the outside world and something to be nurtured rather than destroyed. This means that today, according to the description of language use outlined by Smith (1983), Malay is used in Brunei for intranational purposes and English for international purposes. Of course, actual language use is not inflexible and Malay is sometimes used as the language of international communication with Brunei's Malay-speaking neighbours, Malaysia and Indonesia, while English is usually the medium of communication within Brunei between speakers of different races. Also, it is often more expedient, because of the cosmopolitan nature of Brunei's workforce, for the government and private companies to issue bilingual notices and conduct much of their business in English.

It should also be noted that educational ties between Brunei and Britain had always been close, and that in Brunei English medium study characteristically led to tertiary studies in the U.K. Up to 1974 many Malay medium students enrolled as undergraduates in Malaysian universities, but after this time most of these students were also sent to study in Britain after first receiving intensive English language courses.

With English playing such a prime academic role it is therefore not surprising to see that the 1984 outline for the country's education system goes on to state:

This recognition of the importance of the English language is partly based on an assumption of its importance for academic study, and thus its ability to facilitate the entry of students from Brunei Darussalam to institutions of higher education overseas where the medium of instruction is English. Such a perception may, of course, be subject to review should Brunei Darussalam itself be able, in the future, to provide its own facilities for higher education.

(1984: 2)

Since 1984 Brunei has developed its own institutions of higher education and, apart from the teaching of Religious Studies and Malay Language and Literature, the medium of instruction in these institutions is English.

Language Planning or Nation Building?

At the time of Brunei's independence, in December 1983, there was much talk of 'nation building'. It is not a coincidence that, at the same time, the government introduced Dwibahasa. Language planning and nation building are intertwined and Brunei needed a progressive education system which would produce graduates capable of representing Brunei in the international community. The consensus at the time was that the country could no longer rely on outside help but had to develop its own human resources. However, this need for national assertion generated a new problem for Bruneians: how could Brunei go out into the world, adopt an international language and yet still remain relatively tranquil and conserve its culture and traditions? Brunei needed a unique education system.

Islam and the monarchy have always been the cornerstones of Brunei's political stability and cultural continuity. At the founding of the modern Brunei state, the concept of a Malay Islamic Monarchy was seen as being of paramount consideration in any education system. To some extent this concept is self-explanatory and suggests a unification of the three basic components of Bruneian society: Malay ethnic identity, Islamic religion, and a monarchal system. It is believed that together they constitute a bulwark against excessive outside interference.

The Malay Islamic Monarchy concept can be analysed in its constituent parts. The word 'Malay' in this context is meant to focus on the characteristic aspects of the Brunei Malay race in terms of their culture, attitudes and ways of thinking. 'Islam' focuses on a common and moderate attitude towards the teaching of the Islamic religion according to the tenets of the Sunni sect, which should result in both Muslims and non-Muslims enjoying peace and security. 'Monarchy', or 'Beraja' as it is referred to in Malay, imparts the understanding that His Majesty the Sultan symbolises the unity and commonality of the people and nation in his dual role as the

Yang Dipertuan (supreme ruler) and as the Head of the Official Religion. Therefore the Sultan is seen as the supreme ruling power who at the same time works for the development of the community and nation, as well as for the propagation and growth of the national religion. Thus the Malay Islamic Monarchy concept attempts, through education, to inculcate a sense of national identity which it is hoped will result in a stable, peaceful society claiming undivided loyalty to its ruler.

It is expected that, amongst other things, the Malay Islamic Monarchy concept will offset the cultural intrusions that may result from acquiring a foreign language. Malay may be the language most widely used within Brunei today, but with the emphasis being given to English in the schools there is obviously some risk to its future dominant status, no matter what its official status might be. This in itself would provoke some reaction, if we accept that language is a means of self-identification, as Fishman (1972: 131) contends. If Bruneians were perceived to be strongly identifying with a Western culture, then it could have the effect of undermining the idea of 'Malay' as described in the Malay Islamic Monarchy concept, which would be both socially and politically unacceptable. In this respect, much must depend on the variety of English to be taught and how it is to be presented to the pupils. Within Brunei it is the government Curriculum Development Department which acts as the monitor in this field.

The Brunei Curriculum Development Department inspects textbooks for their cultural appropriateness and is in the process of producing teaching materials within the country based on local themes. Western cultural influences via television, music and travel will continue, but without the supporting influence from the classroom they need not necessarily lead to a fundamental change in the pupils' self-identity. This may be particularly so in Brunei, where family ties and religion continue to play a dominant role in everyday life. Indeed, as can be seen from three of the aims of the 1984 Report, unity was a basic consideration in the planning of the new education system:

2.2 To implement a single, system of education, to be known as the Education System of Negara Brunei Darussalam, which will no longer comprise different mediums of instruction.

2.3 To build a community and nation where the concept of a Malay Islamic Monarchy is paramount, by means of the Education system of Negara Brunei Darussalam.

2.4 To instil solidarity among the people of the nation by means of a single system of education.

(1984: 1)

Thus, the new education system recognises the need to instil cultural values, and tries to do this through the Malay Islamic Monarchy concept. Section 2.4 might suggest that the old dual education system was potentially divisive and certainly under the former system English medium graduates would have been able to work in both English and Malay, whereas Malay medium graduates were restricted to working in one language. In theory at least, a single system of education assures a greater degree of equality and is expected to instil solidarity — goals which any nation would surely wish to strive for.

The Implementation of Dwibahasa

Prior to the implementation of the bilingual education system in Brunei, the country had English, Malay, Chinese and Arabic medium schools, but only the English and Malay schools came under the Education Department. In the new system the old division of English and Malay medium is replaced by one system known as 'The Education System of Negara Brunei Darussalam'. Children in Brunei attend Lower Primary School when they are six years old. They stay in Lower Primary for three years, continuing to Upper Primary and eventually to the Lower Secondary schools when they are 12 years old. They spend three years in Lower Secondary and two in Upper Secondary, taking their General Certificate of Ordinary Level Education when they are 16 years old. Those children that are educationally successful can then continue into Higher Secondary education where, after two years, they can sit for General Certificates of Education at Advanced Level in their chosen subjects. Entry into the higher secondary school, the Sixth Form Centre, is restricted to those pupils gaining five credits at the General Certificate of Education Ordinary Level, including a credit pass in Malay Language or Islamic Religious knowledge. It is important to note here that in order to gain a grant to proceed to tertiary level education, those pupils who have not already done so must gain a credit pass in Malay Language while at the Sixth Form Centre.

The implementation of the bilingual education system began in 1985 and is proceeding in stages. Manpower constraints have meant that the lower primary schools are least affected by the changes and only the English language class is taught in English at this level. All other subjects are taught in Malay.

In 1985 itself only Upper Primary children (10-year-olds) were introduced to the system. In 1986 this group had become Upper Primary

VI and were joined in the bilingual system by their juniors in Upper Primary V. They were also joined by some seniors in Lower Secondary I who were following an abridged version of the bilingual system in an effort to wean them gradually from mono- to bilingual education. In 1987 Dwibahasa extended from Upper Primary IV to Lower Secondary II, thus including all 9- to 13-year-olds in the country, and in 1988 the 9- to 14-year-olds.

The implementation of Dwibahasa came too late for those children already in Lower Secondary I in 1985. Under the present scheme, these children will be the last monolingually educated generation in Brunei and will continue in either Malay or English medium schools until they graduate in 1991. Dwibahasa will be fully implemented to include all school children by 1993.

The breakdown of the different school subjects year by year, as shown in Table 1, seems to indicate clearly that Malay is being all but replaced by English as the medium of instruction in schools. However, the chart does not take account of the non-compulsory subjects from which pupils can make their own choice, and most of these options will be taught in Malay. Nevertheless the overall picture is that Malay is progressively being replaced by English as the medium of instruction for most subjects in the Bruneian school classroom.

Some implications of Dwibahasa

The introduction of a bilingual education policy, with its heavy emphasis on English, has been met with remarkably little opposition within Brunei. Obviously Malay medium teachers who face the prospect of either retraining or early retirement have voiced some discontent, but even this criticism has been muted and has certainly not threatened the adoption of the new system. The general consensus of opinion amongst Bruneians is that Dwibahasa is a progressive step in the right direction. However, many are also concerned that it is to some extent a step into the unknown. The unsettling question as yet unanswered is whether future generations of Bruneians will be truly bilingual or unable to communicate effectively in any language.

By its very stress on English as a medium of instruction, Dwibahasa should ensure that future school leavers are more proficient in the use of English than today's school children. Also, assuming that a credit pass in

TABLE 1 *Compulsory and examinable subjects in Brunei primary and secondary schools*

English medium subjects	Malay medium subjects
Lower Primary	
English Language	Malay Language
	Mathematics
	General Studies
	Islamic Religious Knowledge
	Physical Training
	Arts & Handicraft
	Civics
Upper Primary	
English Language	Malay Language
Mathematics	Islamic Religious Knowledge
Science	Physical Training
History	Arts & Handicraft
Geography	Civics
Lower Secondary	
English Language	Malay Language
Mathematics	Islamic Religious Knowledge
Science	
History	
Geography	
Upper Secondary	
English Language	Malay Language
Mathematics	
Science/Art/Technical subjects (depending on stream)	

Malay Language remains a prerequisite for entry to tertiary level education, then standards in the use of the Malay language should not drop. This is, in effect, a circular safeguard. Therefore, within 10–15 years' time, Brunei should hope to be producing school leavers who are able to work or study in either English or Malay speaking environments. And more importantly, given Brunei's professed desire to diversify its oil-based economy, the country would have available a work force which is able to meet the language demands of international industry and commerce. This is assuming, of course, that Dwibahasa proves to be a successful education system and continues to receive support from all sections of the community, particularly from those with a vested interest in education. This support will primarily be contingent upon pupils' performance in public examinations as these are regarded as providing an objective base from which the education system can be assessed and compared.

Nonetheless, a factor which could have an adverse effect on pupil and hence examination performance is a lack of trained teaching staff. There are already teacher shortages in some subjects and while the country intends to recruit overseas and also develop local manpower it cannot be assumed that these measures will solve the problem, especially not in the short term. In fact, it is possible that in the haste to fill staff shortages both local and expatriate teachers may find themselves filling posts for which they are inadequately qualified.

Another factor that might possibly threaten the future of Dwibahasa is that its success could be perceived as a threat to Bruneian culture in that the relative status of the Malay and English languages may become confused. However, I suspect that this is unlikely because the country's national identity and culture are firmly enough rooted to withstand encroachment from both a foreign language and any possible accompanying culture.

The next few years are going to be crucial for bilingual education and for the development of Brunei Darussalam. It is clear that in spite of having witnessed the experiences of its near neighbours, Malaysia and Singapore — countries which at first must seem very similar in many ways to itself — Brunei's experiences are going to be unique. While it is possible to gather some background information, another country's experiences are in no way transferable *per se* and cannot provide a guaranteed blueprint for success.

References

Brunei Government Publication (1972), *Report of the Brunei Education Commission*. Negara Brunei Darussalam: Ministry of Education.
Brunei Government Publication (1984), *The Education System of Negara Brunei Darussalam*. Negara Brunei Darussalam: Pusat Perkembangan Kurikulum, Jabatan Pelajaran, Kementarian Pelajaran Dan Kesihatan.

FISHMAN, J. A. (1972), *Language and Nationalism*. Rowley, Mass: Newbury House.

— (1977), The sociology of bilingual education. In B. SPOLSKY & R. COOPER (eds.) *Frontiers of Bilingual Education*. Rowley, Mass: Newbury House.

LIM KIAT BOEY (1976), The status of English in relation to the other languages in Primary and Secondary Schools in Malaysia. In R. LORD & B. K. T'SON (eds.) *Studies in Bilingual Education*. Hong Kong: Language Centre, University of Hong Kong, Heinemann.

SMITH, L. (1983), English as an international language. In L. SMITH (ed.) *Readings in English as an International Language*. Oxford: Pergamon.

17 The English language in Malaysia and its relationship with the National Language

CONRAD K. OŻÓG

Introduction

Malaysia is a multicultural, multi-ethnic and multilingual society comprising three main ethnic groups. The estimated population of the country is 15.1 million (1985). Malays account for approximately 50% of the population, Chinese about 40%, with Indians, Eurasians and others making up the rest.

The Malays are the major indigenous ethnic group although smaller native populations exist in Sabah and Sarawak. The standard form of the Malay language, Bahasa Melayu, has become Bahasa Malaysia, the national language. Most of the Chinese in the country immigrated after 1850, while most of the Indian community was brought in by the British to work on rubber estates. The Chinese speak a number of dialects and most of the Indian community are Tamil speakers. Native languages exist in Sabah and Sarawak, Kadazan and Iban being the main ones. The other language of major significance in the country is English. Malaysia can thus be described as a polyglossic society (Platt & Weber, 1980: 7) with many varieties of language used side by side in the community.

This study concerns itself with the role of English in Malaysian education policy and its relationship with the National Language, Bahasa Malaysia. A necessary introduction to this is an examination of the development of the English language in the country.

The Development of English in Malaysia

Like other colonial powers, before and since, the British believed in the necessity of having a small élite fluent in the imperial language (Andaya & Andaya, 1982: 222). Thus, it is not surprising that the development of English as a major language in Malaysia coincided with the extension of British rule. The English language has influenced the Malaysian sociolinguistic pattern in a number of ways.

During the colonial era English became the language of interethnic communication among educated people. In those areas under direct British rule, English became the language of government and administration as soon as the British took control. The British came to Malaya for commercial reasons and English was the language of those branches of commerce which involved British or European traders. Local commerce continued to have the Malay pidgin, Bazaar Malay, as its *lingua franca*. By 1850, the English-speaking population, both local and British had grown to such an extent that English language newspapers had been established in Penang and Singapore and, by 1900, in Kuala Lumpur (Platt & Weber, 1980: 1–43). More and more local people were coming into contact with English, although the official British policy was that if there were to be English medium education then it should be for the élite only. In 1890, colonial administrator Sir Frank Swettenham reflected current thinking when he wrote:

> I do not think that it is advisable to attempt to give the children of an agricultural population an indifferent knowledge of a language that to all but the very few would only unfit them for the duties of life and make them discontent (*sic*) with anything like manual labour.
>
> (Perak Annual Report, 1890, quoted in Sadka, 1968: 292)

The schools that were established charged high fees and were therefore only available to Malay royalty and the urban élite, mostly Chinese. However, as British influence extended, and as government became more and more complex, the demand for speakers of English, and hence English medium schools, grew. By 1931, there were 82 English medium secondary schools in the country. They still charged high fees and were heavily populated by rich urban Chinese. The number of rural Malays in the schools was very small. The English medium schools were considered to be the best in the country and the only avenue into higher education or the professions (Platt & Weber, 1980: 21).

In pre-war British Malaya then, education was viewed largely 'as a means of assuring a people contented in their assigned lot' (Andaya &

Andaya, 1982: 264). The result of this policy was a tendency for separate communal development based on language, rural/urban divisions, employment and contact with trade.

This policy is in direct contrast to that of post-war Malaya after the principle of independence had been accepted. Then, the emphasis of education was widened and instruction became 'chiefly aimed at trying to unify the three peoples — Malays, Chinese and Indians — to form one common nationality' (Wong & Ee, 1975: 52).

It was generally felt by the British that multiracial English medium schools were one way of avoiding communalism. The Barnes Committee (1950) recommended the establishment of a national primary school, bilingual in English and Malay, the first recognition by the British of the national status of Malay. The best pupils from these schools would then proceed to English medium secondary schools. For reasons of finance, and pressure from the Chinese and Indian communities, the plan never got off the ground, but the principle of wider secondary English education was established. This principle was reaffirmed by the Razak Committee (1956) which also recommended that Malay should be a compulsory subject for all, regardless of race, thus paving the way for 'the education system in Malaysia to transform into one that was national in character' (Asmah, 1982: 33).

With independence, Malay and English became the official languages although English was to enjoy this status only for a transitional period of 10 years. English medium secondary education was not threatened; indeed the years immediately after independence saw a rise in the number of both English and Malay schools. Although government support of Chinese secondary schools stopped, Chinese secondary education continued in the form of private schools. Many continued their education at private Chinese schools while others continued in English medium schools. After 1967, the number of English medium schools fell sharply as the number of Malay schools rose. By 1970, every student beginning his or her education in a government school in Peninsular Malaysia was being instructed in Malay and thus the last English medium students finished their school education in 1982.

The Legacy of English Medium Education

English medium schools were a very important factor in the political and socio-economic development of Malaysia. Set up to cater for the needs of the colonial society, they produced graduates who moved into prestigious jobs in both government and commerce. Although it has been replaced, English medium education has left a legacy which continues to influence the education system and language planning policies of the country.

The Malays were suspicious of English medium schools from their earliest foundations (Mahathir, 1986: 22). The early institutions were founded by Christian missions and although proselytisation was not one of their main objectives, the schools were to provide 'a general education and a better standard of moral life based on the tenets of Christianity' (Wong, 1971: 15). The Malays are a Moslem people and shunned the schools feeling 'that education via the English language could lead to a conversion to Christianity' (Asmah, 1983). The British, from their earliest intervention in the Malay Peninsula, had a policy of protecting the Islamic religion. One result of this was that the mission schools were built in urban areas where the Malay population was negligible. Even as late as 1970 only 14.9% of the Malay population was urban (Chandler, 1972: 30). The vast majority of them were peasant farmers. The British had guaranteed their right to own land and one consequence of this was to remove the impetus to migrate to urban areas. Rural Malays were guaranteed free education although only for four years. There was no Malay medium secondary education and it is interesting to note that it was the teachers working in these elementary schools who first took the message of Malay nationalism to the rural population.

In their paternalistic desire to help and protect the Malay land and religion, the British, in fact, excluded all but the élite from English medium education. This was indeed unfortunate as 'the English system of education seemed to be the best in every sense of the word' while the Malay schools took the villagers 'only up to the level of being able to read, write and do some calculations' (Husin Ali, 1981: 124).

English schools were subsidised and therefore well equipped and their students had the opportunity of advancing to tertiary education and thus entering the professions. Even those who did not pursue higher education were guaranteed well-paid positions in government service. These schools created what Watson (1983) has called 'social and economic pluralism'; they conferred advantages from which the largest racial group was effectively debarred.

Until Independence, the vast majority of students in English medium schools were Chinese and, even as late as 1968, over 65% of the students were Chinese or Indian. The Malays looked upon English medium education, and thus the English language, as the preserve of the immigrant races. Already culturally and theologically separated from the Chinese, many Malay nationalists looked upon English as a colonial language which had little or no place in their lives. One, Za'aba (1950, quoted in Heah, 1981) went so far as to suggest that most English concepts were too far removed from the Malay world and experience to be of relevance. He advocated that the Malays develop their knowledge of Arabic instead. (For different reasons some present-day Malays feel the same, see below p.314.) The nationalists saw English as 'a reigning usurper to be toppled and vigilantly kept down to safeguard the position of the rightful monarch' (Adibah Amin, 1987).

The 'rightful monarch' was of course Bahasa Melayu and on Independence it became the national language and was enshrined as such in the Constitution (Article 152). There were advocates of English as the national language but the status of Malay was never in doubt. The Malays were the largest ethnic group and the *perjuangan* (struggle) for independence had been led by them. The Chinese, who may have been expected to oppose the National Language Policy were, in fact, won over by liberal citizenship laws.

The Malay nationalists had won the day and yet English remained an important language. The government, led by the Anglophile, Tunku Abdul Rahman, actively encouraged English. English medium education continued and numbers attending English secondary schools rose from 48,235 in 1957 to 349,121 in 1967 (Federation of Malaya, Aziz Report 1968), although admissions to Malay schools rose even more dramatically as universal secondary education was introduced. English medium education remained one from which rural students were still largely excluded and yet it remained virtually the only road to higher education and career advancement. English came to be regarded as a barrier to Malay social and economic advancement and many must have agreed with Mahathir who described the products of English medium schools as:

> Aggressive, knowledgeable and well-versed in the ways of the world, they are well-equipped to shoulder aside their rural counterparts, even if the latter have equal paper qualifications.
>
> (Mahathir, 1970: 86)

Mahathir and the other Malay 'young Turks' believed that economic and social advancement would only come with a massive restructuring of society. Part of this restructuring would involve a more rigorous application of the National Language Policy. Watson (1983) branded advocates of such policies as extremist but this is surely unfair. It is generally agreed that there was an unequal distribution of wealth among the races and, as Asmah (1982: 55–60) suggests, it is surely not extreme to object to a system of schooling from which over 70% of the total population (of all races) was effectively excluded. There is no doubt, however, that many non-Malays were aggrieved with the rigorous imposition of the National Language Policy after 1970, described by Watson (1982: 99) as 'internal colonialism'.

Much of the linguistic nationalism came about in response to English medium education. The perception of the schools and the language as unattainable for the great majority has had a profound effect on the place of English in Malaysian language planning policies from the 1960s to the present.

English and Malay in Contemporary Malaysia

Since 1970, every student beginning his or her education in a government school in Peninsular Malaysia has had Malay as a medium of instruction (in Sabah and Sarawak the change came later). The National Education Policy was one of the results of the restructuring of society which took place after the serious racial riots of May, 1969. The National Language was in the forefront of this policy whose primary aim was 'to erase the state of racial imbalance [and] . . . provide a uniform type of education for all via the national language' (Asmah, 1983).

English is described in the National Education Policy as the second most important language. While the role of Malay is carefully documented, the planners gave English no official status declaring only that it was to be taught as 'an effective second language'. It was to be a compulsory subject but a pass in it would not be a prerequisite for a school certificate. Thus everyone would, in theory, have access to the language, but no one would be penalised for failing to master it.

At a first glance the National Language Policy has been a success. Today most people under 30 can read, write and speak effectively in Malay. Bahasa Malaysia is the language of government and official documents. Government business is conducted almost exclusively in Malay and there is no question that the National Language Policy has succeeded in its aim of creating an interethnic *lingua franca*. Its right to be the medium of instruction is no longer publicly questioned. In any case all discussion of the aims of the National Education Policy was effectively ended with the Constitutional Amendment Act, 1971, Article 152. To be a successful citizen one needs a knowledge of Malay, although many are calling into question the standard of the language being used (Nik Safiah, 1987). Malay is increasingly being used in other fields, apart from government. Sales of Malay daily newspapers are on the increase and it appears that these are increasingly being bought by non-Malays.

It is obvious then that Malay has regained its position as the most important language which it lost during the period of British colonialism. It has become the high status language with all others being accorded lower status. Despite this apparent success, and the fact that discussion of the National Education Policy is forbidden by law, the *implementation* of the policy remains one of the most widely debated issues in contemporary Malaysia. Part of the debate centres on the initial philosophy of the Policy. The Razak Report (1956) and the Dropout Report (1972) saw education as a means of achieving national unity with a common language leading to a shared culture and a national, rather than a racial, identity (Nik Safiah, 1987). However, others saw it as a means of affirming their political dominance. Language and politics could not be separated. The Malay language would, along with Malay culture, be predominant. The implementation of the National Education Policy would assist this process (Watson, 1983) and any attempt to question it would be illegal. Nevertheless, the language policy was too slow in being implemented. English was still the preferred language of many and this was hindering the spread of Malay to all walks of life.

On the other side of the fence were many, including some Malays, who felt that language and culture did not necessarily go hand in hand. The Indians and the Chinese felt that their culture was under threat and the language issue was tied up too closely with the political power of the Malays.

Many, Malays and non-Malays, felt that the change from English to Malay medium had resulted in a severe drop in standards. Much of the debate was, and remains, subjective and at times hysterical. Hardly a month goes by without a string of letters to the Malaysian press on topics related to educational standards.[1] Academics have entered the debate. Some, such as Asmah (1982: 57), insist that standards have been maintained. In the opposite corner, there is the often expressed, though seldom published, view that standards have indeed fallen and that Malay medium education demands less of the students than did English medium.

What can be said is that there is 'a definite downward movement in the level of proficiency in the English language among the present generation of Malaysians' (Asmah, 1982: 57). This has been seen as inevitable by some (e.g. Abdul Aziz, 1985) and Asmah has suggested that the earlier pride in English was misplaced and that Malaysians should now 'transfer this particular type of pride to a mastery of their own national language' (1982: 57). No impartial observer would deny the need for Malaysians to acquire a proficiency in, and a loyalty to, Bahasa Malaysia. And yet, despite the fact that English is granted no official status in the constitution, it still has an important role to play in contemporary Malaysia. (This is not to say that it *should* have, merely that it has.)

Asmah herself (1982: 53) has called the English language the most valuable legacy of colonialism. English remains a compulsory second language in schools and some proficiency in it is necessary for those who want to join the many thousands of Malaysians who study overseas or enter careers in commerce and industry. Many television programmes are in English and it is the language of — the officially frowned upon, yet growing — Western pop culture. It is visually an important language, in urban areas at least, with many posters and billboards in English. Despite frequent pleas to use Malay more extensively (e.g. *Berita Harian*, 5th August 1987) English remains the dominant language of the private sector. For interethnic communication among educated bilinguals, English is the unmarked language and there is a great deal of English used in the discourse of bilingual Malays. English then remains:

> the code associated with gaining better positions, financial gain, better treatment, etc. English, too has the added feature, that it adds prestige to the one who can use it.
>
> (Platt & Weber, 1980: 146)

The continued prestige and importance of English worries Malay nationalists, politicians and linguists. The views of one academic deserve to be quoted in detail:

> Malay faces stiff competition from English. While the policy is to use the national language in all official instances, in many important domains of language . . . English is still the language preferred. Such being the case, Malay has not acquired control of many important domains of language use, a very important factor in its development process. Malay cannot remain forever a language of basic communication. It has to become a language by means of which complex ideas and feelings are communicated effectively and beautifully; it has to be a language of science and technology and a language of high culture.
>
> (Nik Safiah, 1987)

Perhaps the most important point that Nik Safiah is making is that Malay remains a language of basic communication. English remains the prestige language with a large section of the population. Economic advancement, certainly outside government service, cannot be achieved unless one is proficient in English. Yet Malays still regard the language and the benefits accruing from its mastery as being exploited by urban non-Malays.

Herein lies one of the dilemmas faced by Malay politicians and language planners in the 1980s. If English is important then their people must have access to it, and yet, to admit its importance undermines, in their eyes at least, the status of the National Language.

In the 1970s the level of English in the country was allowed to decline. As has been said before, this was regarded as inevitable. However, by the late 1970s, it was obvious that the situation had gone too far with students being refused entry to foreign universities because their English was so poor, a far cry indeed from the 1960s. Measures were taken to try to promote the language and these have continued to the present. Intensive English language programmes have been introduced for pre-university students going abroad; reading programmes have been developed by local Malay medium universities and English language teachers have been recruited from overseas to teach lower secondary students in rural areas. English campaigns have been conducted in schools and in-service courses have been implemented for teachers. However, the failure rate in rural schools remains high. While in the urban areas English is very much a second or additional language, in the rural schools it is more like a foreign one with students having little or no exposure to it outside the classroom. Yet for the ambitious rural Malay, there is no escape from English; proficiency in it is essential.

Language and curriculum planners recognise the importance of English as a functioning second language within the constraints of the National Education Policy. Malay politicians, on the other hand, who see students fail because of their weaknesses in English, often play a contradictory role. While encouraging students to develop English language skills they criticise Malaysians, especially Malays, who use English outside the classroom. In March 1987, the Deputy Prime Minister castigated professional Malays for using English and not taking pride in the National Language (*Borneo Post*, 7th March 1987). In a similar vein, the Education Minister criticised those Malays who did not use their mother tongue in decision making processes (*Star*, 8th December 1984). Others have expressed dissatisfaction with those who advocate more attention to English and letters to the Malay language press frequently demand a more stringent application of the National Education Policy.

Whether deliberately or not, these statements by politicians and lay people suggest to many Malays that there is something almost disloyal in wanting to learn English and that it is certainly disloyal to use it. The disloyalty is not to Malaysia but to the Malay race and in Malaysia today ethnic loyalty is stronger than national loyalty. The 1980s have seen a renaissance of Malay nationalism and so issues such as loyalty to one's race have taken on a new importance, not least in the classroom. The atmosphere is hardly conducive to the teaching and learning of English.

A contributory factor to the new Malay nationalism has been the increased Islamic identity of the Malays. This is obviously a very sensitive area and one which has been misinterpreted by many non-Islamic observers (e.g. Naipul, 1982). As with the Islamic peoples of the Middle East, the Malays are re-evaluating much of their lives and, in so doing, are rejecting many Western ideas and practices. As we have seen, English has been perceived by the rural Malays to be a Western language with little or no place in their lives. The Islamic movement has reinforced this view. A view expressed by many, although not yet publicly by a politician, is that English is a *kafir* (non-Islamic) language. This is the extreme view but one which gives some comfort to those rural students struggling with an alien tongue. A reflection of this can be seen in a series of interviews I conducted with students at the International Islamic University in Malaysia. Students were asked to discuss what English meant to them and what place it should have in Malaysia. Fifty students' responses were taped and analysed. All were concerned that English was the main avenue through which Western, that is non-Islamic or even anti-Islamic, culture entered the country; 28 of the students wanted to see English replaced completely by Arabic, this despite the fact that they themselves were studying in an English medium institution. The other 22 wanted to see Arabic enjoy equal status with English as a compulsory foreign language. English was viewed as useful but dangerous and therefore had to be very carefully controlled, with special attention given to textbooks.

While the more devout Malays are worried about the threat of Western culture, it is access to that culture that motivates many non-Malays to learn English. A study of school students I conducted in July and August 1985 in two schools in the suburbs of Kuala Lumpur showed that 71% of Malays wanted to learn English primarily to study abroad. The rest wanted to write to pen-pals, watch English films, etc. The non-Malays also wanted English to study abroad but for the vast majority

(85%), the main reason was to enable them to read English books and understand English pop songs.

In Malaysia then, the English language is in a state of flux with many different groups having different views on its position in society. Much of the discussion is political in nature, taking place far from the classroom. But it is in the classroom that one flank of the battle is being fought.

Racial polarisation is a recognised problem of the Malaysian education system, a feature commented on frequently by politicians over the last few years (e.g. *New Straits Times*, August 1985; 28th September 1987). This polarisation causes problems in all aspects of teaching, especially English language, not least because the different communities have such different views on the importance of English and its role in Malaysian society.

In rural schools, the English teacher may be bottom of the time-tabling pecking order with classes either last thing in the morning or afternoon. Teachers must be careful when they produce materials so as not to offend any racial group. (In 1980, a picture card showing a person eating with chopsticks was rejected by the Ministry of Education as being un-Malaysian.) Books written for primary schools are rigorously checked to ensure they conform to 'Malaysian' culture and many references to non-Malay festivals and customs are removed. The lack of inter-racial friendships and the problems of mixing of the sexes also cause problems for the innovative teacher wanting to use group work and pair work.

Because of the contradiction between planners and politicians, it is often left to the classroom teacher to create status for the languages s/he is teaching. The status s/he must create for the language is 'often at variance with its status as perceived by pupils' (Noss, 1986), especially in rural schools. Thus the classroom teacher has considerable problems in teaching English, problems going back over 150 years to the founding of the first English school in Penang.

Conclusion

This paper has attempted to examine the place of English in Malaysia today. Jones (Chapter 16) has discussed its place in Brunei while in Indonesia the importance of English is increasing with it now being a compulsory subject in secondary schools and the universities and the language of degree subjects taught by non-Indonesian speakers (Nababan,

1979: 284; Professor Winarno Surakhmad, in a personal communication). Both countries are predominantly Malay speaking and yet the role of English in each is very different from that of Malaysia. In both Brunei and in Indonesia, the indigenous Malays are in a clear majority[2] and neither Bahasa Melayu in Brunei nor Bahasa Indonesia is perceived by the Malays there to be under threat from an outside force. The security this gives allows them to be generous to the English language and, in Brunei, allows the language to have a very definite place in the language policy.

The situation in Malaysia is very different. English is part of a colonial heritage that the present leadership finds embarrassing. On the one hand, Malays want to be proficient in the language and want to acquire the prestige that goes with the proficiency. On the other hand, the language is seen as a threat to the National Language, and by extension, the Malay culture. This conflict in attitude has caused problems for the teaching of the English language.

It seems that the contradiction can only end when the National Language is secure enough for it to allow English to have a small slice of the cake. Thus, the best hope for revitalising English is for the National Language to share the domains controlled at the moment by English. Only when the National Language battle has been won will there be a *planned* place for English in Malaysia.

Notes

1. This has lessened since the security clampdown of October/November 1987 when several opposition M.P.s and several advocates of Chinese education were arrested under the Internal Security Act for supposedly inciting racial tension.
2. I have included here Javanese and Sundanese although neither have Bahasa Indonesia as a first language.

References

ADIBAH AMIN (1987), English as she is spoke and wrote in Malaysia. *Straits Times*. Singapore, June 5th and 6th.

ABDUL AZIZ IDRIS (1985), The Teaching of English in Malaysia: Its socio-cultural perspectives. Paper presented at National Seminar on Teaching of English, Universiti Kebangsaan Malaysia.

ANDAYA, B. W. & ANDAYA, L. Y. (1982), *History of Malaysia*. London: Macmillan.

ASMAH HJ OMAR (1982), *Language and Society in Malaysia.* Kuala Lumpur: Dewan Bahasa Dan Pustaka.
— (1983), The roles of English in the context of national language planning. In R. B. NOSS (ed.) *Varieties of English in Southeast Asia.* Singapore: RELC.
CHANDLER, R. (1972), *1970 Population and Housing Census.* Kuala Lumpur: Department of Statistics.
Federation of Malaya (1950), *Report of the Committee of Malay Education* (The Barnes Report). Kuala Lumpur: Government Printer.
— (1956), *Report of the Committee of Education* (Razak Report). Kuala Lumpur: Government Printer.
— (1968), *Report of the Royal Commission of Teaching Services* (Aziz Report). Kuala Lumpur: Government Printer.
— (1972), *Mid-Term Review of the Second Malaysia Plan* (The Dropout Report). Kuala Lumpur: Government Printer.
HEAH, C. (1981), Influence of English on the lexical expansion of Bahasa Malaysia. Unpublished Ph.D. thesis, University of Edinburgh.
HUSIN ALI (1981), *The Malays, Their Problems and Their Future.* Kuala Lumpur: Heinemann.
MAHATHIR MOHAMMAD (1970), *The Malay Dilemma.* Kuala Lumpur: Federal.
— (1986), *The Challenge.* Kuala Lumpur: Pelanduk Publications.
NABABAN, P. W. J. (1979), Languages in Indonesia. In T. A. LLAMAZON (ed.) *Papers on Southeast Asian Languages.* Singapore: RELC.
NAIPUL, V. S. (1982), *Among the Believers.* London: Hutchinson.
NIK SAFIAH KARIM (1987), The development of a 'Bahasa Melayu Tinggi' variety in modern Malay. Paper presented to the European Colloquium on Indonesian and Malay Studies, University of Passau, West Germany.
NOSS, J. B. (1986), Sociolinguistics in language planning. In R. NOSS & T. LLAMAZON (eds.) *Sociolinguistic Aspects of Language Planning and Teaching.* SEAMEO Occasional Papers No. 41. Singapore: RELC.
PLATT, J. & WEBER, H. (1980), *English in Singapore and Malaysia.* Kuala Lumpur: Oxford.
SADKA, E. (1968), *The Protected Malay States 1874–1895.* Kuala Lumpur: University of Malaya Press.
WATSON, K. (1982), Education and Colonialism in Peninsular Malaysia. In K. WATSON (ed.) *Education in the Third World.* London: Croom Helm.
— (1983), Cultural pluralism, nation building and educational policies in Peninsular Malaysia. In C. KENNEDY (ed.) *Language Planning and Language Education.* London: George Allen and Unwin.

WONG, F. H. K. (1971), Education and Christian missions: Malaysia and Singapore. In F. H. K. WONG (ed.) *Comparative Studies in South East Asian Education*. Hong Kong: Heinemann.

WONG, F. H. K. & EE, T. H. (1975), *Education in Malaysia*. Kuala Lumpur: Heinemann.

18 Evaluating bilingual education in the Philippines: Towards a multidimensional model of evaluation in language planning

ANDREW GONZALEZ, FSC

The Context of Language Planning and Use in the Philippines

Language planning

Language planning, in the sense of a conscious effort to frame policy and to set down steps for implementation, did not take place in the Philippines until the passage of the National Language Law in 1936 under the Commonwealth government (see Gonzalez, 1980).

However, previous to this formal legislation, a Model of National Language Planning, the Spanish colonial government (1565 to 1898) had drafted many instructions on teaching the *indios* the Castilian language (see Bernabe, 1986 for a detailed account of language policy formulation during this period). However, with so few Spanish-speaking colonials (both peninsulars and insulars) during the period, concentrated only in the Old City (Intramuros) in Manila and in such Hispanized urban centers as Vigan in the North, Cebu in the Visayas, and Zamboanga in the South, there was really little opportunity to learn Spanish among the locals, although a pidgin Philippine-Spanish vernacular evolved, which has become creolized (Chabacano). In many remote areas, away from the urban centers, the only Spaniard available was the Spanish fraile who for evangelization purposes found it more advisable to learn the local language rather than to try to have the population learn his language. Moreover, not until 1863 did the Spanish colonial government really attempt to organize a system of primary schools. The first normal school for teachers — the main task of which was to teach Spanish — did not begin until 1865 at the Ateneo Municipal (for male teachers) and in 1868 at the Colegio de Santa Isabel in Naga (for female teachers).

At the end of the Spanish period, even by the most optimistic estimates, no more than 2.4% of the population could speak Spanish (see Gonzalez, 1980: 3) — although there was an 'overlay' of Spanish in the content words of the Philippine languages including those languages of ethnic groups in the mountains who had been least touched by Spanish influence.

The rapid learning of English by Filipinos came through the mass-based elementary school system which the Americans established almost as soon as they arrived in 1898. The rewards for learning English, including social mobility, and the Filipino's own hunger for education explain the rapid learning of English although President McKinley's instructions to the second Philippine commission enjoined them to use the local vernaculars as languages of instruction. Since none of the languages in the eyes of the government had a sufficiently rich literature and adequate number of speakers to be used for education, the instructions, like the instructions of the Spanish monarchs on the teaching of Spanish in the previous regime, became a dead letter. English dominated the system, although intermittently, especially in the 1930s, a plea for using the local languages as languages of initial education and literacy was sounded by different educational authorities of vision (see Sibayan & Gonzalez, in press, for an account of English language teaching during the American period).

By the time of the drafting of the Constitution of 1935, enough consensus had been built on the desirability of having a national language to be developed from one of the existing languages; in the meantime, the official language continued to be English.

With the passage of the National Language Law in 1936, the National Institute of Language was formed. Its founding commission selected Tagalog to be the basis of the national language. A grammar (in Tagalog) as well as a dictionary (actually, a bilingual Tagalog–English word-list) was ready in 1939, leading to the mandate to begin teaching Tagalog to senior high school students and to students in normal schools by 1940. In 1941, a law was passed making Tagalog (now called *Wikang Pambansa* or

National Language) an official language by 1946, when the Philippines would be granted her independence.

With independence, Tagalog was taught as a subject from Grade 1 all the way to High School. The Institute of National Language was charged with the task of propagating, standardizing and cultivating the language. The period from 1946 to 1973 was marked, however, by disagreements with regard to the choice of Tagalog as the basis of the national language because of the larger numbers of Visayans (speakers of two related Visayan languages, Hiligaynon and Cebuano), which led to the repudiation of Tagalog-based Pilipino[1] as the national language by the 1973 Constitution. The latter constitution mandated that FILIPINO be the national language, a language to be formed from all the existing Philippine languages; in the meantime, Pilipino and English continued as official languages. After the 1973 Constitution, the martial law government of Ferdinand E. Marcos declared Spanish to be a third official language, for legal purposes.

By the time of the 1987 Constitution, there was sufficient consensus that Tagalog-based Pilipino (so named in 1959 to lessen the objections of non-Tagalogs) be renamed Filipino after it had been enriched with lexical elements from the Philippine languages and from other languages, presumably English, Spanish and possibly Arabic. Filipino, thus, has been recognized as the national language. By 1987, however, Spanish no longer received official status but was declared by the Constitution to be voluntary, together with Arabic.

Language use

Life seldom follows legislation, however, especially on such matters as language. While Tagalog was not given constitutional legitimation as the basis of the national language until the 1987 Constitution, it had received some form of legitimation by the recognition of (Tagalog-based) Pilipino as an official language by the 1973 Constitution. Also, of course, the period from 1937 to 1973 saw the rapid spread of Tagalog-based Pilipino not only in the school system but through the mass media and the migration of people to the cities and to other areas of the country (Gonzalez & Postrado, 1976).

Thus, the number of speakers of Pilipino either as a first language or a second language went from 4,064,000 or 25.4% of the total population of 16 million in the 1939 census to 29,998,000 or 77% of the population six years old and over (38,925,000) in the 1980 census count (Gonzalez, 1985: 135–36). Accepted or not as the basis of the national language, Tagalog has spread throughout the archipelago; has developed a rich literature; has been used widely in the domains of inter-ethnic communication and everyday business transactions; and has continued to be taught in school both as a subject and, since 1974, as a medium of instruction for specific subjects because of the enactment of the bilingual education policy by the Department of Education in 1974 (Department Order No. 25, series 1974).

Several surveys (Gonzalez & Bautista, 1986) show that Pilipino spread through the islands (77% of the population six years old and over in 1980 claimed that they spoke some conversational variety of Pilipino) and that by the year 2000, by simple extrapolation, 97.1% of the population is expected to speak it (Gonzalez, 1977). Presently, it is likewise expanding its domains. In Metro Manila and other urban centers, Pilipino is rapidly displacing English in inter-office communications, in informal board meetings (where a code-switching variety, between English and Pilipino, is used), the mass media (including movies), print media, and interaction in business offices and commercial establishments (except at board meetings and the highest levels of management). Because of the influence of and instruction in English for writing purposes, letters were primarily written in English in 1968 (Otanes & Sibayan, 1969). But in a more recent survey done by Sibayan & Segovia (1982), many more letters as well as informal inter-office memos are now written in Pilipino, another indicator of the expanding use of the language into new domains hitherto reserved for English.

The Bilingual Education Policy of 1974

During the period of student activism from 1969 to 1972, suddenly suspended by the declaration of Martial Law, one of the topics which the students constantly referred to was their 'miseducation' as a result of the use of English as the medium of instruction, a continuation, in their eyes, of the cultural and linguistic imperialism of the United States of America.

There were individual and institutional initiatives taken to use Pilipino as the medium of instruction in colleges and universities, even in fields such as science, and to use the language more and more in campus newspapers. Clearly, Pilipino was the language of the 'parliament of the streets' and the 'language of protest'. The Movement for the Advancement of Nationalism (MAN), an umbrella group of social activists of different political persuasions, had a program to use Pilipino in the future as the medium of instruction in schools.

Even with the declaration of Martial Law, in response to the clamor for a more nationalistic education, different language planners in the Department of Education had already talked about a bilingual education scheme. After a hurriedly drafted policy aimed towards the expanded use of Pilipino was enacted in 1973, a more systematic policy was promulgated in 1974 by the Department of Education after a nationwide survey of manpower and materials resources for bilingual education was completed.

The policy, enacted by the Board of National Education, upon the recommendations of a Technical Committee, stipulated that beginning in Grade 1 English was to be used as the medium of instruction for science and mathematics and Pilipino for all other subjects, with the major vernaculars as 'auxiliary' languages. A timetable was set, with some allowance for later implementation in non-Tagalog areas, but the stipulation was that by 1983–84, the first batch of students who had gone through 10 years of the bilingual education scheme in Tagalog-speaking areas was supposed to graduate.

Although there was talk of evaluating the scheme after a decade, it was not until a year later, in 1985, that plans were finally set for a nationwide evaluation of bilingual schooling.

The Bilingual Education Policy Evaluation Project

In the course of 11 years, from 1974–1985, there were ongoing (formative) evaluations of the policy and its implementation; these evaluations, however, were for the most part limited in scope to individual institutions and geographic areas and reported perceived difficulties in implementation (Gonzalez, 1984) rather than objective measures of achievement in learning with the use of two languages as independent variables.

In 1985, the Ministry of Education, Culture and Sports accepted the offer of the Linguistic Society of the Philippines to carry out a nationwide evaluation based on achievement measures and funded the project, together with other international and national funding agencies (see

Gonzalez & Sibayan, in press). The model for evaluation was multi-dimensional and necessitated both achievement test data and perception data from key members of various sectors of the Philippine national community; the studies composing the evaluation consisted of four separate though related studies.

The core of the study tested a national sample of Grade 4, Grade 6 and Fourth Year High School students (the leaving stage at the end of secondary education) in Pilipino and English as language subjects and in Mathematics, Science, and Social Studies as content subjects. The tests for Mathematics and Science were in English, whereas the tests for Social Studies (*Araling Panlipunan*) were in Pilipino, since this language had been used as the medium of instruction for this subject.

Since the evaluators, however, were aware that test results alone would not yield conclusive results on the effects of bilingual schooling, other factors had to be included as variables.

With length of exposure to bilingual schooling as an independent variable, achievement test results in language and content subjects and indices of anchorage to the country (as a measure of nationalism) were considered dependent variables, with the following other factors as intervening variables: the type of community from which the students came (whether Metro Manila or outside Metro Manila — whether rural or urban — whether the community was open to migrant influences or not), teacher factors (the teachers' own competence in the subjects which they were teaching as measured by proficiency tests, their linguistic nationalism and permanency indices measured by five point attitudinal scales); school factors — measured by a team which visited each school involved (whether or not the schools were private or public; whether they were rated by the division superintendent as excellent or poor; institutional characteristics such as the quality of language departments, of library holdings, of laboratory facilities; the attitudes of administrators and faculty towards the bilingual education program; and the quality of teaching as indicated by classroom visitations).

By statistical methods of partialling out and by regression analysis, the team of evaluators was able to determine which factors had the most impact on achievement and permanency indices, which were the best predictors, which explained the greatest amount of variance. Canonical correlations were likewise computed to clarify the relations between clusters of factors, for example, English language skills and achievement in other content subjects.

In three accompanying studies by research teams working under the direction of the evaluation team, parents, administrators, and students were interviewed to obtain indicators of extent of implementation of the policy at the tertiary level; likewise, key officials of government and non-government agencies were interviewed and asked about their awareness and perception of the education department's language policy and the role they perceived for themselves in implementing this policy. Finally, officers of scholarly societies, both language oriented and non-language oriented, were interviewed as members of the 'lead' population on their activities contributing to the implementation of policy and their perceptions about the future language scenario in the country.

Main findings

The main findings of the evaluation were: length of exposure to the bilingual education program (measured by number of years of implementation) was not a significant predictor of student achievement; neither was it a significant predictor for students' anchorage to the country. By partialling out certain factors, it was found that the bilingual education policy (which in effect results in more use of Pilipino) favored only Tagalog and Manila students. The type of community, not the ethnolinguistic affiliation of the students, had more impact on achievement; living in urban Metro Manila, and an open community were plus factors in the achievement of students. The main predictor of student achievement for all subjects was found to be socio-economic status. For Mathematics, Science, and Social Studies, the proficiency of the teachers in their respective subjects was the second most important predictor. Among the findings based on interviews, what emerged was the refusal of Filipinos to equate nationalism with medium of instruction choice. They have accepted Pilipino as the linguistic symbol of unity and national identity, but they refuse to equate mastery of Pilipino with nationalism and still less do they consider their nationalism measurable by the proportion of English or Pilipino used as medium of instruction, although the use of two languages has now been accepted. Filipinos from all sectors and all age groups are of the opinion that Pilipino can be learned as a language not only in school and therefore see less urgency for its expanded use in education, especially for social science subjects at the secondary and tertiary level, where the lack of terminology and difficulties with translation create problems for its use as a medium of instruction, at least for the short term.

Some unexpected findings

Some interesting and unexpected findings of the evaluation are:

(1) The bilingual education program, using both Tagalog-based Pilipino and English, yielded learning dividends and advantages only to Tagalogs and Metro Manilans (where the *lingua franca* is Pilipino), thus widening the gap between Manilans and non-Manilans on the one hand and between Tagalog and non-Tagalogs on the other hand. Initially, the working hypothesis of the evaluation team was that ethnolinguistic membership was the main cause of advantage, namely, being Tagalog. However, more than ethnolinguistic membership, type of community predicted success. The formula for success in Philippine education is to be a Tagalog living in Metro Manila, which is highly urbanized, and studying in a private school considered excellent. And of course, the formula for failure is the opposite: being non-Tagalog, studying outside of Metro Manila, in a rural setting, in a public or government school considered sub-standard!

(2) Using regression analysis, it was discovered that language factors (Pilipino and English) were responsible for 45% of the variance in results; however, when only Pilipino was considered, independently of English, the percentage of variance explained was much, much smaller. This leads to the inevitable conclusion that Filipinos at present, even those learning social science content with Pilipino as a medium of instruction, have to depend on English for their learning! This is easily explained by the fact that up to now, social science teachers in secondary schools who learned their social studies content in English think in English and translate the lesson into Pilipino; moreover, all references except for the textbook are still in English. Hence, switching to the indigenous language in a post-colonial situation will not be enough to develop a language, as the language itself will have to undergo the process of cultivation (or elaboration), one specific aspect of this cultivation being its intellectualization or its use as a language of scholarly discourse.

(3) The very high canonical correlations between English and Pilipino language skills which were found indicate a transfer of skills from one language to another, mostly English language skills transferring to Pilipino, although across levels in the educational system (from grade 4 to Fourth Year High), there was an indication of the increasing proportion of Pilipino language skills transferring to English, thus indicating a trend towards genuine bilingualism, which, based on the data, peaks in Grade 6.

Another unexpected finding was that students achieving well in English likewise achieved well in Pilipino. On the other hand, there were hardly any cases of pupils achieving well in Pilipino but achieving poorly in English; thus, at least for the present, the transfer of skills seems to be mostly in only one direction, from English to Pilipino.

(4) Although previous attitudinal and motivational studies demonstrate that it is difficult to learn a second language unless one's attitude is integrative, the test results indicate that even non-Tagalogs, especially Cebuanos, who are not particularly enthusiastic about Tagalog, do learn it — undoubtedly for purely utilitarian reasons — for the best achievers in Pilipino after the Metro Manilans and the Tagalogs were the Surigao–Cebuanos and Kapampangans followed by Pangasinenses. Undoubtedly, one reason would be the challenge posed to non-Tagalogs to achieve well, being the underdogs.

(5) Schools which are excellent do a good job of teaching both Pilipino and English; in other words, the bilingual education policy can be implemented provided that the institution has the necessary features of a good institution. While the good schools of the country are concentrated in Manila and urban areas, there are nevertheless good schools even in remote areas (one such school was reached by helicopter by the accrediting group because it was not accessible by road).

(6) Pilipino has by now been accepted by most of the citizens of the Philippines as the linguistic symbol of unity and national identity; its status as the national language is no longer in question. Hence, the selection phase of language development is no longer an issue, as it was in the constitutional conventions which drafted the 1935 and the 1973 constitutions. However, acceptance of Pilipino as the national language is not equated by the majority of Filipinos, in fact, by most of them, with the necessity for its mastery (the counter claim is made that one can be a nationalist and still not master Pilipino) and least of all with the necessity of using it as the sole medium of instruction. The Filipino accepts the use of two languages; s/he sees the need for the maintenance of English for economic reasons and sees the limitations of Pilipino as a language of higher cognitive activity at this stage of its development.

(7) In implementing language policy, not only the Department of Education should be involved but all departments of the national government, which should be made aware of the policy and mandated to implement it within their particular spheres of influence. Most necessary as co-operating agencies are the Professional Regulations Commission and the Civil Service Commission, which are charged with

testing and certifying future professionals and civil servants. Likewise, all scholarly organizations, which represent the 'lead' population in language use, must likewise be recruited for the national effort.

(8) The parents were more optimistic than faculty, administrators and officers of government and non-government agencies about the state of competence of the present generation in English and Pilipino; all other groups (except for the parents) saw a 'deterioration' in English competence.

(9) The Filipino community in general is quite sophisticated about its views on the effects of bilingual education, for while the officers of government and non-government organizations and scholarly societies saw a 'deterioration', they did not necessarily ascribe this achievement gap to the bilingual education program alone but to systematic weaknesses of the educational system which have been allowed to develop during the post-war period. Most pessimistic and most condemnatory of the program are English teachers (who feel that more time for Pilipino has resulted in less time for English) and administrators who are worried about the standing of their institutions in achievement tests.

(10) Scholarly societies are more optimistic about the future of Pilipino as a language of scholarly discourse, except for legal societies which cannot conceive of the exclusive use of Pilipino in the legal domain in the future.

(11) Little significant impact was created by the Bilingual Education Program on achievement or on indices of anchorage to the country. In other words, the Philippine experience shows that it is not programming and allocation of time or subjects which will spell success or failure in learning but such factors as socio-economic status, overall quality of schools, competence of the faculty. Nor should the extended use of Pilipino (which is one result of the bilingual education policy) be expected to engender greater nationalism and anchorage to the country. On this latter matter, economic imperatives more than nationalistic aspirations determine decisions, *pace* to Philippine ultranationalists and leftists.

(12) In developing a post-colonial indigenous language as the national language and as the language of scholarly discourse to develop special registers for classroom use, implementation should not start at the bottom, in primary school, but at the tertiary level, at the university, where a creative minority of scholars who are both linguistically versatile and knowledgeable in their fields can do the necessary pioneering work in translation and production of research in Pilipino so as to be able to create an intellectualized variety of the language.

Policy reformulation

On the basis of the findings of the evaluation, the Department of Education, Culture and Sports organized a series of workshops and consultations to draw up a revised scheme. This was finally formulated on 21st May 1987 as Department Order No. 52, known as 'The 1987 Policy on Bilingual Education' with its implementing guidelines spelled out in another Department Order (Department Order No. 54, series 1987).

Essentially, the 1987 policy remains the same as the 1974 policy except that the major vernaculars (specifically the regional languages) have been restored as languages for initial schooling and literacy in areas where in the judgement of the Regional Director, the students entering Grade 1 do not know Tagalog-based Filipino sufficiently to use it as a medium of instruction. These regional languages will therefore serve as transitional languages. Moreover, discretion has been given to the Regional Director to decide on local adaptations of curricula and on the timetable, provided the plan is submitted to the General Office of the Department in Manila. More important, the burden of intellectualizing Filipino has now been turned over to tertiary level institutions, universities, using a filter-down model of language cultivation, supported not by coercion but by a proposed system of incentives. Auxiliary studies necessary for proper implementation (e.g. a revised co-ordinated curriculum for Filipino and English to avoid needless repetition and to provide for planned reinforcement and the transfer of skills from one language to another; a body of materials and techniques for teaching Filipino to non-Tagalogs; a body of materials and techniques for retraining teachers who hitherto have used English for teaching social studies to enable them to teach the same subjects in Filipino; a restructuring of pre-service education courses in Colleges of Education and Normal Schools to reflect the bilingual scheme and for the students to take their undergraduate courses in Filipino) have been planned and an appropriation made to fund these programs.

Implications

Some theoretical and methodological innovations

Based on the Philippine experience and the unexpected and somewhat surprising findings of the evaluation, and their rich theoretical and practical implications, future evaluations of systems-wide programs implementing language policy must develop a multidimensional model to make sure all relevant and significant factors impacting on results are taken into account.

Not only must one's equations include as many possible dimensions as possible to obtain a fair description of what real impact a program has had, but likewise the evaluation exercise must use not only one single model but a bundle of studies using different models to take into account not only quantitative data (test results) but qualitative perceptions of both implementors, clientele and beneficiaries (or victims) of such programs. In-depth interviews therefore on perceptions, which ideally should be verified by empirical data of a more objective nature, are needed to obtain a holistic account of the impact of the scheme on the learning process.

Such evaluation must likewise take into consideration not only the views and perceptions but also the behavior of administrators, teachers, parents, representatives of scholarly societies, and officers of key government and non-government agencies if language planning is to succeed. Moreover, in predicting success, community type (whether metropolitan or not; whether urban or rural; whether closed or open to migrants and therefore a 'melting pot') must be considered. Socio-economic status has already been discovered in previous studies to have a crucial influence on achievement, but other economic factors which have to do with motivation and the language of aspiration for social mobility must likewise be considered. In the Philippine case, one foresees that even with the drumbeating of die-hard nationalists and pro-Filipino advocates, the general public will continue to want to learn English as long as English is economically rewarding, and the public will therefore demand the maintenance of English in the system not only as a language subject but as a medium of instruction, for pragmatic, instrumental, and financial reasons.

Finally, evaluation cannot be done from the comforts of one's office based on test results administered by evaluators in the field. In addition to final product measures, the process itself must be observed first-hand, through visitations of institutions and most important of all, through classroom observations of even remote schools where both media of instruction are in use, to gauge real results and to contextualize the numbers that will be churned out by the test results.

Sociolinguistic implications

Taking a holistic view and assuming long-term considerations, more general implications for language planning and language use may be gleaned from the 11 years' experience.and its formal summative evaluation.

Perhaps the most important insight that can be gleaned is that two languages, one indigenous, the other one exogenous (a colonial language), can be learned by a school population provided these languages are taught well. Good schools did an excellent job of teaching both languages well, and poor schools did a poor job of teaching the two languages.

One factor that consistently explained the variance was the socio-economic level of these schools; in other words, success in Philippine academic achievement depends on being in Manila and studying in an excellent private school that charges high tuition.

Filipino as a language of scholarly discourse can be developed in a good school with adequate teaching materials and a linguistically versatile and subject-competent faculty, but until the language has been adequately intellectualized (best done at the tertiary level in universities), more time devoted to it does not result commensurately in higher attainment of language skills for higher cognitive activity. A plateau of achievement in Pilipino was reached, with little improvement beyond this plateau. As long as the local indigenous language is not yet sufficiently developed, then the transfer of skills is more from the developed dominant language (English) to the less developed language (Filipino) than the other way. Clearly, language is a major factor in predicting achievement, but the language which predicted success was English more than Pilipino even for the subject (Araling Panlipunan/Social Studies) taught in Pilipino, simply because in this transitional period, materials in English and the training of teachers have been in English rather than in Pilipino.

Thus, in a bilingual scheme where the two languages are not at the same level of cultivation and do not command the same social prestige (unlike the more or less equal status of French and English in Canada, for example) the indigenous language in the process of intellectualization and cultivation is bound to suffer in comparison with the hitherto dominant and socially and economically rewarding language in the system, even if more time is given to the indigenous language in the school curriculum.

To succeed in the second language requires resources which often most schools in a developing country do not have. Those who suffer in the process will be the less culturally advantaged in society and they may end up in a state of semi-lingualism by not mastering either English or Filipino and therefore be unable to carry on higher cognitive activities in any language.

Hence, the success or failure of any language policy depends on the education system itself, which in the Philippines, because of circumstances specific to it, is badly in need of improvement especially at the secondary level.

Language planning and language policy formulation cannot be done in a vacuum but must take the entire context of the system into account and make plans for compensatory programs so that those less advantaged will not suffer from any change or innovation; this applies specifically to minority language speakers (in this case, non-Tagalogs), who are bound to be even more disadvantaged with the increasing dominance of the language of the majority.

Moreover, perhaps as a caveat to those planning drastic changes in any system because of the imperatives of nationalism, it must be emphasized that the utility of a language as a learning tool (in this case, an indigenous one) depends on the state of its cultivation. Hence, side by side with school language formulation should be a larger well-planned and systematically funded program of language cultivation for the entire society, involving all ministries, government and non-government organizations, learned societies, and the universities and their scholars. The problem, of course, is that the cultivation of a language even for registers referring to concrete social realities closer to the speakers than the more distant abstract realities of science and mathematics, takes about a generation to develop. Few countries in the process of nation building have the luxury of waiting for a language to develop before using it as a medium of instruction. In such a case, one can hope at best that the two phases of language development, the expansion of the language as a medium of instruction in the system and the cultivation and intellectualization of the language as a language of scholarly discourse, will be in tandem; otherwise, there will be a repeat of the Philippine situation and its less than felicitous consequences.

In countries contemplating a bilingual education scheme, where the status and stage of development of the two languages is not the same because of a post-colonial situation, the experience of the Philippines should be carefully weighed lest the same mistakes be committed.

Nationalism alone cannot make up for the intellectual immaturity of a language in the process of development. Nor is nationalism sufficiently strong in some polities to take priority over economic needs. To equate nationalism and love of country with loyalty to a national language can be a questionable juxtaposition which the majority of the society may not accept. In other words, language is only one among many indicators (and sometimes a weak one) of nationalism.

Note

1. In this paper, for purposes of clarity, FILIPINO, the approved national language of the Philippines since the ratification of the 1987 Constitution is defined as Tagalog-based Pilipino enriched with lexical items from other Philippine languages and other languages. In referring to the languages, PILIPINO is used for legislation and policy enacted and events which occurred before 1987 and FILIPINO for those which took place beginning in 1987.

References

BERNABE, E. F. (1986), *Language Policy Formulation, Programming, Implementation and Evaluation in Philippine Education (1565–1974)*. Manila: Linguistic Society of the Philippines.

GONZALEZ, A. B., FSC (1977), Pilipino in the Year 2000. In B. S. SIBAYAN & A. B. GONZALEZ, FSC (eds.) *Language Planning and the Building of a National Language. Essays in Honor of Santiago A. Fonacier on his Ninety-Second Birthday*. Manila: Linguistic Society of the Philippines and Language Study Center, Philippines Normal College.

— (1980), *Language and Nationalism. The Philippines Experience Thus Far*. Quezon City: Ateneo de Manila University Press.

— (1984), Evaluating the Philippine bilingual education policy. In A. GONZALES, FSC (ed.) *Panagani. Language Planning, Implementation and Evaluation. Essays in Honour of Bonifacio P. Sibayan on his Sixty-seventh Birthday*. Manila: Linguistic Society of the Philippines.

— (1985), Bilingual Communities: National/Regional Profiles and Verbal Repertoires. In R. B. KAPLAN (ed.) *Annual Review of Applied Linguistics, Vol. 6*. Cambridge: Cambridge University Press.

GONZALEZ, A. B., FSC & BAUTISTA, M. L. S. (1986), *Language Surveys in the Philippines (1966–1984)*. Manila: De La Salle University Press.

GONZALEZ, A. B., FSC & POSTRADO, L. T. (1976), The Dissemination of Pilipino. *Philippine Journal of Linguistics* 7 (1/2), 60–84.

GONZALEZ, A. B., FSC & SIBAYAN, B. P. (In press), *Eleven Years of Bilingual Schooling in the Philippines*. Manila: Linguistic Society of the Philippines.

OTANES, F. T. & SIBAYAN, B. P. (1969), *Language Policy Survey of the Philippines*. Manila: Language Study Center, Philippine Normal College.

SIBAYAN, B. P. & GONZALEZ, A. B., FSC. (In press), English language teaching in the Philippines. In J. BRITTON, R. E. SHAFER & K. WATSON (eds.) *Teaching and Learning English in the World*. London: Multilingual Matters.

SIBAYAN, B. P. & SEGOVIA, L. Z. (1982), Language and socioeconomic development: Perceptions of a Metro Manila sample — implications for Third World Countries. *Philippine Journal of Linguistics* 13 (2), 63–103.

19 Language planning and education in Southeast Asia: An annotated bibliography

BO YIN

Introduction

Language is an essential element in social communication and nation building. However, in most Southeast Asian countries, the linguistic situation is complex and multilingual. Some countries, like Malaysia and Singapore, have chosen to embark upon massive programs of linguistic, cultural and political reorganization. These developments have meant that in schools there are at least two languages which have important roles in education: the national language and English. Because of the centrality of language to communication and nation building, these language problems and their implications are a common concern among social scientists from different disciplines.

In order to understand the language situation which exists in Southeast Asia better, papers related to the language and education situation in five typical countries in the region are reviewed here. Indonesia, Malaysia, the Philippines, Singapore and Thailand are all multicultural, multi-ethnic and multi-religious, but each has chosen a radically different approach to language modernization and educational development. To achieve the goal of national unity, language policy and planning via educational policy and practice have been emphasized. Furthermore, a number of readily accessible recent studies have been done in these areas.

Readers also should be aware of several classic books on language planning in the region (Alisjahbana, 1976; Asmah, 1979). An anthology of materials relating to ASEAN (Association of Southeast Asian Nations) by Asmah & Noor (1981), and Watson (1982) are also worth consulting.

ALISJAHBANA, S. T. (1976), *Language Planning for Modernization — The Case of Indonesian and Malaysian*. Mouton: The Hague.
ASMAH, H. O. (ed.) (1979), *Language Planning for Unity and Efficiency*. Kuala Lumpur: Penerbit Universiti Malaya.
ASMAH, H. O. & NOOR, N. E. M. (eds) (1981), *National Language as Medium of Instruction*. Kuala Lumpur: Dewan Bahasa dan Pustaka.

Asmah (1979) includes 30 papers presented at the Fourth Conference of the Asian Association on National Languages (ASANAL). It is a valuable document of language planning in Southeast Asia, especially in Malaysia. Its|eight|parts are |closely|related|to|national language policies, situations and problems, e.g. 'The implementation of national language policy' and 'National language — in bilingual and diglossic situations'.

WATSON, K. (1982), The contribution of mission schools to educational development in South East Asia. In K. WATSON (ed.) *Education in the Third World*. London: Croom Helm.

Watson (1982) describes the influence of the Christian missions in the field of education in Southeast Asia. The development of modern education in this area is a direct result of missionary influence. This involvement began in the sixteenth century and expanded in the nineteenth and twentieth centuries. The achievements and contribution of mission schools to local educational development in the region are major. The most lasting influence is that the mission schools helped to produce an educated élite capable of formulating ideas based on Western humanism and liberalism. However, major critiques of the mission schools are also noted by Watson: they replaced the existing schools — 'instruments of civilisation' with 'instruments of economics'.

Indonesia

ALISJAHBANA, S. T. (1984), The concept of language standardization and its application to the Indonesian language. In F. COULMAS (ed.) *Linguistic Minorities and Literacy*. Berlin: Walter de Gruyter.

After giving a general overview of modern language standardization and related problems in Asian countries, this paper analyzes the linguistic situation in Indonesia. Further it discusses the historical and contemporary problems of Indonesian language standardization, covering aspects of spelling, vocabulary, and grammar. Concepts of modernization and characteristics of modern culture are summarized. The emphasis here is on the advantages of the co-ordination and standardization of the Indonesian and Malaysian languages.

ALISJAHBANA, S. T. (1984), The problem of minority languages in the overall linguistic problems of our time. In F. COULMAS (ed.) *Linguistic Minorities and Literacy.* Berlin: Walter de Gruyter.

The language situation in Indonesia, including language choices and decisions, is examined. This paper first discusses the relationship between the national language and the minority languages. In order to provide a picture of the place and meaning of the minority languages in the total linguistic situation, the paper summarizes the present world language situation.

ANWAR, K. (1980), *Indonesian: The Development and Use of a National Language.* Indonesia: Gadjah Mada University Press.

This book deals mainly with the problems of the adoption, development and use of Indonesian in modern Indonesian society. The first three chapters discuss the Indonesian cultural-linguistic background, political situation, and the development and role of the Indonesian language. In Chapter Four, aspects of language planning and the interaction of language are discussed. Chapter Five examines the cultivation of Indonesian by language teachers in schools as well as by writers in their handling of the national language. Chapter Six focuses on problems of language use. The last chapter summarizes the book and concludes by arguing that Indonesian has never been intended to replace regional languages but only to add to them.

GRIJNS, C. D. (1981), Jakartan speech and Takdir Alisjahbana's plea for the simple Indonesian word-form. In N. PHILLIPS & K. ANWAR (eds.) *Papers on Indonesian Languages and Literatures.* London: Indonesian Etymological Project.

This paper examines language planning in Indonesia, which has concerned itself particularly with written language reform. The purpose and intention of the latest spelling system are cited and the spelling rules are introduced. Additionally, varieties of spoken Indonesian are discussed.

JIYONO, & JOHNSTONE, J. N. (1983), The influence of out-of-school factors on the determination of achievement levels in the Indonesian language. *Journal of Multilingual and Multicultural Development* 4 (1), 29–40.

To explain and analyze the influence of out-of-school factors on language achievement levels, a model tested among a group of Indonesian students is presented. The authors recommend to Indonesian policy makers strategies they might adopt in out-of-school domains to promote competence in their national language.

NABABAN, P. W. J. (1985), Bilingualism in Indonesia: ethnic language maintenance and the spread of the national language. *Southeast Asian Journal of Social Science* 13 (1), 1–18.

This paper introduces the Indonesian language situation and reports some findings of the 1980 survey of bilingualism in Indonesia. The survey, conducted by the National Centre for Language Development, covers a sample of about 3,000 respondents. It shows a shift from vernaculars to the national language and confirms the spread of Indonesian throughout the nation. Nonetheless, the paper also provides results which indicate that the vernaculars will continue to be used.

THOMAZ, L. F. F. R. (1981), The formation of Tetun-praca, vernacular language of East Timor. In N. PHILLIPS & K. ANWAR (eds.) *Papers on Indonesian Languages and Literatures*. London: Indonesian Etymological Project.

Historical background and social changes have great influence on languages used in Timor. As a result of local warfare, Tetun, one of the Indonesian languages, has become a kind of *lingua franca* in East Timor. This paper discusses the development and formation of Tetun and shows the influence of Malay and Portuguese on the lexicon and syntax of Tetun. Illustrations of the interdependence between linguistic and historical evolution are cited.

Malaysia

ASMAH, H. O. (1982), Language spread and recession in Malaysia and the Malay archipelago. In R. L. COOPER (ed.) *Language Spread*. Bloomington: Indiana University Press.

Noting some characteristics of Malay, the paper analyzes the development of Malay, especially at three different levels: the *lingua franca*, the cultural, and the educational-scientific. The historical, political and geographical reasons for the spread and recession of language influence both Malay and English are discussed.

ASMAH, H. O. (1982), *Language and Society in Malaysia*. Kuala Lumpur: Dewan Bahasa dan Pustaka.

Asmah presents the sociolinguistic situation in Malaysia and the issues and problems arising from the use of language in society. Particular stress is given to those that are related to the use of the Malaysian national language, including the problems of instituting a language planning program and spreading the use of Malay. Asmah brings 10 essays together in this book which deal with the various statuses, roles and manifestations of the languages spoken in Malaysia.

ASMAH, H. O. (1985), Patterns of language communication in Malaysia. *Southeast Asian Journal of Social Science* 13 (1), 19–28.

Malaysia features a variety of patterns of language use, depending on situation, ethnic group membership, and educational background of the speakers. Although the national language policy establishes Malay as the national and sole official language of the country, many problems still exist. The paper analyzes the situation in Malaysia and argues that in order to bring about effective communication among Malaysians, the national language needs to be more widely spread.

GAUDART, H. (1987), A typology of bilingual education in Malaysia. *Journal of Multilingual and Multicultural Development* 8 (6), 529–551.

Malaysia is a multi-ethnic, multilingual country with a population of about 15.8 million people and at least 100 languages. This article introduces relevant historical background and focuses on a description of the language and education policies in Malaysian schools. The national curriculum for schools encourages bilingualism, and a number of forms of bilingual education have emerged. The article identifies four main types of bilingual 'transfer' programs: initial transfer, re-transfer, circular transfer, and gradual transfer. Each of these four types has a number of sub-types. This typology describes the choices for children's language education that are available in Malaysia.

LE PAGE, R. B. (1985), The language standardization problems of Malaysia set in context. *Southeast Asian Journal of Social Science* 13 (1), 29–39.

This paper discusses language standardization in Malaysia. Comparing the linguistic situations in England and Malaysia, the paper analyzes the standardization possibilities in Malaysia. Malaysia is seen as an example of the interplay between ideological commitments, linguistic theory, and individual interaction under social and psychological constraints.

MUKHERJEE, H. & SINGH, J. S. (1983), The new primary school curriculum project: Malaysia, 1982. *International Review of Education* 29, 247–256.

The major goal of the Malaysian education system is to promote national unity among ethnic groups. This paper gives some background information on Malaysia and its education system. Further, it introduces events and conditions which led to the planning and limited implementation of the new curriculum in 1982. Personnel interviews and observations are included.

PRENTICE, D. J. (1987), Malay. In B. COMRIE (ed.) *The World's Major Languages*. London: Croom Helm.

A description of Malay use, situation and development in Malaysia, Indonesia and Singapore is presented in this paper. An analysis of Malay phonology, morphology and syntax is also provided.

SURYADINATA, L. (1985), Government policies towards the ethnic Chinese: a comparison between Indonesia and Malaysia. *Southeast Asian Journal of Social Science* 13 (2), 15–28.

Following a short introduction to Malaysia and Indonesia, the government policies towards ethnic Chinese in the two countries are analyzed with special reference to issues of citizenship, language, culture, education, economics and politics. The paper argues that contradictory policies and socio-political conditions cause the ethnic Chinese to be particularly aware of their own identity. Suryadinata concludes that the complete integration or assimilation of Chinese in both countries has still a long way to go.

WARD, C. & HEWSTONE, M. (1985), Ethnicity, language and intergroup relations in Malaysia and Singapore: A social psychological analysis. *Journal of Multilingual and Multicultural Development* 6 (3), 271–296.

Both Malaysia and Singapore are multicultural, multi-ethnic and multi-religious, but they have chosen radically different political solutions to multiculturalism and nation-building. Following a historical and socio-political background, this paper examines the two countries from a social psychological perspective, presenting an overview of ethnic relations and intergroup processes. The available data are integrated with a focus on the Chinese and Malay ethnic groups in both countries. The limited research on language issues is also reviewed, including work on language policy, attitudes and usage. In summary, it argues that these two countries are particularly appropriate for multilingual and multicultural research. Directions for further investigation are noted.

WATSON, K. (1982), Education and colonialism in Peninsular Malaysia. In K. WATSON (ed.) *Education in the Third World.* London: Croom Helm.

This paper surveys educational policies in Peninsular Malaysia both before and after Independence. The colonial influence on education is divided into three parts in this paper: traditional 'classical' colonialism; British control of Malaya and internal colonialism; Malay political dominance over the Indians and Chinese within Malaysia, and neo-colonialism. Besides educational policies, language policy is also discussed and analyzed.

WATSON, J. K. P. (1984), Cultural pluralism, nation-building and educational policies in Peninsular Malaysia. In C. KENNEDY (ed.) *Language Planning and Language Education.* London: George Allen & Unwin.

The paper seeks to explain historically how Malaysia became a multi-cultural and multilingual country. It examines how successive post-Independence governments have sought to use the educational system as a means of creating a sense of national unity. Finally, it argues that educational policies in and of themselves cannot bring about social harmony or cultural unity.

The Philippines

DeCICCO, G. & MARING, J. M. (1983), Diglossia, regionalism, and national language policy: A comparison of Spain and the Philippines. In A. W. MIRACLE, Jr (ed.) *Bilingualism.* Athens: University of Georgia Press.

By comparing the language issues and policies of Spain and the Philippines, DeCicco and Maring point out the importance of history and of the interplay between ethnic, national, and international identity in national language decisions. In both nations, the dominant language is the one that holds the centre of the geographic stage. The paper provides substantial detail about the actual language structure and attitudes in the two nations. Social factors relating to diglossia are noted.

GONZALEZ, A. G. & BAUTISTA, M. L. S. (eds.) (1981), *Aspects of Language Planning and Development in the Philippines*. Manila: Linguistic Society of the Philippines.

This is a collection of papers presented at a series of conferences held in 1977. The collection summarizes discussions on aspects of language planning and development in the Philippines, and includes 11 papers on topics such as 'The institute of national language and the present and future of Pilipino' and 'The role of linguistics and allied disciplines in the development of Pilipino'.

GONZALEZ, A. (1985), Sociolinguistics in the Philippines. *Southeast Asian Journal of Social Science* 13 (1), 52–60.

The paper traces linguistic history beginning with the nineteenth-century Spanish missionaries who compiled grammars and word lists of Philippine languages. In the twentieth century, linguists and philologists made attempts at language planning and language development. Descriptive and applied linguistics flourished in the Philippines. By describing how these two have developed, the paper introduces the language teaching movement in the 1950s, which led to a growth in applied research. The paper also focuses on the nationwide language survey work which provides empirical data as a rational foundation for language planning and development.

KAPLAN, R. B. (1982), The language situation in the Philippines. *The Linguistic Reporter* 24 (5), 1–4.

Accompanied by a brief description of the Philippine geographic distribution and population, this paper mainly discusses the language situation in the Philippines. The spread of Tagalog, encouraged by the mass media, and the spread of Pilipino, supported by movies and the educational system, are covered.

MILLER, J. R. (1981), The politics of Philippine national language policy. *Language Problems and Language Planning* 5 (2), 137–152.

This paper first provides an overview of language planning from the end of the last century to the present in the Philippines. Miller then describes the major problems of choosing a national language. The situation and attitudes of Filipinos towards the language spoken in the Philippines are included. Since World War II government support in promoting Pilipino has slackened. The paper thus analyzes national language policies in their political contexts.

RANDALL, R. A. (1983), Ten languages or two? Southern Philippine multilingualism and inadequacies in the Philippines' policy on bilingual education. In A. W. MIRACLE, Jr (ed.) *Bilingualism*. Athens: University of Georgia Press.

Randall argues that the bilingual policy in the Philippines needs reconsideration. He examines the linguistic situation in the Zamboanga City area, describes the history of each language in the area, indicates the present status of each language in the city, and discusses the importance of each. Arguing that linguistic diversity can create major communication problems, Randall cites a few examples of what such facts can mean in people's daily lives. More generally, the Philippine policy on bilingual education is discussed.

SCHACHTER, P. (1987), Tagalog. In B. COMRIE (ed.) *The World's Major Languages*. London: Croom Helm.

This paper discusses the Tagalog phonology and orthography, syntax and morphology. However, the paper also reviews the historical background of Tagalog, the language family to which Tagalog belongs, other languages' influence, and its current position in the Philippines today. The development of Tagalog as a national language is presented and it is estimated that by the year 2000 over 98% of all Filipinos will speak Tagalog as either a first or second language.

SIBAYAN, B. P. (1984), Survey of language use and attitudes towards language in the Philippines. In C. KENNEDY (ed.) *Language Planning and Language Education*. London: George Allen & Unwin.

This paper presents the survey conducted by the Language Study Center of the Philippine Normal College in 1968. A total of 6,622 people were interviewed. The results of the questionnaires were closely related to the respondents' background, their preferences regarding language use in schools and their attitudes towards variation in language. The paper deals with the most important findings from the survey and points out that the

Filipino faces the problem of reconciling the demands made by personal goals, ethnic loyalty, modernization and nationalism. Finally, the author concludes that with intelligent language planning, the demands of ethnicity, nationalism and modernization can be harmonized.

SIBAYAN, B. P. (1985), Reflection, assertions and speculations on the growth of Pilipino. *Southeast Asian Journal of Social Science* 13 (1), 40–51.

This paper summarizes the development and growth of Pilipino during the last five decades. Then it comments on the contribution of nationalists and others towards the use of Pilipino. Nine domains of use are identified. Next, the paper argues that in order to develop Pilipino, the most important task in Pilipino's modernization and intellectualization must fall on the colleges and universities, learned societies, and individual scholars. Finally, the paper considers the future dialects of Pilipino, which at present has four main varieties. The paper predicts that modernized and intellectualized Pilipino will become Taglish.

SMOLICZ, J. J. (1984), National language policy in the Philippines: A comparative study of the education status of 'colonial' and indigenous languages with special reference to minority tongues. *Southeast Asian Journal of Social Science* 12 (2), 51–67.

Beginning with an overview of the world multilingual situation, the paper places special emphasis on the analysis of national language policies in the Philippines. For historical and linguistic reasons, the country has encountered educational problems. Thus as early as 1908, the Philippine Commission made a recommendation to establish a language institute in order to develop a national language. A bilingual policy was adopted, but problems and difficulties still existed. Some children finished school without being fully literate in any language. Specific problem areas are taken as examples of the application of bilingual policy. After describing the disadvantages of the language policies, the paper points out that other home languages cannot be neglected in this multilingual and multicultural country. Suggestions are given relating to languages of instruction and for study in primary schools, secondary schools and universities.

Singapore

CHEE, F. S. (1982), Every Singaporean can be adequately bilingual. *Speeches* 6 (3), 83–87.

Through a discussion of the borrowings of languages, especially those of Malay, this article states the importance of bilingual policy for all Singaporeans.

CHEONG, O. T. (1981), Make Mandarin a living language. *Speeches* 5 (5), 40–42.

Based on the surveys of evaluating the impact of the Mandarin Campaign in Singapore, the paper comments on objectives of the campaign, problems, advantages, and effects of the Chinese press.

KUO, E. C. Y. (1984), Mass media and language planning: Singapore's 'Speaking Mandarin' campaign. *Journal of Communication* 34 (2), 24–35.

This paper focuses on the important roles and functions of the three major types of mass media, namely the press, radio and television, in Singapore's 'Speak Mandarin' campaign. It illustrates the close relationship between language planning and mass communications planning in Singapore.

NEWMAN, J. (1986), Singapore's speak Mandarin campaign: the educational argument. *Southeast Asian Journal of Social Science* 14 (2), 52–67.

The purpose of this paper is an analysis of the public rhetoric in support of the 'Speak Mandarin' campaign in Singapore. Starting with historical background on the education system to the present language policy, the paper then discusses educational and dialect problems.

ONN, L. C. (1982), Chinese Singaporeans must speak Mandarin while at work. *Speeches* 6 (5), 55–58.

Reasons and purposes for speaking and promoting Mandarin among Chinese Singaporeans are cited. Examples are given which show ways of spreading the use of Mandarin.

PECK, E. S. (1985), Educational policies in Singapore: background to parity of treatment. *Forum of Education* 44 (2), 35–43.

The present educational situation in Singapore features a system of schools using different languages (e.g. English, Mandarin, Malay and Tamil) as media of instruction. This is attributed to historical and political developments. With a brief discussion of educational development, the paper provides an historical backdrop for the problems faced by the Malays and describes the dilemma faced by locally elected government in policy decisions.

PENDLEY, C. (1983), Language policy and social transformation in contemporary Singapore. *Southeast Asian Journal of Social Science* 11 (2), 46–58.

This paper focuses on the role that language policy plays in transforming the communicative structure of Singapore society. The paper examines the economic policies, and political and communicative problems which relate to the formulation of concrete language policy. Also some comments are made concerning the nature and functions of ideology in Singapore and some aspects of language policy are analyzed in terms of their implications for social change and the political and economic interests they represent.

PLATT, J. T. & LIAN, H. M. (1982), A case of language indigenization: Some features of colloquial Singapore English. *Journal of Multilingual and Multicultural Development* 3 (4), 267–276.

By describing and discussing the features of colloquial Singapore English, the paper presents an overview of language development and change in Singapore.

SOON, T. E. (1982), English is our bridge language. *Speeches* 5 (1), 63–65.

Soon provides a brief introduction to the language use, teaching and learning in schools in Singapore.

Thailand

AKSORNKOOL, N. (1985), *An Historical Study of Language Planning.* Singapore: Singapore University Press.

The teaching of English as a foreign language (EFL) has been a part of Thai education for more than 13 decades. This volume presents the EFL problems and the important causes for the failure of EFL teaching in Thailand in recent years. Through a historical investigation of EFL teaching, it shows the relevance of language planning to EFL teaching in Thailand. Teacher-related factors are also illustrated. Additionally, the book provides background information on field study. Recommendations for future work on the planning and teaching of English in Thailand are forwarded.

HUDAK, T. J. (1987), Thai. In B. COMRIE (ed.) *The World's Major Languages*. London: Croom Helm.

Along with the description of phonology, the writing system, morphology and syntax of Thai, the paper introduces the historical background of Thai, including its origin, distribution and development. The situational use of Thai in Thailand is also detailed.

HUGKUNTOD, U. & TIPS, W. E. J. (1987), Planning and implementation of nonformal education projects in rural Thailand. *International Review of Education* 33 (1), 51–73.

This is a study of the factors that cause success and failure of implementation of rural education projects. The paper analyzes non-formal education in Thailand, noting problems and presenting a brief discussion of some important issues for present research. The paper argues that the successful implementation of 'non-formal' education projects should be based upon eight principles and approaches.

KETUDAT, S. & FRY, G. (1981), Relations between educational research, policy, planning and implementation: The Thai experience. *International Review of Education* 27 (2), 141–152.

The major focus in this paper is on the research and educational policy relationship in the Thai experience. The paper briefly describes the political and administrative system. Then it notes the approaches and strategies used to enhance the policy and planning relevance of educational research. Finally, lessons to be learned from the Thai experience are summarized.

PROPAT, B. (1985), Language barriers to rural development: a note on the Thai experience. *Southeast Asian Journal of Social Science* 13 (1), 106–111.

The paper examines the problem of language barriers of rural development communication in developing countries, especially in Thailand where there is almost no research on language problems. The paper examines a case of adult education and argues that the adult population carries the major responsibility of village life and that educational programs for adult literacy provide the answer to the communication problems. The paper suggests some solutions to these problems.

SUNGSRI, S. & MELLOR, W. L. (1984), The philosophy and services of non-formal education in Thailand. *International Review of Education* 30, 441–455.

After providing a historical background of Thailand education from 1940 to the present, the paper examines the philosophy and curricula of adult and non-formal education, and describes the activities offered by the non-formal Education Department and other involved agencies. It concludes with suggestions for the future education in Thailand.

20 Language planning and education: A critical rereading

ALLAN LUKE and RICHARD B. BALDAUF, JR

The initial papers in this volume posed several alternative ways to 'read' the various case studies of language planning and education herein. One view stressed the need to reconstruct language planning to address better the needs of those for whom language was being planned; it concluded, somewhat ironically, by noting the paucity of indigenous voices represented in this volume. The second argued that the very practice of language planning stood as a denial of group and interethnic interests and needs, and, describing it as a discursive means for social control, called for its utter deconstruction. Yet another view pointed to methodological limitations in existing models and, with reference to comparative cases, provided guidelines for a more 'technical' adjustment.

Regardless of whatever theoretical and practical reservations we may have about the courses and consequences of current efforts, language will indeed be planned. As evidenced in this volume, the processes of language planning, whether official or unofficial, formal or informal, are already well underway in Australasia and the South Pacific. However, this situation can only partly be attributed to the evolution of 'language planning' as a formal, codified set of disciplinary assumptions and procedures to be used as an instrument of language change by international development agencies, national governments and others. Whether planning has occurred through the media of education and governmental systems, regional cultural change and conflict, international aid and tourism, superpower intrusion or multinational expansion — language change, death and maintenance have taken place and will continue to take place.

Taken together, the essays here place at least three crucial caveats on current and further planning: first, there is a need to consider more directly aspects of historical, social and economic forces in a manner which examines the contribution of context critically, and thereby goes beyond the interest-related constraints imposed by specific governments and groups. While this is not a new observation (e.g. Fishman, 1983), many of the essays in this volume begin to tackle this issue directly. Second, the overreliance on outside, external 'expertise', whether linguistic or governmental, has been placed under scrutiny here. This observation begins to define some of the constraints within which language planning must work. Third, several contributions here have pointed to the tenacity of the ostensibly 'unplanned' in the face of a range of attempts to enforce a technical order on language change, attempts variously consensual and authoritarian, centralized and localized.

It is all too tempting to conclude this rereading with the proverbial call for further research. But given the consistent scepticism expressed throughout the volume towards taken-for-granted assumptions on which language planners and educators have operated, such a call may in fact be in order. For, whatever else they may signal, these essays suggest not only that language-related matters in Australasia and the South Pacific remain problematic and dynamic, but as well that the very disciplinary discourses of language planning, language education and social policy have entered a period of flux and debate.

One area in need of further work is the tracing of what might be termed patterns of 'resistance' and 'contestation' (cf. Giroux, 1983). In his survey of European minority languages undertaken for the European Parliament, Verdoodt (1987) describes the range of languages which have survived loss of economic viability, loss of population, ethnic rivalry, politically-based attempts at destruction or displacement, and so forth. Perhaps to understand better how languages are maintained, we need to attend further to those languages, dialects, registers, and indeed discourses which have survived *without*, or in spite of, state intervention or control. This would include not only studies of pidgins, creoles and dialects as presented here, but as well studies of specific speech registers and codes which are used for purposes of social boundary maintenance. The notion of language as discourse which runs counter to attempts at control, and thereby signifies social solidarity in the face of authority, bears further examination (cf. Halliday, 1978: 164–82).

Second, the matter of the relationship between language and cultural identity requires continual reappraisal in specific regional and local contexts. Several of the essays here have shown the historically and socially complex character of the language/identity relationship, particularly among groups and classes in the midst of rapid socio-economic change. Edwards' (1985) argument that the two are distinct runs counter to Smolicz's (1980; 1981) claim that language is a 'core value' at the heart of the cultural identity of at least some ethnic groups in the region (cf. Clyne, 1988). If indeed economic and social factors are more significant than language *per se* in the maintenance of minority cultures, then the operant assumptions of much contemporary educational policy and language planning bear reexamination. At the very least, this matter deserves reinvestigation in light of Edwards' hypothesis.

Finally, several papers here have reiterated the need for comprehensive sociolinguistic surveys of language use and distribution. It should be noted, however, that such surveys need to keep pace, perhaps better than they have in the past, with theoretical and methodological developments in the ethnography of communication, ethnomethodology and discourse analysis, pragmatics, applied educational linguistics, and other related areas of research. In the English-speaking world, an emergent literature on daily, lived 'ways with words' in communities and work places, home and school contexts is generating a reappraisal of the role of institutions in the teaching, learning and use of language and literacy (e.g. Heath, 1983; Cook-Gumperz, 1986). This research is leading to a revision of various longstanding presuppositions of language and educational policy, and of related institutional practices, many of which had been substantiated by decades of large scale quantitative research. Accordingly, it seems imperative that further research go beyond the traditional precedents set by many large scale surveys of language status, and that researchers look beyond the numbers generated by attitude and use surveys towards fuller, qualitative descriptions of language in use.

Kuhn's (1962) insight that paradigms shift when their practitioners have succeeded in generating anomalies which apparently defy explanation through the application of existing theories and methods may be significant here. But it must be juxtaposed to Foucault's (1972) position that there are no *a priori*, universal problems in the phenomenal and sociocultural world which exist independently of their disciplinary articulation. It would appear that it is impossible to speak |of| sociocultural/ linguistic situation, without at the same time speaking of our own assumptions about how to 'read' that situation (McHoul & Luke, in press/1989). Regardless of how readers choose to frame this text and its portrayal of current and historical situations, it seems evident that language planning and education — like the peoples, languages and nation states of Australasia and the South Pacific — are in the midst of a period of change. The former, apparently, will be marked by paradigm shift and discursive reformation; the latter, hopefully, will themselves create situations marked by increasing linguistic and political self-determination.

References

CLYNE, M. (1988), Review of Edwards, 'Language, society and identity'. *Language in Society* 17, 103–108.

COOK-GUMPERZ, J. (ed.) (1985), *The Social Construction of Literacy.* Cambridge: Cambridge University Press.

EDWARDS, J. (1985), *Language, Society and Identity.* Oxford: Basil Blackwell.

FISHMAN, J. A. (1983), Progress in language planning: A few concluding sentiments. In J. COBARRUBIAS & J. A. FISHMAN (eds.) *Progress in Language Planning.* Berlin: de Gruyter & Co.

FOUCAULT, M. (1972), *The Archaeology of Knowledge.* Trans. A. M. SHERIDAN SMITH. New York: Harper and Row.

GIROUX, H. A. (1983), *Theory and Resistance in Education: A Pedagogy for the Opposition.* London: Heinemann.

HALLIDAY, M. A. K. (1978), *Language as\Social Semiotic.* London: Edward Arnold.

HEATH, S. B. (1983), *Ways with Words.* Cambridge: Cambridge University Press.

KUHN, T. (1962), *The Structure of Scientific Revolutions.* Chicago: University of Chicago Press.

MCHOUL, A. W. & LUKE, A. (in press/ 1989), Discourse as language and politics: an introduction to the philology of political culture in Australia. *Journal of Pragmatics* 13:3.

SMOLICZ, J. J. (1980), Language as a core value of culture. *RELC Journal* 11 (1), 1–13.

SMOLICZ, J. J. (1981), Core values and ethnic identity. *Ethnic and Racial Studies* 4, 75–90.

VERDOODT, A. (1987), Minority languages in Europe. Paper presented at the Australian New Zealand Association for the Advancement of Science Annual Congress, Townsville, Queensland.

Contributors

Richard B. Baldauf, Jr is Associate Professor in the Department of Language and Arts Studies in Education at James Cook University of North Queensland. His research interests include scientometrics, education and language planning, measurement, and culture and language learning in the Pacific Basin. He has published a number of chapters in books and articles in journals like *Educational and Psychological Measurement, Australian Review of Applied Linguistics, Language Planning Newsletter*, and *Australian Journal of Psychology.*

Paul Black is a lecturer in the School of Australian Linguistics of the Darwin Institute of Technology, where he trains speakers of Aboriginal languages in literacy worker skills, interpreting and translation. His current research interests include bilingual education, schema theory and applications of linguistics to Aboriginal languages. Before taking up his current position in 1982, he completed comparative research on the Eastern Cushitic languages of the Horn of Africa, for which he received a Ph.D. from Yale in 1974, and then spent several years undertaking descriptive and comparative research on Aboriginal languages of Northern Queensland with funding from the Australian Institute of Aboriginal Studies.

Bo Yin, a recent graduate student in language studies in education at James Cook University, is an English language lecturer in China.

William Eggington is an Assistant Professor in English Language at Brigham\ Young University, Provo, Utah. He\ was previously a Senior Lecturer and Head of Division, Division of Language Studies at the Darwin Institute of Technology. His research interests include language policy and planning, contrastive rhetoric, English language pedagogy and English as a world language. He has published in these areas.

Andrew Gonzalez, FSC, is Professor of Language and Literature at De La Salle University, Manila, which is run by the Brothers of the Christian

Schools (Fratres Scholarum Christianarum). He is Executive Secretary of the Linguistic Society of the Philippines and editor of its journal, the *Philippine Journal of Linguistics*. He has published extensively in Philippine and foreign journals in the fields of language planning and sociolinguistics in the Philippines.

Gary Jones is a lecturer in English at the Universiti Brunei Darussalam. His research interests include bilingualism and language planning in Brunei Darussalam, the topic of his Ph.D. thesis, and ESP and language teaching methodology on which he has presented a number of papers. He has previously taught at a University for Buddhist monks in Sri Lanka, established a language teaching unit for a Middle Eastern oil company and worked as a language consultant in Britain, West Germany and Abu Dhabi.

Christine Jourdan teaches Anthropological Linguistics at the State University of New York in Cortland. She obtained her Ph.D. in Anthropology and Linguistics at the Australian National University in 1986. Her research focus has moved from Quebec language planning policies to the creolization and urbanization of Solomon Islands Pijin. Recent and forthcoming publications deal with the creolization of Solomons Pijin and the emergence of an urban culture in the Solomon Islands.

Joan Kale is a lecturer in linguistics and language arts in the Department of Social and Cultural Studies in Education at James Cook University. She works primarily with Aboriginal and Torres Strait Islander students in the Diploma of Teaching (Early Childhood Education). Essentially an applied linguist, her areas of interest include: Aboriginal education, bilingual education, pidgin and creole studies, and first- and second-language learning.

Roger M. Keesing, Professor of Anthropology at the Australian National University, completed his B.A. at Stanford (1956) and his M.A. (1962) and Ph.D. (1965) at Harvard. His research has been focused on the Solomon Islands and also the Indian Himalayas. He is the author of *Cultural Anthropology, Kin Groups and Social Structure, Kwaio Religion, Kwaio Grammar, Kwaio Dictionary, 'Elota's Story* and *Melanesian Pidgin and the Oceanic Substrate*. He is the co-author of *Lightning Meets the West Wind: The Malaita Massacre* and has published about 80 professional papers in anthropology and linguistics.

Robert B. Kaplan is Professor of Applied Linguistics in the Department of Linguistics at the University of Southern California, where he is also

Director of the American Language Institute. In addition to serving as Editor-in-Chief of the *Annual Review of Applied Linguistics* series, he has also contributed a number of articles and monographs in written discourse analysis, language policy and planning, and language teaching.

Don J. Lewis is a lecturer in Statistics in the Department of Mathematics and Statistics at the Papua New Guinea Institute of Technology in Lae. Besides teaching statistics, he provides advice and consultant help in a wide range of projects. A recent relevant publication is 'There's a lot of it about': Self-estimates of their use of Tok Pisin by students at the Papua New Guinea University of Technology, in Laycock and Winter, *A World of Language: Papers presented to S. A. Wurm on his 65th Birthday* (ANU, 1987).

Joseph Lo Bianco, Australian Advisory Council on Languages and Multicultural Education, Canberra has been involved in many aspects of language policy development in Australia.

Allan Luke teaches language in education at James Cook University of North Queensland. He currently is undertaking research on literacy in Australia. He is author of *Literacy, Textbooks and Ideology* (Falmer Press, 1988) and co-editor of *Literacy, Society and Schooling* (Cambridge, 1986), *Language, Authority and Criticism: Readings on the School Textbook* (Falmer Press, 1988) and *Towards a Critical Sociology of Reading Pedagogy* (John Benjamins, 1989).

Alec W. McHoul teaches discourse analysis and cultural theory at Murdoch University in Perth, Australia. He has published books on ethnomethodology and reading, Wittgenstein and the social sciences and will shortly publish a book on the American novelist Thomas Pynchon (with co-author David Wills). He is currently working towards a textbook on contemporary social and cultural theory.

Jacob Mey is Professor of Linguistics at the Rasmus Rask Institute of Linguistics, Odense University, Denmark. He is author of *Whose Language? A Study in Linguistic Pragmatics* (John Benjamins, 1985) and editor of *Pragmalinguistics* (Mouton, 1981). Professor Mey is founding editor of the *Journal of Pragmatics* (North-Holland/Elsevier) and continues to work in the field of socially and politically based pragmatic theory.

A. Conrad K. Ożóg is a lecturer in English language at Universiti Brunei Darussalam. He is interested in varieties of English and the relationship between languages in multilingual societies. Publications include a dictionary, textbooks and readers, as well as articles in journals. Previously he has taught in universities in Norway and Malaysia.

Geoff P. Smith is a Senior Lecturer in the Department of Language and Communication Studies at the Papua New Guinea University of Technology at Lae, Papua New Guinea.

John Swan has taught English in his native Scotland, in Turkey, Zambia, New Zealand and Papua New Guinea. Before taking up his current position as Senior Lecturer in English at Universiti Brunei Darussalam, he was Senior Lecturer in English for Specific Purposes at the PNG University of Technology. His research interests have been in the area of applied linguistics and sociolinguistics and he has published a number of articles in the area of English for Specific Purposes and on the developments in the use of Melanesian pidgin.

Vicki Teleni is a TESOL teacher in the Townsville College of Technical and Further Education and a graduate student in language studies in education at James Cook University. Her research interests include the appropriate use of statistics in language research and the role of affective variables in the comprehension of second language speakers' oral expression.

Andrew Thomas is Head Teacher at Sydney English Language Centre. He has taught in the United Kingdom, France, Greece, and Vanuatu. His interest in contact languages developed while he was lecturer in English at the University of the South Pacific Centre in Port Vila. His M.A. dissertation at London University Institute of Education (1986) focused on contact language and literature in the South Pacific.

Index

Note: L1=first language; L2=second language. Numbers in italics refer to tables and figures.